W9-DAX-234

Drugs **II**

Students and Drugs

A publication of the

INSTITUTE FOR THE STUDY OF HUMAN PROBLEMS

Stanford University

NEVITT SANFORD, Director

Drugs II

College and High School Observations

Richard H. Blum & Associates

Jossey-Bass Inc., Publishers
615 Montgomery Street • San Francisco • 1969

Students and Drugs

STUDENTS AND DRUGS
Drugs II: College and High School Observations

by Richard H. Blum and Associates

Copyright © 1969 by Jossey-Bass, Inc., Publishers

Copyright under Pan American and
Universal Copyright Conventions

All rights reserved. No part of this book may be
reproduced in any form—except for brief quotation
in a review—without written permission from the
publishers. Address all inquiries to:

Jossey-Bass, Inc., Publishers
615 Montgomery Street
San Francisco, California 94111

Library of Congress Catalog Card Number 73-75936

Standard Book Number SBN 87589-034-2

Manufactured in the United States of America
Printed by York Composition Company, Inc., York, Pennsylvania
Bound by Chas. H. Bohn & Co., Inc., New York
Jacket design by Willi Baum, San Francisco

FIRST EDITION

Code 6904

THE JOSSEY-BASS BEHAVIORAL SCIENCE SERIES

General Editors

WILLIAM E. HENRY, *University of Chicago*

NEVITT SANFORD, *Stanford University and Wright Institute, Berkeley*

Preface

*D*rugs I, *Society and Drugs* and Drugs II, *Students and Drugs* provide information on the use of psychoactive drugs, including marijuana, LSD, heroin, alcohol, and the like. The work presented here, we hope, will help the reader to develop a perspective about these drugs, the conditions associated with their use, the kind of people most likely to use them, some of the results of their use, and the milieu—including attitudes, anxieties, and ideologies—in which drug use, especially social and personal drug use, is embedded. The need for additional information about drugs is apparent, for the United States and other Western nations are experiencing, especially among young people, dramatic changes in drug use habits. The information we have developed is by no means complete, nor does it assure an understanding of the rapidly changing drug scene; yet we trust that our observations—which embrace the history of drug use, cross-cultural comparisons, normal, hippie, and high school and college student use, along with data on drug effects, drug associations with crime, religion, educational status, and the like—will be useful.

Society and Drugs and *Students and Drugs* together represent an important portion of the investigations conducted by our psychopharmacology group at Stanford University and by our cooperating colleagues in other institutions. These drug endeavors began in 1960 with a cultural case study in Greece, reported in Drugs I, which was part of a larger program of investigation and innovation in public health and cultural medicine (see *Health and Healing in Rural Greece,* 1964). Beginning in 1962, our interests extended to a social-epidemiological study of LSD use and users (see *Utopiates,* 1964), went on to include an evaluation of treatment methods and problems for one group of drug disorders (see *Alcoholism: Modern Psychological Approaches to Treatment,* 1967), and embraced an appraisal of the relationship between drug use and crime, suicides, and accidents (see President's Commission on Law Enforcement and the Administration of Justice, *Task Force Report: Narcotics and Drug Abuse,* 1967, and *Task Force Report: Drunkenness,* 1967). The present two volumes represent further inquiries. These attend primarily to the social use of psychoactive drugs, the correlates, background, and short-term consequence of that use, and the cultural, attitudinal, and interpersonal milieu in which sentiments and conduct focused on drugs arise and are expressed.

In all of these endeavors we have been seeking to identify factors associated with changing patterns of drug use, ones associated with observed constancies or similarities in use, outcomes, or associated beliefs, and to place the phenomena of individual drug use and reactions into a broad perspective. Thus, over the years, we have sought to specify the variety and patterns of drug use by individuals, groups, or populations; to compare persons in similar settings; to compare common cultures; to examine similarities and differences among cultures in their drug use; and to inspect historical patterns associated with drug diffusion, acceptance, and social reactions. We have sought to consider treatment in something of the same fashion as we did in our *Alcoholism* book—that is, comparatively, in terms of the efficacy of methods, and contextually, by examining social, moral, and administrative factors as well as clinical ones that affect treatment operation and outcomes. Throughout we have tried to maintain contact with individual cases and to link them—not forgetting the unique nature of the person, drug, group, or culture—to the larger context.

Even though the total number of individuals interviewed, observed, or completing questionnaires for the data reported here runs to about 20,000, and even though we have studied about 250 cultures as well as a variety of nations, historical events, and special groups, we are still in the frustrating position of having studied samples at moments in time rather than total populations continuously over time. Given such conditions, we must be cautious in generalizing, for our Western college students are not Midwestern rural ones, our hippies are in San Francisco and not in Boston, our cultural case study is of rural Greeks, not of Malayans or of people from Timbuktu, and our follow-up studies measure discrete rather than continuous events. Even so, we do generalize and imagine the reader will do the same, for in the absence of better data, one has to make do with the data at hand. As we trust that what we offer will open the door to greater understanding, so also do we trust that others will come through that open door with more and better information in the future.

Our study was made possible by grants from the National Institute of Mental Health (MH-12286) and was conducted in cooperation with the Pharmacology Service Center and the Center for Drug Abuse of NIMH. Coordinators from the Pharmacology Service Center were Mitchell Balter, Ph.D., and Jerome Levine, M.D., and from the Center of Drug Abuse, Roger Meyer, M.D. The coordinated study was directed by Richard Blum. In addition to support by NIMH, the project received on-campus financial support from the Urban Life Institute of the University of San Francisco, and the Office of the Dean of Humanities and Sciences at Stanford University.

RICHARD H. BLUM

Stanford, California
January 1969

Contents

The Associates

Jean Aron, B.A.; research associate, Community Mental Health Services, San Jose, California; executive secretary, Santa Clara County Council on Drug Abuse

Mary Lou Funkhouser Balbaky, M.A.; graduate student in anthropology, Brandeis University

Diane Bausek, B.A.; research assistant, Institute for the Study of Human Problems, Stanford University

Philip E. Beal, Ph.D.; dean of men, Pacific Lutheran University, Tacoma, Washington

Eva M. Blum, Ph.D.; co-director, Psychopharmacology Project; Institute for the Study of Human Problems, Stanford University

Richard H. Blum, Ph.D.; director, Psychopharmacology Project, Institute for the Study of Human Problems, Stanford University

Roland Bonato, Ph.D.; chief, Biometrics Laboratory, George Washington University

Robert Bowlin, Ph.D.; dean of men, University of Oregon

Lauraine Braunstein, M.A.; research assistant, Institute for the Study of Human Problems, Stanford University

Jack H. Curtis, Ph.D.; professor of sociology; director, Urban Life Institute, University of San Francisco

Robert A. Ellis, Ph.D.; professor of sociology, University of Oregon

Sanford Feinglass, Ph.D.; program coordinator, National Education Association Drug Project, Marin County, California

Bruce Ferguson, M.A.; student, Stanford University Medical School

Joel Fort, M.D.; lecturer, School of Social Welfare, University of California, Berkeley; co-director, National Sex and Drug Forum, San Francisco

Mervin B. Freedman, Ph.D.; professor of psychology, San Francisco State College

Emily Garfield, B.S.; research assistant, Institute for the Study of Human Problems, Stanford University

Thirza Hibner, B.S.; staff assistant, Institute for the Study of Human Problems, Stanford University

Kristine Hooper, undergraduate assistant, Institute for the Study of Human Problems, Stanford University

Peggy Joseph, B.A.; research assistant, Institute for the Study of Human Problems, Stanford University

Richard Joyce, Ph.D.; professor of pharmacology, London Hospital Medical College, London

Helen Nowlis, Ph.D.; dean of students, State University of New York at Rochester

Frances Orr-Nitzberg, Ph.D.; consulting psychologist, Institute for the Study of Human Problems, Stanford University

James Paulsen, M.D.; chief psychiatrist, Student Health Clinic, Stanford University

Charles E. Richardson, Jr.; computer programmer, Stanford University

A. Rinker, B.A.; graduate student in psychology, San Francisco State College

Alma Stone, M.S.; psychiatric social worker in private practice, Palo Alto, California

Richard Switalski, M.A.; staff member, Biometrics Laboratory, George Washington University

Thomas Tutko, Ph.D.; professor of psychology, San Jose State College

Drugs **II**

Students and Drugs

Prologue: Students and Drugs

Richard H. Blum

I

Over the past several years, public concern has greatly increased over mind-altering drug use among students. That concern has been evoked by a flow of reports from individuals, mass media, the police and other governmental agencies, educators and, only incidentally, from social scientists. The reports are consistent in telling of a remarkable expansion of student interest in and use of drugs which are illicit or exotic.[1] It is an expansion which is nation-wide and which, at this date, is rapid. In the period to 1963 or so, the students who were primarily interested in these psychoactive substances were, it appeared, mostly graduate students (Blum and Associates, 1964), but as the years have passed, the statistics as well as clinical and journalistic observations

---

[1] The illicit drugs are those whose acquisition, sale, and (sometimes) possession are prohibited by law, such as LSD, marijuana, and heroin; also illicit are those drugs which are lawful to use under medical supervision or prescription but not privately—for example, the amphetamines and barbiturates. Exotic drugs are those which are so newly developed that they are not covered by existing statutes—for example, STP, MDA, or natural plants whose use is novel, such as morning-glory seeds, banana peel, seaweed, mimosa bark, and catnip.

have implicated increasingly younger student groups. Undergraduates first became—and remain—a focus of concern, then high school students, and nowadays even some grade school pupils are also described as prone to use illicit-exotic drugs. The very young children of drug-using parents are also being "turned on." In addition, there has been, since about 1966, the rise of the hippie movement, comprised of young people who are not in school and who have proclaimed a way of life which, among other aspects, centers on the use of illicit and psychoactive compounds.

Public concern about our rapidly changing patterns of drug use stems from many factors. Some of these have been considered in *Drugs I*. Undoubtedly, there has been much anxiety lest young people suffer direct damage to their physical or mental health. There has also been concern about their safety in terms of accidents occurring because of drug-induced deficits in judgment or coordination, worry about the ability of students to study effectively, about their wanting to stay in school, or their engaging in unwise social activities, such as sexual indiscretion or the disruption of friendships arising out of drug-related impulsiveness. Parents and others have also been rightfully concerned about the risks their children take in engaging in illicit acts. The latter is no small matter in view of the stigma attached to being called a "drug user" and the penalties upon being convicted, which can range up to twenty years in some states for a first offense. In two states even the death penalty can be applied to a young adult if he is convicted of drug sales to a minor.

Beyond these specific and, in some cases, quite justifiable worries, public concern has a broader focus. People wonder what the meaning of this preoccupation with drugs is, the social significance and the implications for the lives of the young people involved. Why should students intentionally violate the law and take drugs widely believed to be a hazard to health, to psychological adjustment, or to personal reputation? More than that, what does it signify when students emulate the hippies, those exemplars of the "drug movement," and wear long hair and beads, walk about unkempt and perhaps unwashed, and espouse philosophies or platitudes which jar the ear of conventional people? Why do students bother to listen to Leary's invitation to "turn on, tune in, and drop out" and why have some few accepted that invitation? Parental and public concern is also expressed another way in the question "Why are intelligent and supposedly respectable young people doing things which bring on the extreme disapproval of their elders?" One also may ask—in view of much that has been said in praise of hippies, marijuana, and the like—how much of the public "concern" is, in fact, admiration of the new dissent and fascination with the possibility of delightful drug effects?

Even if there were adequate—or at least consoling—explanations for the appeals and persistence of drug taking itself, these would not suffice to divert public attention from the college campus, for the campus "scene" provides a good deal of other excitement for the older generation—stimulation ranging from admiration to fright and fury—which seems to have nothing to do with drug taking. On many campuses a variety of student activities have surprised and sometimes confronted conventional society. In addition, these activities have also surprised a large number of student peers as well.

It is our impression that of the several forms of student conduct which have been perturbing to some if not most citizens, activism as such has received a greater share of public interest and mass-media attention—possibly because it is visible, dramatic, and sometimes verges on violence—than has student drug use. Activism, which includes a variety of protest demonstrations, the construction of experimental programs (for example, free universities), the development of fledgling political movements, and the enunciation of several distinguishable ideologies (for example, the New Left, pacifism, and anarchism), has also had the advantage of a great deal more scientific study and scholarly comment. The response to student surprises—whether activism and/or hippie styles—on the part of public officials, journalists, and probably millions of unquoted adults appears to have been more immediate and their characterizations more negative and sweeping than those of the scholars. Since the former have a wider audience than the latter, the general public has been encouraged, if not induced, to adopt pat judgments as to what is going on. One hears the words "rebellion," "social rejects," "escapists," "outlaws," "anarchists," "self-indulgence," and that old standby, "communists." Such descriptive diagnoses of students make it easy for the self-appointed critic to feel that understanding has been achieved and that he has insights which close the circle linking such diverse events as the violation of drug laws, activism, and dropping-out.

However satisfying it may be to feel that things fit together after all, this sense of closure may be premature. Certain features of student behavior are not accounted for by any easy diagnosis, however qualified. In the first place, *most* students do not appear to be interested in illicit-exotic drug use, in the New Left, or in dropping-out. Consequently, any diagnosis of student drug experimentation or activism which says "students are . . ." misses the fact that *most* students are not. In the second place, even the students who are (activist, drug-oriented, or drop-outs) are by no means—as we shall later see—a homogeneous group. As the semanticists used to warn, student$_1$ is different from student$_2$, is different from student$_3$, and so on. So even if some students are . . . something . . . others in the groups which attract attention and/or concern are likely to be something else. A third point is that the espoused beliefs of many students who do subscribe to drug use, activism, and dropping-out proclaim a number of positive values which sound so much like the things that conventional people say they also want that one wonders why so much emphasis is on differences. To say, "They are . . . but *I* am not . . ." overlooks that old and young share a great deal in common. Consider that among the revolutionaries of the inner world, the drug-oriented, the goals espoused read much like a Christian sermon —fellowship, love, peace, religious experience, personal expansion, and artistic development, among others. Consider that the revolutionaries of the outer world, the activists, espouse goals which sound like a presidential campaign speech—peace and international accommodation, freedom at home and abroad, democratic sharing of power, justice for all, opportunity for all, and so on. How can these young ministers and politicians worry us so? Is their rhetoric so different from that of the conventional world?

A fourth problem in a premature assessment is the insufficiency of quick easy labels or quick explanations to provide any genuine understanding of even part of what is happening. Whatever labels may tempt us—whether they be disapproving ones such as "anarchist" or "addict" or even laudatory ones such as "progressive" or "idealistic" —insofar as they lead no further than classifying young people as good or bad, they do no service toward understanding. Neither damnation nor praise of young persons tells us who among students can be accurately characterized in the above manner. Such labels tell us nothing of the correlates of a particular condition, they tell us nothing of how the students came to be that way, nor do they indicate how any one group of students views the world.

The alternative to a premature sense of closure, to resting contentedly on our labels, is to remain uncertain while gradually throwing light on the matter through study and thought. Fortunately, many citizens have been willing to tolerate the distress of uncertainty and, as a result, have encouraged objective appraisal. Consequently, there have been both a stimulus to and an audience for studies and inquiries undertaken by school administrators and other educators, civic groups, governmental agencies, and social or behavioral scientists. People have been attentive to what the students themselves have had to say and, through student speeches, newspapers, and, of late, books, they have enjoyed first-hand appraisals. Going to the source itself is a good practice and conforms to a fundamental rule for all lost travelers, policy planners, detectives, or examining physicians: "If you want to know something from someone, ask him!" Asking may not be enough, but it is a splendid beginning.

STUDIES ON COLLEGES AND YOUTH

In addition to the good beginnings of inquiry and attention, there have been in recent years a number of advanced steps as well. For the most part, these have been studies of the characteristics of various student groups conducted by psychologists, sociologists, political scientists, and educators. There has also been a rapidly expanding literature of research and commentary which has dealt with closely related topics. A few examples are as follows: (1) college-student development and the impact of schools on students (Freedman, 1967; Jacob, 1957; Katz and Associates, 1968; Newcomb and Feldman, 1968; Sanford, 1966, 1967); (2) the history and characteristics of universities, including studies of them as organizations and of faculty-administrative roles (Morison, 1966; Rudolph, 1962); (3) studies of high school functions and needs, such as Conant's, 1959; (4) studies of adolescent development and psychology (Adams, 1967; Douvan and Adelson, 1966; Erikson, 1963); (5) studies of social movements as such (Kohn, 1935; Toch, 1965; Weakland, 1968); (6) evaluations of students, their values, characteristics, and so on (Butz, 1964; Goldsen, Rosenberg, Williams, and Suchman, 1960; Sutherland, 1962; Pervin, Reik, and Dalrymple, 1966); and (7) works aimed at placing student drug use in perspective for the education of school administrators (Nowlis, 1967).

The foregoing are but samples of areas and work which aid in providing perspectives on contemporary student behavior. The activists themselves have written (Cohen and Hale, 1967; Draper, 1965; Jacobs and Landau, 1966). They have also been objectively studied and have stimulated much scholarly commentary (Bay, 1967; Block, Haan, and Smith, 1967; Fishman and Solomon, 1964; Flacks, 1967; Katz, 1967; Keniston, 1967; Lipsit, 1966; Lipsit and Wolin, 1965; Miller and Gilmore, 1965; Newfield, 1966; Peterson, 1966; Sampson, 1967; Trent and Craise, 1967; Watts and Whittaker, 1966; Westby and Braungart, 1966).

The foregoing are by no means all of the studies. More complete bibliographies will be found in the *Journal of Social Issues* (1967, volume 13), in Katz (1967), and in most of the articles cited above. Attention in the literature to activists as such should not obscure the fact that at least some studies have concentrated on conservative students or have compared one group with the other (for example, Barker, 1963; Schiff, 1964; Westby and Braungart, 1966).

For our purposes three principles emerge from the work done on activists. One principle is that simple explanations do not account for what has occurred, but rather that—as with most human social behavior—a complex set of factors within the student, his family, his peer group, his university, and society at large have all contributed to the development of activism. The second principle is that those who surprise conventional people need not be bad, incompetent, or "sick." To the contrary, the findings on activists are reasonably consistent in showing that, on the average, they are good students, are psychologically "healthy," and probably are more independent, more mature, more egalitarian, more dedicated to helping their fellow man, and more responsive to the ideas imparted by teachers than are their inactive peers. They can also be close to their families rather than rebellious and can reflect intellectual, humanistic, and democratic ideals fostered in the home. The third principle is that students differ and student groups differ; all those who are changing, who are unconventional, who shock, or who intentionally challenge laws cannot be lumped together.

Various observers propose different typologies; for example, Block *et al.* (1967) identify six groups among whom are the alienated (hippies or "beats"), the antisocial, the activists, the individualists or conservatives, the constructivists, and the apathetic. Sampson (1967), following Keniston (1967), differentiates the alienated (such as hippies) from the activists but notes there may be brief united fronts; within these groups Sampson notes the need to distinguish on the basis of motives, leadership vs. followers, and kind of commitment. It is Keniston's thesis that the activists are basically optimistic, socially concerned, and traditionally American in the sense of democratic values, whereas the alienated are pessimistic, private, nonconforming, incapable of responsibility, and likely to be psychologically disturbed even if they may also be talented and artistically gifted. Keniston sees the protesting student as promoting his parents' democratic values and, in contrast, the hippie as rejecting them. His own finding is that the child who becomes a student hippie comes from a family where there is schism between father and mother, where the father is depreciated by mother and son, and where mother and son have a special alliance of understanding and maternal control. Keniston finds the attraction of alienated youth to drugs compatible with their social withdrawal and their interest in intensifying subjective experience. These youth reject basic American values, are apolitical, and do not become involved in organizations or long-range activities. Keniston (1965), in a sensitive and comprehensive study, presents the details of his case studies of alienated and nonalienated students. Interestingly enough, he finds that dropping out of school is not related to activism and dissent, although it may be associated with alienation.

As to how many collegians may be alienated in Keniston's sense, there can only be estimates. Boyd (1967) proposes that 4 per cent "suffer from severe alienation." With about six million students enrolled in colleges and universities, that would mean 240,000 estranged and unhappy students. In public-health terms one would expect this 4 per cent—*if* that estimate is accepted and *if* alienation is predisposing to illicit-exotic drug use—to be "at risk" of symptomatic centering of their lives around such drug use.

Keniston's work, based on a careful study of individual subjects as well as on an appraisal of group studies, is one of the few which focuses on the drug-using student, although his emphasis is on the basic syndrome of alienation rather than on drug use for itself. Our concern in this book is, on the other hand, directed toward the use of drugs by students. There have not been many studies which bear directly either on styles of drug use or on the correlates of that use among students. These few relevant investigations, along with several commentaries that have come to our attention, will now be considered.

Goldstein (1966) observed drug use on fifty campuses from the vantage point of a journalism graduate student. His casual interviews with students, police, and administrators led him to conclude that marijuana was used by one out of seven students but that use of illicit or exotic drugs was rare. He considers most students simply to be dabblers or occasional (for example, week-end) smokers while only a very few are potheads. He views the latter to be psychologically disturbed individuals who are ethnocentric, anti-authority, vulnerable to progression to more dangerous drugs, and preoccupied with being "cool"—that is, with not being involved or emotional. Goldstein cites a number of stated goals for taking marijuana, among which seeking pleasure is the most frequent. Taking it out of curiosity, to achieve status or prestige in a social group, to relieve boredom, to express rebellion, and to have intense personal experiences are also common. He points out that the incidence of drug use varies greatly by campus and he attributes this to the location and orientation of the university or college and the composition of its student body. He notes that sophisticated urban schools initially had the highest student use of marijuana and other illicit-exotic substances but that there is now a spread to rural and less elite institutions. Whatever the prevalence on campus, the emphasis is on smoking as a social experience—one learned from others, done with others, and meaningful because it is a shared value and experience. Because it is a group activity and one which binds students together in expressing a style of living—even if it is only a fad —any student group may employ it. Smoking pot, he says, is not the prerogative of hippies or swingers on campus; instead, any strong ingroup, whether in an Ivy League residence house, a Midwestern fraternity, or a California cooperative may take up smoking. Thus, outward signs, beards or beads, are not enough to signal who may employ marijuana and who may not. Goldstein makes the important observation that alienation insofar as it is displayed by costume and pronouncement may in itself simply be a campus fad to which the students conform. Students may strive to appear alienated, but as an explanation for what they do, Goldstein holds such "alienation" suspect. The student "has adopted the style of alienation without assuming its emotional attitudes. . . . His connection with drugs . . . is just as fad-

dish. He is one of the crowd, not one of the disturbed. . . . The big
beat now brings us alienation a go-go" (p. 231).

Simmons and Winograd (1966), a sociologist and a journalist
respectively, have offered a portrait of the youth scene. They describe
the hang-loose ethic, the phenomenon of tripping out, the idea of the
happening, the psychedelic-drug scene, new politics, new music, and
related activities. Their thesis is that the university, or at least the
California university, "is a showplace of what is happening throughout our society" in the sense that it is the leading front of social
change. They suggest that irreverence toward conventional Americana
is the theme, a theme stressing humanism, the value of personal experience, distrust of dogma, primacy of spontaneity, tolerance, and
social equality. Property as the highest value is repudiated and so is
duty or obligation as such—that is, the hang-loose people will not do
what they "should" but only what they want to. "Concretely, this
means that they will break a law they disagree with, will desert a
spouse or friend they no longer love . . . ."

Regarding trips, of which the drug trip is one variety, they
are any "raw sensuous-emotional experiencing" and "tripping out is
the most definitive and the most controversial thing that happeners
are doing." Today's happenings are attributed by Simmons and Winograd to rapid social change with origins in the social fringes and with
a high negative correlation between "fringiness" and morality-legality
according to conventional standards. As to what is "happening," the
authors propose that there are "a million joints (marijuana cigarets)
a day smoked in California and an increase of about five percent per
month." They state that "The greatest participation is among West
Coast youth, then the East, then the Midwest, and the least in the
South." Discussing drug use, the authors propose that "the majority
of those involved are otherwise ordinary people" (except for their
fringe activities which are labeled illegal), that extralegal organizations, stirred by profit motives, have grown up to meet the demands,
and that "happenings are a spontaneous groundswell." There is, they
say, wide geographical spread for making connections for drugs, sex,
and friendship within the new circles, so that the university-hippie-
new world atmosphere is like "folks getting together for a big party";
yet, both beat and conventional society move toward each other, "so
that the lines between hip and square, cool and straight, philistine and
bohemian are blurring and more people slip back and forth or inhabit

the many-shaded areas between." The authors discard the notion of alienation as applicable, suggesting that the happeners are comfortable and lighthearted and enjoy good fellowship even while opposing the established order and feeling demoralized in the process of growing up.

Simmons and Winograd consider the drug scene central to what is happening in America, the "crossroads of conflicting ideologies," the place where "generational change . . . most vividly thrusts itself forward. . . ." Drug use is, they say, an escape from the conventional world, a "kick" of an experience. Discussing the many forces producing drug interest, they note that smoking marijuana has become the thing to do, that drug users are the children of the Establishment liberals who run things, that they are seeking a new and different inner world, that drug experiences do change people, and that some changes of the sort which happeners demand in the conventional world are in order. They quote Aldous Huxley: ". . . widespread training in the area of cutting holes in cultural fences is now the most urgent of necessities. . . ."

The authors consider the role of education as a force producing the youthful drug users. They note criticisms that education functions to produce people to meet the demands of the social order, not the needs and potentials of students. In essence, educational institutions are molds for plastic plants, not nurseries for growing flowers. The authors appear to agree with Paul Goodman—and with many students—that middle-class children are educational slaves. The university is criticized for being a service center for society, one which reflects the wishes of the "power elite" rather than being a student-centered cultural fair which is rich, nurturant, and uninhibited in its offerings.

Simmons and Winograd have much more to say—all of it provocative and insightful, none of it cursed or blessed with statistics or any of those other scientifically "respectable" devices for developing or proving a point. Their descriptions of hang-loose youth conform to what many other observers have also seen; yet one does not know "for a fact" that either their estimates of drug-use incidence or their characterizations of causes, feelings, and life styles are objectively the case. Theirs is an interpretation of what is happening, and for many it would *feel* correct.

With reference to the increase in drug use itself, all of the data are in support of the trends—if not the numbers—which Simmons and Winograd propose. Consider, for example, that in California in 1967 juvenile arrests for marijuana went up 181 per cent over 1966 and dangerous-drug arrests (mostly amphetamines or amphetamine-barbiturate combinations) went up 89 per cent. There were only a few "hard" narcotic arrests in the state among juveniles, but the increase for these was over 300 per cent. The rise in juvenile drug interest is by no means limited to the United States—any more than is the rise of student activism on campus or of hippie or "provo" groups. Reports from Great Britain, Japan, and Sweden, reviewed in *Drugs I,* show widespread illicit use; for example, Herulf (1967) in a total sample survey of all ninth-grade Stockholm students found that one child in three had access to drugs and that one in five had tried illicit drugs. Hashish was most often used by casual experimenters, but among the heavier users Preludin (phenmetrazine hydrochloride) was more popular.

In the United States, scandals and arrest statistics have been more often reported than study data with regard to drug use among high school students. Fortunately, a few studies are available. Miller (1967) sampled 2,600 students in a Great Neck, New York, high school. Findings indicated that 8 per cent had tried marijuana, 6 per cent had taken barbiturates without medical advice, 6 per cent had tried glue sniffing and cough syrup, and 2 per cent had experimented with hallucinogens. Most users reportedly intended to continue illicit use; ill effects from drugs were reported by only a few students. Settings for the illicit user were most often the home, parks, and parties, in that order. Students participating in school organizations reported illicit use less often, as did students with better grades. In California two 1967 studies in the San Francisco Bay Area are available. One Castro Valley questionnaire survey (Price, 1967) was directed to eleventh- and twelfth-grade students in two high schools. The results showed the following: 43 per cent of the boys and 33 per cent of the girls smoked tobacco; 50 per cent of the boys and 38 per cent of the girls had been drunk upon occasion; 35 per cent of the boys and 22 per cent of the girls had tried marijuana, and over three fourths of these had used it three or more times; 15 per cent of the boys and 9 per cent of the girls had taken LSD, and three fourths of the boys and half of the girls had taken it three times or more; 22 per cent of the boys and 18 per cent of the girls had taken amphetamines, with three fourths of both groups having used them three times or more. Settings for use were said to be either when out with "the gang" or at home; the average age of first use was fifteen to sixteen years; and the use of most drugs was initiated by classmates who were also the source of supply. Most students apparently felt there was "nothing wrong" with taking drugs. A study in a San Mateo high school (1967) found 8 per cent had used LSD, 4 per cent more than three times, and 18 per cent had used marijuana, 11 per cent more than three times. The per cent using these drugs increased the higher the grade level. A total of 20 per cent had used either LSD or marijuana. In a companion study, all juveniles referred for "narcotic" use (all drug offenses) in San Mateo County (a very wealthy county) were compared with a sample of delinquents engaged in other than "narcotic" offenses. Base data showed that narcotic-offending juveniles were more often older girls. Matching for age and sex to control these variables, researchers found that the narcotics-using juvenile who was apprehended was more likely to come from a stable middle-class home than were other offenders. The drug offenders were, in almost half of the cases, above average or intellectually superior; most had not been discipline problems in school, although the majority of boys had prior records (nondrug complaints) of police or probation contact. The girls, on the other hand, who were drug offenders did not, for the most part, have prior records. School-attendance problems were common for both boys and girls who were drug offenders.

Two final entries in the statistical parade describe results from questionnaire surveys conducted in the San Francisco Bay Area in 1968. One, by a Marin County high school paper, indicated that 46 per cent of all students in that suburban San Francisco Bay Area school had tried marijuana and 45 per cent said they were still using it. The other, the largest scale survey done to date, covered all students in San Mateo County high schools. It indicated that 32 per cent of the students surveyed said they had tried marijuana and 17.6 per cent said they had used it more than ten times. More than 10 per cent of those questioned said they had tried LSD, and about a sixth of the students said they had used amphetamines. Only 24 per cent said they had never used a psychoactive drug—including alcohol and tobacco.

None of these high school statistics can be taken at face value. Not only are they affected by sampling bias, possible underreporting and overreporting, but, more importantly, they are outdated by the time they are printed. Since marijuana use is primarily a social phenomenon and its adoption is part of a series of rapid changes in the youth culture, it responds to those kaleidoscopic events which shape social movements, fads, symbolic expressionism, and other features of the high school age.

COLLEGE STATISTICS

More survey data are available at the college level, although few studies are based on carefully conducted random samples. A San Mateo County (California) junior college sampled 700 students (Devonshire, 1967) and reported that 23 per cent had smoked marijuana, most more than once, and that 8 per cent of the students had used it more than twenty times. Another 7 per cent of the students intended to try it; 18 per cent were not sure whether they would try it or not. Seven per cent of the students had tried LSD, most more than once. About 12 per cent of those with LSD experience had taken it more than twenty times. Ten per cent of the students had had experience with other hallucinogens, including mescaline, banana peels, and *catnip*. Among nonusers, 6 per cent intended to try the so-called psychedelic drugs and 19 per cent were not sure. Regarding alcohol, 62 per cent of the students said they drank upon occasion and one in four among the drinkers have become drunk. Only 40 per cent of the students smoked cigarettes; among that group about a third smoked more than a pack a day. Asking about the age when the use of various drugs had begun, Devonshire found that a third of the LSD-experienced sample had begun its use in high school as had 22 per cent of the marijuana-experienced students. More than half of those using alcohol and tobacco had begun before the age of sixteen. Most students wanted more information about drugs.

Drawing by unspecified methods a sample of a hundred students from San Francisco State College, Harrison (1965) states that 60 per cent of the student body used drugs illicitly during their college career, pep pills being the most common. One fifth to one fourth reported smoking marijuana and about 3 per cent said they had had experience with LSD. Eells (1967) sampled students at the California Institute of Technology and found that 20 per cent had tried marijuana and 9 per cent LSD. Eells reports that the highest per cent of users was in the junior class, whereas there was little use by graduate students. With respect to future intentions, half of the undergraduates and about three quarters of the graduate students stated that they did not expect to use marijuana, whereas 65 per cent of the undergraduates and 85 per cent of the graduates were not interested in beginning the use of LSD. There was no evidence of "hard" narcotics use on campus.

Demos and Shainline (1967) administered a questionnaire to 540 students at California State College at Long Beach. They report that 50 per cent of the students had taken some type of drug without medical advice, that 11 per cent had taken LSD, mescaline, or marijuana, and that 21 per cent of the students who had not used marijuana or hallucinogens were not sure whether they would begin such use. Two thirds of the students indicated that they had learned about illicit drugs during their teens, while a quarter of them had learned about them before the age of twelve. Most students were interested in receiving more information about drugs.

A Princeton survey conducted by student journalists with unspecified sampling procedures reported in 1967 (newspaper account) that 15 per cent of the students had taken one or more illicit drugs. The majority of users were academically superior, among the upper fifth of the students, and a third of the users were said to be varsity athletes.

A special student group in Oregon replied to an anonymous questionnaire (Smith and Blachly, 1966). These were medical students asked about their amphetamine use. Of the two thirds replying, almost half had employed amphetamines and most of those doing so had used them several times. For student physicians the source had often been a physician (although that does not imply a medical need or formal prescription), friends, or available samples employed for self-administration. (The latter brings to mind the common route to drug dependency among physicians, who have access to narcotics and the opportunity for private employment.) Most using amphetamines described beneficial effects; some combined them with barbiturates, tranquilizers, or caffeine.

Pearlman (1966) at Brooklyn College has been critical of unsubstantiated off-the-cuff estimates of student drug use, of inadequate surveys, and of the alarmist sentiment underlying statements by some police, journalists, and academic personnel. His 1965 survey of all Brooklyn College seniors employed an anonymous questionnaire mailed to students, which was returned by only 51 per cent of those receiving it. Among those responding, about 6 per cent admitted to the use of (apparently) illicit-exotic drugs during their college careers. Replies by these illicit-drug users indicated that most began experimentation while in college, that most were not currently using illicit drugs, and that friends had been the major source of supply with "pushers," doctors, and others relatively unimportant.

In spite of the lack of sophisticated methods for surveys—as, for example, the bias introduced by nonresponse to mailed questionnaires or by loaded or leading questions—there has been a range of agreement that among urban college students somewhere between 15 per cent and 25 per cent had tried marijuana by mid-1967. At that time less than half had ever been regular users; about a fourth of the non-using students were toying with the idea of trying it. Our impression, based on the studies in School I conducted one and a half and two years after our initial survey there and reported in Chapter Six, is that from 1967 to 1969 a rapid increase occurred in the number of college students experimenting with marijuana. Hallucinogens appear to have been consistently less popular, although their use also has increased. Hard-narcotics use is rare but if opium is so classified, their use is also expanding markedly.

OFF-CAMPUS STUDIES

We see that the survey information about college students has been, for the most part, rather superficial and especially vulnerable to that sampling error which arises when one relies on the voluntary return of anonymous questionnaires. In such research it is generally the case that those who do not return their questionnaires are different from those who do, just as in door-knocking, opinion-poll work those who are consistently not at home are different from the stay-at-homes. Just how the nonresponders would affect incidence and prevalence rates is unknown. Within their limitations it is clear that the college surveys through 1967 showed that most users of illicit drugs had begun their experimentation in college, that most such use was learned from peers—and inferentially from upperclassmen—and that successful and active students could be involved in illicit use fully as much as "deviant" or fringe-element students. Graduate students, especially married and career-oriented people, appear to have been less involved in illicit-drug use.

In the 1968 studies—admittedly very limited in scope and method—one senses expansion of illicit use not only very considerably downward in age and "sideways" in the sense of within college-age or class groups but also upward as well into the echelons of unmarried graduate students. There is also the appearance of increased regular use of marijuana as opposed simply to experimentation. The importance of proselytizing—that is, a missionary zeal in "turning on" others—is implied in several studies, and it is perhaps that mission which is associated in part with evidence that increasing numbers of students are involved in the sale as well as the use of marijuana. All these findings stress the importance of marijuana rather than hallucinogens in terms of the numbers of students involved; they also imply the immense amount of marijuana which must be physically available in our major cities. The LSD and other-hallucinogen users must not be discounted simply because there are fewer of them. It is that fact which makes one focus on their individual characteristics as likely to be more unusual as compared with the diversity of personalities which must exist within the marijuana-using groups. It is also not to be discounted that perhaps up to 15 per cent to 20 per cent of undergraduate students in some colleges—and more in some high schools—have taken LSD or want to take it in spite of the fact that it is the most powerful psychoactive drug known to man and that its activity is unquestionably associated in at least some students with very bad outcomes, including psychosis, suicide, judgment deficit, and unlooked-for personality change.

OBSERVATIONS ON YOUTHFUL DRUG USERS

In recent years a number of observations made on drug-using youths have focused not on incidence or prevalence by school but, rather, on the social or psychological factors associated with individual propensities and group conduct. For the most part, these investigations have been a rich source of data on drug "abuse" as such and have enriched our knowledge particularly of heroin users, a group of young people found predominantly in big-city slums. Because our focus here is on students—and, in correlation, on advantaged rather than slum-dwelling youngsters among whom heroin plays a very small role—we shall not review the many excellent investigations that take as their cases identified "addicts." The reader is referred, for a good background, to such works as those by Chein, Gerard, Lee, and Rosenfeld (1964), Finestone (1960), O'Donnell and Ball (1966), and Stevenson (1956). Attention is also directed to the recent paper by Gordon (1967) on the widespread presence of psychopathology in gangs and to the role of drugs as possible facilitators of gang interaction and cohesiveness among these otherwise inadequate youngsters. There are also some early works on marijuana use, perhaps the most relevant of which is the La Guardia Report (1944).

Some important current studies provide a bridge between the foregoing focus on addicts or identified deviants and our interest here in student drug behavior.[2] Howard Becker (1963) in his study of jazz musicians and marijuana users describes important aspects of how one learns to smoke marijuana, how that drug use is related to membership in a group, and how the group sentiment constitutes simultaneously an in-group which rejects the square world and, in turn, as a deviant group is rejected by the square world. Becker examines the beliefs and drug conduct of these "outsiders" in a way which provides insight into the functioning of student drug-using society.

Another set of studies, our own (1964), describe some of the social and psychological antecedents, correlates, and consequences of the use of LSD and other psychoactive drugs among a group of intensively interviewed Californians during the years 1962 through 1964. Among them was a small sample of "informal black market" users (the study was done during a period when LSD use was legal but supplies were controlled), some of whom were graduate students and all of whom were part of a swinging crowd which associated with university teachers and with artists and intellectuals outside the university. Theirs was a history of use of many substances—peyote, marijuana, methedrine, mescaline, and so forth. Self-styled "heads" in the sense that they spent most of their time with other drug users, they were, nevertheless, professionally ambitious young people who appeared well adjusted to life and work and whose use of drugs emphasized pleasure and partying as well as freedom from internal restraints and conventions, and the enhancement of creativity. During this period, the males especially were proselytizers; we have followed some

---

[2] We see that student drug use is frequent enough that it must be considered within the "normal" range of behavior, at least on some campuses. We can also assume that since much of this behavior is experimental and focuses on drugs—many of which do not produce physical dependence—the concept of "addiction" is thoroughly inappropriate as a conceptual basis for its evaluation.

of them over the years and seen them become temporary leaders of
local drug-oriented groups, become suppliers of drugs and supporting
philosophies to graduate and undergraduate students, become professionally successful while still continuing drug use (especially marijuana), and we have seen one prominent young person in the group
convicted of drug offenses. In that study we identified some of the
social and personal features associated, in those "early" days, with
accepting or rejecting LSD, with ceasing its use or becoming a "regular" user, and with the natural history of use. We shall not cite that
work further here, but in those days the common phenomenon was
missionary zeal in initiating others to use, of the formation of drug-
interested social groups, of the use of a variety of drugs as a common
practice, and of a relationship between taking LSD and personal-life
dissatisfaction, desire for inner adventure, lack of concern about loss
of self-control, and the nature of prior information about the drug.

Blumer (1967), a sociologist, began a rehabilitation pilot project with youthful users of marijuana, LSD, and other "mod" drugs
in Oakland, California. That program turned into an inquiry about
these users, who ranged in age from seven to twenty-five, and evolved
a typology. The student investigators discriminated among the crimi-
nally oriented, aggressive, and undisciplined (rowdy) children who
came early to illicit-drug use. Starting out with alcohol, and glue,
gasoline, or lighter-fluid sniffing, they progressed to marijuana and,
in high school, to barbiturates, amphetamines, and more marijuana.
Experimenters of an extraordinary order, they might also try nutmeg,
sniff burning plastic, crush aspirin in cokes, soak inserts from inhalers
in beverages, inject wine intravenously, and smoke genuine tea. Curiously, this sample, even though lower class in origin, did not use
heroin. As late adolescents, the rowdy group might become hoods or
members of a motorcycle gang; they might begin to use drugs in
preparation for criminal activities (fights, robbery, and terrorizing)
and through underworld contacts become, the authors suggest, suscep-
tible to later use of heroin.

Contrasted with the unusual rowdy were those with a "cool"
(self-controlled) style, although, the authors state, many rowdies might
switch over to become cool. "Coolness" implies that the user controls
his drug use and his drug reactions and becomes neither dependent
nor openly intoxicated. Among these youth, the potheads—those who
limit themselves to marijuana—were from lower-class origins, were

alert, well informed, well dressed, and inconspicuous socially. In contrast, youth from middle and upper classes were more likely to use marijuana in protest (and presumably to dress in protest costume as well) and to become interested in LSD. Youth whose primary use was marijuana were not troublemakers, were not known to the law, were not otherwise delinquent, and, according to the investigators, most were likely to move into conventional society. It is our inference that some of this group would be represented in middle-class high schools and later in colleges.

The majority of the sample observed in the Oakland study belonged to a class the investigators labeled as "mellow." They were cool but ready to try anything once. Interested in parties, sex, and pleasure, they primarily used marijuana but they also employed pep pills, hallucinogens, and methamphetamine (crystal). Egalitarian, tolerant, and interested in good fellowship, the mellow user does not seek out drugs and does not orient his life around them, in contrast to the pothead, whose marijuana use is more intense and more central to his life. The mellow user is more discriminating in his drug tastes and shares a group lore as to which drugs are best at producing which effects; marijuana, for example, is best for music and for sex. The mellow users are seen as moving into conventional society, and it is our inference that they, too, will be in high school and college where, when interviewed about drug use, they will be identified as experienced but not intensive drug users who began before or during their teen years.

The investigators emphasize that drug use is learned from peers and older associates, that it occurs as a group activity imbued with group meanings, and that drug use does not necessarily signify rebellion, escape, or alienation. Instead, it is, the investigators contend, one of the things which a young man living in an already illicit-drug-using society learns to do. The study did not utilize controls of any kind, and so the question as to why some learn about drugs and do not use them, others learn and use drugs sparingly, and some learn and use drugs intensively remains unanswered. In any event, the Oakland investigation reveals that among preteen and teen-age children there is an established and sometimes compelling society of drug lore, drug availability, drug sales, and drug use. Apparently, depending upon background and personality factors, those recruited into drug use will take one of several alternatives—and by no means irrevocable—routes, the most common of which appear to emphasize self-control and conventional, external appearances along with either intensive use of marijuana or extensive use of multiple drugs. Many of these youth are in high school, some will attend college, and, while there, may be expected not only to continue their own drug interests but, as highly experienced users, to introduce others into "what's happening."

One assumes that some of the Oakland children described by Blumer are on their way to becoming full-fledged hippies and that others may already be "teenyboppers," some of whom wear flamboyant costumes and show precocious involvement in a variety of illicit or adult activities other than drugs. What about the hippies or flower children, who flagrantly advertise alienation, the love ethic, and the "hang-loose" style? Regrettably, they have been understudied even though overobserved, if we take free-swinging journalistic one-day immersions as illustrative of the latter. Nevertheless, a few scholarly studies and some statistics on drug use are available. Weakland, in *Drugs I,* discusses "what the scene means" and emphasizes the importance of the "trip" as a means of leaving a life which is felt to be insufficient or downright damnable and of finding a more satisfying life and self—but in a way which thumbs noses at the distressed elders. He notes how both hippie child and square parent are likely to be caught in a web of convention and failure to understand, to communicate, and—we infer—to enjoy life or one another. In this and in the use of drugs as a means to alleviate pain or, optimistically, as tools by which to search for something better, hippie children and square—but aspirin-using, heavy-drinking—elders share the same assumptions and, in the vernacular, "hang-ups."

Other thoughtful observations on the hippie culture include those of Berger (1967), Davis (1967), and Lettvin (1967), who emphasizes questions of morality and judgment. Simmon and Trout (1967) reported on a casual study of hippies *in* college. They distinguished within the on-campus hippie community between the goal-oriented "politicals" in the New Left and the apoliticals, called "skuzzies" by their Midwestern peers. A further group of teenyboppers were freshmen (whereas in California a "teenybopper" is any child in hippie dress from age eleven to fifteen to sixteen, some of whom are extremely active on the drug and love-in scene). In the Simmon and Trout observations, campus hippies were often scholarship holders, social-science majors, Jewish, and from middle-class or upper-middle-class intact urban or suburban homes. Without social spirit or athletic interests, the skuzzies recruit from among young students who tire of left-wing political activities and who are intrigued by hedonism. A further step in their initiation is to oppose parents, drop out of school, and then, later, return. It is the younger skuzzie who smokes the most marijuana and engages more in sex; older ones are cooler and do better in school. The average skuzzie period is a year and a half with two paths out: one is by aging, working, and getting married and the other is by becoming deviant hippies—that is, heavy drug users who are promiscuous or homosexual. The authors note the speedy change in the campus hippie culture, in its spread to high school, in its spread outward from a core group of students with personal problems—arising possibly out of a difficult social environment —to a broader movement. Furthermore, the New Left, which was, to Simmon and Trout, at least partly hippie though never skuzzie, will play, they say, a decreasing role as the New Left suffers "moral unemployment," and more students will become hippie without passing through a New Left phase. They believe the hippie appeals of pleasure, self-knowledge, drugs, and hanging loose, coupled with new music and art—plus a new sexual morality—are so great that this is no longer limited campus Bohemianism but possibly a permanent appeal for many students who, responding, will change the face of the campus for years to come.

Many of these and other observations are sympathetic to the desire of young people to improve the quality of their individual lives and of society as a whole. Yet many observers criticize the efficacy and safety of the drug orientation which they display. (Lettvin's [1967] remarks are particularly apt.) The extent of the importance of drugs for hippies is suggested by the replies to a few incidence inquiries. An "underground" newspaper, *The East Village Other* of New York City, published (January 1–16, 1968) results to a late 1967 questionnaire inquiry to which 1,200 "villagers" replied anonymously. Among the findings: 98 per cent had taken marijuana, 85 per cent hashish, 77 per cent LSD, 70 per cent methedrine, 50 per cent DMT, 41 per cent peyote, 31 per cent cocaine, 21 per cent heroin, 23 per cent laughing gas (nitrous oxide), 18 per cent barbiturates-tranquilizers, 12 per cent psilocybin, and so on. Methedrine and amphetamines were most often nominated as the worst trips, with heroin second and LSD third. Marijuana was elected most often as the best trip. Marijuana smoking for half of the sample had begun by age eighteen; a quarter smoked every day, most denied pot hang-overs, over half had a steady source of drug supplies ("a connection"), two thirds had themselves sold drugs, and half spent $20 or more per month for marijuana alone. Only 13 per cent had been arrested for drug offenses, most had at least some friends who were not drug users, and 14 per cent supported themselves by selling drugs; most of the rest worked at legitimate jobs. Most of the sample were between seventeen and twenty-five years of age, two thirds were male, three fourths had at least some college education, and two fifths were college graduates. It appears that over a fourth were college drop-outs.

Buckner (1967), a San Francisco sociologist, conducted interviews with fifty Haight-Ashbury hippies and received returns from 200 (of 500) mailed questionnaires as well. Most of his sample were found to be from out-of-state, to have been in California less than a year, to have had some college education, to be from middle- or upper-class homes, to be under age, and to be disassociated from conventional Christianity. Ninety-six per cent had smoked pot and 90 per cent said they had taken LSD. Regarding sexuality, 42 per cent of the males reported homosexual experience, as did 24 per cent of the females; these latter figures suggest a "polymorphous perverse" capability as much in opposition to convention as is their drug use. McNamara and Keller (1968) observed 232 Haight-Ashbury summertime hippies whose average age was twenty-one; they found them to be poor, friendless, and without skills or initiative. Half of their subjects moved once a week or oftener, a fifth had had no place to sleep the evening prior to the interview; half lived on less than $20 a week, a third on less than $10. These life styles are reflected in severe psychological disturbance in the clinical cases, in individual futility, and, we infer, social disorganization in this community of despair. Further observations on psychopathology in the Haight-Ashbury residents are offered by Hensala, Epstein, and Blacker (1967).

OBSERVATIONS ON STUDENT DRUG USERS

It is apparent that what is "happening" socially can be evaluated not only by statistics of drug use, mobility, and economics, or from the standpoint of cultural importance but individually in terms of either the effects of drugs on people or in the appraisal of kinds of people who are attracted to the drug scene. We have already discussed Keniston's (1965) fine case material which is so instructive.

Another psychiatrist, Kleber (1965), carefully observed twenty-one students at Yale who had taken peyote, half of whom had also taken marijuana. Kleber observes that both psychologically stable and unstable students experiment with drugs and that for the unstable ones the reasons offered—"wanting new experience," "seeking religious meanings," and so forth—were superficial and concealed serious problems of adjustment. Even admissions of rebellion were capable of more psychodynamic interpretation, specifically acting out of hostility to parents by doing a disapproved act and also experimenting with independence in risk situations. Among the unstable students using a hallucinogen, as compared with the psychologically stable and otherwise average undergraduates he observed, Kleber found more adverse effects, fewer reports of pleasant experiences, and less intention to repeat use. Among psychologically adjusted students, the reasons offered for drug use were more likely to be more accurate, showing self-awareness and not reasons which concealed adjustment problems. Many subjects reported anxiety during the drug experience; half felt drug use had improved their lives; a fourth (these confined to the maladjusted students) were observed to have long-lasting adverse effects, including anxiety, persistent hallucinations, worsened symptoms, or drug dependency.

Kleckner (1968) administered the Cattell 16PF Test to forty college students who were psychedelic drug users and compared them with a matched sample of forty non-users, all from the same college. Users were significantly more aloof, anxious, paranoid, and had less ego strength and super ego. The 16PF interpretation also termed them brighter and more dominant interpersonally. Nevertheless, the scales were further interpreted as indicating that users were more creative, less leader-like, more isolated, and more accident prone. No other test data or life-history data were brought to bear to validate these at times inconsistent interpretations.

A very careful psychological study of LSD effects by McGlothlin, Cohen, and McGlothlin (1967) tells us much that is important about the characteristics of students who are interested in hallucinogens. The investigators recruited subjects for an experiment without telling the volunteers what the study would be. A large battery of tests was given prior to a series of three LSD sessions at intervals of two weeks and then six months after the last LSD session. Among 122 male graduate students qualifying as subjects (not prepsychotic, not in therapy, or so forth), 25 refused to take LSD when they were told what the experiment would be and another 11 remained but were fearful. These negative students were compared with neutral and positive (toward LSD) ones. On tests the students who were against taking LSD proved to be more extroverted, more organized and given to making plans, and more conventional and factual. The students who were in favor of taking LSD were more capable of regressive experience (related to hypnotic susceptibility), more intuitive, more introverted, more casual and spontaneous, more psychopathic (amoral, careless of the rights of others), more bizarre, and more excitable. Almost all of those favorable toward taking LSD had had marijuana, and fewer were married and attended church. After taking 200 mcg of LSD, students were compared with controls who took either minimal LSD (25 mcg or 20 mg amphetamine). Two weeks after taking LSD, the experimental group felt they were less tense and anxious compared with others, but objective tests did not consistently bear out "real" differences in anxiety; tests did show they were less emotional in response to laboratory stress. Six months after taking LSD, experimental subjects appeared on tests to be less defensive and reported in a questionnaire that they felt greater musical appreciation and creativity. On the other hand, tests of aesthetic appreciation, imaginativeness, and originality showed no changes.

A study by Brehm and Back (1968) identifies important personality factors associated with student drug use. Using 333 college freshmen and focusing on the broad spectrum of psychoactive drugs, the investigators identified five factors derived from the attitude questionnaire which they employed. One factor was insecurity, another was fear of loss of control, the third was sick role, the fourth was denial of drug effects, and the fifth was curiosity. The first factor contained items related to symptoms of distress and their alleviation through chemical means, as well as feelings of inadequacy and hypochondriasis. These factors were found to be related to reported drug usage. Correlations existed between the use of several classes of drugs; for example, for males especially, social stimulants, sedatives, and the use of hallucinogens and opiates were correlated. As a result, the authors conclude that there is a general orientation toward the use of pharmaceutical controls to change oneself (a conclusion in keeping with our findings). Insecurity was found to be a factor related to the use of all agents, from aspirin through opiates. Curiosity was related to the use of hallucinogens, opiates, and energizers, whereas fears about loss of control were negatively related to the use of these illicit substances. Brehm and Back conclude that ". . . the combination of doubt about and wish to change the self plus a general confidence in the effectiveness of drugs is related to using *any* type of physical agent, whereas a combination of curiosity about one's potentialities and an absence of fear of loss of control relate more specifically to using that complex of agents known as 'releasors.' "

The authors then went on to construct self-concept scales focusing on external self (appearances), ideal self, and hidden self. They found that the "hidden" self was the one which corresponded most closely to drug use when a discrepancy measure was employed comparing the hidden with the ideal self. Combining this with a factor analysis, they conclude that two aspects of self-perception are associated with a desire for self-modification through the use of chemical agents: "One is general dissatisfaction with oneself . . . the other is the absence of any defenses or restraints against taking this route, be it fear of loss of control, (primarily in males) or defense through denial (primarily in females)." Using these variables as classifiers in that same sample was found to produce an accuracy ranging from 51 per cent (drug use in females) to 97 per cent (nonuse in females). Reduced success in classification occurred in subjects whose characteristics suggested either apathy about chemical agents or conflict about their use. Brehm and Back suggest that it is in this group that social, situational, and additional psychosomatic conditions may affect the use of the more powerful (and illicit) psychoactive agents.

Reviewing these diverse studies of prevalence and incidence, as well as of social and psychological features associated with drug use, we conclude that illicit-drug use is an exceedingly important activity for many young people, that the styles of student use differ considerably from the heroin involvements of slum dwellers, that the intentions and functions for drug use vary considerably within the student population which is involved and embrace phenomena as diverse as individual psychopathology and personal idiosyncrasy, leadership and followership in social movements, the accident of being on particular campuses or in particular social or resident groups, personal curiosity and exploration, and, of course, responsiveness to the pharmacological effects of psychoactive drugs as such. We also conclude that not only is there a rapidly expanding social phenomenon but that it has increasingly important implications for individuals involved in drug-centered living. For those who are interested in that drug use, it is apparent that issues ranging from the moral and ideological through the neurophysiological and biochemical must be confronted and, further, that by focusing on drug use one elucidates a host of events and problems which are intimately linked to critical issues in many disciplines and professions—as well as to our very philosophies of government and of man's relationship to nature and to his fellow man. Drug use is also linked to most of us quite personally, not only because we are ourselves likely to be users of drugs, albeit probably legal ones, but because the youthful drug user is someone most of us know and for whom we have responsibilities and affection. More than that, the youthful drug user—or the phenomenon itself— is someone to whom we *react* in highly intense and personal ways. Whether we respond with admiration for the pioneering or rebellious spirit, with titillation over drug effects we ourselves might like to experience, with indignation over violation of law and convention, with anxiety over the consequence for those we know, or simply with wonder about what it all signifies, our own reactions are critical and compel us not only to seek understanding of student drug use but possibly even to examine our own responses with more than ordinary reflection.

Drugs on
Five Campuses

Richard H. Blum

II

O ur own study as reported here focuses on drug-using conduct and on some social and psychological correlates among students in five Western colleges or universities. There is also information on drug use among students in four California high schools. Our data on students include information on bad outcomes; this means ill effects reported by students and bad outcomes as identified by official school case finding—the records of school administrative and health authorities. This book also includes an assessment of the psychiatric aspects associated with bad outcomes, an appraisal for school administrators of the implications of drug use, a commentary on the relationship between drug use and one set of predominant religious values, and an overview of the findings from ours and other on-going or recently completed student and youth studies.

The methods we employed were several. The study, which we later called *Utopiates* (Blum and Associates, 1964), really began in 1962 with our observations on LSD users, some of whom were faculty members, teaching assistants, research workers experimenting on students, and graduate students. These observations were completed in 1964 but began again in 1965 through 1966 as we prepared the ground for the college survey. The method of preparation was to be with student drug users so as to get to know them well. More formally, this is called "participant observation." Much of that work was done by Funkhouser-Balbaky (1966). A second simultaneous set of observations, extending from 1962 to the present, were those of the intensive clinical case study. Some of these observations appear in *Utopiates*, a few are presented in Chapter Fifteen, but others unreported constituted a source for the questions asked during the surveys and for the speculations advanced as we pondered upon what we had found.

Once the interview schedule for the survey work itself was constructed—a process of pretesting which took over a year—the business of its administration was relatively straightforward (a statement which takes no notice of the difficulties involved in running a survey in five different colleges). In each of the schools, a sample of undergraduates was randomly drawn from the registrar's lists of matriculated (day) students. In one school a small graduate sample was also drawn. Interviewers were trained in the use of the schedule, including its precoded answer-recording sectors. In two schools, following the administration of the interview, a reliability check was conducted.

All the results of the interviewing phase represent the reports of students about themselves. Although we presume that skillful interviewing reduced the likelihood either of exaggeration or denial of illicit-drug use per se, we must assume that some such distortion occurred. How much we cannot estimate. The reader will see that our data conform to the range of reports from other schools as cited in Chapter One and to subsidiary samples drawn at the same time on one campus (see Chapter Eleven). All this may imply is that the errors of underreporting and overreporting remain fairly constant across campuses. We do have some reasonably heartening evidence, cited in Chapter Sixteen, to the effect that what students say they will do in regard to drug use in general is, in fact, what they will do when given an opportunity to use illicit drugs in particular, $r = .78$.

Another method employed involved the selection of special samples as used in the students described in Chapter Eleven. Chapters Twelve through Fourteen report on groups of students with intense interests in illicit-exotic drugs, left-wing politics, right-wing politics, and religion who were identified on the basis of membership in organizations, visible involvement in issues, and nomination by faculty, college ministers, and peers. These students were interviewed and given psychological tests. In Chapter Sixteen, two fraternity houses constituted the sample and the endeavor was to predict individual drug use—specifically "turning on" or being initiated into illicit-exotic use—over the course of a year. The methods employed here were rating scales of experience and attitudes, a brief questionnaire, and sociometric devices. A fourth method employed, reported in Chapter Ten, was the panel. Panelists in two schools comprised randomly drawn subsamples selected from the initial, larger random sample. In a third school—this time intentionally—sampling differed and was based upon the selection of identified users of illicit-exotic drugs. The device used in the panel study was a weekly and monthly drug-use diary kept on a daily basis by students and collected from them monthly. A fifth method employed was use of psychiatric interviews and observation, as reported in Chapter Seventeen. A sixth device, though hardly a method in any elaborate sense, is found in Chapter Nine and consisted of gathering case-finding data from the official— and unofficial but recorded—records of institutions, school administrators, school health services, and local and state police agencies. To varying degrees all of the foregoing devices for identifying and selecting students and for assessing their conduct were processed and elaborated by means of coding, quantification, computer processing, and, when deemed appropriate, the application of statistical tests.

Our plan called for a sample of 300 undergraduates to be drawn randomly only from registrars' lists in each of four schools and a sample of 200 from the junior college in our study. The plan also called for professionals in each school to be in charge of sampling, interviewer training, and interviewer supervision, with all of them using the same interview schedule and receiving the same instructions in sampling, interviewing, and coding procedures. The plan, however, did not work out quite that way. In School I, 2 out of the sample of 300 refused to participate and were replaced by further random drawing. In School II, a sample of 275 was drawn out of which there were five refusals, so that the final sample was 270. In School III, local personnel were unable to perform the work, so that interviewers from School I did so instead. There, a sample of 207 was drawn; because there were six refusals, the final sample was 201. School IV drew an initial sample of 300 but failed adequately to supervise the work so that only 192 were interviewed; a second sample of 300 was drawn, but work was not completed in time so that a final sample of 250, heavily weighted with upperclassmen, was the outcome. School V, because of local needs, required a sample of graduate students as well; 75 graduate students and 218 undergraduates comprised the final selection. These 218 were drawn from a list of 251. There were thirty-three refusals.

In each school all information was collected from students who were personally contacted and privately interviewed. Students were assured of anonymity if they were concerned, and they were shown the coding procedure designed to guarantee that anonymity. Interviews were conducted over a period of three to six months in each school; all work was done in the 1966 to 1967 academic year. The interview schedule, which standardized question format, question order, and recording and coding had been developed and pretested on several campuses over the prior eighteen-month period. The average interview time was one hour; it was rarely less than forty-five minutes, rarely more than ninety minutes.

The accuracy of the information collected depended upon what the student was able to remember of his own lifetime drug use and what he was willing to report to the interviewer. There was only one student who accepted the interview and then refused to answer some of the questions. We have seen that the rate of refusal varied from less than 1 per cent (the private university) to 34 per cent (the state college). During interviews the interviewer could raise additional queries if a student appeared to be giving inconsistent or unclear information about his drug-use history; however, there was no way for the interviewer to know whether the student was lying. It was the impression of the interviewers—all of whom were either graduate students themselves or older persons who enjoyed and were sympathetic to students—that most students were interested in the interview discussions and were open about their own views and experiences with mind-altering drugs.

The 39 inquiry areas and 215 questions or index items which constituted the interview were derived either from the need for specific descriptive data about the students and their history of drug use or from expectations that particular characteristics of students would be associated with varying styles of drug use—that is, that there would be regular psychological relationships. We do not claim that these expected relationships, ones which emerged as expected differences among students in their drug use as a function of some other personal or social characteristics, verify anything as elegant as "hypotheses." Rather, these relationships, most of which were found to operate as anticipated, are consistent with what any thoughtful observer would expect. The fact that drug use does turn out to be reasonably predictable simply confirms that people—their experiences, personalities, and actions—are not composed of unjointed and disparate parts but rather that they are of a piece, articulated, coordinated, or otherwise a systematic whole.

In presenting these findings, we have been faced with a typical problem of our technological age, that of computer output amounting to many thousands of tables. We have taken it as our task to identify those findings which were linked to our expectations or which were otherwise meaningful and to translate them into expository prose. We have not used the shotgun or random method of discussing—or even paying attention to—much of the inevitable computer output that was unrelated to our general expectations. We have tried to avoid tables, for the sake of readability as well as of publishing costs. Any reader who wishes to have more details on numerical distribution is invited to write to us. Finally, we have strongly limited the use of statistical tests. We feel that, for the most part, interview data which consist of hundreds of interrelated subitems interpreted for the most part in terms of trends and major links are not to be gilded with statistical testing. The latter are procedures we prefer to apply to the rigorous test of hypotheses under controlled experimental conditions. Such statistical tests as we apply are demonstrative or, occasionally, helpful to inference.

Repeat interviews were conducted in two schools on a small sample of twenty-two students (ten on one campus, twelve on the other) randomly drawn from the basic sample. The second interview was conducted by a different interviewer. The repeat interviews took place from one to five months after the initial interview and were designed to test the reliability of the information gained. One set of interviews was conducted in the school where interviewer supervision had been poorest, although the interviewers there had also been trained and were considered competent. The other school was one where interviewer supervision was considered satisfactory.

The 215 replies or indices were coded for computer analysis. That meant for the ten students reinterviewed in one school 2,150 agreements were possible between the original and the repeat interview; for the twelve students in the other school, there were 2,580 opportunities for agreement or disagreement. The actual rate of agreement in the first school was 86.4 per cent and in the second 84.4 per cent. The agreement between the two rates of consistency was such as to indicate that our assessment of poorer interview supervision in the second school was not actually related to any important difference in what the interviews yielded. A check was made of the items which were the basis for the greatest inconsistency between the initial interview and the repeat interview. There were twenty-five items where more than seven of the twenty-two students gave a different reply in each of the two interviews. Two items were shifts within one question (q. 12) which required the ranking of several potential activities as to their current importance to the student. Here, his political and "other" activities changed rank over time. Another item (q. 17) was related for it inquired about the direction of the student's political beliefs and whether they were, in fact, shifting. The implication here is that more than 30 per cent of those who made up the reliability sample experienced some shift in the importance and direction of their political activities during the school year. In the lifetime drug-history sector, inconsistency showed up in replies to inquiries about events associated with stopping or decreasing use of tobacco (which could be related to starting or stopping use in the between-interview interval) and about major events associated with increasing or decreasing alcohol consumption and with the source of alcohol when first consumed (the latter is either clear error or represents students beginning to drink during the interval between interviews). In the lifetime drug history, there were also inconsistencies in sedative reports, both in intentions to use again and in reports of parental use; with tranquilizers there was also inconsistency in reports of parental use. No major inconsistencies existed on any items regarding lifetime drug histories of amphetamines, marijuana, hallucinogens, opiate-narcotics, or special substances used for kicks. With no drug were there major inconsistencies, as defined here by 30 per cent or more disagreement, on any feature or age of onset of use, on amount of use during any year of life, on beneficial or ill effects, on dependency worries, or on reports of friends' or relatives' reactions to a student's using a drug. Further inconsistency did show up, however, in the area of common drugs in regard to "yes-no" reports of experience with strong (opiate) pain-killers and characteristics of the present amount of use of mild stimulants (coffee, tea, chocolate and cocoa, Coca Cola and other cola drinks, and No-Doze and other over-the-counter stay-awakes). This latter item—amount of present use of any one of these subclasses of minor stimulants—was the least consistent of all, with fifteen of twenty-two students reporting a shift in amount of use between the first interview and the repeat interview.

In reference to the functions or aims for which drugs were used, changes took place in the "yes-no" reporting of having taken something to satisfy cravings or compulsions, or to relieve boredom or monotony, or to make the student feel healthier or stronger. There were also changes in "other" reasons (spontaneous) given to account for the use of drugs by the student. There were inconsistencies in elaborations or replies to an inquiry as to beliefs which guided the student in regard to his personal use of illicit drugs. These guiding principles, complexly coded because of the open-ended question, accounted for three unreliable subitems (out of a set of eighteen such subitems). Inconsistency also appeared in responses to the question as to how ready the student's parents were to give medication when he was ill as a child, in the evaluation of advantages to being sick as a child, on the final score given mother-father-student consonance on a list of nineteen issues of potential disagreement (this subitem, in fact, made up nineteen questions, each with three sectors; reliability scoring provided a "disagreement" score whenever there were three or more shifts in reply out of the fifty-seven possible). The final inconsistencies were in self-ratings of satisfaction/dissatisfaction with present teachers and in the degree of optimism the student had about how likely he and people of similar belief could bring about the changes in the world (technological, social, and so on) that he would like to see happen.

Excluding these items with relatively high inconsistency, we find the overall consistency for the remaining majority of (190) items to be high. These included nearly all aspects of lifetime drug use, self-descriptions, background data, relationships with others, and so forth. With regard to the inconsistent items, it is possible to speculate, but not to know, as to what contributed to variability. In each instance the repeat interviewer was a different person from the initial interviewer, so that some direct interpersonal influence may have operated. Several of the items were sensitive to any shift over time in what the student was doing politically or how particular patterns of current drug use were changing. Some items were possibly sensitive to mood changes or to intervening events, as in relations with parents. If lies about drug use were told, we would expect them to have centered about the illicit substances. Since no great inconsistencies occurred in reporting any aspect of illicit-drug use, we may at least conclude that if lying did occur, it was done with consistent sophistication.

Table 1 below sets forth major characteristics of the student

Table 1

CHARACTERISTICS OF SAMPLES DRAWN FROM FIVE SCHOOLS*

	School I	School II	School III	School IV	School V
			Percentages		
Per cent male	68	61	59	50	59
Per cent female	32	39	41	50	41
Per cent aged					
18 and below	15	15	18	5	4
19	25	27	35	13	21
20	21	28	26	14	17
21	26	17	5	18	12
22	9	6	4	15	12
23	1	2	4	11	7
24 and over	2	5	8	25	27
Year in school					
Freshman	27	34	53	12	20
Sophomore	19	26	44	12	19
Junior	25	22	1	32	17
Senior	29	16		44	17
Graduate					26
Unclassified		1	2		
Major field					
Technological,					
hard sciences	24	29	10	16	22
Arts, humanities	10	13	20	28	18

* All per cents are rounded off to nearest whole number in all tables.

Table 1—Cont.

CHARACTERISTICS OF SAMPLES DRAWN FROM FIVE SCHOOLS*

	School I	School II	School III	School IV	School V
			Percentages		
Biological sciences	9	18	4	10	12
Social sciences	30	39	19	38	38
Other majors	1	1	34	4	9
General studies or undecided	25	0**	10	4	1
Several majors	0	0	1	1	1
Family annual income					
Under $5,000	4	6	6	8	8
$5,000 to $10,000	14	29	27	39	34
$10,000 to $15,000	25	34	31	32	26
$15,000 to $25,000	19	23	22	14	19
Over $25,000	32	7	6	5	6
DK/NA***	5	1	7	3	7
Present religious affiliation					
Protestant	43	6	42	31	62
Catholic	14	88	28	26	14
Jewish	5	0	0	8	2
Other religion	2	1	3	4	1
No religious affiliation	31	5	25	30	19
DK/NA***	0	0	0	1	1
Sample size N =	300	270	201	250	293

* All per cents are rounded off to nearest whole number in all tables.
** Because we are rounding off, a zero entry can conceal cases belonging in that category whenever the number of cases are fewer than half of 1 per cent (0.5%). Whenever such otherwise unentered cases are of special interest, or whenever actual Ns are of interest, the tables will include the actual N in parentheses.
*** DK/NA = "Don't know" or "No answer."

samples randomly drawn (with the exception of School IV as noted) for each school.

The information in Table 1 allows the inference that the student populations vary from one school to another in reputation and structure of the college. Students from School I, the private university, come from the wealthiest families. Social sciences predominate as a major along with a large undecided or general-studies group. Most of the students are either Protestant or deny any current religious affiliation. Most students at School II, the Catholic university, are Catholic and come from middle-income families. Social sciences and the hard sciences (including technology) are the most popular majors. The senior class at School II is small; there is a consistent attrition from early to later school years. School III, the junior college, has the youngest population and the greatest number of students in non-academic majors (vocational programs). Most of its students are Protestants or deny current religious affiliation. School IV, the state college, has the largest number of older undergraduates in its sample, the largest proportion of Jewish students, more students from lower-income families, and the highest proportion in arts and humanities. The large number of upperclassmen in the sample represents, we believe, a sampling error. School V, the state university, located in a small city in a rural area, includes the graduate-student sample. Social and hard sciences, plus technology, are the most popular majors. It has the highest proportion of Protestant students. These student characteristics are consistent with differences in the reputations, traditions, and locations of each of the schools.

Table 2 below presents gross data on drug experience among the samples in each school. More detailed information on how drugs are used is presented in later chapters; our purpose here is simply to compare experience with each class of mind-altering substances by school. Experience in this instance is defined by the statement on the part of the student that he has had one or more experiences with any drug in the class of drugs inquired about; thus, any experience with wine, beer, or hard liquor constitutes an affirmative statements for alcohol. Similarly, any experience with LSD, DMT, STP, mescaline, peyote, psilocybin, and so on would classify the student as having had experience with hallucinogens.

Table 2, with its lifetime or one-or-more drug experiences, shows that in each school alcohol is the drug most often cited, nine out of ten or more students in all schools (except 89 per cent in one) reporting use. Alcohol use is greatest in the state colleges. Tobacco is consistently second with from two thirds to over four fifths reporting

Table 2

PER CENT OF STUDENTS IN EACH SCHOOL REPORTING
ANY EXPERIENCE WITH DRUGS

School	Tobacco	Alcohol	Amphet-amines	Sedatives	Tranquil-izers
I	76	94	25	31	18
II	72	91	11	18	11
III	83	94	26	29	21
IV	81	97	32	25	28
V	68	89	13	21	19

School	Marijuana	Hallu-cinogens	Opiates, cocaine, other narcotics	Special substances*
I	21	6	1 $(N = 4)$	6
II	11	2	1 $(N = 4)$	4
III	21	7	2 $(N = 4)$	11
IV	33	9	1 $(N = 3)$	8
V	10	2	1 $(N = 3)$	3

* Special substances include materials used for kicks, such as glue, gasoline, and nitrous oxide (for the purpose of sniffing), cough syrups, and so on.

use. Tobacco has been used by fewest students in the state university, while the junior college has the greatest number of students reporting its use. The medically available compounds—the amphetamines, sedatives, and tranquilizers—show more between-school diversity than either alcohol or tobacco. The state college is highest on amphetamine experience and tranquilizers; the Catholic university is lowest on both of these and shares the lowest frequence of tranquilizer experience with the private university. The junior college students report the greatest experience with sedatives. In terms of numbers of students reporting experience, marijuana ranks about the same as the medically available stimulants, sedatives, and tranquilizers, with from one tenth to one third of the students reporting experience. The state college is highest on marijuana use (perhaps reflecting the sample bias with its greater number of upperclassmen), while the state university and the Catholic university are lowest. Hallucinogen use is markedly less than marijuana experience for all schools; again, the state university and the Catholic university are lowest and the stage college is highest. Hallucinogen experience is, in terms of ranked averages, slightly less than use of special substances, although with both groups less than 10 per cent of the students (with one exception, 11 per cent in the junior college reporting special-substance experience) stating any experience. Least often used are the opiates with 2 per cent as the highest figure—that, too, in the junior college. For opiates, Table 2 also shows actual numbers of students reporting since our rounding-off procedure for presenting percentages does not allow exact calculations of numbers involved. It is to be kept in mind that the opiate classification is exclusively illicit for it excludes any opiates (for example, morphine) administered under medical supervision.

On the basis of the data in Table 2, one may conclude that genuine differences exist among schools in the (reported) drug experience of students. There are also across-the-board or "cross-campus" consistencies in average ranking of one-time-or-more drug use, ranging from alcohol and tobacco as everywhere most common to hallucinogens and opiates as least common. It would not be wise to generalize about kinds of institutions as such on the basis of our one-of-a-kind samples. It is interesting simply to see that a state college located in a metropolitan center is highest or shares the highest frequencies for alcohol, amphetamines, tranquilizers, marijuana, and hallucinogens and that a suburban junior college ranks highest on tobacco, sedatives, opiates, and special substances. These rankings raise questions as to the relationships of drug experience to the characteristics of the student body and, specifically, of the relationship of kind of drug experience to the characteristics of students. The rankings also pose the possibility that there will be correlations among drug experiences—that is, persons reporting use of one unusual drug might also be more likely to report use of another unusual drug. We shall explore these likely possibilities in later chapters.

Another way of comparing drug use by schools was to examine the intensity of drug use as measured by the distribution of individual scores in contrast simply to experience. An intensity score was developed for each student on the basis of his statements about his lifetime history of the use of each drug in the nine categories. Scored intensity of use would increase for each year the student had taken the drug and by the amount taken, classified as "intermittent," "occasional," "regular," or "considerable" (definitions of these classifications were specific for each drug). Most of the intensity comparisons we made were based on the score equivalent of the "mean drug-use score."

That score was obtained by first summing up all the entries in the drug-use table (individual drug profile) for a given drug, then dividing by the number of age categories which applied to that individual. For example, a total of fourteen categories is applicable to an individual who is twenty-eight years old or more; therefore, the sum of entries would be divided by 14. For a person eighteen years old, the divisor for each drug-use score would be 8. By dividing in this fashion, one prevents overweighting of the drug use of older students when developing use-intensity scores for students of different ages.

Table 3 below gives the distribution of total drug-use scores on each campus. From Table 3 we see that there are considerable dif-

Table 3

INTENSITY OF DRUG USE FOR STUDENTS ON EACH CAMPUS
(As per cent of student body)

Score	School I	School II	School III	School IV	School V
0 (No drug use ever)	3	5.6	2.6	2	7.2
1–25	72	77.4	68	46	64
26–50	21	14.8	22	39	24.5
51–75	3.7	2.2	5.5	11.6	4
76–100	0.3	—	0.5	1.2	0.3
101–125	—	—	—	0.4	—
126–150	—	—	0.5	—	—
151–175	—	—	—	0.4	—

ferences among schools in the distribution of scores. School IV has the fewest students in the zero-score category and by far the greatest number in the over 26-, over 51-, and over 100-score categories. School II has the greatest proportion of students in the range of scores of 25 and under. Except for School IV (which suffered from sampling inadequacy and bias), we see that the majority of students are in the very low range of drug-intensity scores.

To refine the scores for drug-use intensity for each campus, the two drugs which most students on every campus have used, alcohol and tobacco, can be excluded. Thus, what is left are the prescribed drugs (amphetamines, sedatives, and tranquilizers) and the illicit drugs (marijuana, hallucinogens, illicit opiates, special substances—and, again, amphetamines[1]). Table 4 below presents the distribution of drug-intensity scores when such an exclusion is made.

Table 4

DRUG-USE INTENSITY SCORES FOR EACH CAMPUS,
EXCLUDING ALCOHOL AND TOBACCO

Score	School I Per cent	School II Per cent	School III Per cent	School IV Per cent	School V Per cent
0*	39.5	61.8	42	33.6	58
1–10	48.8	35.3	48	51.5	35.6
11–20	10.3	2.6	7	10.8	5.5
21–40	1	.4	2	3.2	1.1
41 and over	.3		1	.8	.3

* The zero category now includes all students who have taken no drugs except alcohol and tobacco.

The data in Table 4 above are consistent with Table 3 in placing School II as the lowest in intensity of use, for only one third of its students report the use of any psychoactive drug (in our major categories) except for alcohol and tobacco. School II is closely followed by School V in this respect. We may infer that most of the drug experience which constitutes the drug-history intensity score for students in Schools II and V was with alcohol and tobacco, for with these drugs removed from consideration, the majority in both schools have zero-intensity scores. School IV is in the first rank in terms of the percentage of students with intensive drug-use histories, but now we see that School I ranks a close second in intensity and that School III is not far behind. Combined with data from Table 3, this implies that students in these three schools are considerably greater users of both prescribed and illicit drugs. Such is exactly the case, of course, as shown in Table 2. Recall that School IV ranks first in marijuana use, followed by Schools III and I; a similar ranking obtains for hallucinogens. These are the schools that are also highest in reported experience with the amphetamines, sedatives, and, with one reversal, tranquilizers. What this shows is that the experience measure is related

---

[1] Amphetamines are obtained by students through both legal and illegal channels.

to the intensity measure,[2] a relationship which will be considered in further detail in later chapters. In the meantime, we are assured that there are differences among schools whether drug use is measured in terms of reported student experience—"yes" or "no"—with each class of drugs or whether overall intensity of drug use is recorded over a lifetime and includes all the major psychoactive-drug classes or, alternatively, limits the measure of intensity to illicit and prescribed drugs.

Table 5 below expands on the information in Table 2 to give data elicited from inquiries supplemental to the detailed life histories of the nine major classes of drugs. These less comprehensive inquiries covered experience with common other drugs, including general anesthetics.

Examination of Table 5 shows a consistent pattern across campuses. Nearly all students currently employ mild painkillers and/or tranquilizers and drink cola beverages. Over three quarters in all schools drink coffee, tea and chocolate/cocoa beverages, and two thirds to three quarters in all schools have undergone general anesthesia. About half in each school, except for the junior college, have had medically prescribed or administered opiates, and from one quarter to two fifths are presently employing over-the-counter stay-awakes.

Compared with these quite constant across-campus figures, marijuana and amphetamine experience shows in Table 2 a very considerable variation from campus to campus; there is also a variation —though slightly less wide—in tranquilizer experience. Proportionately, very considerable differences exist in special-substance and hallucinogen experiences. One campus, for example, has almost four times as many students as another whose students have taken special substances; one campus has almost five times as many students as another reporting the use of hallucinogens. These comparisons lead to the proposition that student behavior, regardless of campus, is very similar with regard to the culturally sanctioned and freely available minor stimulants, painkillers, and social drugs. On the other hand,

---

[2] That there should be a relationship between reported experience with a drug or lifetime prevalence of use and measures of intensity is not surprising; experience as such contributes to the intensity score (although one-time experience would contribute very little by way of magnitude), and we have already shown, in our pilot study of normal-population drug use (see companion volume *Drugs I*) that past experience is related to present use. Given both past and present use the intensity score necessarily increases.

Table 5

Experience with Common Drugs

School	Any past experience: Strong painkillers (opiates medically administered or prescribed)	Any past experience: General anesthetics	Any present use of mild stimulants: Coffee	Tea	Chocolate Cocoa	Cola drinks	Stay-awakes	Any present use of mild painkillers and tranquilizers: Aspirin Compoze Endin, and comparable drugs
I	51	70	80	80	79	90	26	96
II	35	73	81	76	76	90	35	99
III	55	65	73	76	77	90	35	98
IV	52	65	86	86	86	91	30	92
V	54	74	78	81	86	91	38	97

the campus "culture"—that is, the school's special environment composed of different kinds of student populations, traditions, location, and so on—is reflected in the use of the illicit-exotic substances and in presumed patterns of medical care as inferred from the differential prescription of tranquilizers. What emerges, on the one hand, is an overriding general culture or style of drug conduct which determines the level of use of painkillers, mild stimulants, and social drugs, and also some prescribed psychoactive drugs (sedatives) compared with a much more specific and variable sensitivity by campus to illicit-exotic drug use and to some kinds of prescribed drugs—the latter reflecting, we presume, medical-care variation.

This chapter has presented an overview of the methods employed in the college study, as well as gross characteristics of the student populations in the five samples studied, information on the prevalence of experience with each of the major classes of drugs, and data on intensity of use. The samples and, inferentially, the colleges, show considerable differences in student-body characteristics, differences which are presumably associated with differences in illicit-drug use. Differences among campuses are slight with regard to the use of the culturally sanctioned and easily available minor drugs, are greater for the approved social and prescription drugs, and are greatest, proportionately, for illicit substances. What is implied is that across-campus conduct with regard to over-the-counter analgesics, minor stimulants, and so forth is much the same as that of our national drug-use culture, of which it is a part. Furthermore, differences in student characteristics and campus milieu are beginning to play a stronger role in the use of alcohol, tobacco, and prescription psychoactives, and student characteristic and campus milieu are emerging most strongly as determinants of the use and non-use of illicit-exotic drugs. These features may be identified generally as cultural, social-environmental, and family-individual factors, all of which affect drug conduct.

Those Who Do, Those Who Do Not

Richard H. Blum

III

The purposes of this chapter are threefold. It aims to establish an anchor for the consideration of drug use among students by examining that extreme group of students who have never had any of the major drugs with which our investigation was concerned. These total abstainers deny any use of tobacco, alcohol, amphetamines, sedatives, tranquilizers, marijuana, hallucinogens, illicit opiates, or special substances for kicks. Their characteristics are necessarily of interest, and because they are an anchor group, their characteristics should be kept in mind since descriptions will be offered in later chapters of those using various drugs. The second purpose of this chapter is to provide a perspective on the anchor group of total abstainers by comparing them with the total sample of students. Thus, what the trends in differences are should become apparent and, since the percentage differences are presented, just how great those differences may be. The third aim of this chapter is to provide a different perspective on later chapters by providing the base-line data showing—in major ways—how the total sample is distributed on those items of background, activity, interest, and ideology about which we inquired. Thus, the statistics which are provided in the comparison of abstainers with the total sample give, at the same time, the percentage distribution for that total sample.[1]

There are some differences among schools in the presence on campus of these total abstainers, although these do not prove to be significant at the .05 level. School V, the large state university, accounts for nearly two fifths of all abstainers; School II, the Catholic university, accounts for another fourth. In contrast, School IV, the big-city state college which has the highest proportion of illicit-drug users, has the fewest abstainers; there are also only a few at School III, the junior college, which ranks second in hallucinogen and marijuana use. There may be an inverse relationship between the experience rates for illicit drugs and the presence on campus of total abstainers. Presumably, the differences, if not chance variation, reflect demographic variables—in the case of the state university, the only one that is not located in a metropolitan area—variables associated with rural and conservative population characteristics. The image or tradition of a campus probably attracts and recruits students who expect the institution to be compatible with their background and views. There are likely to be social dynamics on a campus which consist of forces (for example, fundamentalist church groups) supporting the perpetuation of abstinence or protecting abstainers from drug proselytism. As we shall see, that "protection" is only temporary for most abstainers.

Looking at individual characteristics, we see that there are proportionately more abstainers among younger students than older ones (a sharp reduction occurring at age twenty-one and over), and among underclassmen. We find abstainers are also more heavily concentrated in technology and the hard sciences (29 per cent vs. 21 per cent) and less concentrated in humanities and arts (13 per cent vs. 17 per cent) as major fields of study. They come from families in the lower-income group—not from the poorest families (under $5,000

---

[1] The total sample as presented includes the 4 per cent of the students who are in the abstainer group. This is advantageous in the sense that total-sample statistics are not made erroneous by the subtraction of a subgroup. On the other hand, the comparisons with the abstainer group are always slightly inaccurate and attenuated, since the abstainer group is still within the total sample with which it is compared. Keep in mind that all contrasts would be greater were the total sample not to include abstainers.

income are 4 per cent abstainers and 6 per cent of the total sample) but mostly from those in working- and lower-middle-class brackets (48 per cent in the $5,000 to $10,000 range vs. 28 per cent for the total population, only 13 per cent in the $15,000 to $25,000 range, and 4 per cent in the over-$25,000 family-income bracket vs. 19 per cent and 12 per cent for the total sample). They also come from intact families with both parents living and are from settled rather than mobile families, just as are most of the total sample. They differ from the total sample in religious affiliation, being much more often Protestant (54 per cent vs. total sample 39 per cent).

The abstainers are much more interested in religion than are students as a whole (36 per cent deeply interested vs. 19 per cent; 41 per cent mildly interested vs. 36 per cent; only 2 per cent with no interest compared with 5 per cent; only 2 per cent "intellectually" interested in religion compared with 8 per cent; and 16 per cent "philosophically" interested compared with the total population's 25 per cent). Abstainers are also slightly more likely to share their father's religion, 70 per cent doing so compared with 66 per cent in the total sample. More important, they share their mother's religion, 88 per cent doing so in contrast to 73 per cent in the total sample. As an outcome of the above, it is not surprising to see more abstainers in religious agreement with both parents—68 per cent—than students as a whole, who agree with both parents only 58 per cent of the time.

Participation in activities differs somewhat. Abstainers less often find athletics extremely important (16 per cent vs. 24 per cent) but join the majority in moderate participation (65 per cent terming athletics very important, important, or occasionally important vs. 58 per cent among the whole population; only 16 per cent of abstainers and 15 per cent of the total call athletics of very little or "no importance").

As would be anticipated from the earlier items on religious interests, the religious activities of abstainers are greater. Thirty-six per cent say participation is extremely or very important compared with 18 per cent of the total sample, while at the other extreme 20 per cent say such activities are of very little importance as do 19 per cent of the total sample, but none among the abstainers says he is totally uninterested. On the other hand, 15 per cent of the total sample say such activities are of no interest at all. Political participation is less among the abstainers; 37 per cent consider political participation of very little importance or of no interest at all compared with 29 per cent among the total population. Activities involved with seeking new experiences are also less important, for while only 23 per cent of the abstainers find it extremely important to seek new experiences, 44 per cent of the total population say these activities are important. At the other extreme, 7 per cent of the abstainers find activities that are part of seeking new experiences to be of little importance, whereas only 3 per cent of the total sample find them of little or no importance. The two groups are about the same in regard to the importance of activities which further their academic-scholastic and future careers (getting good grades, school projects, and so on); 45 per cent of the abstainers and 46 per cent of all students find these extremely important and 52 per cent vs. 46 per cent find them very important or important. On the other hand, none among the abstainers is uninterested in school-career activities, whereas 3 per cent of the total sample say they find academic pursuits of very little importance or of no importance whatsoever.

On the political spectrum which reads from right to left, one finds the abstainers consistently more conservative. The table below presents the progression for the abstainers and the total sample on the scale which we used.

Political involvement is also reduced among the abstainers, 34 per cent of them being active or strongly interested in politics com-

Table 6

ABSTAINERS COMPARED WITH TOTAL SAMPLE ON
POLITICAL POSITION

	Abstainers Per cent	Total Sample Per cent
Very conservative	5	4
Republican	30	24
Democrat	30	23
Independent–conservative	9	8
Independent-liberal	16	25
Independent-radical	0	3
Left-of-center	5	3
New Left	0	3
Marxist	0	0.15
No preference	4	7

pared with 39 per cent among the total sample. In the range of mild or moderate interest are 59 per cent of the abstainers and 55 per cent of the total sample, while in the extreme range of apathy and no interest are 7 per cent abstainers and 5 per cent of the total sample. Forty-six per cent of both groups say their ideas are undergoing change. The directions differ however. Only 11 per cent of the abstainers see themselves as moving left, whereas 19 per cent of the total sample say their trend is leftward; 2 per cent of the abstainers are moving right and 14 per cent center compared with 5 per cent right and 11 per cent center in the total group. There is more political agreement between fathers and student abstainers than in the total sample; of the former 34 per cent are in complete agreement and 39 per cent in partial agreement with their father; among the students as a whole, 27 per cent are in total political agreement and 43 per cent in partial agreement. The complete disagreement figures are 11 per cent vs. 20 per cent. We also find more political agreement with mothers and student abstainers as follows: full agreement 39 per cent, partial 45 per cent, and none 11 per cent, whereas in the total sample the figures are 28 per cent, 44 per cent, and 18 per cent.

Students were asked whether their parents were quick to give medicines or home remedies to them as children or whether, instead, they were reluctant and medicated only if they were really very sick. In answer we find 16 per cent of the abstainers reporting that their parents were quick to medicate, 66 per cent considering them average, and 16 per cent reluctant to say. Students as a whole, compared to abstainers, view their parents as having been somewhat more ready to medicate, 23 per cent consider them quick to medicate, 57 per cent consider them average in this area, and 19 per cent are reluctant to say. Asked whether, in looking back on childhood illnesses, they recall any advantages to having been sick, 75 per cent of the abstainers say "no." Compare that with only 47 per cent of the total sample recalling at least some advantages in childhood illness. A third parent-evaluating question in regard to illness revealed nothing. One may wish to consider the abstainers' replies to these questions as indicative of a response tendency on their part to take the middle ground rather than the extremes in reviewing parent-child health factors. Estimating how much their parents worried about their health as children—from paying little attention to being very much concerned—36 per cent of the abstainers and 34 per cent of the total consider their parents as having been very much concerned—63 per cent and 61 per cent as having had an average concern and 2 per cent and 5 per cent as having had an overconcern.

In another question we listed nineteen issues, stands, values, or ways of life and asked students to rate their parents as for or against that value and to rate themselves the same way. The topics were political/religious pacifism, socialism-Marxism, the radical right, liberals, integration of Negroes, getting out of Vietnam, escalating the war in Vietnam, patriotism, sexual freedom, psychiatry and psychiatrists in general, atheism, religious mysticism, organized religion, prayer, taking prescribed medicine, birth control, abortion, admitting Red China to the United Nations, and making money. The sum of topics in this grouping on which father-mother-student all agreed became an agreement or family-homogeneity score. The sum of items on which father and mother agreed but the student disagreed became a student-to-parent-opposition score. The range of possible scores on both was from 0 to 19. Our findings show that among abstainers 50 per cent agree with their parents on twelve or more topics. Only 11 per cent agree on six topics or fewer, and 18 per cent agree on sixteen topics or more. For the sample as a whole, 50 per cent agree with their parents on eleven topics or more with 15 per cent agreeing on only six topics or fewer and 8 per cent agreeing on sixteen topics or more. In regard to oppositional tendencies, 50 per cent of the abstainers disagree with the common stand of their parents on four or fewer topics, 7 per cent disagree on ten or more, and 13 per cent disagree on only one or on no topics. For the sample as a whole, 50 per cent disagree with a common parental stand on six topics or fewer, 14 per cent disagree on ten or more, and 7 per cent disagree with both their parents on only one or on no topics. We conclude that abstainers tend to be in agreement with their parents on major issues more often than does the total sample.

We asked three questions about school satisfaction: satisfaction with course work and subject matter, with teachers, and with school as a whole. These inquiries correspond to some industrial morale measures which have as components satisfaction with work, supervision, and company. Answers indicate that 59 per cent of abstainers are completely satisfied with course work as are 53 per cent of the total sample; among abstainers 5 per cent are thoroughly dissatisfied compared with 7 per cent among students as a whole. Satisfaction with teachers is complete for 63 per cent of the abstainers compared with only 50 per cent of the total sample; total dissatisfaction affects 7 per cent of the abstainers and 6 per cent of the total; a mixed reaction characterizes 30 per cent of the abstainers and 44 per cent of the whole. Abstainers are satisfied with their school as a whole in 71 per cent of the cases, have mixed reactions in 27 per cent of the cases, and 2 per cent are completely dissatisfied. The total sample figures are as follows: satisfaction, 62 per cent; mixed, 29 per cent; dissatisfaction only 9 per cent. The dissatisfaction component is clearly less among abstainers; whether this reflects higher morale as such, comfort with the status quo, or simply a reluctance to complain or "bitch" can be argued.

A number of items focused on school performance. With regard to the number of incomplete grades within the last year, abstainers indicate they had almost none; only 4 per cent took incompletes and in each case only one incomplete grade was taken. The total sample performed less well; 10 per cent took incompletes and among these students 3 per cent took two or more incomplete grades. On grade points ($A = 4$, $B = 3$, $C = 2$, $D = 1$) the average grade point for abstainers in the past year was 2.7 or $B-$. For the whole sample it was 2.8, which is also $B-$.

Students were asked whether they had ever dropped out of school for other than health reasons. Two per cent of the abstainers indicate that they had once dropped out as compared with 14 per cent of the total sample. Asked whether they were seriously thinking now of dropping out, 89 per cent of the abstainers report "no," 9 per cent are considering it, and 2 per cent are really serious about doing so. Among students as a whole, 89 per cent say "no," 6 per cent are considering it, and 4 per cent say they are intending to drop out of school. One question asked students what the relationship was between the way they wanted to live and their present course of studies. Among abstainers 68 per cent report their studies are relevant for *both* their life *and* career goals, 18 per cent say they are relevant only to career goals, 7 per cent to life goals, and 5 per cent say they are unrelated to either. The total sample yields 64 per cent seeing their studies as relevant to life and career, 15 per cent related to career only, 13 per cent to life goals, and 6 per cent saying studies are irrelevant for either. (We suspect the larger per cent in the total sample relating college to life goals would be arts and humanities or social-science majors.) Asked whether they were optimistic or pessimistic about really doing what they would like once school was finished, 86 per cent of the abstainers report they are optimistic and 9 per cent are pessimistic; among the total sample the figures are 79 per cent and 12 per cent. Students were also asked whether their life plans included efforts to make changes in the world so that the lives of many people would be different (and presumably improved). Such plans are claimed by 39 per cent of the abstainers and 44 per cent of the total sample. Those who do plan to work for a greater good—if we may call it that—were asked how optimistic they were that they—and people like themselves—could bring about the desired changes. Abstainers in 50 per cent of the cases are optimistic and 29 per cent uncertain; the total sample of constructive idealists—we think that is what they are—are optimistic only in 22 per cent of the cases and are uncertain 23 per cent of the time. The pessimists account for 16 per cent of the abstainers and 7 per cent of the sample. What accounts for the missing proportion among the total sample are 48 per cent who are indifferent or who neither can say or are unwilling to reply. Thus, indifference or uncertainty characterizes the plans of most idealistic students in the total sample, whereas the abstainers are much more optimistic. Students were asked—on another dimension of optimism-pessimism or hope vs. reality—to compare life as they now knew it with what they had expected it to be like when they were younger. We find that 29 per cent of the abstainers say it is as they expected, 20 per cent say it is better, 5 per cent say it is worse, 32 per cent say it is both better *and* worse, and 13 per cent say it is different without being either better or worse. Total-sample figures are as follows: as expected 14 per cent, better 22 per cent, worse 9 per cent, better and worse 30 per cent, and different 23 per cent. The abstainers emerge as at least seeing themselves as having been more realistic and less often surprised.

Students were asked about their relationships to groups, their views and involvements in them. Membership in organized groups was held, at the time of interviewing, equally by both samples with the abstainers as follows: no groups 52 per cent, one group 25 per cent, two or more groups 23 per cent. The total sample figures are: no group 50 per cent, one group 27 per cent, two or more 23 per cent. Students were given a list of groups, some of them close to them and real and others classifiable as abstract entities, with which they might or might not identify or feel sympathy. They were asked, after an explanation of the intent of the question, to indicate how they felt about each—either as an insider or an outsider. The groups listed are as follows: their own families, the student body at their college, the people living in their residence unit (home, dorm, and so forth), the majors in their department, the intellectual-creative community (professors, writers, poets, scientists), the student revolt and New Left on campus, the student government, adults who hold power in the university, people holding power in the United States, being an American, traditional middle-class values, Western culture, and the age of technology. We find scores from this expanding universe (or hodgepodge) of groups ranging from being "out" (alienated, unsympathetic, and so forth) with from zero to thirteen. Abstainers average being an outsider on three of the thirteen with only 4 per cent feeling outside of seven or more groups. The total-sample average is to feel an outsider on four groups, with 10 per cent feeling outside of seven or more groups. Another question asked students what they considered to be the most dangerous group in the United States today. Among abstainers 7 per cent identify those presently in power, the Establishment; 55 per cent say left-wing or other change-oriented groups, 2 per cent identify middle-of-the-roaders, 45 per cent say right wingers, and 5 per cent identify criminal elements. In the total sample the distributions are: those in power 7 per cent, left wing 46 per cent, middle-grounders 4 per cent, right wingers 53 per cent, and criminal groups 3 per cent.

Another group of questions asked about the use of minor drugs and experience with strong painkillers and anesthetics. We find none of the abstainer group reporting ever having received medically prescribed or administered opiates—Demerol, Percodan, morphine, codeine, or the like. In contrast, 51 per cent of the total sample have received narcotics under medical supervision. Twenty per cent of the abstainers have undergone general anesthesia, another major mind-altering event. This compares with 70 per cent of the total sample who have had general anesthesia. These two sets of differences are remarkable and suggest very different experiences of the two samples either in illness, in medical care, or in the acceptance of medical intervention.

With reference to minor drugs, we find no abstainers who use coffee more than a few times a year; those who use it at all ("intermittently," defined as four times a year or less) constitute 38 per cent of the abstainer sample. In comparison, in the total sample only 20 per cent do not drink coffee, 14 per cent use it intermittently, and the remaining 67 per cent use it more often, either occasionally, regularly, or considerably.

Abstainers are also low on tea consumption. Sixty-one per cent do not drink it, 9 per cent take it intermittently, 7 per cent occasionally (less than once a week but more than four times a year), 9 per cent regularly (once a week or more), and 14 per cent considerably (daily or more). The total sample drinks much more tea. Only 20 per cent do not drink it, 14 per cent drink it intermittently, 29 per cent take it occasionally, 20 per cent regularly, and 18 per cent considerably.

Chocolate and cocoa drinks find the two samples closer in habits. Thirty-two per cent of the abstainers do not drink chocolate or cocoa whereas 21 per cent of the total sample do not. Intermittent use for abstainers occurs in 20 per cent and in the total sample 21 per cent, occasional use 23 per cent vs. 34 per cent, regular use 14 per cent vs. 17 per cent and considerable use 11 per cent vs. 7 per cent.

Cola drinking by the two groups shows heavier use among the total sample. Abstainers include 21 per cent who do not drink cola beverages, 20 per cent taking them intermittently, 34 per cent drinking them occasionally, 18 per cent regularly, and 7 per cent considerably. In the total sample the figures are: none 10 per cent, intermittent 9 per cent, occasional 26 per cent, regular 33 per cent, and considerable 23 per cent.

The use of stay-awakes (No-Doze and other caffeine-containing, over-the-counter stimulants) differs considerably and in an unexpected direction. Eleven per cent of the abstainers claim not to use stay-awakes compared with 64 per cent of the total sample. Thirteen per cent of the abstainers use them intermittently whereas 26 per cent of the total sample so employ them. Occasional use is by 29 per cent of the abstainers and 9 per cent of the total sample; regular use is by 36 per cent of the abstainers and only 1 per cent of the total; considerable use is by 13 per cent of the abstainers compared with only 0.3 per cent use by the total sample. These differences are dramatic and show that, in spite of their abstinence in almost all other areas, the "abstainers" do have a drug of choice and it is a stay-awake.

Asked about their use of mild painkillers and mild tranquilizers (aspirin, Bufferin, Bromo-Seltzer, Compōz, Cope, Endin, and so forth) 84 per cent of the abstainers deny any use; none reports regular or considerable use. In contrast, only 4 per cent of the total sample (which means that members of the abstainer group account for almost all of the no-aspirin group in our entire sample) deny use of mild analgesics. Twenty per cent of the total sample report intermittent use, 60 per cent occasional use, 14 per cent regular use, and 2 per cent considerable use.

The final question, to be discussed here, asked students to state their beliefs about drugs that guided their own conduct in regard to their personal use of LSD, marijuana, and the like. Answers were coded in terms of positive-valence replies—those setting forth reasons for using these drugs or facilitating conditions for use—and negative-valence replies—those giving reasons why such drugs should not be taken, including barriers and restraining forces in the environment. Examining the replies, we find that no abstainers speak only of positive-valence principles; 88 per cent speak only of negative ones; and 12 per cent speak of both positive and negative ones. In the total sample, 61 per cent speak only of negative-valence factors, 8 per cent speak only of positive ones, and 31 per cent speak of both.

SUMMARY

Four per cent of the sample are total abstainers—students who have not tried alcohol, tobacco, or any other major drug. The proportion of abstainers varies by campus; fewest are found in the big-city college and the greatest proportion in a school which appears to draw more heavily from rural conservative families. As a group, abstainers tend to be—as compared with the total sample—young, from poorer but close-knit families, majoring primarily in technology or hard sciences, deeply religious (mostly Protestant), politically conservative but inactive, generally satisfied with what they are doing, and optimistic about the future. As for minor-drug use, abstainers rarely use coffee or tea but show very great use of stay-awakes in comparison with most students. As they stay in school, their abstinence tends to disappear and they blend into the majority (older) and approved drug-using group.

The total sample of students upon which this study is based are predominantly male (59 per cent) and from middle- and upper-middle-income families making $15,000 or over per year. About a third of the students are nineteen years old or younger, a third are twenty and twenty-one, and slightly less than a third are twenty-two years of age or older. Half of the sample are underclassmen. Majors are, by rank, the social sciences, technology and the hard sciences, the arts and humanities, and the biological sciences. Protestants are most common in the sample (38 per cent), Catholics rank second (33 per cent), and those claiming no religious affiliation are third (22 per cent). Three per cent are Jewish. The majority of the students describe themselves as moderately or "philosophically" interested in religion, with 5 per cent claiming no interest whatever. Most are in religious agreement with both parents; however, 18 per cent claim religious disagreement with both parents. Ninety-one per cent say that activities related to school work and future careers are important to them, 67 per cent say athletic participation is important to them, 44 per cent say political participation is important to them, 44 per cent say seeking new experiences is important, and 36 per cent say religious participation is important. Politically, more than three fourths are middle-of-the-roaders, 16 per cent are inclined to the radical left, and only 4 per cent to the radical right. The majority are in political agreement with both parents, although 20 per cent claim disagreement with both parents.

About half of the students are completely satisfied with their course work and teachers and 60 per cent with their school. Seven per cent express total dissatisfaction with courses, 6 per cent with teachers, and 9 per cent with the school as a whole. Ninety per cent took no incompletes the prior year; the grade-point average for all was a $B-$. Half of the students are members of one or more organized groups. Fourteen per cent dropped out at one time for other than health reasons and 10 per cent are thinking of doing so. Only two thirds of the sample see their courses as relevant to both their future lives and careers but 79 per cent are, nevertheless, optimistic about getting to do what they want to upon leaving school. The majority do not intend to change the world. Few find life to be as they expected it; yet only 9 per cent find it worse than they anticipated.

We would characterize the total sample as one comprised of diverse elements and subgroups—these differing markedly from campus to campus—but for whom the dominant trends are middle- and upper-middle-class backgrounds, family agreement, and middle-of-the-road politics. Science majors (including behavioral sciences) predominate, as do Protestant or Catholic religious affiliations. Most find school activities and athletic participation important and most are at least partly satisfied with courses, teachers, and school. They are generally optimistic, are not world shakers, and are pursuing their interests in preparing for lives and careers.

We would characterize abstainers as like the majority of the total sample except for being younger, poorer, more conservative and religious, and more satisfied with present and future prospects.

Student Characteristics
and Major Drugs

Richard H. Blum

IV

*T*his chapter examines our student population—the five campuses combined—in terms of their background characteristics, their interests, their activities, their performance, and their perspectives on politics, family, school, and the future. It then shows how such characteristics are related to the propensities of students to use drugs. (The "use" of drugs refers here to any reported lifetime experience with designated classes of drugs.) The aim of this chapter is also to show that a wide variety of student characteristics are, in fact, associated with having had drug experience—not just with one group of drugs but with almost *all* classes of psychoactive substances. We shall also see that there are consistent trends, so that the use—that is, any lifetime experience —of certain kinds of drugs bears a more dramatic relationship to student characteristics than other classes of drugs do; thus, we see that such trends become more extreme when illicit-exotic substances are involved. In a later chapter, we will focus attention on the users of particular drugs to see, for example, how those who use them heavily differ from those whose use experience has been less intense.

CHARACTERISTICS

Male students more than female report somewhat more use of tobacco, marijuana, hallucinogens, and special substances for kicks. The sexes are equally experienced ("equal" defined here as within two percentage points of one another) with alcohol, amphetamines, and illicit opiates. Females more often than males have had experience with sedatives and tranquilizers. In fact, the greatest difference between men and women in terms of percentage points occurs with tranquilizers, 15 per cent of the men and 26 per cent of the women employing them one or more times in their lives. The greatest proportional difference between the sexes occurs with hallucinogens; twice as many men (6 per cent) as women (3 per cent) have employed them.

For all drugs, without exception, the younger undergraduates report less experience than do older ones. The age groups reporting the most experience vary somewhat from one drug to another; for example, more twenty-two-year-olds than any other group report experience with marijuana and with sedatives. More twenty-three-year-olds report amphetamine and hallucinogen experience and also the use of special substances for kicks. The students who are twenty-four years old and more report the most experience with tobacco, alcohol, tranquilizers, and illicit opiates. We take these differences to indicate that drug-use patterns were changing during the period of the study as well as that a differential rate of incidence is a function of age. Perhaps the oldest students "missed out" on all but the "old-fashioned" drugs and the youngest had not yet been exposed and turned on, but members of the twenty-two- and twenty-three-year-old group were both old enough to have been initiated and young enough to have been part of a "new wave" of drugs. We shall further consider the age factor in later discussions.

Without exception lowerclassmen report less experience with all classes of drugs than do upperclassmen, and graduate students consistently report—with one exception—less lifetime drug experience than do undergraduates. (Remember that the undergraduates come from five campuses but that the graduates are a small sample from one university.) Seniors report more lifetime drug experience for alcohol, tobacco, amphetamines, tranquilizers, and marijuana and match juniors on hallucinogens and special substances. A very slight variation in this pattern occurs for opiates where one finds sophomores (2.31 per cent) and graduates (2.60 per cent) reporting lifetime experience which is greater than other classes—for example, seniors report 0.68 per cent, juniors 1.13 per cent. Keeping in mind the age findings (older students have greater experience with certain drugs) and the school-year findings (graduate students are consistently low in drug use), we may say that it is the older undergraduate who has the greatest lifetime incidence of drug use. Recall from Tables 2 and 3 in Chapter Two that School IV, the state college, has the greatest number of older undergraduates and also the largest number of both juniors and seniors sampled. (School V, the state university, because of its graduate sample has the greatest number of older students, although only slightly more than School IV.) According to these tables, School IV has the highest reported lifetime-experience incidence with all classes of drugs except tobacco, sedatives, and illicit opiates (the latter showing only a trace of difference). School III, the junior college, is highest in these latter three classes of drugs.

It appears that a concentration of older, upperclass undergraduates is associated with high lifetime-drug-experience incidence on a campus, but it is obvious that age and class standing of the male student are not predictors of overall campus experience for all drugs since a junior college with few older students and no upperclassmen has the highest overall rates for certain drugs.

There are consistent differences in rankings for drug experience among students classified by their major subjects. Those in the arts and humanities report the greatest experience with tranquilizers, hallucinogens, and opiates and share the highest experience of tobacco, alcohol, amphetamines, marijuana, and special substances. Furthermore, they rank a close second on sedatives. Students who are undecided as to major or who are in "general studies" are highest on sedatives and share with others the top ranking for special substances. Students in biological sciences share a high rank only on amphetamines and are lowest on marijuana. Students in the social sciences share high rankings on tobacco, marijuana, and special substances. Students majoring in hard sciences and technology have no high rankings. (A very few students [N = 9] who have several majors also rank high or highest on nearly all classes of drugs but because of the small N are not ranked with the major fields.)

Students from the wealthiest families—incomes of over $25,000 per year—report the greatest drug experience for all drugs with the slight exception of special substances, where 1 per cent more from families in the $15,000 to $25,000 bracket report experience, and of opiates, where all income brackets are about the same, ranging from 1 per cent to 2 per cent. Nevertheless, the lowest-income bracket, under $5,000, is highest on opiates, its 2.38 per cent use being 1 per cent higher than any other, which is, in relative terms, twice as great.

We anticipated that students with one or both parents dead might be higher on drug experience. Our error is reflected in the fact that in no drug class are differences between the two groups greater than a few percentage points.

Students who have lived in more houses by the time of high school graduation are higher in drug experience than those with parental housing stability. Students living in six or more houses report the greatest experience with tobacco, alcohol, amphetamines, sedatives, tranquilizers, marijuana, hallucinogens, and special substances. The only exception is with opiates where 2 per cent (compared with 1 per cent, rounded off, in all other mobility categories) have the greatest housing stability, having lived in only one or two houses. In percentage terms parental mobility makes the greatest difference for amphetamine use, with 17 per cent of the most stable and 31 per cent of the least stable students, as measured by housing mobility, having had drug experience.

Students with present affiliations to Protestant or Catholic faiths consistently report less drug experience than do those who say they have no religious affiliations. One finds that the no-affiliation group has the greatest proportion reporting experience with every class of drugs except sedatives; Jewish students are highest in sedative experience and are second in the proportion reporting experience with amphetamines, tranquilizers, and marijuana.

Students describing their present interest in religion as "deep" are least likely to report drug experience for all classes of drugs. Those saying they have no interest in religion most often report experience with amphetamines, marijuana, and hallucinogens and they share high rankings for tranquilizers and alcohol. Those with "philosophical" interests in religion most often say they have had experience with opiates and tobacco; those with "intellectual" interests are markedly higher on use of special substances and share high hallucinogen, tobacco, and alcohol ranking with others.

We expected that students not sharing their parental religious values would more often have experience with exotic-illicit substances. Findings indicate that this is the case for all classes of drugs. Students not sharing their father's religion more often report experience with all classes of drugs than do students who share their father's religious values. The greatest differences in proportions obtain for marijuana (9 per cent difference between groups) and amphetamines (8 per cent difference). Not sharing the religion of the mother appears much more important in the sense that differences in proportions between the two groups are greater; for example, 15 per cent (rounded off) of those sharing the mother's religion report marijuana experience, while 32 per cent not sharing the mother's religion report such experience. For amphetamines the figures are 16 per cent vs. 35 per cent, for tranquilizers 16 per cent vs. 27 per cent, for hallucinogens 3 per cent vs. 10 per cent, for opiates 1 per cent vs. 4 per cent, and for special substances 5 per cent vs. 11 per cent.

We also expected that students disagreeing with the religious faith of both parents would more often report experience with illicit-exotic drugs than students disagreeing with only one parent or sharing religion with both parents. Our expectation was borne out. We find that for all classes of drugs (the only exception being a 1 per cent difference for sedatives) students sharing religions with only one parent do not differ essentially from those sharing a religious faith with both. The greatest differences obtain between the groups for amphetamines (16 per cent spread), marijuana (15 per cent spread), and hallucinogens (3 per cent low vs. 10 per cent high).

We expected that students participating in various organizations and activities would show a smaller proportion with drug experience than those not participating. Participation was defined in terms of a 7-point rating scale which required the student to rank the importance to him of a pursuit ranging from extremely important to totally uninterested. We also expected that there would be differences in drug experience by activity for those expressing interest—for example, that those "seeking new experience" would more often report illicit-exotic drug use in their lifetime histories than would students interested in athletics. These expectations were, for the most part, confirmed.

Regarding *athletics,* students for whom sports are either of very little or no importance report proportionately more experience with all classes of drugs. Those for whom athletics are extremely important tend to be the least experienced with amphetamines (a shared low ranking) and marijuana, whereas those saying athletics are of little importance tend to have low rates of use for alcohol, amphetamines (shared ranking), and tranquilizers. We surmise that this latter low-use group is comprised of persons for whom athletics are personally unimportant but who do not resort to extreme ratings in contrast to the greater drug-experience group for whom ratings may reflect ideological or emotional rejection of the collegiate athletic ethic, or possibly an extremist tendency for negative ratings.

Regarding *religious* participation, those saying it is of very little or no interest consistently report more experience with all classes of drugs. The spread on this item is considerable. For example, 51 per cent of those for whom religious participation is "extremely important" have one-time-or-more tobacco use whereas 76 per cent have alcohol experience; 80 per cent or more of these with very little or no religious participation report tobacco use and 96 per cent alcohol use. For amphetamines the proportions are 16 per cent vs. 36 per cent; for sedatives 13 per cent vs. 28 per cent; for tranquilizers 17 per cent vs. 31 per cent (although the lowest experience at 11 per cent is among those saying religious participation is "important"); for marijuana 11 per cent vs. 32 per cent; for hallucinogens 3 per cent vs. 9 per cent (with a low of 1 per cent in the "very important" group); and for special substances 6 per cent (with the low at 3 per cent among the "important" group) vs. 11 per cent. All opiate users fail to participate in religion.

For *political* participation a strikingly differentiated pattern emerges. Those who say political participation is "extremely important" comprise the highest proportion reporting experience with amphetamines, marijuana, hallucinogens, opiates, and special substances. The lowest-experience group is at the uninterested end of the scale except for opiates where persons rating participation as "very important" are lowest. Tranquilizer use, on the other hand, is highest among students uninterested in political activity; tobacco is highest among those saying political activity is very important and lowest among those saying it is occasionally important. Very little variation occurs among the groups in regard to alcohol experience.

Regarding action to *seek new experiences,* an unusual bimodal distribution is found. Students saying it is extremely important to seek new experience are highest, or share the high ranking, on all classes of drugs. There is a tendency for the proportion reporting drug experience to become smaller as one moves down the scale to those saying it is of little importance to them to seek new experience. However, those in a small group ($N = 13$) who say seeking new experience is of very little or no interest are also quite high on all drugs except hallucinogens and opiates. The incongruity could arise from extremist rating tendencies in a small (nihilist?) sample. If that small group is excluded, then there is a consistent relationship between saying that seeking new experience is very important and reporting drug experience of all kinds. Indeed, most drug users unequivocally rate "seeking new experience" as extremely important and the more "illicit" the drug, the higher the proportion emphasizing new experiences. Thus, 72 per cent and 66 per cent of the opiate and hallucinogen users are among those saying new experiences are extremely important; 58 per cent and 57 per cent of the amphetamines and marijuana users do so, whereas all other drugs have fewer users falling in the group emphasizing new experiences. Note that this phenomenon is even more pronounced when high-intensity users are compared with low-intensity users (a comparison we shall make in later chapters).

As for activities to further one's academic-scholastic career, the tendency is for students for whom such activities are important to report less drug experience. However, since for three fourths of the total sample these school activities are important, the comparison is a weak one. It is clear that fewer users of illicit drugs find school-career activities important; for example, only 58 per cent of hallucinogen users, 60 per cent special substance users, 66 per cent opiate users, and 68 per cent marijuana users describe scholastic activities as important.

POLITICAL POSITIONS

We expected drug experience to be associated with political position, anticipating that left-of-center students would reveal more use of illicit-exotic substances. Students were presented with ten political alternatives, the list having been developed after extensive pretesting experience. The findings not only bear out our expectations but extend them. With all classes of drugs, experience is greater as one continues to move left, commencing with the position of the independent-liberals. Drug experience is less on the right, moving right from the independent conservatives. Thus, if one treats the list of political positions as a scale, moving from right to left ((1) very conservative; (2) Republican; (3) independent-conservative; (4) independent-liberal; (5) Democrat; (6) independent-radical; (7) left of center (8) New Left; (9) Marxist, with an unscaled "no-preference" category as well), one finds illicit-exotic drug users underrepresented among conservatives (groups one through three) and overrepresented in the left and radical groups. As we have indicated, the other accepted drugs also show shifts in these same directions. As for exceptions, among the very conservative sedative use is high. At the other extreme, neither of the two Marxists in the sample reports any use of marijuana, opiates, or special substances. Members of the "no-preference" group show no remarkable characteristics.

We expected political involvement, or activism, to be linked to greater drug experience. That by no means remarkable expectation proved correct. On every class of drug the students who describe their political involvement or commitment as active are in the group with the highest proportion of drug experience. The trend for drug experience to diminish with each step of reduction in political involvement varies occasionally; for example, students who say they have no interest, participation, or involvement in politics are second highest in tranquilizer, opiate, and hallucinogen use but lowest or next-to-lowest on all other drugs.

We expected that students who felt that their political position was changing would be more likely to report use of illicit-exotic drugs. (Our rationale expected the common and liberal-leftward undergraduate shift to lead to challenges to many conventions in the inner and outer worlds.) The expectation was supported for every class of drug. We find that those students who say they are undergoing a political shift have a higher proportion reporting drug experience than those not shifting. Interestingly, those not shifting have had, in turn, more drug experience than the smaller number ($N = 46$) who do not know whether they are shifting or not.

Those undergoing a political-ideological shift ($N = 605$) were asked in what direction they felt they were moving. We anticipated that those moving left, and, thus, more liberal or change-oriented, would report a higher proportion of drug experience than those moving to the right or center (of course, a rightist moving to center is moving left). For the most part, our expectation was borne out. The left-moving students report the highest experience on tobacco, amphetamines, tranquilizers, marijuana, and hallucinogens and share the first rank for opiates, tranquilizers, and alcohol. A group characterizing its direction not as right, left, or center—that is, fluctuating in direction according to issues involved (not polarized)—is also high, relative to right- and center-moving students, in the proportion reporting drug experience, ranking first on special substances and sharing high ranks for amphetamines, hallucinogens, marijuana, and opiates. Curiously, those who do not know the direction of movement they are taking or who are otherwise unable to describe the political shift they have already claimed share the highest ranking for tranquilizer experience.

We expected that students who disagreed with their father's political position would report more drug experience; in this expectation we were correct. On all classes of drugs, students who say there is no agreement between themselves and their fathers report more drug experience than students reporting some agreement or those saying they are in agreement with their fathers. Those with some agreement and, necessarily, some disagreement, report proportionately more drug experience, in turn, than those in full agreement; this holds for each class of drugs. The group (N = 167) who do not know or refuse to say how they stand regarding their fathers' politics are unremarkable except for their having slightly more (1 per cent) tranquilizer experience than even the "no-agreement" group. The spread of differences among the groups is greatest for tobacco (no disagreements, 67 per cent experience; no agreement with father, 84 per cent experience), marijuana (12 per cent vs. 29 per cent) and, proportionately, for hallucinogens (2 per cent vs. 10 per cent).

We also expected that students disagreeing with their mothers on political grounds would report greater drug experience. However, given the relative unimportance of American women in family political leadership (Lane and Sears, 1964), less consistent relationships might be anticipated. The major expectation was borne out; the qualification was not. Students stating no agreement with their mothers on political matters report the highest drug experience—or share the first rank—on all drug classes compared with students reporting some agreement and with those saying there is complete political agreement between them and their mothers. The group members who say there is some agreement and some disagreement are more likely to report drug experience on all classes of drugs compared with the students in full agreement with their mothers' politics. In the case of tranquilizers and opiates, the full-agreement and some-agreement groups share the same proportion of drug-experienced persons. The spread of differences is greatest again for tobacco (full-agreement students reporting 68 per cent experience; no-agreement students, 84 per cent experience), for marijuana (13 per cent vs. 30 per cent), and proportionately for hallucinogens (3 per cent vs. 9 per cent). It is evident that disagreement with mothers' politics and fathers' politics is the same in terms of the relationship between drug experiences.

Using the father-student and mother-student positions, we categorized students as having some, if not full, agreement with both parents, one parent, or neither parent. One anticipates that disagreement is related to drug experience. For all drugs—except sedatives, where the difference is slight—students in agreement with both parents report least drug experience and students in disagreement with both parents report the highest proportion of drug experience for all drugs but sedatives (except a slight shift of 1 per cent on special substances, giving them second rank compared with students disagreeing with one parent). Amphetamines, marijuana, hallucinogens, and special substances stand out as drugs with the greatest absolute of proportional percentage spread among the agreement-disagreement groups.

We asked students which they regarded as the most dangerous groups in the United States today. The replies were categorized in terms of their identifying as dangers or enemies groups holding real power, groups on the left (or change-oriented groups), groups in the middle, those on the right, those with particular ways of thinking (not politically homogeneous or specifiable), or criminals as such. Given the rejection of the Establishment by hippies and distrust of the middle and the right by activists, we anticipated that drug experience would vary with those identified as the greatest danger to the country.[1] These expectations were supported.

Most students identify both left and right extremes as dangerous. Those students identifying the Establishment and middle-of-the-roaders as dangerous consist of a greater proportion of drug users, especially of illicit-exotic drugs, on the other hand, those focusing on

[1] We are indebted to Nevitt Sanford for proposing that we ask students about the "enemy."

left-wing dangers tend to be lower in drug experience. To be specific, we find that all other students are more experienced with all classes of drugs except sedatives and alcohol. The differences are considerable for marijuana (45 per cent vs. 17 per cent), amphetamines (36 per cent vs. 20 per cent), hallucinogens (20 per cent vs. 4 per cent), opiates (4 per cent vs. 1 per cent), and special substances (13 per cent vs. 6 per cent).

Students identifying the left wing or others seeking change as the greatest danger are consistently lower in drug experience than all other students. The biggest differences between these two groups obtains for tobacco (33 per cent vs. 42 per cent), alcohol (42 per cent vs. 51 per cent), and marijuana (6 per cent vs. 13 per cent).

Students who label the middle-grounders (middle-of-the-road, middle class, the comfortable masses, average citizens, and so on) as the most dangerous have more drug experience on all drug classes except tranquilizers than those students who do not perceive the middle-grounders as enemies. The greatest differences are on tobacco (88 per cent vs. 75 per cent), amphetamines (33 per cent vs. 21 per cent), and hallucinogens (18 per cent vs. 4 per cent).

Students considering the right wing (conservatives, reactionaries, fascists, and so on) as the most dangerous force have more drug experience on all drug classes than students not perceiving the right wing as dangerous. Differences between the groups are slight except for alcohol (50 per cent vs. 43 per cent) and tobacco (41 per cent vs. 34 per cent).

Those identifying various criminal groups (not used rhetorically but referring to persons violating the criminal codes) tend to report less drug experience—with one important exception—than students not labeling criminals as such as dangerous to the country. The exception is tranquilizers; those concerned about criminals report 29 per cent experience compared with the less concerned remainder reporting 19 per cent experience. Marijuana, on the other hand, had been used by 19 per cent of the remainder, and only 6 per cent of the students label criminals as most dangerous. All other differences in drug experience are slight.

FAMILY HOMOGENEITY

To get information about the agreement on values not only between student and parents but between parents themselves (that is, family homogeneity), we asked each student to indicate how each of his parents stood on a list of nineteen topics and then to state his own position on each of the issues. (See Chapter Three for details.) Recall that all these perceptions were summed for both agreement and disagreement and were expressed by two scores—one being the number of values or issues on which the whole family were in accord and the other scoring the number of points on which father and mother were in accord and the student was in disagreement with both.

Inspection of the distribution of scores for family agreement indicates a normal curve with a median family agreement on eleven issues and the mode at eleven as well. The distribution of scores for father-mother agreement and student agreement with both is skewed so that modal number of disagreements is on four issues only; the median is at six issues.

Comparing mother-father-student agreement in terms of those students experienced with each class of drug as compared with those without any experience, we find that non-users of each class of drugs report more family agreement than do users. Family agreement occurs least often among the hallucinogen users, followed by marijuana users. Family agreement is reported most often among students who have never drunk alcohol.

The other measure we employed was the number of issues on which the student stood apart from both his parents—that is, the parents agreed with one another and the student was in opposition. One may recall that this measure gauged opposition, rebellion, isolation, progress, or whatever one fancies. The results show that non-users of each group of drugs perceive and report fewer issues on which they stand in opposition to both parents than do users of drugs. The groups perceiving the greatest number of issues on which they stand apart from parents are hallucinogen users, marijuana users, and opiate and special substance users, in that order. We see that on both measures of family solidarity and of student agreement with parents, the hallucinogen users stand out as the most extreme group as measured by their view of themselves as apart from their families on matters of value, policy, and social perspective. At the other end, on both measures, the teetotallers see themselves and their families as the most homogeneous in terms of agreement.

OUTSIDER-INSIDER DIMENSION

Implicit in the opposition of student to parents, as well as in some of our political-position measures, is the notion of being with—

in contrast to being outside of or against—social institutions. We pursued this dimension further for we anticipated that illicit-drug-using students would feel outside of more groups than would others. Students were presented with a list of thirteen groups—including several abstract identity classes—beginning with their family, the people in their own residences, and majors in their department, and expanding outward to include the student body, the intellectual community, the university administration, then, the broader concept of Americans, and the more abstract concepts of middle-class values, Western culture, and this age of technology. Students were asked, after a discussion of the items, whether they felt like an insider (that is, as a member of the group, sympathetic to it, or identified with it or the concept) or like an outsider (feeling outside, being left out, or desiring to be disassociated). A score was constructed by summing the number of times the student replied that he was an outsider.

Inspection of the distribution of scores shows an exaggerated normal curve skewed toward low outsider scores. The median score is four—that is, listing oneself as an outsider on only four of nineteen groups. The mode is also four. Ten per cent of the students feel outside of seven or more groups or abstract classes.

There are no important differences in feelings on the insider-outsider dimension when one contrasts users to non-users on any of the legitimate (that is, medical or social) drugs. However, on all of the illicit drugs, differences do emerge, so that we find hallucinogen users most "outside" by their own account, with opiate, special-substance, and marijuana users trooping behind. In no cases are the differences extreme.

UNIVERSITY AND STUDENTS

Three questions were directed at satisfactions with course work, teachers, and the institution as a whole. These constitute a morale measure roughly akin to industrial-morale inquiries which, to produce morale indices, ask about satisfaction with work, supervisors, and company. We expected that students with greatest dissatisfaction—that is lowest morale—would report more drug experience than others. This expectation was consistently supported.

Students expressing themselves as (entirely) dissatisfied with the subject matter in courses report more drug experience for all drug classes than those students who are both satisfied and dissatisfied or those who are satisfied. Very slight differences exist, for the most part, between the students both satisfied and dissatisfied with their courses and the fully satisfied ones; the greatest difference obtains for marijuana—the satisfied students reporting 15 per cent experience, satisfied-dissatisfied students reporting 23 per cent experience, and totally dissatisfied students reporting 28 per cent experience.

Students entirely dissatisfied with their teachers report proportionately more drug experience for all classes of drugs, except for alcohol, than students who are quite satisfied or who say they are both satisfied and dissatisfied. These latter two groups do not differ in any marked way on drug experience. The greatest differences between the entirely dissatisfied students and the quite satisfied students are on marijuana (35 per cent vs. 16 per cent), amphetamines (32 per cent vs. 19 per cent), hallucinogens (11 per cent vs. 4 per cent), special substances (13 per cent vs. 6 per cent), and opiates (4 per cent vs. 1 per cent).

Students satisfied with the institution as a whole report comparatively less drug experience for all drugs; the entirely dissatisfied students report most experience; students both satisfied and dissatisfied occupy an intermediate position. Illustrative differences are amphetamines, 18 per cent vs. 34 per cent, with the ambivalent group at 25 per cent; marijuana at 15 per cent vs. 38 per cent vs. 22 per cent; hallucinogens at 3 per cent vs. 18 per cent vs. 7 per cent; and opiates at 0 per cent ($N = 4$) vs. 5 per cent vs. 2 per cent.

Students were asked how many incompletes (taking a course but not completing it—for example, not taking the final exam, with permission of the instructor) they had taken during the last year. We expected drug experience to be higher among those students taking more incompletes. We find that the majority of students report no incompletes and are lower on the use of all classes of drugs in comparison with students taking one or more incompletes the previous year. When we look at the students who, as a group, have the greatest proportion of incompletes, we find them to be first in use of opiates, hallucinogens, and amphetamines, closely followed by use of special substances and marijuana. About 20 per cent of all students in these groups have taken one or more incompletes compared with a maximum 15 per cent taking incompletes among any of the other medical- or social-drug users. In terms of the number of incompletes, the hallucinogen users have had more than any other group, 9 per cent having taken two or more incompletes.

Students were asked whether they had ever dropped out of school for other than health reasons. On all drugs members of the drop-out group report greater use than those who have never dropped out. Figures are as follows: tobacco, 86 per cent vs. 73 per cent; alcohol, 98 per cent vs. 92 per cent; amphetamines, 41 per cent vs. 18 per cent; sedatives, 35 per cent vs. 23 per cent; tranquilizers, 31 per cent vs. 17 per cent; marijuana, 34 per cent vs. 16 per cent; hallucinogens, 8 per cent vs. 4 per cent; opiates, 2 per cent vs. 1 per cent; and special substances, 13 per cent vs. 5 per cent. Looking at the data from another aspect, we can say that students who have tried hallucinogens rank first in the proportion who have dropped out of school for other than health reasons. Students who have used special substances rank second, and amphetamine-experienced students third.

Students were asked whether they were now seriously thinking of dropping-out. On all drugs except alcohol, those not considering dropping out (88 per cent) report less drug experience than those who say either that they intend to or are considering dropping-out. The greatest difference between the group not intending to drop out and the group intending to do so is for marijuana experience, 31 per cent vs. 18 per cent. Looking at this item, too, from the standpoint of experience with particular drugs and drop-out plans, we find that students who have used hallucinogens have the greatest proportion (23 per cent) thinking about dropping-out, with opiate users, special-substance users, and marijuana users following in that order.

The grade-point average ranges from 1, an average D grade, to 4, an average A grade. A small group interviewed as first-semester freshmen have no grade-point average as yet. Distribution of grade points for the others shows a flattened skewed curve with the mode at 3.0 or straight B and with high frequencies at 2.5 and at 2 (straight C). The average grade point for the total sample is 2.8. Ten per cent of the total sample have grade points of 3.5 (A−) or better. Table 7 below gives the distribution of grade points for non-users and users of each drug. All differences are small. The major inference is that drug experience does not constitute a predictor of grades. Minor observations are that non-users of alcohol and tobacco have slightly higher grades, whereas students experienced with amphetamines, tranquilizers, and several of the illicit-exotic substances have slightly higher grades.

Students were asked what the relationship was between their

Table 7

DISTRIBUTION OF GRADE POINTS

| | Grade Points | |
Drug	Non-Users	Users
Tobacco	3.0	2.8
Alcohol	3.5	2.8
Amphetamines	2.7	2.8
Sedatives	2.8	2.85
Tranquilizers	2.8	3.0
Marijuana	2.8	2.75
Hallucinogens	2.8	2.9
Opiates	2.6	2.72
Special substances	2.6	2.7

course of studies and how they wanted to live their lives. The question aimed at the relevance of school for their future. Replies were divided into categories indicating relevance or necessity for career goals, life goals, both life and career goals, and school as being irrelevant for either life or career goals. Our findings show that the students for whom school is relevant for both career and life goals are the ones who report least drug experience on all drugs. The students for whom school is unrelated to either life or career goals report the greatest experience with most drugs—alcohol, tobacco, amphetamines, hallucinogens, and opiates (the latter a shared ranking)—and also share second highest ranking on sedatives and marijuana. Those for whom school is relevant for career goals alone cluster on the low-experience side for all drugs except sedatives and opiates, and with these the differences among groups are slight. Students relating school only to life goals, a more diffuse concept, are highest on alcohol (a shared ranking), sedatives, and tranquilizers, and share high experience on marijuana.

Students were asked whether they were optimistic or pessimistic about doing what they'd like to do once school was completed. Students who are optimistic about their futures are uniformly low on all drug experience, sometimes sharing that low ranking with those in the "other" reply category, most of whom express frequent fluctuating shifts between optimism and pessimism. The pessimistic students are high on all classes of drug experience, although they share high experience on some drugs (tobacco, alcohol, and tranquilizers) with the "other" reply group.

Students were asked whether their life plans included efforts to make changes in the world—technology, the environment, social or political systems, and so forth—so as to change the lives of many persons. The aim of the question was to identify students with what others have called "constructivist" goals that are broadly humane and ambitious as well. These, of course, would focus on idealistic students oriented toward innovation. Although students who indicate they are idealistic innovators, or even revolutionaries, are higher than others in drug experience for all classes of drugs, except sedatives, the differences are not great. Those not interested in changing the world are more experienced in drugs than the "maybe"-group members who report consistently lowest usage (we must keep in mind, of course, that the percentage spread is slight).

Students were asked how many different campus clubs, teams, or recognized groups or organizations they held membership in at the moment. The group with the greatest experience with drugs report being members of no organization at all. They offer the highest proportion of experience with amphetamines, tranquilizers, marijuana, hallucinogens, opiates, and special substances (sharing these latter two rankings with others). A very small group (combined $N = 15$) with the greatest proportion reporting experience with tobacco and alcohol is comprised of members of the largest number of college organizations, five or over. These extremely busy students are lowest on sedatives, tranquilizers, marijuana, opiates, and special substances. There is little order to the remaining groups; for example, students holding membership in two or three organizations are low in tobacco, alcohol, and amphetamines but highest in sedatives, fairly low on marijuana and hallucinogens, but high on opiates and special substances. Persons holding membership in one group consistently appear in the middling range of drug experience.

LIFE AS STUDENTS VIEW IT

We asked students to compare what they now knew about life with what they had expected it to be like when they were younger. Replies were coded in terms of those who found it as expected, those who found it better than expected, those who found it worse, those who found it both better and worse, and those who found early expectations utterly unmatched by the present and could only say it was "different."

Students expecting life to be just as it has turned out (at least so they say) comprise the group with the lowest proportion reporting drug experiences for all classes except tranquilizers and opiates, but these latter are only a few percentage points from the lowest group. Students finding it both better and worse, but not the same as expected, are also low on drug experience or sometimes middling. Students finding it "different"—thereby abstaining from value or emotional connotations—are, it turns out, the ones with the greatest proportion of drug experience. Those finding life better than anticipated are consistently a middling group (except for sharing with others an opiate high ranking differentiated from the low by only 2 per cent), whereas those finding it "worse" present a mixed pattern— high on alcohol, highest on amphetamines, high on sedatives, highest on special substances, but lowest on tranquilizers and opiates. Because the spread of differences is small among the middle groups, it is best not to make much of these relative positions, except to wonder about the consistently higher experience of those finding life so much different than anticipated and to keep in mind the relatively (but not remarkably) lower drug experience of the self-styled realists. To illustrate maximum differences, the figures show the realists reporting 13 per cent marijuana experience whereas the "it's-different" group report 21 per cent; realists report 16 per cent amphetamine experience with the "it's-different" group reporting 25 per cent; realists report 65 per cent tobacco experience and the "different" group 80 per cent.

SUMMARY

On almost every student characteristic which we expected to be associated with trends in drug use, we found differences in the expected directions. For the most part, these differences were consistently related to the use of all drugs, although the differences in characteristics became more marked for the less-often-used drugs and especially for the amphetamines, hallucinogens, and marijuana. The drugs appearing most often to be inconsistently linked to these characteristics were sedatives and tranquilizers. The characteristics inquired about included the following: student age, sex and school year; family mobility and wealth; student position vis-à-vis parents, as well as family homogeneity on major values and issues; student interest and participation in activities, politics and religion; student political ideology and religion; shifts in student ideology; school majors; student dissatisfaction with and morale in school; student school performance; conceptions of the relevance of their present lives for the future; and student involvement in organizations and their conceptions of themselves as part of or outside of ordinary groups providing membership, identification, or models for young people. Of all measures, grade averages proved the least consistent.

The differences observed, although not always of great magnitude, are certainly not to be assumed as creating either-or dichotomies or necessarily to be assumed as concealing considerable differences within groups of users and non-users of drugs; nevertheless, they show that drug use as such is related to student background, interests, activities, viewpoint, and performance. These differences (more marked for the illicit drugs and amphetamines, much use of which is also illicit or at least informal) suggest that at the time of the study students with illicit-drug experience were generally wealthier and older upperclassmen; irreligious; in opposition to their parents; politically left wing and politically active; in arts and humanities or social sciences; undergoing ideological shifts; generally dissatisfied and with lower school morale; and more surprised about their life as they found it and more pessimistic about the future.

We cannot be sure what components or dynamics underlie these trends. We suspect one feature—as evidenced in the age and class data—simply represents exposure to drug availability and pro-drug arguments the longer the student is in school. Tied to acceptance of those arguments is a willingness to denounce and distrust conservatism and convention and to embark on a variety of new ventures, some of which are ideological and intellectual and some of which are private and personal. Drug use is at the same time ideological, social, and individualistic. The dissatisfaction, pessimism, incomplete grades, drop-out trends, and major concentration in arts, humanities, and social sciences imply, we believe, not only the "alienation" of some student drug users but also flexibility, lessened commitment to institutional goals and rules, and an interest in unusual personal experiences, in new social experiments, and in the improvisation of new life styles. For some we suspect these trends also imply personal depression, confusion, anger, rebellion, inadequacy, and uncertainty. For others—whatever temporary psychopathological labels may be tempting—the essence of dissatisfaction and experimentation is, we believe, a creative and challenging personal and social ethic.

Student Characteristics, Minor Drugs, and Motivation

Richard H. Blum

V

*T*his chapter continues the comparison, begun in Chapter Four, of students who have had one or more lifetime experiences with any of the major classes of mind-altering drugs to students who have never used that class of drugs. The focus of interest here is on correlated drug activity—that is, on students' use of minor stimulants, their exposure to anesthetics, their use of prescription painkillers, their self-medication with mild painkillers and mild tranquilizers, the variety of functions which drugs have had for them, the principles which guide their drug conduct, and their view of sickness and parental sick-care behavior when they were children. The aim of the chapter is to show that students differing on these activities and viewpoints differ consistently on all drug use. It also shows that users of illicit-exotic drugs constitute a set of special cases.

MINOR DRUGS

Students who have undergone general anesthesia constitute a group with proportionately more experience with every class of drug than students not having had general anesthesia. In no instance are the differences greater than a few percentage points. The maximum difference obtains for sedatives; here, 27 per cent of those having had anesthesia have sedative use and 20 per cent of those not having had anesthesia report sedative use. It is possible that routine sedation administration before anesthesia accounts for this fact. The consistent slight differences in anesthesia experience may be interpreted in terms of more exposure to medical care by the higher-income group, which, as we know from Chapter Three, is more drug experienced, or it may reflect either resistance to anesthesia among the nondrug users or, conversely, readiness to accept anesthesia as one feature of a life pattern that accepts, teaches, or otherwise exposes people to the use of chemical agents to affect their minds.

Students who report having received strong painkillers (morphine, Demerol, Percodan, codeine, among others) under medical supervision demonstrate a higher proportion of experience with every class of drug compared with the students who have not received strong painkillers medically. The most marked differences are seen for tranquilizers; here, 26 per cent of those having used painkillers have also used tranquilizers as opposed to 12 per cent among the no-opiate group, and for sedatives where the figures are 33 per cent and 16 per cent. For amphetamines the figures are 27 per cent experience among students for whom painkillers have been prescribed as compared with 15 per cent amphetamine use among students who have neither had medical opiates prescribed nor been given them directly.

Students were asked to describe their use of nonprescription mild painkillers and mild tranquilizers (aspirin, Bufferin, Bromo-Seltzer, Compōz, Cope, Endin, and so on) in terms of "none," "intermittent" (four times or less per year), "occasional" (less than once a week but more than intermittent), "regular" (once a week or more), or "considerable" (daily). Our findings show that those who characterize themselves as regular or considerable self-medicators with these compounds constitute the group having the highest proportion of experience with sedatives and tranquilizers as compared with the other categories of analgesic use. The most outstanding difference among all drug classes obtains for sedatives where 56 per cent of the heavy ("considerable") self-medicators also have sedative experience, 30 per cent of the "regular" self-medicators do, compared with 16 per cent and 21 per cent among those who use mild painkillers and tranquilizers only on an "intermittent" basis or not at all. Regular self-medicators are the group with the greatest amphetamine experience; curiously, those who never self-medicate with analgesics or tranquilizers rank second in amphetamine use, while the heavy self-medicators rank third.

To summarize, we find that the heaviest users (daily) of analgesics have the greatest experience (defined as ranking either first or second) with alcohol, sedatives, tranquilizers, hallucinogens, and illicit opiates. The "regular" (weekly) users of analgesics and over-the-counter tranquilizers appear among the most experienced users of tobacco, amphetamines, sedatives, tranquilizers, marijuana, hallucinogens, and special substances. The group members who never self-medicate with analgesics are nevertheless high, proportionately, in tobacco, alcohol, amphetamine, hallucinogen, opiate, and special-substance use and are quite low only with reference to sedatives and tranquilizers. Many of these subgroup differences might not obtain statistical significance since the N's for both the heavy self-medicators and the no self-medicators are small, twenty-five and forty-eight respectively. Nevertheless, we think it worth noting that those who reject self-medication with mild analgesics can be proportionately high in use of other drugs, two of which (alcohol and the illicit opiates) are also usually analgesic in action. What makes better sense is that the heaviest self-medicators with mild analgesics are also heaviest in experience with the stronger sedative-tranquilizer compounds.

Students were asked to describe their use of coffee (caffeine), tea (theine), chocolate and cocoa (theobromine) drinks, cola drinks and No-Doze (both caffeine), or other stay-awake preparations in terms of "none," "intermittent," "occasional," "regular," and "considerable" for each as in the previous question. Our findings indicate that the daily users of coffee are also the students with the greatest experience with tobacco, alcohol, amphetamines, tranquilizers, and marijuana. Regular users are also high on alcohol and hallucinogens. Those who drink no coffee are lowest, proportionately, on use of tobacco, alcohol, and amphetamines. The most marked difference in drug experience occurs with tobacco where 84 per cent of the daily coffee drinkers have smoked in contrast to 58 per cent of those who have never used coffee. Our impression from the data is of an association between coffee-drinking habits and the use of social and stimulating drugs.

With reference to tea, those who drink no tea also have the lowest proportion of use of tobacco, alcohol, amphetamines, sedatives, tranquilizers, marijuana, and hallucinogens; those who are daily or weekly tea drinkers rank high for alcohol, amphetamines, sedatives, tranquilizers, and special substances. The most marked differences—about 10 percentage points—obtain for sedatives, tranquilizers, and marijuana. The importance of not drinking tea as a correlate of low use of other drugs is suggested.

Regarding chocolate and cocoa drinks, there are no consistent trends, although reversals over the expected occur. For example, those who drink no chocolate or cocoa are highest on tobacco, alcohol, amphetamine, and marijuana while those who are daily drinkers are lowest on amphetamines, sedatives, tranquilizers, and marijuana. Differences among groups are slight; the greatest is the 9 per cent difference in amphetamine experience between those who do not drink chocolate (24 per cent) and the drinkers (17 per cent). One wonders whether one might find other substances which, like chocolate, are primarily foods, the use of which would be negatively correlated with drug use.

Cola drinking is linked to little. The weekly and daily imbibers rank neither highest nor lowest on any drug except sedatives where 30 per cent of the daily cola drinkers are experienced compared with the 23 per cent average for the other groups.

Stay-awake preparations are used daily or weekly by only a few students (19/1,314) whereas the majority (838) do not use them at all. Consistently, those who do not use the stay-awakes are lowest in the proportion having experience with every class of drugs; the small group of weekly or daily users rank high in the use of every drug and the differences between them and the rest of the population are considerable. The proportions of reported drug use by the heavy stay-awake users (combined daily and weekly groups, $N = 19$), and intermediate group of occasional users, and the non-users of stay-awakes are, in order, as follows for each drug class: tobacco 85 per cent, 85 per cent, and 17 per cent; alcohol 100 per cent, 97 per cent, and 91 per cent; amphetamines 26 per cent, 31 per cent, and 18 per cent; sedatives 53 per cent, 30 per cent, and 21 per cent; tranquilizers 32 per cent, 21 per cent, and 18 per cent; marijuana 37 per cent, 21 per cent, and 15 per cent; hallucinogens 16 per cent, 6 per cent, and 4 per cent; illicit opiates 11 per cent, 3 per cent, and 2 per cent; and special substances 16 per cent, 10 per cent, and 5 per cent. It can be seen that the greatest differences occur with respect to sedatives.

We conclude that stay-awakes, even though they contain only caffeine, are an important index of the use of other drugs.

FUNCTIONS AND INTENTS

Each student was asked whether he had ever taken anything to achieve a variety of specified effects for which drugs are sometimes used. Our expectation was that those with more variety of drug use would have used drugs for a greater number of purposes—a finding we (Blum and Associates, 1964) have already reported elsewhere and which has also been reported by Aberle (1966).

With reference to having taken something "to make you feel less afraid or more courageous," students answering "yes" report more experience with every class of drug than those answering "no." The biggest differences between the two groups obtain for tobacco (89 per cent vs. 71 per cent), amphetamines (32 per cent vs. 18 per cent), tranquilizers (30 per cent vs. 16 per cent), and marijuana (27 per cent vs. 16 per cent).

Asked whether they had ever taken anything "to find out more about yourself" (personality, problems, or potentials), the students showed striking differences. According to our findings, those few answering "yes" have had more experience, proportionately, in every drug class than those saying "no." The differences are large: for marijuana 80 per cent vs. 12 per cent; for hallucinogens 34 per cent vs. 2 per cent; for illicit opiates 7 per cent vs. 1 per cent; for special substances 19 per cent vs. 4 per cent; for amphetamines 49 per cent vs. 18 per cent; for tranquilizers 34 per cent vs. 17 per cent, and so on. It would appear that this item reflects the presumed motives, justification, or drug-goal consensus especially of marijuana users, but also for those employing other drugs.

Asked whether they had ever taken anything "to have a religious experience or to come closer to God," the students showed equally striking differences—this time applicable to the amphetamine and hallucinogen groups. Among the "yes"-reply group, 55 per cent have used hallucinogens compared with 4 per cent among the "no" group. The figure for marijuana use among "yes" responders is 72 per cent and 18 per cent among the "no" group. Other figures are as follows: amphetamines 62 per cent vs. 20 per cent; tranquilizers 45 per cent vs. 18 per cent; and special substances 31 per cent vs. 5 per cent. These data suggest that the religious inquiry is also a very important item in the catalogue of motivations which users of illicit substances ascribe to themselves.

"Have you ever taken anything to satisfy a strong craving or a compulsion, something you just had to have?" We find those replying "yes" have had more experience with all classes of drugs than those answering "no"; however, differences are not great—an average 10 per cent difference obtains for sedatives, tranquilizers, and marijuana.

"Have you ever taken anything to relieve your boredom (break up monotony or a dull time)?" We find the "yes"-reply group have had more experience in every class of drugs; the biggest difference obtains for tobacco, 86 per cent compared with 65 per cent.

"Have you ever taken anything to make you feel less depressed or sad?" Results show that the "yes"-reply group have had more experience with all drugs. The biggest difference is with reference to amphetamines, 31 per cent vs. 17 per cent, tranquilizers, 28 per cent vs. 15 per cent, and marijuana, 31 per cent vs. 14 per cent.

"Have you ever taken anything to relieve tension or nervousness?" We find that the "yes" group have had more experience with all drugs; the biggest differences obtain for tobacco, 83 per cent vs. 64 per cent; amphetamines, 28 per cent vs. 11 per cent; sedatives, 31 per cent vs. 16 per cent; tranquilizers, 29 vs. 5 per cent; and marijuana, 24 per cent vs. 12 per cent.

"Have you ever taken anything to make a good mood last longer or to make a fine feeling into an even better one?" The "yes" group have had more drug experience in all classes; the biggest difference on this item obtains for marijuana, 34 per cent vs. 13 per cent, and amphetamines, 30 per cent vs. 18 per cent.

"Have you ever taken anything to relieve or counteract anger or irritability?" The "yes"-reply group have had more drug experience in all drug classes. The biggest difference is for tobacco, 90 per cent vs. 72 per cent; for amphetamines, 34 per cent vs. 19 per cent; and for tranquilizers, 31 per cent vs. 17 per cent.

"Have you ever taken anything to make you more friendly

or loving toward others?" The "yes" group have had more drug experience across the board; the largest differences occur in respect to amphetamines, 33 per cent vs. 19 per cent, marijuana, 36 per cent vs. 16 per cent, and special substances, 14 per cent vs. 5 per cent.

"Have you ever taken anything to change your appetite for food, either to increase it or reduce it?" The "yes" group have had more experience with drugs in all classes; the biggest differences are for amphetamines, 44 per cent vs. 13 per cent, and for sedatives, 34 per cent vs. 22 per cent.

"Have you ever taken anything to make you feel stronger or healthier?" Results show this item to be of little value, even though the "yes" group tend to have more experience with most drugs; differences are slight except for amphetamines, 26 per cent vs. 17 per cent, and sedatives, 30 per cent vs. 21 per cent.

"Have you ever taken anything to make you feel less dull or sluggish?" Again, the indication is that the "yes" group have had more experience with all drugs. The biggest differences are for amphetamines, 31 per cent vs. 14 per cent, marijuana, 24 per cent vs. 15 per cent, and tobacco, 81 per cent vs. 71 per cent.

"Have you ever taken anything to improve your sexual appetite, sensitivity, or sexual capacities?" Findings show that, with the exception of sedative experience, the "yes" group have had more experience with all drug classes. Some of the differences are striking; for example, marijuana experience is 59 per cent for the "yes" group compared with 17 per cent for the "no" group; hallucinogen use is 29 per cent compared with 4 per cent; amphetamine use is 44 per cent compared with 20 per cent; tranquilizer use is 31 per cent compared with 18 per cent; special-substance use is 19 per cent compared with 5 per cent, and illicit opiates use is 7 per cent compared with 1 per cent. It is clear that the item on sex, like the earlier ones on self-exploration and religion, taps into functions and drug uses of special interest to drug-experienced students.

"Have you ever taken anything to reduce sexual desires or sexual sensitivities?" Only a few students (14) are in the "yes" group but they are, in the proportion of drug experience reported, higher for all classes except opiates than the majority of the "no" group. Their experiences compared with others are as follows: tobacco 100 per cent vs. 75 per cent; alcohol 100 per cent vs. 93 per cent; marijuana 71 per cent vs. 18 per cent; amphetamines 43 per cent vs. 21 per cent;

sedatives 43 per cent vs. 24 per cent; tranquilizers 36 per cent vs. 19 per cent; hallucinogens 7 per cent vs. 5 per cent; opiates 0 vs. 1 per cent. This sexual reduction item is particularly relevant for some of the marijuana-use group.

"Have you ever taken anything to keep yourself from going into a panic or perhaps to keep you from going crazy?" The "yes" group (N = 83) have had more drug experience in all classes than the "no" group. Tranquilizers stand out as the drug class showing the greatest difference between the two groups; 52 per cent of the "yes" group have taken tranquilizers compared with 17 per cent of the "no" group. Other figures are: sedatives 47 per cent vs. 23 per cent; amphetamines 45 per cent vs. 20 per cent; marijuana 36 per cent vs. 18 per cent; hallucinogens 8 per cent vs. 5 per cent; and special substances 17 per cent vs. 5 per cent.

"Have you ever taken anything to kill yourself?" Thirteen students, or 1 per cent of the total population, say they have tried to kill themselves via substance ingestion. These group members are high on all drug experience compared with the others (except illicit opiates). The drug-class experience showing the greatest difference between the two groups is, not unexpectedly, sedatives; 69 per cent of those attempting suicide have used sedatives compared with 24 per cent among those not attempting suicide (at least via ingestion). Other differences include tobacco 92 per cent vs. 75 per cent, amphetamines 46 per cent vs. 21 per cent, tranquilizers 54 per cent vs. 19 per cent, and marijuana 46 per cent vs. 19 per cent.

"Have you ever taken anything to make you smarter or improve your ability to learn or to remember things?" We find that the "yes" group have more drug experience across the board. The biggest difference is for amphetamines: 61 per cent of the "yes" group have used them compared with 17 per cent of the "no" group. Other figures are tobacco 88 per cent vs. 74 per cent, tranquilizers 30 per cent vs. 18 per cent, marijuana 45 per cent vs. 16 per cent, hallucinogens 13 per cent vs. 4 per cent, and special substances 16 per cent vs. 5 per cent.

"Have you ever taken anything to improve your performance in something physical (athletics or work)?" The "yes" group have had more drug experience, but the item does not reveal strong differences between these members and the "no" group.

"Have you ever taken anything to get you ready or put you

'up' for some stress (exam, meeting)?" The "yes" group have had more drug experience across the board. The biggest difference is in amphetamine experience, 35 per cent vs. 15 per cent; tranquilizers 30 per cent vs. 15 per cent; and sedatives 32 per cent vs. 22 per cent.

"Have you ever taken anything to shut things out, to help you put something out of your mind or keep something from intruding?" The "yes" group have had more drug experience in all classes. Differences obtain for marijuana, 40 per cent vs. 16 per cent, amphetamines 40 per cent vs. 19 per cent, sedatives 35 per cent vs. 23 per cent, tranquilizers 33 per cent vs. 17 per cent, hallucinogens 10 per cent vs. 4 per cent, and special substances 15 per cent vs. 5 per cent.

We can look at self-ascribed drug motivations to learn whether different functions apply to different drugs. For the drug-using population as a whole, we learn that people say they employ drugs to relieve tension, to feel stronger, to feel less dull, and to satisfy a strong craving. We see that opiate users answer "yes" to almost every possible motive (four excepted) and in doing so suggest that they use opiates for almost any felt need. One might also ask whether opiate users have the least clearly delineated states of feeling and the closest linkage between arousal states and drug gratifications. If such is the case, one would expect to find a much reduced level of need differentiation among opiate users and a broad substitution of opiates as a source of polyvalent gratification. Examining replies to the motive questions still further, one finds that users of tranquilizers more than any other class of drug users employ these substances to relieve tension and avoid panic. Amphetamine users emphasize the use of drugs to feel stronger and to be less dull.

If, on another tack, we take the outstanding differences between the "yes" and "no" groups regarding purposes of use, we find that marijuana use is twice as great among those who say—as opposed to those who don't—that they employ drugs for self-exploration, religious seeking, combatting of depression, mood elaboration, enhancement of friendliness, sexual improvement, sexual reduction, avoidance of panic or psychosis, suicide attempts via drugs, enhanced learning or recall, and insulation from stimulation.

Using the same criterion for identifying motives for drug use among hallucinogen users (this criterion requires that at least twice as many assert their motives as deny them), one finds the principal self-ascribed motives of hallucinogen users to include self-exploration, religious seeking, relief from boredom, combatting of depression, mood elaboration, sexual-appetite enhancement, learning facilitation, stress preparation, and insulation from stimuli.

Sedative users claim the following motives more than twice as often as nonsedative users: tension relief, reduction of sexuality, and suicide attempts via drugs.

In summary, we find that the greatest variety of motives obtain for the illicit-opiate users, followed, in turn, by special-substance users, amphetamine users, and pot smokers. Our selection of motives for inquiry was not balanced between positive and negative but implies some sense of deficit on the part of the user. Perhaps it is for this reason that the catalogue of motives claimed by the drug-experienced students, as compared with the inexperienced ones, implies so much distress. Nevertheless, we would not wish to overlook the implications of the fact that persons laying claim to drug uses based on functions reflecting psychological pain emerge as having used psychoactive drugs considerably more often than those not claiming to have used drugs for these distress-reducing reasons.

PRINCIPLES GUIDING DRUG USE

Students were asked what beliefs about drug use guided their own conduct in regard to their personal use of LSD, marijuana, and similar substances. Replies to this open-ended item were content coded. Our findings show that the majority (61 per cent) of students say they are guided primarily by negative considerations, dangers, disapproval, and the like. Seven per cent emphasize only positive features in the use of these drugs, and 31 per cent offer both positive and negative considerations. Only 1 per cent are unable to set forth their own rules for drug use. Among the negative valences, the risk of undesirable changes in the self tops the list (46 per cent); next, in order, are the following: danger of physical harm; sheer disinterest in taking drugs; a sense of inappropriateness in terms of the student's view of himself and his position or responsibilities (". . . responsibility toward my family—they would disapprove and I care what they think of me," or "I should serve as an example to my younger brothers and sisters"); the disapproval of others; incompatibility with the student's morality; risk of changes in social relations as a consequence—that is, loss of friends or becoming a member of a druggie group; or, for 4 per cent, the lack of opportunity to take these drugs.

On the positive side—that is, reasons for taking the drugs—the most often cited (by 21 per cent of the population) is to satisfy some personal motive, such as curiosity and the desire for self-exploration, followed by the recommendation by authority figures (teachers, ministers, writers, and so forth) to use them, compatibility of drug use and/or effects with the student's own philosophy (for example, "I'm not sure about LSD but marijuana I use socially; it also gives occasional glimpses about yourself that you can't get with alcohol"), in response to encouragement, or facilitation from the immediate environment (for example, to please a friend or be in the spirit of a party, to respond to the recommendation of friends as to beneficial effects, or to facilitate moods).

Considering that almost 40 per cent of the students do have reasons for taking LSD and marijuana—although only about 20 per cent report taking them—one suspects the existence of a strong "ready reserve" who, under some circumstances, will "turn on." Indeed, the shifts in use reported in Chapters Eleven and Sixteen give every reason to believe that many may have begun drug experimentation after our survey. We would presume such students were drawn from among those who had positive reasons for using drugs although they had not yet used them then. We shall further consider the ready-reserve group when presenting information on the stated intentions of students with regard to further drug use.

As one examines the distribution of positive-, mixed-, and negative-valence principles guiding drug use, one finds, as expected, that students using the illicit-exotic drugs emphasize positive features to a far greater extent than do students inexperienced with those drugs; for example, the ratio of negative to positive to mixed valences for marijuana users is about $1:2:5$, and for hallucinogen users it is about $1:8:12$ compared with the total-population (less the marijuana-hallucinogen group) ratio, which is about $23:1:8$. What these ratios show is that the illicit users are oriented to benefits and facilitating features of drug use, that hallucinogen users are far less concerned than marijuana users (by a factor of 4) about negative effects or other barriers or threats surrounding use, and that hallucinogen users are also most extreme in the sense that they have the least ambivalence internally or are least aware externally of both attracting and repelling forces surrounding illicit use.

The distribution also suggests that there are a number of features which control drug use even among those experimenting with illicit-exotic substances, especially among the marijuana group. Thus, there are negative-valence factors reported by three fourths of the marijuana smokers and by three fifths of the hallucinogen users; what is more, about one tenth of the marijuana users (one twentieth of the hallucinogen users) report only negative-valence principles. We presume that these are experimenters who are no longer using illicit drugs. Among the negative features noted, one fourth of the marijuana and LSD groups mention the danger of physical harm, some show concern over their reputations and responsibilities, an interesting 10 per cent claim disinterest in these drugs, and a few (about 6 per cent) comment that their use is contrary to their morals. Almost half of the marijuana users—and over one fourth of hallucinogen-experienced students—seek to avoid undesirable changes in themselves which they believe may occur in consequence of drug use, and almost one fourth of the marijuana users—as opposed to only a tenth of hallucinogen users—limit their use because of social disapproval—including legal sanctions. As for positive reasons for use, the satisfaction of personal motives and compatibility with personal beliefs rank first among both marijuana and hallucinogen users.

CHILDHOOD SICKNESS AND CARE

We expected that adult drug use would be related to childhood experience with illness, the presumption being that if illness—accompanied in America by the common application of medications—had been in any way pleasant there would have been some learning of drug use as a feature of the sickness role. Similarly, if parents had given medicines quickly, the child could later learn self-medicating habits which would also be generous ones. One could, of course, take the same expectations and translate them simply into exposure to medical care and medication as a function of the socioeconomic differences we have already shown to characterize drug propensities. One could speculate in terms of pre-existing personality traits that would lead a child to influence his parents to give medicine or to allow him to play the sick role or one could speak of justification of present habits in terms of a reconstruction of data relevant to childhood experience. In any event, we had already obtained data supporting these expectations in the normal-population study (reported in Chapter Eleven of *Drugs I*) and we sought to replicate those findings here.

Among students characterizing their parents as quick to give medicine or home remedies (about one fourth of the sample), a higher proportion have used tobacco, alcohol, amphetamines, sedatives, and tranquilizers—in other words, the sanctioned medical or social drugs —than those characterizing their parents as "reluctant" or "average." On the other hand, among the offspring of parents viewed as quick to medicate, there stands the lowest proportion of marijuana and hallucinogen users. The differences are, however, small.

Asked whether there were advantages to being sick as a child, the students saying "yes" (over one third of the sample) consistently indicate the most experience with all classes of drugs compared with students saying "no" or those describing both advantages and disadvantages in childhood illness. The greatest differences obtain for sedative, tranquilizer, and tobacco use.

Students were also asked to evaluate their parents' level of worry about their health when they were children. We wanted to know whether the student perceived his parents as overconcerned about health or, in contrast, underconcerned. We anticipated that those perceptions of the parents as extreme—and implicitly unsatisfactory—would be related to variations in drug use. Our findings show that those few students (total $N = 68$) reporting their parents as having shown little concern about their health in childhood have the highest proportionate use of all drugs compared with students evaluating their parents either as very concerned or overconcerned or as average. Differences in drug experience among these groups of students differing in their views of their parents are sometimes considerable; for example, those seeing parents as underconcerned vs. average (which is how the majority replied) use tobacco 93 per cent vs. 74 per cent, amphetamines 38 per cent vs. 21 per cent, sedatives 37 per cent vs. 22 per cent, marijuana 44 per cent vs. 19 per cent, and hallucinogens 12 per cent vs. 5 per cent. It is noteworthy that almost no differences show up between students reporting their parents as having shown average concern and those reporting overconcern.

Reviewing these reconstructed views of what parents were like in childhood—a recollection likely to be strongly colored by current student views of what parents *are* like—one sees first that the most unusual students statistically—that is, those few seeing their parents essentially as uninterested in their childhood health (an inferential measure of rejection or, equally likely, a justification for student counterrejection)—are the heaviest drug users for all drugs. Secondly, one sees a tendency—and only that—for perceived readiness to give medicines as being associated with more experience with all drugs except illicit-exotic ones when compared with the drug experience of those who believe caution was used in home dispensing. Thirdly, one sees a clear relationship between recollection of gain in the sickness role and the use of all drugs. The relationships are obviously complex as well as partial. It does appear clear that perceptions of childhood illness and parental care are linked to drug-use history. Perhaps one thread in the data is that the notion of being apart from one's parents —as is the alienated or rebellious student, who we have already seen is more experienced with illicit-exotic drugs—is linked to a group of views, one of which is that parents were not loving, that they did not even "give" medication, that they did not "care." Would the advantage in the sickness role, then, be a way of forcing parents to care? Perhaps another thread in the data is for students who do use conventional drugs more heavily to recall a family orientation that played a part in their learning to use drugs readily; perhaps parents accounted directly for part of that drug history by introducing the student to some compounds. At another level one wonders whether early personality features developing out of family interaction may have led not only to the utility of being sick as a way of gaining satisfaction but perhaps to early gratifications from drugs administered in childhood. This would have been a first step in learning drug use, as well as an expression still extant of the passive manipulation of the environment —that is, by altering oneself through drugs and by assuming a less active role. One wonders, too, whether heavier drug use might not be regressive in the sense that by self-medication one returns to an earlier problem-solving mode which once worked in childhood by forcing parents to care. Certainly, the social consequences of illicit-drug use at the very least are that elders are made to sit up and take notice! We shall carry these speculations no further at the moment. What must remain clear is that how students report their childhood may have little to do with how others observing parent-child interactions would have characterized these. We hope to follow up on some of these issues by working directly with families, observing how, in fact, the parents of children who are or become heavy drug users differ in their views and behavior from other parents.

SUMMARY

There is a consistent trend for users of all drugs, whether social, medical, or illicit, to have had more experience with other psychoactive agents whether strong or mild. Thus, anesthesia, medical
opiates, coffee, tea, and stay-awakes are all more commonly employed
among drug-experienced—as contrasted to non-using—students for
almost all classes of drugs. The differences are more extreme for users
of certain drugs; for example, tobacco smokers are most often coffee
drinkers and stay-awake users.

Inquiry into the variety of functions (desired effects, reasons
for use) of drugs reveals that illicit users claim the use of drugs to
accomplish more things than do non-users. This multiplicity of drug
functions for those committed to use has been reported elsewhere
(Aberle, 1966; Blum and Associates, 1964). We suspect it represents
a rosy-colored view of what drugs are, a justification of why drugs
are important, and an optimism about drugs as tools to change one's
own inner nature, moods, cycles, and social relationships. The specific
functions more often accepted by drug users and denied by non-users
include the following: combatting fear; exploring one's self; achieving religious experience; satisfying cravings; relieving boredom; combatting depression, sexual impulses, tension, anger, dullness, panic,
and psychosis; elaborating moods; facilitating friendliness, learning,
and sex; preparing for stress; changing or reducing appetite; shutting
out the world, and killing oneself.

Upon inquiring as to the personal principles which guide conduct in respect to illicit drugs, one finds that most students are guided
by negative considerations, the fear of ill-effects, inhibiting or coercive
social forces, inappropriateness of use, and so on. Mixed positive and
negative guidelines more often characterize drug users, while positive
values primarily guide illicit users—for example, in the ratio of negative to positive to mixed valences (principles) for hallucinogen users
is 1 to 8 to 12 compared with the reverse ratio of the remainder of the
students, which is 23 to 1 to 8.

Inquiry into aspects of parental medicating habits and of recollections of childhood illness reveals as the most important finding
that users of all classes of drugs consistently recall the advantages of
being sick as a child. Too, that small group of students who believe

their parents had little concern over their health in childhood were high in their use of all drugs in comparison with other students. These latter reconstructions of childhood as to what illness and parents were like represent, we believe, a perception of parents as not caring—a position compatible with other critical views of parents as expressed by drug users. Whether parents did not, in fact, care, we cannot say. As to the gains from childhood illness, the speculations that emerge are tantalizing. Were these gains an introduction to passivity compatible with adult drug-induced states? Were the self-indulgences in staying away from school and responsibility compatible with dropping-out, taking incompletes, and enjoying pleasure-giving drugs? Were they early exposures to drugs which helped teach drug pleasures, now elaborated in late adolescence? Were they periods of rest from excessive demands by ambitious parents or periods of attention from parents otherwise too busy to care? Were they, perhaps, early expressions of preoccupations with inner states—including symptoms—which foretold later investments in self-exploration through drugs? Are the data simply compatible with McGlothlin and Cohen's (1965) finding to the effect that drug-interested students enjoy regressive states? Or is adult drug use simply a new way of gaining adult attention that was, in earlier years, accomplished by being sick? We believe these questions are important enough to prompt further inquiry.

Correlations and Factor Analysis

Richard H. Blum

VI

*I*n the preceding chapters we have seen that the characteristics of students—background, activities, interests, viewpoints and the like— are linked in some consistent ways to differential use (experience with) drugs. These trends show not only that students who use one drug tend to differ from those who do not use it but, more generally, that one set of characteristics—for example, family wealth or mobility or student school dissatisfaction—are linked to the use of all or nearly all drugs which constitute our spectrum of interest. There are exceptions. It is also important to realize that students with diverse characteristics are included in user and non-user groups; the larger the group, the more diverse the characteristics therein within the range of characteristics in the sample. Nevertheless, what emerges from these chapters is the impression that the use of drugs as such is a general phenomenon, that particular drugs, alike in either the style of use (that is, social, medical, illicit) or in their presumed probable pharmacological effects, "go together" in the sense that people who use one also use another and, conversely, that people who reject one also

101

reject another. What these observations imply is that certain drugs are correlated or, expressed differently, that a regular association exists between a person's use of one drug and his use of another. Secondly, since it appears that there are subgroups of drugs in which the use of one is linked to another but not to drugs in a different subgroup, one may posit that intercorrelations exist among subgroups. Put another way, this means that clusters of people use certain groups of drugs. The search for intercorrelations specific to one subset and not to another is the search for factors and can be accomplished through factor-analytic procedures.

In this chapter we present results of a factor analysis showing the intercorrelations which stand out and demonstrate subsets or clusters of drugs that show communality in their use. Our factor-analytic procedures are based on normalized scores which correct for age—that is, on the z scores derived from the drug-profile scores of each person's lifetime drug history. Note that the significance of correlations rests, in some cases, upon the high number of cases, many of which may be zero cases. For example, a correlation of .07 can be significant at the .05 level because there are 1,312 degrees of freedom.

We see that each drug or drug class is significantly correlated

Table 8

INTERCORRELATIONS AND FACTOR ANALYSIS ON NINE DRUGS
(Significant at .05; rounded off to nearest hundredth)

TOBACCO:

Alcohol	$r = .42$	Illicit opiates	$r = .13$
Amphetamines	$r = .17$	Special substances	$r = .20$
Marijuana	$r = .31$		
Hallucinogens	$r = .14$		

ALCOHOL:

Tobacco	$r = .42$	Marijuana	$r = .22$
Amphetamines	$r = .19$	Hallucinogens	$r = .11$
Sedatives	$r = .07$	Illicit opiates	$r = .12$
Tranquilizers	$r = .13$	Special substances	$r = .17$

AMPHETAMINES:

Tobacco	$r = .17$	Marijuana	$r = .33$
Alcohol	$r = .19$	Hallucinogens	$r = .18$
Sedatives	$r = .09$	Illicit opiates	$r = .24$
Tranquilizers	$r = .16$	Special substances	$r = .27$

Table 8—Cont.

INTERCORRELATIONS AND FACTOR ANALYSIS ON NINE DRUGS
(Significant at .05; rounded off to nearest hundredth)

SEDATIVES:

Alcohol	r = .07	Marijuana	r = .08
Amphetamines	r = .09	Illicit opiates	r = .25
Tranquilizers	r = .11	Special substances	r = .15

TRANQUILIZERS:

Alcohol	r = .13	Hallucinogens	r = .06
Amphetamines	r = .16	Illicit opiates	r = .25
Sedatives	r = .11	Special substances	r = .16
Marijuana	r = .11		

HALLUCINOGENS:

Tobacco	r = .14	Marijuana	r = .55
Alcohol	r = .11	Illicit opiates	r = .13
Amphetamines	r = .18	Special substances	r = .23
Tranquilizers	r = .06		

MARIJUANA:

Tobacco	r = .31	Tranquilizers	r = .11
Alcohol	r = .22	Hallucinogens	r = .55
Amphetamines	r = .33	Illicit opiates	r = .24
Sedatives	r = .11	Special substances	r = .41

ILLICIT OPIATES:

Tobacco	r = .13	Tranquilizers	r = .25
Alcohol	r = .12	Marijuana	r = .24
Amphetamines	r = .24	Hallucinogens	r = .13
Sedatives	r = .25	Special substances	r = .46

SPECIAL SUBSTANCES:

Tobacco	r = .20	Tranquilizers	r = .16
Alcohol	r = .17	Marijuana	r = .41
Amphetamines	r = .27	Hallucinogens	r = .23
Sedatives	r = .15	Illicit opiates	r = .46

with most, if not all, other drugs and that the order of correlation ranges from a low .07 (alcohol and sedatives, alcohol and tranquilizers) to highs of .55 (marijuana and hallucinogens) and .46 (illicit opiates and special substances). Note that the correlation with other drug use is least and lowest for sedatives and tranquilizers and highest for marijuana. What this shows is that use of sedatives and tranquilizers, while related to the use of other drugs, is a more independent phenomenon than in the case of marijuana; here, it is evident that marijuana users are also likely to be users of all other drug classes.

These preliminary observations on intercorrelations now lead us to the examination of common factors—that is, clusters of drug-use habits that link one class of drugs to another.

Table 9 below presents the principal-components solution, using as a criterion that the second last latent root (eigenvalue) be equal to or less than 1. (The latent root is the square root of the sum of the squared loadings for a given factor.) These calculations are used to determine whether the maximum (residual) variance is being accounted for by a given factor. With this method of factoring, each factor extracts the maximum amount of variance (that is, the sum of squares of factor loadings is maximized on each factor) and gives the

Table 9

FOUR-FACTOR PRINCIPAL-COMPONENTS SOLUTION*

Drug	Factor I	Factor II	Factor III	Factor IV
Tobacco	.501	−.376	.547	.055
Alcohol	.478	−.235	.663	.066
Amphetamines	.558	−.002	−.051	−.171
Sedatives	.313	.624	.110	.362
Tranquilizers	.378	.560	.168	.379
Marijuana	.733	−.324	−.289	.176
Hallucinogens	.532	−.378	−.468	.435
Illicit opiates	.591	.424	−.113	−.406
Special substances	.679	.121	−.195	−.421

Sum of latent roots = 6.015. Percentage variance explained = 66.83.

Proportion of total variance explained by each root: 1 = .296; 2 = .149; 3 = .126; 4 = .097.

Proportion of cumulative explained variance accounted for by each added root: 1 = 1.000; 2 = .335; 3 = .221; 4 = .145.

* Here, and in the following two tables, negative as well as positive signs appear. The negative covariance should be examined in contrast to positive covariance only within columns. What is expressed is the relationship between the drug use and each factor. It may be conceived as an arbitrary description with a factor which is a vector in an n-dimensional field, thus the sign of the loading implies drug use and factor compatibility or antagonism. It is the magnitude which occupies our attention.

smallest possible residuals. Thus, the correlation matrix is condensed into the smallest number of orthogonal factors. This method, applied to our data by Switalski and Bonato at the George Washington University Biometrics Laboratory, has the advantage of giving a mathematically unique (least squares) solution.

From Table 9 we see that Factor I is found to account for the greatest proportion of the variances—that is, it yields the highest intercorrelation, one which accounts for about 10 per cent of the observed drug-use patterns. We see that tobacco, amphetamines, marijuana, hallucinogens, illicit opiates, and special substances all have high loadings on Factor I. Another cluster finds sedatives and tranquilizers with high loadings; these are the only two drugs sharing Factor II. Alcohol and tobacco share high loadings on Factor III to the exclusion of all other drugs. (Note the consistent negative loadings on Factor III for all illicit drugs, plus amphetamines.) There is no important fourth factor; the highest loadings are in the .40 to .44 (rounded) range and are shared by hallucinogens, illicit opiates, and special substances.

The next step, presented in Table 10, offers the four-factor principal-components solution with rotations for four-, three-, and two-factor coordinate systems. Rotation is a procedure in which coordinates (factors) are moved so as to transform the data to optimize meaning—that is, interpretation—by virtue of getting greater precision.

Using a cut-off level obtained by calculating the mean of the

Table 10

PRINCIPAL-COMPONENTS SOLUTION WITH ROTATIONS

Drug	Factor I	Factor II	Factor III	Factor IV
Tobacco	−.126	.057	−.809	.142
Alcohol	−.050	−.131	−.839	.061
Amphetamines	−.238	−.064	−.205	.491
Sedatives	−.006	−.786	.013	.116
Tranquilizers	−.047	−.778	−.088	.117
Marijuana	−.772	−.024	−.220	.335
Hallucinogens	−.911	−.033	−.010	.055
Illicit opiates	.023	−.251	−.001	.802
Special substances	−.196	−.027	−.092	.802

means for the two highest loadings of each drug across all factors, a value of .476, one sees four clear factors emerge. Factor I has high loadings for marijuana and hallucinogens only. Factor II has high loadings for sedatives and tranquilizers; Factor III for tobacco and alcohol, and Factor IV for amphetamines, illicit opiates and special substances. These are reasonably precise factors and differ from the results of Table 9 by differentiating out of Factor I in Table 9 two different substructures of illicit-exotic drug use, one linking marijuana and hallucinogens, the other among amphetamines, opiates, and special substances. We already know, from Table 8, that significant correlations do link marijuana with the amphetamines ($r = .33$) and with special substances ($r = .27$), which is why Factor I in Table 10 must be interpreted to represent substructures in illicit use rather than a dichotomy. It remains of interest that, on the most precise factor analysis, the amphetamines are linked to hard narcotics, volatile intoxicants, and other unusual materials. We cannot by means of factor analysis identify the underlying variables which account for this link, whether these be drug action, settings for use, personality of users, or what-have-you.

Although we reject it as a less than optimal solution, a three-factor rotation was also conducted, the results of which are presented in Table 11.

Underlined are loadings near or above the cut-off point of .453. We see in Table 11 that amphetamines and special substances are grouped with marijuana and hallucinogens under Factor Ia. These, however, are split loadings which, when combined with the

Table 11

THREE-FACTOR ROTATION

Drug	Factor Ia	Factor IIa	Factor IIIa
Tobacco	.197	.013	−.808
Alcohol	.068	−.113	−.840
Amphetamines	.452	−.260	−.206
Sedatives	−.034	−.706	.002
Tranquilizers	.003	−.689	−.098
Marijuana	.825	−.035	−.209
Hallucinogens	.792	.132	.006
Illicit opiates	.369	−.637	−.013
Special substances	.583	−.406	−.097

fact of the high correlation between special substances and opiates ($r = .46$), point to the four-factor solution of Table 10 as optimal. Nevertheless, the three-factor solution in Table 11 merits comment, especially the high loadings under Factor IIa for sedatives, tranquilizers, *and* illicit opiates. We see that Factor IIIa with its high tobacco and alcohol loadings is identical to Factor III in Table 10.

From the foregoing analysis, we believe it reasonable to propose that there is, first, a general drug-taking disposition. This is inferred from the consistent positive correlations found in Table 8 and is compatible with the distributions set forth in preceding chapters. The notion of a general drug-taking disposition is imprecise, and by factor analysis a set of discrete subordinate clusters of patterns emerge. The unrefined Factor I of Table 9 and Ia of Table 11 allow the presumption of one subordinate pattern which is of illicit-exotic drug use as such. Upon more precise analysis, Table 10, this is found to consist of at least two separate substructures.

There is Factor I on which marijuana and the hallucinogens have high loadings and there is Factor IV on which amphetamines, illicit opiates, and special substances have high loadings. Sedatives and tranquilizers, two medically prescribed classes of psychoactive drugs, have high loadings on Factor II. In regard to Factor II, note that another prescribable class, the amphetamines, are not to be found. Thus, although we are dealing with drugs capable of being prescribed, Factor II cannot be considered a prescription factor per se. This is a limited interpretation for, as we shall see later, amphetamines are often obtained by students under nonprescription circumstances. A potential link between Factor II and the amphetamines, one found among persons heavily involved with drugs on the up-and-down cycle (sedatives as "downers" and methamphetamines as "uppers"), does not appear. The implication is that the cycle has not made its appearance among students.

In discussing Factor II, we should not overlook the correlation appearing in Table 9 which shows that among all drug classes correlated with sedatives and tranquilizers, the illicit opiates yield the highest, $r = .25$ in both cases. Looking at Table 11, we see that all three drug classes share high loadings on Factor IIb. Given the fact that tranquilizers, sedatives, and opiates have much in common in terms of probable pharmacological effects (Irwin, 1968) in reducing arousal-excitability, fighting behavior, responsiveness to pain, activity, learning, and probably anxiety, we posit that Factor II has a behavioral component, the desire for these suppressive effects. Factor IIb bridges legal- and illicit-drug use whereas the final Factor II does not. We shall consider either factor as the distress- and activity-diminishing factor.

Factor III is found to underlie only tobacco and alcohol. It is obviously not linked to illicit-drug use, to prescription drug taking, or—given our assumptions about Factor II—to depressing central-nervous-system effects. Were there to be a component related to pharmacological alerting or stimulation, one would expect some strong link between these drugs and the amphetamines. In the absence of these presumed components, we shall consider Factor III a conventional social-drug-use cluster.

Returning to Factors I and IV, we are uncertain as to their interpretation. Both embrace illicit-exotic drug use, although the amphetamine loadings in Factor IV may bridge into prescription and informal amphetamine use as well. One can only speculate, suggesting, for example, that the marijuana-hallucinogen Factor I may reflect the psychedelic enthusiast or drug "intellectuals" or the curious drug-experimenter, whereas Factor IV may be a drug-immersion factor. Consider, for example, that from the findings in Chapter Five, the greatest number and variety of self-ascribed drug motives occur among users of opiates, special substances, and amphetamines, in that order. Given the high intercorrelations and the motivational polyvalence, we prefer the immersion construct. If so many functions are linked to drugs or if so many gratifications are connected to them, one may presume that the user's life is centered about drugs as such, a phenomenon implying dependency or addiction. If in this light one infers from the data reported in Chapters Eleven and Nineteen the increasing likelihood that students will be using methamphetamine and heroin intravenously, it would follow that Factor IV will be of increasing interest to epidemiologists. Manner of drug administration should also be considered as a possible component in Factor IV, since methamphetamine and heroin are both injected while heroin and the volatile intoxicants can both be sniffed. Consideration of Factors I and IV should also mark well the psychology of the street—that is, the characterizations which drug users apply to persons fancying one drug over another. Thus, there are acid heads, potheads, speed freaks, junkies, drunks, and others. It is possible that psychological components in the two factors include typologies which can be constructed on the basis of drug preferences, these preferences in turn probably being related to personality, social settings, and biochemical constants. We offer the foregoing as speculations; what is required is further investigation into the variables accounting for the observed factors.

CONCLUSIONS

Intercorrelations and factor analysis, supported by data from the other chapters, reveal a number of relationships capable of interpretation as patterns, communalities, or substructures linking drug use. We propose that there is, first, a *general disposition* toward psychoactive drug use as such. Although of a low order statistically, such an orientation reflects the widespread willingness to use a variety of drugs as tools to alter states of consciousness, biological cycles, and social relations. Much more precise are the subsets of dispositions which link particular drugs and exclude others. One factor tentatively identified is *style of drug use by source,* which has as separate components *conventional social-drug use,* the *employment of illicit-exotic substances,* and, less well supported, *reliance on prescription drugs.* Given the data in Chapter Five on home-remedy use, we would posit self-medication as a behavior linked to the prescription-drug cluster. A second factor tentatively identified concerns *seeking similar drug effects* among several classes of substances. In particular there is a component interpreted as pharmacological effects which diminishes activity and anxiety.

With regard to the more uncertain Factors I and IV, we propose—as a basis for exploration rather than final explanation—alternative components: *immersion* in drug use, an interpretation based on the multiplicity of after-the-fact functions said to be met by drug use along with high intercorrelations with other drug classes; a *typology of users,* which we presume reflects personality and social circumstances and is based on street types such as acid head, speed freak, junkie, and the like; and also *manner of drug administration.* The special reference is to the intravenous injection and sniffing ("snorting") which link methamphetamine, heroin, and the volatile intoxicants. Among these constructs, immersion is probably most closely linked to what is ordinarily considered addiction. The clusters revealed by factor analysis show the importance of discriminating among a variety of components in drug use.

Users of
Approved Drugs

Richard H. Blum

VII

*I*n this chapter we focus on the users of particular drugs, the approved medical and social ones, to identify differences among students using each drug intensively compared with those using it less intensively. Users will also be contrasted with non-users. Comparisons will be made of the same characteristics which have been shown in preceding chapters to be linked to drug experience. Additional descriptive data derived from individual histories of drug use will also be presented.

The comparison in this chapter between less and more intensive users of a drug abandons the criterion of "experience" defined as any use over a lifetime in favor of an intensity measure showing how much use over a lifetime. The intensity measure is derived from the individual's lifetime drug history, or profile, which indicates for each drug or class of drugs how much a student has used the drug over each year of his life. The how-much-each-year replies are coded as "none," "intermittent," "occasional," "regular," or "considerable." These codes were defined for each drug on the basis of pretest findings as to the distribution of replies. For example, "considerable" alcohol use means four drinks each day on most days for six months or more during the year; "considerable" hallucinogen use is daily use. The scoring procedure leads to higher scores either if the student has used the drug a lot during a given year or if he has used it over any number of years. The highest scores are obtained if someone has used a drug frequently each year over many years. The maximum score of 56 for any one drug profile or history would represent "considerable" use each year of life beginning with age six and continuing through age twenty-eight. (Obviously, since most students in the study were not twenty-eight and most had used drugs rather less intensively than the maximum, we expected no maximum scores.) Two students beginning drug use at the same age and continuing to the same degree could receive different intensity scores if one student were older than the other. This distortion source has been controlled by the use of z scores based on mean drug-use scores, so that persons whose z score for any drug falls above the mid-point are classified as intensive or high users.

Once a set of intensity scores has been obtained for each sample member on each drug, the next step is to order the distribution of all scores on one drug, to identify the median, and to classify all persons above the median as intensive or high drug users and all persons with scores below the median as less intensive drug users. Since the median often falls in a category containing many subjects, the median category itself becomes classified as either high or low, depending upon whether the theoretical median falls in the lower or upper half of the actual median-frequency category. Keep in mind that our classification of intensity is divided into low and high users and excludes those who have never taken the drug. This means low-intensity users are people with at least one-time use.

In presenting the relationship of student characteristics to the patterns of use of a drug, we have proceeded in the discussion by three routes. The first has been to present a brief review of the trends differentiating users and non-users as reported in earlier chapters. The second has been to report trend differences identified in comparisons of high- and low-intensity users. The third has been to test some of those differences by means of the Kolmagorov-Smirnov Test, a statistic which rests upon cumulative score differences. When we describe "significant" differences, we refer to a difference at the $P = .05$ level by this test. The limitations of such a test are several. One is that it does not discriminate or identify the direction of differences—a flaw remedied by simply observing the distribution. The second limitation is that it performs best when there is a range of scores within the limits of 4 to 10. Since only one fifth of our variables are coded within that range, the test must be considered as having been applied only to a (probably representative) sample of our findings. Recognize that there is nothing absolute in these tests of significance; for example, given the vast differences in N for various non-user, high-user, and low-user groups, small differences can emerge as either significant or nonsignificant. Similarly, consistent differences are to be taken as meaningful even if significance at .05 is not achieved. Consider, too, that out of every hundred tests run, five must be expected by chance to achieve significance at the .05 level. In reading each section in this and the following chapter, keep in mind that all students are considered under each drug—that is, the total student sample is examined in terms of characteristics associated first with use and non-use of tobacco and then the smaller sample of users are compared for intensive vs. less intensive use. For brevity we have not repeated the comparison group's classification each time a trend is noted. For example, when we write, "More tobacco users are found among students who are older," the implicit comparison group for "older" is "younger"—that is, more than 75 per cent of all students over age twenty-one smoke, whereas less than 75 per cent of all students under age twenty-one smoke, and so on.

Some drugs, like the sedatives, are employed by people who are not so readily discriminated by the variables upon which this study has focused; thus, because we have not elucidated their special features (assuming they have some associated with taking prescription sedatives), these people more often appear to be distributed throughout the student population. As we examine trends and are aware that drug use is simultaneously intercorrelated overall, intercorrelated on particular factors, and independent of any intercorrelations we have seen fit to try, it is apparent that each person and each group of drug users present a slightly different picture, some aspects of which may simply be chance variations. On the other hand, there is another phenomenon which tends to unify the data; it is the concept of "scaling" in the Guttman sense of predictability of step sequences, or even of a stochastic process. We have met it before in the normal-population pilot study (Chapter Eleven of *Drugs I*) when we found that the greater the use of unusual drugs, the more likelihood there is of the use of ordinary ones. We shall see this again in the next chapter when we find that opiate users are highest of all in their experience with usual *and* unusual—but more "usual" than opiates—drugs. What is implied is a pyramid of the sort that the chap sitting on the top using the most unusual class of drugs is likely to have tried everything else along the way.

Something else which happens to the data is that as the size of the groups (classifications) under consideration grows larger or smaller, then the group itself is likely to become more or less like the population as a whole. For example, since alcohol and tobacco users comprise most of the student population, it is inevitable that they demonstrate the dominant (normal, modal) features of that population. On the other hand, alcohol abstainers and LSD users are rare and, as deviants, are likely to be different in terms of their characteristics vis-à-vis the total sample. Such an expectation, of course, underlies the philosophy of this sort of study. Also, as groups get smaller, it becomes more difficult to get power out of the statistics we employ for testing differences. This means that, ordinarily, when a small group of intensive users—let us say of opiates—are compared with a small group of less intensive users, one cannot expect much in the way of statistical significance. Another problem arises from the method employed in the survey which emphasizes differences among students classified by drug experience or intensity but does not analyze within-group differences. Thus, we have only occasional hints about the interesting clinical or social subgroups which may lie within a classification of users—for example, the high yield of the "craving" item among illicit-opiate users, the curious emphasis on strength and prowess among intensive special-substance users, the athletes, who are conservatives among intensive drinkers, or the odd lack of influence of an alcoholic parent on student drug behavior. Our methods, geared to the gross, deny us the pleasure of subgroup identification or the postulation of psychodynamics following such identifications.

APPROVED DRUGS

Tobacco. Reviewing trend data regarding differences between users and non-users (see Chapters Four and Five), we find that proportionately more tobacco users than non-users are found among students who are older, upperclassmen, arts-humanities or social-science majors, come from wealthier and less settled (more mobile) families, are without current religious affiliation or deep religious interests, differ from their father's or mother's religion (or from both), are in disagreement with their parents on major issues, and are not athletic participants but are political participants. Users are also more extreme in either seeking or in not seeking new experiences, are more often not interested in academic-scholastic-career-related activities, more often are left, politically involved, members of many organizations, are undergoing political change to the left, and differ with fathers and mothers on politics. Proportionately more tobacco smokers will be found among students who perceive their parents as quick to medicate, who recall advantages in childhood illness, and who feel their parents worried less than most about their early health. Regarding school, proportionately more smokers are found among students who are dissatisfied with their courses, their teachers, and the school itself, have taken recent incompletes, have dropped out of school in the past for other than health reasons and are now thinking of dropping-out, see studies as unrelated to future life or career, are not optimistic about getting to do what they want, and find life as it is either worse or totally different from what they have expected. Proportionately more smokers than nonsmokers will be found among students with lower grade-point averages. They will also more often be found, proportionately, among students who consider as the most dangerous groups in the United States today those holding real power (the Establishment), middle-of-the-roaders, and right wingers. Finally, more smokers than nonsmokers occur, proportionately, among students who see benefits from or facilitating reasons for the use of illicit drugs.

Reviewing correlated use of minor drugs, we find that the trends suggest a greater prevalence of tobacco users among students who drink coffee often and use mild painkillers (aspirin, and such), mild tranquilizers (Compōz, and so forth), and over-the-counter stay-awakes. With reference to drug functions, more smokers are among those who use (compared with those who do not use) drugs to build courage, to explore self, to seek religious experience, to satisfy cravings, to relieve boredom, to combat depression, to relieve tension, to facilitate good moods, to counteract anger, to enhance their own friendliness, to induce appetite changes, to combat feelings of dullness, to improve sexuality, to reduce sexuality, to combat panic, and to use in suicide attempts. Tobacco smokers are also more prevalent among those who use drugs to enhance learning, to improve physical performance, to prepare for stress, and to exclude stimuli.

It is important to keep in mind that the foregoing trend descriptions are, for the most part, descriptions of percentage-point differences of a very small order. These statements about trends by no means imply that all smokers are to be so characterized while all non-smokers are not. To the contrary, since most students have tried tobacco, the overriding observation is of diversity within the characteristics of users and the very limited utility of predicting who is a smoker simply on the basis of any one of the characteristics set forth above.

We now turn to the comparison of intensive smokers to less intensive smokers. There are differences by school: School IV has the greatest proportion of high-intensity users (46 per cent of its students are high-intensity users whereas 34 per cent are low), and School I has the highest proportion of low-intensity users (46 per cent are low-intensity, only 30 per cent high-intensity). High-intensity smokers are more often males, older students, upperclassmen, and social-science or arts-humanities majors, come from wealthier families, have parents living, are from unsettled families, and are without religious affiliation, while low-intensity users are more often Protestant or Catholic with a deep religious interest that they share with their parents, who have the same religion. Intensive tobacco use is found more often among those uninterested in athletics or in religious participation; less intensive use is more often found among those for whom athletics is extremely important. Conversely, political participation is more important for intensive smokers than for less intensive ones. Activities such as seeking new experiences are important to intensive smokers, less so to nonintensive ones. The highest proportion of intensive smokers is found among students considering themselves left-of-center politically; the highest proportion of nonintensive smokers is among those having no political preferences. Similarly, political involvement and intensive use are linked, as are noninvolvement and low use. Among students who find their political ideologies shifting, intensive smoking is most often found among those moving left; low tobacco use among those moving right. Political disagreement with father and mother is also linked to more intensive smoking. Intensive smokers more often see their parents as little worried about their present health. Dissatisfaction with teachers and with school as a whole more often characterizes intensive users, who also have more recent incompletes, more often dropped out of school, and are planning to drop out. As for the relationship between studies and life desires, intensive smokers more often occur, proportionately, among students seeing school related to career, while—a deviation from ordinary trends—less intensive smokers more often occur among those finding school unrelated to desires for living. Intensive smokers are more often among the pessimists about getting to do what they would like in life and among those who intend to change the world; less intensive users are more often among those uncertain about trying to change it. Even so, intensive users are also more often pessimistic about seeing changes brought about and more often are students who find life worse than they have expected. Intensive smokers, more often than less intensive ones, are not members of any official organizations. The intensive smokers are among those seeing the Establishment as a menace; less intensive users more often are found among those considering middle-grounders dangerous to the country. Intensive smokers have used other drugs for a greater variety of reasons and think in terms of the benefits of illicit drugs, so that the valence of their guiding principles contains positive elements.

Applying the Kolmagorov-Smirnov test to those variables amenable to it, we find significant differences on eight out of twenty-eight tests and, in comparing users to non-users, significance on an additional eight variables. Of the trends noted, significance is inferred for differences between intensive and less intensive smokers in age, school year, religious affiliation, religious interest, participation in athletics and religion, organizational membership, and valence of principles guiding drug use. For user/non-user differences, significance is inferred for the variables of political participation, seeking new experiences, political involvement, shifting political ideology, current political affiliation, advantages in childhood illness, school satisfaction, and realism of life expectations. Applied to minor-drug-use habits, significant differences between intensive and less intensive smokers emerge for coffee drinking and the use of stay-awakes.

In reviewing the Kolmagorov-Smirnov results, one finds only one instance[1] in which a variable is shown to yield a significant differ-

---

[1] The higher proportion of less intensive smokers are among those finding school unrelated to future ideal-life plans—yet this "unrelatedness-of-stud-

ence between users and non-users in which a trend in the same direction was not also present between intensive and less intensive smokers, even though significance was not achieved. Conversely, when significant differences between intensive and less intensive smokers obtained, there was in each case a trend in the same direction between users and non-users even if it was not significant. What is implied is that relationships are continuous, so that heavy users are at one extreme and non-users are at the other with the less intensive users in the center. We shall find this kind of a distribution characterizing most drugs —but not sedatives—on almost every variable.

With reference to salient points in the history of use, we find regarding associated-drug use that 98 per cent of the smokers drink alcohol, 42 per cent of these beginning with alcohol, 39 per cent with tobacco, and the remainder beginning use of both about the same time. Among smokers, 26 per cent have taken sedatives, 24 per cent have used amphetamines, 21 per cent tranquilizers, 23 per cent marijuana, 7 per cent special substances, 6 per cent hallucinogens, and about 2 per cent opiates. In almost all cases, alcohol or tobacco preceded the use of the other drugs. Comparing intensive users with less intensive users, one finds the average age for beginning use for low users is sixteen and for high-intensity users fifteen. Regarding the source of the drug for initial use, there are no important differences between the high and low groups. As for parental smoking habits, no strong differences emerge, although slightly more (6 per cent) parents of heavy smokers (84 per cent of these parent smokers) also smoke. It is to be noted, as much other research has shown, that the parents of nonsmokers are less likely to smoke, although, interestingly enough, 65 per cent of the parents of non-smokers have at one time smoked. In regard to student intentions either to begin or to continue smoking, we find that almost none of the 25 per cent of the population who are nonsmokers intend to start. Two thirds of the low-intensity group do *not* expect to use tobacco again, whereas only one fifth of the intense smokers intend not to smoke in the future. Clearly, among students only a history of low intensity of use in the past is associated with the expectation not to smoke in the future.

Alcohol. A review of characteristics shows trends suggesting

---

ies" trend does appear in Chapters Four and Five as linked to drug use compared with non-use.

that proportionately more students have alcohol experience among those who are older, are upperclassmen, come from wealthy families, have no religious affiliation or deep interest in religion, differ from their mother's religion, do not participate in religious activities, have a great interest in seeking now experience, are not interested in furthering their academic future careers, are politically active, differ politically with their fathers and mothers and on many other major issues, recall advantages in childhood illness, report their parents were less than ordinarily worried about childhood illness, are dissatisfied with their school, took incompletes in school last year, have dropped out of school previously and are thinking of dropping out, are pessimistic about getting to do what they want in life, are uncertain about whether desirable world changes can be brought about, find life different or worse than they expected, and see benefits or facilitating features for the use of illicit-exotic drugs.

Reviewing correlated minor-drug use, one finds drinkers are more prevalent among those who drink coffee often, drink tea, and use stay-awakes. Regarding drug functions (goals, effects of drugs), one finds more drinkers among those who use drugs for courage, for self-exploration, for a religious experience, to satisfy cravings, to relieve boredom, to combat depression, to relieve tension, to facilitate moods, to enhance their own friendliness, to alter appetite, to combat feelings of dullness, to improve sexual appetites, or to reduce sexual desires, and to combat panic; there are also more drinkers among those who have used drugs to attempt suicide, to enhance intelligence, to prepare for stress, and to combat stimuli.

Using the Kolmagorov-Smirnov Test, we find seven out of twenty-eight of the foregoing trends in characteristics to discriminate between users and non-users beyond the .05 level, and another three of the associated comparisons (tea, coffee, and so on) out of six achieve significance in comparing users and non-users. If we take these tests as a sample of significance, one would estimate that about one quarter of all trends identified as existing are "real" in the sense of being valid inferences not likely to be chance variations. However, if one examines the consistency with which these trends appear—not only in Chapters Four and Five but in this and the next chapter as well—then another feature to be considered in estimating probabilities is the likelihood of the same trend's appearing repeatedly, even if on each occasion or on some occasions it does not achieve independent significance. What we are proposing is that trends which appear repeatedly in the data are not to be ignored whether or not significance at the .05 level is achieved in any one comparison of drug users vs. non-users or of intensive users vs. less intensive users.[2]

On the other hand, and equally important, even the occurrence of significant differences and the prevalence of consistent trends should not lead to overlooking the generally small magnitude of the differences between the various user groups. With alcohol, for example—as with tobacco—most students are users, which means that there will be considerable diversity within the user group. The total abstainers, described in Chapter Two, are the unusual people, and it is no surprise that theirs are unusual characteristics as defined by the characteristics of the student population as a whole.

Within the large sample constituting alcohol drinkers, the two subgroups of drinkers, the intensive and less intensive ones, have been compared. On the Kolmagorov-Smirnov Test, twelve[3] differences out of twenty-eight are significant on the descriptive variables as are three of six associated-drug-use items. When we look at trends, we see the following. Intensive drinking varies by school. In School IV, our heavy illicit-drug-use school, 65 per cent of its drinkers are intensive drinkers, whereas in School II, the Catholic university, only 43 per cent are intensive drinkers. Other characteristics associated, in trend data, with intensive drinking are being male, older, and an upperclassman, as well as having a social-science major; less intensive drinkers are more concentrated in the biological sciences, have a wealthy family, housing mobility, no religion or are Jewish (theirs is usually the long-term, safe-drinking pattern), are without religious interests (those with deep interests have the highest concentration of less intensive users), and differ with father and mother on religion. Intensive drinkers are also proportionately more often found among those who are either very much interested or totally uninterested in participating in athletics and are uninterested in participating in religion but interested in political participation, whereas less intensive drinkers are more often politically uninterested or find participation important but not vital and stress new experiences as exceedingly important. Intensive drinkers are more often politically very conservative or left-of-center; low-

---

[2] As a corollary, a significant outcome in a direction inconsistent with major trends may well be ignored as a chance deviation.

[3] We include one that misses the .05 level by .002.

rate drinkers are more highly concentrated among independent-conservatives and Democrats. Intensive drinking and political activity are linked; less intensive drinking and little activity are linked; intensive drinking and political disagreement with both parents are also linked. Regarding other drugs, intensive drinking is associated with the use of strong painkillers and mild stimulants, with offering a greater variety of reasons for the use of other drugs, and with having positive valences for guiding principles for illicit-drug use. Intensive drinkers more often recall advantages to sickness in childhood than do less intensive drinkers and say their parents were little worried about their childhood health. In school, characteristics linked to intensive drinkers more than to less intensive ones include being dissatisfied with courses, teachers, and school as a whole, having recent incompletes, having dropped out, and thinking of dropping out. More intensive users are more often in the group finding studies unrelated to the way they want to live. Pessimism about doing what they want to do in life and about bringing about world change, as well as finding life worse than expected also characterize the intensive drinkers more than the less intensive ones, as does the view that the Establishment, middle-of-the-roaders, and the right wing are a menace to the nation. Less intensive drinkers more often see the left wing or criminals as such as a menace. Intensive drinkers report fewer major issues on which their whole family is in agreement; there are also more issues on which the student stands in opposition to the position both parents have taken together. Teetotallers report the greatest amount of family homogeneity on major issues of value and belief of any student group classified by drug use. On grade points both intensive and less intensive drinkers average 2.8, whereas the nondrinkers average 3.5.

Testing twenty-eight of the foregoing variables in the Kolmagorov-Smirnov Test, one finds, as noted earlier, significance on twelve of them and, as with tobacco, in the same directions as in the comparison of users and non-users. Significant variables are age, school year, religious affiliation, interest and participation, political participation and involvement, desire for new experiences, childhood-sickness advantages, satisfaction with school, and positive valences for illicit-drug use. Intensive drinkers drink significantly more coffee than less heavy drinkers, use more stay-awakes, and drink more chocolate.

Regarding drug histories and correlated-drug use, one finds that 79 per cent of the drinkers have smoked tobacco, 26 per cent

have used sedatives, 23 per cent amphetamines, 20 per cent marijuana, 20 per cent tranquilizers, 6 per cent special substances, 5 per
cent hallucinogens, and about 1 per cent opiates. As noted earlier,
alcohol is most often the first drug used by any student. Students asked
whether either parent were alcoholic report as follows: 5 per cent say
"yes," 33 of these being among the 600 intensive users and 30 among
the 620 less intensive users. It is possible that if we had clinically selected a "drinking-problems" group, something more interesting would
have emerged. Intensive users report that they began drinking at an
average age of fourteen; light drinkers at age seventeen. For the in-
tensive-use group, parents are more often the first source of alcohol
(59 per cent vs. 40 per cent); for a different subgroup, older friends
are somewhat more often the source for intensive contrasted to light
drinkers (15 per cent vs. 10 per cent). Nearly all the parents are
drinkers; there is a small difference showing a few more parents of
the intensive users in the nondrinking group (8 per cent vs. 4 per
cent). One is reminded of other research (Cisin and Cahalan, 1966)
suggesting two kinds of heavy drinkers: those from middle-class origins who drink safely and whose parents—our inference—also drink;
those from Fundamentalist origins whose parents—again our inference—do not drink and whose offspring when they drink get in trouble
with alcohol. With reference to drinking plans, more of the intensive
users will continue to drink (97 per cent) than lighter users (90 per
cent). Interestingly enough, over one third of the (7 per cent) nondrinkers intend to begin. Considering tobacco intentions, it is evident
that drinking is more universal than smoking, and while drinking will
expand among the few teetotallers on campus, smoking will not.

Sedatives. When we review experience with sedatives in relationship to individual characteristics, we find that sedative users are
more prevalent among students who are upperclassmen, are majors in
general studies or arts and humanities, come from wealthy families,
come from unsettled families, have no religious affiliations or are Jewish, differ from their mother or both parents in religion, do not participate in athletics or religious activities, seek new experiences, are
not interested in activities relevant to scholarship or future careers, are
very conservative politically or New Left, are members of several organizations, are politically active, are not in political agreement with
their parents, disagree with them on other major issues, see their parents as having been quick to medicate them when they were children,

and recall advantages in childhood ills. Sedative users are more dis-satisfied with their school course work, their teachers, and their school, have taken incompletes recently, have dropped out of school in the past for other than health reasons, are thinking about dropping-out, are pessimistic about doing what they want to in life, are uncertain whether they want to change things in the world, are optimistic about world changes being brought about, and see benefits and facilitating reasons for illicit-drug use.

A review of correlated minor-drug habits shows a greater prev-alence of sedative users among those who drink coffee—as opposed to noncoffee drinkers—among those who drink tea and cola drinks, and among those who take stay-awakes and use mild painkillers. In regard to drug functions, the suicide variable stands out among sedative users; nine out of thirteen (70 per cent) students admitting to suicide at-tempts via ingestion are sedative users.

Only a minority or 24 per cent of the students have used seda-tives. Insofar as trend differences are noted, these individuals are like the majority of all students, which means they are also like drinkers and smokers. One does see emerging a subgroup of sedative users who are politically conservative, do not emphasize differences with their parents, and are reasonably optimistic about the world. In these char-acteristics they remind one of the total-abstainer sample of Chapter Three. In this independence of sedative users from the trends found in other drug use, we see operating the independent prescription-drug-use factor identified in Chapter Six. Since none of the rates of preva-lence of characteristics reviewed for differences emerges as strong—usually a matter of a few percentage points (see Chapter Four for those)—the major conclusion must be that most sedative users, except for the interesting clinical groups (would-be suicides, those who at-tempt to reduce panic, and so on) identified by drug functions, are not distinguished from the total student group on the basis of special features. On only one variable, religious affiliation, is significance achieved.

Looking over differences among sedative users for the high- and low-intensity classification, one finds little difference by school except that School IV has more of the less intensive users. On individ-ual characteristics the intensive users more often than low users are not distinguished by a single difference that achieves significance in the Kolmagorov-Smirnov Test on twenty-eight variables. While some of the trends found in the user–non-user comparison are discernible, they are slight enough not to be worthy of repetition. On the other hand, differences in mild-drug habits are not only discernible but significant; intensive users do use more stay-awakes and more mild painkillers than do non-users. For the record let it be noted that intensive users have an average grade point of 2.9 while less intensive ones have an average 2.8.

In associated-drug histories, we find that 97 per cent have taken alcohol, 82 per cent have smoked tobacco, 31 per cent have used tranquilizers, 29 per cent amphetamines, 25 per cent marijuana, 9 per cent special substances, 8 per cent hallucinogens, and 4 per cent illicit opiates. The initial average age for beginning use is eighteen for the light users, sixteen for the heavy ones. Initial sources of the drug differ only slightly, with the intensive users more often (24 per cent introduced by their parents as compared with 18 per cent among less intensive users. About half of the parents of the students have used sedatives, but more of the parents (69 per cent) in the intensive-user group have used them as compared with parents of the less intensive group (57 per cent) or non-user group (38 per cent). Some students (10 per cent) not yet experienced with sedatives expect to take them; one third are not sure. Among intensive users 71 per cent intend to continue sedatives; among less intensive users only 37 per cent do.

Tranquilizers. Those who have used tranquilizers, upon review, are more prevalent proportionately among students who are older, are upperclassmen, are arts and humanities majors, come from wealthy families, have one or both parents dead, are from unsettled-mobile families, are without religious affiliation or interest and differ from their fathers' and mothers' religion, do not participate in athletics or religion, do *not* participate in politics, do seek new experiences, are politically left of center, are organization members, view parents as having been quick to medicate, recall advantages in childhood sickness, are dissatisfied with school or are contemplating dropping out, are pessimistic about doing what they hope to do in life, and see benefits and facilitating reasons in illicit-drug use.

Reviewing associated mild-drug use, we find tranquilizer users more prevalent among those who drink tea, take stay-awakes, and use the mild analgesics. Regarding drug functions, tranquilizer users are more prevalent among those who do, rather than do not, use drugs to gain courage, to explore themselves, to have religious experiences, to satisfy strong cravings, to combat depression, to relieve tension, to counteract anger, to alter appetite, to seek to feel strong, to combat feelings of dullness, to improve sexual appetite, to reduce sexual desire, to combat panic, to try to kill themselves via ingestion, to enhance intelligence, to prepare for stress, and to shut out stimuli.

Only a minority of students have used tranquilizers, 19 per cent. The trends discernible in the comparison of characteristics of users and non-users are rarely dramatic and usually constitute percentage-point spreads of small magnitude. Nevertheless, when tested on twenty-eight variables, eleven achieve significance. These are on age, major field of study, religious affiliation, interest and participation, political affiliation, childhood-sickness advantages, organizational membership, pessimism about life as they find it, school satisfaction, and perception of benefits in illicit drugs.

When we begin to compare intensive tranquilizer users with less intensive ones, the same variables identified as showing trend differences and as achieving significant differences are observed. However, when tested not one of the twenty-eight is significant at the .05 level. We do find that intensive users use significantly more mild painkillers as well—this significant beyond .05. When grade points are compared, both intensive and less intensive users have an average of 3.0, compared with an average 2.8 for non-users. Because there are so few significant differences in student characteristics, we shall refrain from repeating the catalogue of variables for which trend differences may be observable. Such that occur are all in the by-now-familiar direction.

With reference to associated-drug histories, 96 per cent of tranquilizer users have used alcohol, 84 per cent tobacco, 40 per cent sedatives, 36 per cent amphetamines, 26 per cent marijuana, 12 per cent special substances, 12 per cent hallucinogens, and about 4 per cent illicit opiates. Among those who have used both tranquilizers and sedatives, tranquilizer use precedes the latter at a rate of over 4 to 1. Among those who have used both amphetamines and tranquilizers, amphetamine use precedes the latter at a rate of $1\frac{1}{2}$ to 1. Among intensive users of tranquilizers, it is somewhat more common to have an alcoholic parent than among less intensive users. As for age of onset of use, it averages eighteen for less intensive users and sixteen for intensive ones.

For intensive users a physician is much more often the initial drug source (75 per cent) than for less intensive users (46 per cent). Parents are more often the initial source for lesser users (23 per cent vs. 16 per cent). Although 40 per cent of the parents in the total sample reportedly have used tranquilizers, the distribution shows fewest tranquilizer-using parents in the non-user student group (38 per cent) compared with less intensive users (55 per cent) and intensive users (68 per cent). Expectations for future tranquilizer use show the same shifts: among non-users 30 per cent are uncertain and 17 per cent expect to begin; among less intensive users 33 per cent expect to continue and among intensive users 67 per cent do.

Amphetamines. We consider the various amphetamine compounds under the approved drugs even though it is well known that much of this use is informal or frankly illicit. Our only measure of the extent of informal-illicit use comes from data on initial sources of the drug. Counting physicians and parents as "sanctioned" sources, friends as informal or illicit sources, we find that 55 per cent of our sample of users were first supplied through informal or illicit sources. Even so, it is our impression that most college use—under the laws prevailing through 1968—was not initiated through buying and selling in such a fashion as to be illegal under dangerous-drug codes but simply resulted from friendly give-and-take as occurs among students with many things, whether books, clothes, or what-have-you.

A review of the different rates of prevalence for characteristics among students classified as users or non-users of amphetamines indicates that higher prevalence occurs among students who are older, are upperclassmen, are arts, humanities, and biology majors, come from wealthier families, have one or both parents dead, are from unsettled families, are either without religious affiliation or are Jewish, are without interest in religion, have a religion different from their father's and their mother's, find athletics unimportant, do not participate in religion or in politics, seek new experience, find academic-career activities unimportant, are politically left wing and actively involved in politics, are undergoing a political change to the left, differ politically from their fathers and mothers, are not in agreement with their families on issues. Amphetamine users are also more often found, in proportion, among students who perceive their parents as having been reluctant to give drugs—or in other cases quick to do so—who found childhood illness satisfying, see parents as having been little concerned over their health as children, and are dissatisfied with their school courses, their teachers, and the school as a whole. Furthermore, amphetamine experience is more prevalent among those students who have recently taken incompletes, have dropped out of school earlier, are thinking of dropping-out, see little relationship between school and life or career goals, are pessimistic about doing what they want to do in life and about bringing on world changes, and disappointed in having found life worse than expected. Prevalence of amphetamine experience is greater among students who view as nationally dangerous the Establishment, other presently powerful cliques, or middle-of-the-roaders, and who are also among those students seeing good reasons to take illicit-exotic drugs.

Reviewing minor drugs, we find a greater prevalence of amphetamine users among those who drink coffee often, drink tea, and take stay-awakes. Regarding drug functions, there is a greater prevalence of users among those who take drugs to gain courage, to explore themselves, to have religious experiences, to satisfy strong cravings, to relieve boredom, to combat depression, to relieve nervousness, to facilitate moods, to combat anger, to facilitate friendliness, to alter appetite, to seek to feel stronger, to combat feelings of dullness, to improve sexual appetite, to reduce sexual desire, to combat panic, to attempt suicide, to enhance intelligence, to improve performance, to prepare for stress, and to exclude stimuli.

Only a minority of students (about 21 per cent) have taken amphetamines. Those who have do differ rather markedly from others in terms of proportionate distributions on many of the variables considered. Compared with users of other approved drugs, the amphetamine-using students appear more pervasively different from their peers. Testing by the Kolmagorov-Smirnov procedure, we find significant differences achieved on fourteen out of twenty-eight variables. These are age, year in school, major subject, family income, family mobility, religious affiliation, interest and participation, desire for new experiences, political involvement and affiliation, satisfaction with courses and school, and benefits perceived in illicit drugs. Amphetamine users also differ significantly from others in drinking more coffee and in using more stay-awakes. In respect to several characteristics not previously discussed, we find the amphetamine users to come from families with less homogeneity on family issues; in addition, these students perceive themselves more at odds with the combined parental stance on a variety of issues more than non-users. Grade points for users (both intensive and less intensive) average 2.8 and for non-users 2.6.

Within the amphetamine-user group, no significant differences emerge between intensive and less intensive users in the Kolmagorov-Smirnov Test on the twenty-eight amenable variables. Inspection of the distribution suggests that a few trends may be discerned but, as in the case of sedatives and tranquilizers, these are not worthy of repetition. The conclusion is that intensive users do not differ much from less intensive users; rather, the important distinction is between those with use experience and those without such experience.

With reference to drug histories and, specifically, to correlated-drug use, 99 per cent of amphetamine users have also used alcohol, 87 per cent have smoked tobacco, 44 per cent have used marijuana, 33 per cent have used sedatives, 32 per cent tranquilizers, 17 per cent hallucinogens, 17 per cent special substances, and 4 per cent illicit opiates. Considering the sequence of use of illicit substances for amphetamine-using students, one finds that amphetamine precedes marijuana twice as often as marijuana precedes amphetamine, and amphetamine use precedes hallucinogen use at a rate five times greater than hallucinogens precede amphetamines. Proportionately more amphetamine users use marijuana than do users of any other approved social or prescription drug.

When we look at the high-intensity amphetamine group compared with the low-intensity group, we find that most (62 per cent) intensive users were introduced to the drug by physicians whereas most (64 per cent) light users were supplied by friends. Intensive users begin earlier; the average initiation age is eighteen whereas lesser users begin at an average age of nineteen. Most parents of users have not used amphetamines, but the ratios differ; 31 per cent of the intensive users report their parents have used them, but only 19 per cent in the less intensive category report such a fact. Only 5 per cent of the non-using group say they have parents who have taken amphetamines. Regarding future plans, only a few non-users (5 per cent) expect to try amphetamines, while 34 per cent of the lesser users and 68 per cent of the intensive users intend to continue with amphetamines.

Only 8 per cent of those using amphetamines report any difficulty in obtaining a supply. For half of those few having difficulty, it means a temporary reduction in use.

SUMMARY

A review of the characteristics of users of medically and socially approved drugs compared with those of non-users was undertaken to show differences among users who employ such drugs intensively versus those employing them less intensively. Statistical testing of significance was limited to those variables capable of being handled by the Kolmagorov-Smirnov Test. Our findings show that consistent differences appear for each drug when users are compared with non-users. When intensive users are compared with less intensive users, differences are pronounced for drinkers and smokers, are not less easily discernible among tranquilizer and amphetamine users, and are rare in the case of sedative users. Insofar as differences exist—as, for example, with drinkers and smokers—intensive users occupy one end of a continuum, moderate users a mid-point, and non-users an extreme opposite position. In capsule, the satisfied, close-to-family, moderate, religiously active, ideologically stable, technologically oriented, younger lowerclassmen are in the non-using groups. As one moves into using groups—with the exception of sedative users—these characteristics begin to shift in the direction of religious noninvolvement and political interest, with students also being older, more advanced in school, in opposition to parents and conventional values, and so on. These are, of course, common characteristics of the student sample and insofar as drug users, drinkers, and smokers, for example, are a majority, that majority will necessarily be like the total sample. On the other hand, as one moves to more extreme groups—whether intensive smokers, drinkers, amphetamine users, or, to a lesser extent, tranquilizer users—but rarely sedative users—the exaggeration of the statistically normal traits of the total population is evident, and the extreme users are more often found to be "deviant," very dissatisfied, in opposition to their parents, and politically very active and left wing; often they take incompletes, have a lot of drop-out experience, have considerable faith in drugs as tools to achieve a variety of personal and interpersonal purposes, are irreligious, pessimistic, and the like, and often have considerable associated use of such minor drugs as coffee or stay-awakes. The mix and proportions of these extreme users depend entirely upon the accident of sampling which has made our total population comprised of students from five diverse schools.

Since our data-analysis procedures do not lend themselves to sub-group identification, one is hard pressed to define and conceptualize the many subgroups which probably do exist within any given group of students classified by their history of use of any one or group of drugs. On the other hand, there are hints in the trend data which suggest—as seen earlier in Chapters Four and Five—a socially and totally uninterested radical subgroup among intensive users, a con-servative-athletic subgroup among heavy drinkers, and a psychologi-cally disturbed-depressed and suicidal group, on the one hand, and, perhaps on the other, an excitement-seeking and hyperactive group.

With reference to drug histories, we see what we have seen before, both in this book and in other books (see Blum and Associates, 1964, 1969): people do not ordinarily use one drug but many. How-ever, individual patterns do vary. For example, most students use alco-hol but only one quarter of the alcohol drinkers take sedatives; on the other hand, 64 per cent of the sedative users drink. Clearly, most stu-dents begin their psychoactive drug use with alcohol and tobacco, some not going beyond that. Of all the approved drugs, ampheta-mines are the most closely linked to illicit use; indeed, amphetamine use tends to precede marijuana experience. Intensive users of all the approved drugs start at an earlier age than less intensive users. Among tranquilizer, sedative, and amphetamine users, parental habits regard-ing the same drugs influence intensity of use, but this is not true for alcohol and tobacco—probably because most parents are users them-selves. Student intentions to continue or begin use vary with their present habits; for example, low-intensity users do not intend to con-tinue use—with the exception of alcohol—while an important number of now-"naive" students plan to begin drinking. The first source of the drug does seem to make a difference in terms of intensity of use; in the case of alcohol, parental introductions are associated with in-tensity, whereas with tranquilizers and amphetamines a physician's prescription is linked to intensive use. With amphetamines less inten-sive use is associated with peers as a first source; using this as a meas-ure, one estimates that about half of amphetamine use on campus is unsanctioned—that is, informal or illicit.

In conclusion it appears that intensive users of the psychoac-tive prescription drugs—even if they are used informally, as in the case of amphetamines—do not differ from less intensive users. On the other hand, users of any degree of intensity do differ from non-users, although sedative takers stand out the least (except for clinical sub-groups) and amphetamine users are most distinct from amphetamine non-users. The differences of the greatest magnitude between intensive and less intensive users are for the approved social drugs, alcohol and tobacco; less intensive users resemble the average for the total population.

Users of
Illicit Drugs

Richard H. Blum

VIII

Ihe focus of this chapter is on students who use the illicit-exotic drugs marijuana, hallucinogens, opiates, and the special substances. In review users are compared with non-users of each drug, intensive users of each are contrasted with less intensive users, and drug-history data are examined.

ILLICIT DRUGS

Marijuana. Reviewing materials presented from a different point of view in Chapters Four and Five, we find that marijuana-experienced students are more prevalent among students who are older, upperclassmen, arts and humanities or social-science majors, come from wealthier families, have one or both parents dead, are from unsettled families, are either without religious affiliation or are Jewish, have no interest in religion, differ from their fathers' and mothers' religion, find athletics of no importance, do not participate in religion, do participate and are involved in politics, do seek new experience, do not participate in activities related to academic or future careers, politically are strongly left, are undergoing political change further to the left, and are in disagreement with the politics of their fathers and mothers. Marijuana users are also proportionately more often found among those who view their parents as quick to medicate but little concerned about their childhood health, recall advantages in childhood sickness, are dissatisfied with course content, with teachers, and with their school, have taken incompletes in the last year, have dropped out of school for other than health reasons, are thinking of dropping-out, are pessimistic about doing what they want in life, plan to work for changes in the world but are pessimistic about their realization, consider dangerous to the country present groups in power, middle-of-the-roaders, and right wingers, and see exclusively benefits and good reasons for illicit-drug use.

Reviewing correlates to marijuana use among minor-drug-use habits and among the functions for drug use, we find that users are more prevalent among students who drink coffee often, drink tea, do not drink chocolate or cocoa, do not drink cola beverages, do use stay-awakes, and do not use mild analgesics. Marijuana users are more prevalent among students who do, rather than do not, use drugs to achieve courage, to gain self-knowledge, to satisfy strong cravings, to combat depression, to relieve nervousness, to facilitate good moods, to counteract anger, to enhance their friendliness, to alter appetite, to combat feelings of dullness, to improve sexual appetites, to reduce sexual desires, to prevent panic, to attempt suicide, to enhance intelligence, to improve physical performance, to prepare for stress, and to shut out stimuli.

As in the preceding chapter, these trends, while important, do not allow one to decide that the marijuana smoker (some take it orally or sniff it as well) is a different kind of person from the non-user, for the proportionate distribution of traits is rarely so extreme that most users share a trait whereas most non-users do not. Rather, we are dealing with apparently continuous distributions on a variety of interrelated social and personal features where the most that can be said is that marijuana users are as a group different from non-users but at the same time share many features with them. If we look at the significance of trends identified, we find that about half achieve significance at the .05 level—that is, fifteen out of twenty-eight amenable variables do so when tested by the Kolmagorov-Smirnov procedure. In addition, three out of six associated-drug-use variables (more coffee and stay-awakes, less chocolate drinking) differentiate significantly between users contrasted to non-users.

Approaching the contrast of intensive users vs. less intensive users, we find these same trends visible although not as often significantly so, for on twenty-eight tests only four discriminate. These are year in school, lack of religious affiliation, political affiliation, and the positive valence of principles guiding illicit-drug use. We think that there are other differences—or similarities—which are observable —even if the inference as to their reality vis-à-vis chance distribution is open to question—or worthy of comment. For example, intensive use varies by school; 53 per cent of the total population of students in the School IV sample are heavy users, more than twice as many as at any other school. The greatest concentration of less intensive users, 36 per cent of the sample, is in School I. With reference to sex, it is important to note that no differences exist between males and females in the distribution of intensive vs. less intensive use. Intensive more often than less intensive users are arts-humanities majors, come from more unsettled families, are totally uninterested in athletics and in academic or career-related activities, are left-of-center, politically are very active, are opposed to fathers' and mothers' political stance, and have used drugs specifically to gain self-knowledge, to have religious experiences, to improve sexual appetites, to attempt suicide, and to enhance intelligence. Intensive users are also more dissatisfied with course work, find life worse than expected, and fear the Establishment and middle-roaders as menaces to the nation. They also report less family agreement—themselves included—on issues, more often say they oppose the stance of their parents, and feel like outsiders with various groups such as family, student body, and nation. On grade points, intensive users average 2.8, less intensive users 2.7.

Looking at drug histories, we find that most marijuana users begin with alcohol and/or tobacco as their first psychoactive drug. In terms of correlated-drug use, 99 per cent also drink, 94 per cent smoke tobacco, 50 per cent have used amphetamines, 33 per cent sedatives, 29 per cent tranquilizers, 24 per cent hallucinogens, 19 per cent special substances, and 6 per cent opiates. The average age for initiation into marijuana use is nineteen for intensive users, for less intensive users it is age twenty. No remarkable differences in the source of the first experience occur. Only 1.8 per cent of the parents in the total sample are described as having used marijuana. In the heavy-smoker group, 9 per cent say their parents have used marijuana; in the light-smoker sample, 2.4 per cent say their parents have used marijuana. With reference to plans for future use, 13 per cent of the nonsmokers say they intend to begin smoking and 28 per cent are not sure. Among less intensive users, 45 per cent intend to continue and 10 per cent are uncertain. Among heavy smokers 87 per cent are sure they will continue to smoke marijuana. Only 15 per cent of those who say they have used marijuana ever state having any difficulty obtaining it and for only half of these suffering limitation in supply has there been any reduction in use.

Hallucinogens. Reviewing earlier data, one finds hallucinogen users are more prevalent than non-users among the following groups (compared with implicit contrast groups on that same characteristic): older students, upperclassmen, arts and humanities majors, those who are from either wealthy or very poor families, from unsettled families, those who are without religious affiliation, those who differ with their mothers on religion, those who do not participate in religious activities, who do seek new experience, who do not engage in extra activities related to academic or future careers, are politically left wing, politically involved, and differ with their fathers' and mothers' political positions. Users are also found proportionately more often among students who are dissatisfied with course work, with teachers, and especially with the school as a whole, who have taken recent incompletes, have dropped out of school or are thinking of dropping-out, and see little relationship between their studies and how they want to live. More hallucinogen users are also found among those students who see persons presently in power as dangerous to the nation along with middle-of-the-roaders and who see benefits in illicit-drug use.

Reviewing minor-drug habits and total drug functions, one finds that hallucinogen users more than non-users are found proportionately more often among students who do, rather than do not, take stay-awakes. With reference to drug functions, more hallucinogen users are found, proportionately, among those who do, rather than do not, use drugs to achieve courage, to gain self-knowledge, to have religious experiences, to relieve boredom, to combat depression, to relieve tension, to facilitate moods, to enhance friendliness, to alter appetite, to improve sexual appetite, to combat panic, to attempt suicide, to enhance intelligence, to improve physical performance, to prepare for stress, and to shut out stimuli.

Nine out of twenty-eight tested variables demonstrate significance of differences between the user and non-user groups. Those variables are age, year in school, religious affiliation, religious interest, seeking of new experience, political affiliation, recall of childhood-illness advantages, dissatisfaction with school, and the valence of principles guiding drug conduct.

Approaching comparisons between intensive and less intensive hallucinogen users, one finds there is, on the twenty-eight test variables, only one significant discriminator, which is age, and in this instance intensive users are younger rather than older. On items not tested, intensive users report more family disagreement on issues, and there is more student opposition to positions taken by both parents. Grade-point averages for intensive and less intensive users are 2.9. Other items perhaps worthy of mention (even if tested and found wanting or not subject to statistical test) show practically no difference by school or sex in intensity of use. One does observe—with caution—proportionately more intensive use among freshmen, less intensive use among technology and hard-science majors, no intensive use among Jews and little among Catholics, the critical importance of seeking new experience set forth by intensive users, greater disagreement with the mother on political issues, and among intensive users more specific use of drugs to satisfy cravings, to counteract anger, and to shut things (stimuli) out. Intensive users more often say life is worse than they expected, distrust the Establishment, and are guided only by positive valences in illicit-drug use.

With reference to drug history, one finds that alcohol and tobacco are the first psychoactive drugs for most hallucinogen users. Looking at correlated-drug experience, we find that 100 per cent also drink, 94 per cent smoke tobacco, 91 per cent use marijuana, 73 per cent have used amphetamines, 46 per cent tranquilizers, 40 per cent sedatives, 29 per cent special substances, and 14 per cent illicit opiates. As for the order of use of illicit drugs, marijuana usually (6 to 1) precedes hallucinogen use. We recall that marijuana, in turn, was usually preceded by amphetamines. Carrying that analysis further, one finds that among those using special substances and marijuana, there is nearly a half-and-half split as to which came first. In the case of those using marijuana and illicit opiates, 14 per cent took opiates first, 50 per cent marijuana first, and the remainder began to use both during the same period of time.

The drug histories reveal that the average age for intensive users' initiation to hallucinogens is twenty; that of less intensive users is twenty-one. No remarkable differences occur in sources of that first experience. Only eight parents in the sample (8/1,314) are said to have tried these drugs; five of these are parents of non-users, one of a less intensive user, two of intensive users. Ten per cent of the non-users state they intend to try hallucinogens; another 25 per cent are undecided. Among the less intensive users, 45 per cent intend to continue to use hallucinogens and 6 per cent are uncertain; among more intensive users, 60 per cent do plan to continue and 19 per cent are not sure. (That high undecided figure among non-users is surprising in view of the wide reports of ill effects from LSD, DMT, and STP use about which students are presumably informed.) Only 17 per cent of the hallucinogen users say they have ever had difficulty in obtaining supplies of these drugs; for the majority of those having supply difficulties, the problem did lead to (temporary) reduction in use.

Opiates. The sample of opiate users is so small, 18/1,314, that we shall refrain from any review of the existing percentage differences while comparing students on various viewpoints, activities, or background features. For the same reason of a small N buried in large groups, the Kolmagorov-Smirnov Test cannot be expected to reveal much. Inspecting these outcomes, one finds significant differences among opiate users when compared with non-users only on religious interest (philosophical among users), school dissatisfaction, and the valence of guiding principles for drug use. There is also a significant difference between users and non-users with stay-awakes. Intensive users have a grade-point average of 2.7, less intensive users of 2.8.

It is also hardly likely that the division of the eighteen opiate users into ten intensive and eight less intensive ones would yield significant differences on multiple-coded variables and they do not, in fact, emerge. Inspection of distributions for the two groups is also a rather barren enterprise. Discernible but nonsignificant differences occur on age with intensive users consistently older but *not* further along in school, on income with intensive users coming from poorer families, on the importance of seeking new experiences—greater for intensive users, and, for them also, on the importance of activities involved with academic or career affairs; the latter is a switch from the usual trends. We find half of the less intensive users to be Republicans—also an oddity—and more than half of the intensive users to be independents. Intensive users are moderately involved in politics and are more often in political disagreement with their mothers and fathers. On correlated-drug use, intensive illicit-opiate users have twice as much experience with strong painkillers (medical opiates), have undergone anesthesia more often, do not use stay-awakes, and have used drugs for a greater variety of specific functions: in particular, finding courage, fighting depression, counteracting anger, altering appetite, and shutting things out. Important is the fact that no difference exists between intensive and less intensive users in the use of drugs to satisfy cravings—perhaps more important, about two thirds of the illicit-opiate sample do report use of drugs for just that purpose. Only among the intensive group are school drop-outs found, but none of the other school-dissatisfaction or pessimism measures show differences of any remarkable sort.

From drug-use histories, one finds that, like all other drug users, opiate users also first began psychoactive drug use with alcohol and tobacco. As far as correlated-drug use goes, 100 per cent also drink, 95 per cent smoke tobacco, 78 per cent use marijuana, 73 per cent use sedatives, 66 per cent amphetamines, 62 per cent tranquilizers, 50 per cent hallucinogens, and 33 per cent special substances. In terms of the order of use, marijuana precedes opiate use in the majority of instances. In individual histories one sees that the intensive users average initiation into illicit opiates at age eighteen, the lesser users at age nineteen. Drug sources differ; intensive users more often (40 per cent) began use legally—that is, on prescription from physicians—compared with less intensive users (20 per cent starting). Less than 2 per cent of the parents of non-users are said ever to have used illicit opiates; 16 per cent of the less intensive users say their parents (actually one set of parents, 1/8) have used them, whereas 40 per cent (4/10) of the intensive users state their parents have used illicit opiates. Regarding future intentions, 1 per cent (15/1,314) of non-users say they intend to try opiates; 16 per cent of less intensive users (again an N of 1) will continue; three out of ten intensive users will continue; and another two are unsure. Only 16 per cent of the opiate users (3/18) report any difficulty at any time in getting an opiate supply; when difficulties did arise it meant, for two out of these three, a reduction in illicit-opiate use.

Special Substances. We are again faced with a small group, 79/1,314 or 6 per cent, who have tried sniffing glue, gasoline, paint thinner, nitrous oxide, and the like or have consumed such things as cough medicine, ground anti-asthma cigarettes, catnip, and hyacinth leaves for, as they say, "kicks." Reviewing the distributions for these special-substance users on the various characteristic variables, one finds rarely more than a few percentage-point differences, these a function of the small N. Nevertheless, the trends are in the direction of such users being more prevalent among students characterized as being older, upperclassmen, from wealthier families, from unsettled families, without religious affiliation, having only an "intellectual" interest in religion, differing from their mothers in religion, not participating in religious activities, participating politically, seeking new experience, not participating in activities related to scholarship or future career, being politically left of center and politically involved, holding a different political position from their mothers', recalling advantages in childhood illness, being dissatisfied with coursework, teachers, and their school, having taken incompletes recently, having dropped out of school, thinking of dropping-out, being pessimistic about doing what they would like to do, finding life worse than they expected, and seeing as dangerous to the country persons now holding power, or middle-of-the-roaders, and seeing positive reasons for taking illicit drugs.

Reviewing minor drug use and the functions of drugs, one finds special-substance users more prevalent, proportionately, among those who use stay-awakes and mild analgesics. They are more likely found among those who do, rather than do not, employ drugs to obtain courage, self-knowledge, religious experiences, satisfaction of strong cravings, and relief from boredom, to combat depression, relieve nervousness, facilitate moods, counteract anger, enhance friendliness, alter appetite, combat feelings of dullness, improve physical performance, improve sexual appetite, reduce sexual desires, prevent panic, enhance intelligence, prepare for stress, and shut out stimuli.

The Kolmagorov-Smirnov Test shows a significant difference obtaining between users and non-users on only seven of twenty-eight tested variables. (These are age, year in school, seeking new experi-

ence, engaging in activities related to school or career, political affiliation, not seeing a relationship between present studies and way they
want to live, and valences of drug-use principles.) There are no significant differences on minor-drug use—that is, coffee, and so forth.

When intensive users are compared with less intensive ones,
only three variables emerge as significant out of twenty-eight tested.
These are younger age, lower year in school, and the importance of
seeking new experiences among intensive users.

Inspection of other differences, either nonsignificant or un-
tested ones, shows intensive special-substance users to be concentrated,
proportionately, in School III, the junior college, and also in School
IV. Although there are somewhat more male than female users, the
females report slightly more intensive use. Less intensive users are
found more often among wealthier families, social-science majors, and
those very active politically; intensive users are among Democrats,
independents, and those more often in agreement with their parents
on religious and political matters. Among intensive users the use of
drugs for self-exploration, religious experiences, combatting anger,
making oneself feel stronger, improving physical performance and
sexual appetites, and preparing for stress and shutting things out loom
as more-often-reported reasons for use. It is the less intensive users
who report more course-work and teacher dissatisfaction, although
many of the usual pessimism-activism variables yield nothing by way
of difference. On other items intensive special-substance users report
less whole-family agreement on major issues and have an average
grade point of 2.6 compared with 2.8 for less intensive users.

With regard to drug histories, special-substance users also had
alcohol or tobacco as their first drug. With reference to correlated-
drug use, 100 per cent also drink, 94 per cent smoke tobacco, 58 per
cent use amphetamines, 58 per cent marijuana, 38 per cent sedatives,
38 per cent tranquilizers, 24 per cent hallucinogens, and 8 per cent
opiates. We have noted earlier that marijuana use is preceded by
special-substance use as often as following it; the same is true for the
hallucinogen-vs.-special-substance sequence priority. As for age of
onset of use, it averages seventeen for intensive users and eighteen for
less intensive ones. No remarkable differences exist in terms of the
first sources of drugs; for both groups, peers were most often the initiators. Only three students report that their parents have used any
of the special substances—two of these are parents of intensive users

(2/37), while the other is a parent of a non-user (1/1,235). Only three users say it has ever been difficult to obtain the substances of their choice; for two of these interference in supply led to a temporary reduction in use. Regarding future intentions, only 1 per cent intend to try special substances among the non-user group, whereas among the less intensive users 12 per cent intend to continue and 7 per cent are not sure, as compared with 14 per cent who intend to continue among intensive users and 3 per cent who are not sure. Note that it is only among the special-substance users of all classes of drugs that a minority intends to continue that particular form of drug use.

SUMMARY

The users of illicit-exotic drugs are unusual in that they represent but a minority of students. This unusualness is reflected in the distribution of their characteristics, which, for the most part, indicate that they are older upperclassmen, from wealthy families, arts-humanities or social-science majors, in opposition to parental stands, politically active and left wing, irreligious, dissatisfied, have had drop-out experience, are pessimistic, heavy users of mild stimulants, and are users of drugs for a variety of personal and interpersonal purposes. Nearly all drink alcohol and smoke tobacco and, far more than the average student, they have used prescription psychoactive drugs and a variety of illicit ones. The more unusual the drug used, statistically speaking, the more that the student using it will also have used most other psychoactive drugs examined here; thus, hallucinogen and opiate users stand at the far extreme in terms of their experience with all varieties of drugs. In spite of their anti-Establishment views and school-related pessimism, there is evidence of poorer school performance than for any of the other groups of students using particular illicit drugs.

When intensive users of each illicit-drug class are compared with less intensive users, few findings that lead to a cohesive impression emerge. Marijuana users give the clearest impression; of the extreme (intensive) users, many represent the same trends cited above but carried to an even further degree. Like intensive users for most drugs, they are earlier initiated into use—although that very duration of use puts them at greater risk of being in our intensive sample. More of their parents also use marijuana—a surprising 9 per cent. It is this group which also intends almost universally to continue using marijuana, although about half of the less intensive users also plan to continue—as we saw in an earlier chapter—and, perhaps, 40 per cent of the non-users as well. As with other illicit drugs, getting a supply is rarely difficult and if it is difficult this is not often a deterrent to use.

Among hallucinogen users, few characteristics stand out to mark the more intensive users. Among possibly interesting ones is the apparent comparative youth of the heavy users—in contradiction to usual trends. Disagreements with the mother, having new experiences, using drugs to combat anger and overstimulation, distrust of authority, the use of drugs to satisfy cravings, and being disappointed in life as they find it are all items which appear to characterize the heavier hallucinogen users. Combined with the inference that conventional religion and politics, a harmonious family life, and satisfaction with school and optimism about the future seem to "immunize" against intensive use, certain clinical and social speculations are stimulated. The intensive opiate user, on the other hand, is suspected of being a different chap. There, the disillusionment–anger–lost-child syndrome is not dramatized; rather, it is the emphasis on past medical opiate exposure, the existence of cravings for drugs, the more conservative and even optimistic social bent, the poorer economic background, and inferred slow school progress (although grades are only slightly poorer) which give pause. Combine these with the overriding earlier anti-authority attitudes, depression, and left-leaning trends for most drug extremists and one suspects the existence of two syndromes, both implying individuals pushed by the need for "new inner experiences," as they call it—but one group being the furthest explorers on the drug fringe after using hallucinogens and the other, a less privileged but still struggling group who, importantly, may have learned from example in their own homes since 40 per cent of the intensive opiate users say their own parents have used opiates illicitly. The intensive users of special substances, admittedly a wastebasket classification in itself, seem also to be a special set of cases within the larger wave of the dissatisfied and disillusioned fragmented idealists, whose optimism is limited to what they believe drugs can do for them. These students are younger, stress physical and sexual prowess—or rather what drugs can contribute to these—and are less dissatisfied, pessimistic, and antifamily than less intensive users. Perhaps, among them is a syndrome of hopeful immaturity. Perhaps, theirs was this syndrome;

we say "was" because among all drug classes the special subtances are the only ones that are in the users' past rather than their future; few even among intensive users show any wish to continue their use. This, of course, implies that the special substances are those associated with earlier adolescence, even if our sample did take them at an average age of seventeen or eighteen. Presumably, the various gasolines, airplane glues, shoe polishes, drug-store remedies, garden plants, and catnip collections which constituted their experiments are not worthy —either in terms of drug effects or status appropriateness—of further attention.

Bad Outcomes
on Campus

Richard H. Blum

IX

*T*his chapter looks at the bad outcomes arising from drug use as reported by students. It examines the official cases as well to see what kinds and how many instances of ill effects came to the attention of school administrators, local police, and school medical services during the study period. It also compares the rate of these official cases with the unofficial rates of illicit use as indicated by our survey findings and considers other indices or estimates of student drug experience. In this task the focus is on average estimates of illicit use on each campus by non-users and less intensive and intensive users of drugs. The chapter also looks at the students who reported bad effects and compares them with students using the same drugs who reported no ill effects.

In discussing the data, we cannot assume that all bad effects were reported; perhaps, the students suffering the worst ones could not stay in school to be included in our sample or, perhaps, they were the noncooperators on the several campuses where noncooperation occurred. It is also likely that students did not report all of their ill effects—some because they could not recall them, others because they were embarrassed, and still others because they may not have recog-

147

nized an ill effect when it happened to them. Ill effects, like other forms of unpleasantness, depend upon the standards of the beholder. This is true even for medical diagnosis where unreliability can be quite high (see Blum, 1964) even for well-known disorders. In the case of drugs, where the acute effects themselves can impair judgment and recollection and where no "objective" observer is recording outcomes, the underreporting of ill effects is taken as a foregone conclusion. Consider Hollister's (1968) work, for example, in which he found subjects taking LSD reported a number of distressing physical symptoms during the acute phase. These same subjects asked about their LSD experience a few weeks later could not recall the transient ill effects. A more complex case centers about personality changes which a conventional psychologist or psychiatrist would term undesirable; a drug user experiencing these changes might disagree. This phenomenon was encountered in our earlier study (Blum and Associates, 1964). It is illustrated in the extreme by the contention of Leary and some others that a toxic psychosis or other longer-term psychosis following LSD is a good thing. Another illustration arises from arrest and incarceration which most conventional people would consider an undesirable consequence of drug use. Some of the students we have met have claimed otherwise, saying that jail was a good experience. The foregoing problems are all part of the larger dispute over "drug abuse" as such and cannot be resolved here. There is one virtue in the subjective standard employed here: it represents the conviction of the drug user himself that something bad has occurred. Most observers would agree that such an evaluation represents at least anxiety if not something worse and, as such, deserves attention.

It should be kept in mind that the ill effects reported here are based on lifetime experience. They do not represent any count of the frequency of such effects per person—that is, they are not incidence figures. Rather, they are prevalence figures showing simply the number of persons who have experienced an ill effect one or more times in their lives. Under this system no person can report more than once any one ill effect; he can, however, report as many different ill effects as we have different codes to record them. We had 30 different codes.

BAD OUTCOMES REPORTED

To begin with, let us report that among the 75 per cent of the students who have used tobacco, only 55 per cent replied when asked whether there were any benefits, gains, or pleasures to be had from the drug. What that implies is that 45 per cent find nothing good about it after trying it. How many say there are specific bad or unpleasant effects? Forty-nine per cent, or about half the users, report unpleasantness. These are, in order of frequency for physical difficulties, headache (35 per cent of all users), other physical distress (13 per cent), and appetite difficulties (5 per cent). Among psychological and social problems, the criticism of smoking by friends and relatives ranks first (36 per cent) followed by the student's worry about his own overuse (27 per cent), troubles with friends arising from smoking or smoking incidents (8 per cent), emotional upset perceived as a tobacco effect (3 per cent), and discipline by (lower-grade) school authorities for smoking (3 per cent). We shall not list other less-often-mentioned troubles.

Are the variety of bad effects dependent upon how much tobacco one uses, or, at least, are they reported by the kinds of people who also report heavy tobacco use? The answer is "yes." The average number of different ill effects reported by heavy smokers is one per person; for light smokers it is .5 per person.

First asked about benefits, 74 per cent of the student population who have used alcohol (92 per cent) say there are gains and pleasures from drinking. As for ill effects, 63 per cent of the drinkers report them. Among physical effects reported are headache and/or nausea (89 per cent) of all drinkers, slurred speech (57 per cent), appetite problems (11 per cent), unconsciousness (11 per cent), other physical effects (3 per cent), and physical injury incurred while drinking (2 per cent). Among major or formal social problems there are fights (8 per cent), school discipline for drinking (5 per cent), automobile accidents (5 per cent), moving-violation arrests (including tickets) (3 per cent), jail (3 per cent), and criminal offenses or acts while drinking (2 per cent). Among drinking problems more intimately social or psychological in nature are trouble in thinking as a consequence of drinking (21 per cent), sensitivity to the criticism of friends about one's drinking (18 per cent), loss of self-control (19 per cent), worry about one's own loss of control over use of alcohol (14 per cent), emotional upset due to drinking (11 per cent), trouble with friends (8 per cent), sexual difficulties or unfortunate sexual incidents arising from drinking (6 per cent), study problems (5 per cent), insomnia (4 per cent), and hallucinations (.08 per cent). We shall not specify less frequently occurring troubles here.

Are the variety of bad outcomes associated with the intensity of drinking? In our comparison of heavy drinkers with lighter drinkers, the average number of different ill effects reported per person for heavy drinkers is 2.3 and for light drinkers is 1.1.

Twenty-one per cent of the students have used amphetamines. Of these, 80 per cent report benefits and gains and 61 per cent report bad outcomes. Of the ill effects reported, emotional upset is the most common (35 per cent), followed by insomnia (25 per cent), headache or nausea (19 per cent), other physical distress (11 per cent), appetite problems (9 per cent), worry about one's own overuse (8 per cent), sensitivity to friends' criticism of one's amphetamine use (7 per cent), troubles in thinking when using the drug (6 per cent), loss of self-control (2 per cent), hallucinations (2 per cent), and troubles with friends arising out of incidents when using the drug (1 per cent). Are intensive users likely to report a greater variety of ill effects? Yes, for the average number of different bad outcomes reported by intensive users is 1.6 and for less intensive users is 0.8.

About one fourth of the students report they have taken sedatives. Of these, 83 per cent report benefits from use and 23 per cent report bad effects. Ill effects include worry about overuse (8 per cent), headache and/or nausea (7 per cent), other physical distress (11 per cent), sensitivity to criticism of friends or relatives about use (4 per cent), insomnia (*attributed* to the drug) (3 per cent), slurred speech (2 per cent), emotional upset due to the drug (2 per cent), bad dreams (2 per cent), difficulty in thinking (2 per cent), drug-induced incidents leading to trouble with friends (1 per cent), unconsciousness (1 per cent), and appetite problems (1 per cent). We find that intensive users report more diverse ill effects than less intensive users; the former average .4 ill effects per person, the latter .24.

About one fifth of the students (19 per cent) use tranquilizers. Among these 80 per cent report benefits and 17 per cent report bad outcomes. These latter are as follows: worry about overuse (8 per cent), headache-nausea (4 per cent), other physical distress (for example, sweating, dizziness) (6 per cent), trouble in thinking (4 per cent), insomnia (2 per cent), difficulty in studying (2 per cent), criticism by friends or relatives of use (2 per cent), other psychological distress (inability to be alert when with others) (2 per cent), appetite problems (1 per cent), slurred speech (1 per cent), and unconsciousness (1 per cent). Once again, intensive users report more diverse ill effects than less intensive users; the average for the former is 0.34 per person and for the latter 0.15 per person.

About one fifth (19 per cent) of the students have had experience with marijuana. Seventy-seven per cent report benefits from the drug and 46 per cent report ill effects as follows: headache and/or nausea (21 per cent), sensitivity to criticisms of friends or relatives regarding use (16 per cent), emotional upset due to the drug (15 per cent), other physical distress (11 per cent), trouble in thinking (9 per cent), hallucinations (regarded as unpleasant) (8 per cent), appetite problems (8 per cent), slurred speech (6 per cent), worry about overuse (6 per cent), loss of self-control (4 per cent), incidents leading to trouble with friends (4 per cent), (other) psychological distress, for example, "remoteness" (3 per cent), study problems (2 per cent), jail (2 per cent), bad dreams (2 per cent), insomnia (2 per cent), school discipline arising from drug use (1 per cent), car accidents arising from use (1 per cent), other social problems (1 per cent), unfortunate sexual incidents or difficulties (1 per cent), and criminal acts attributed to the drug-influenced state (1 per cent). Intensive users report more diverse complaints than less intensive users; the former average 1.3 different ill effects per person, the latter 0.8.

Five per cent of the students report experience with hallucinogens. Among them 79 per cent report benefits and 56 per cent report bad outcomes. These latter include unpleasant hallucinations, including recurring ones (23 per cent), emotional upset (22 per cent), headache/nausea (20 per cent), sensitivity to criticisms of friends or relatives about use (17 per cent), insomnia (15 per cent), trouble in thinking (15 per cent), (other) psychological difficulties (9 per cent), slurred speech (8 per cent), other physical disorders (8 per cent), bad dreams (6 per cent), loss of self-control (6 per cent), psychosis (5 per cent), worry about overusing hallucinogens (6 per cent), appetite problems (3 per cent), problems in studying (3 per cent), unconsciousness (3 per cent), and incidents leading to troubles with friends (2 per cent) (one case reporting). In the case of hallucinogens, intensive use is not linked to the report of more diverse ill effects, for the average number of different bad outcomes listed by intensive users is 1.3 compared with 1.6 for less intensive users.

One and three-tenths per cent ($N = 18$) of the students report illicit opiate use. Among these eighteen students, 56 per cent ($N = 10$) report benefits and 72 per cent ($N = 13$) ill effects. Bad outcomes reported include headache/nausea (44 per cent, $N = 8$), sensitivity to the criticism of friends or relatives (28 per cent, $N = 5$), worry about overuse (22 per cent, $N = 4$), troubles in thinking (17 per cent, $N = 3$), emotional upset (17 per cent, $N = 3$), other physical disorders (17 per cent, $N = 3$), slurred speech (11 per cent, $N = 2$), appetite problems (11 per cent, $N = 2$), hallucinations (6 per cent, $N = 1$), problems in studying (6 per cent, $N = 1$), and car accidents (6 per cent, $N = 1$). Intensive users report more diverse ill effects than less intensive users; the average for the latter is 1.7 different bad outcomes per person, and 0.8 for the former.

Seventy-nine students (6 per cent) report experience with special substances; 42 per cent report benefits and 42 per cent report bad outcomes. These latter include headache and/or nausea (24 per cent), other physical disturbance (11 per cent), sensitivity to criticism of friends or relatives about use (5 per cent), hallucinations (4 per cent), incidents leading to troubles with friends (3 per cent), appetite problems (3 per cent), trouble in thinking (3 per cent), slurred speech (3 per cent), (other) social problems—for example, finding it hard to be with a group (3 per cent), loss of self-control (1 per cent), car accidents (1 per cent), emotional upset (1 per cent), psychosis (1 per cent), (other) psychological disorders—for example, impatience with others (1 per cent), and worry about overuse (1 per cent). There is no difference between intensive and less intensive users in the average number of different bad outcomes; the former average .5 per person and the latter 0.6 per person.

OFFICIAL CASES

We wanted to compare the prevalence of kinds of bad outcomes and the inferred minimal incidence of bad outcomes as reported by students using drugs with official cases—that is, the kinds of troubles and numbers of students in trouble known to school, police, and school medical authorities. The question in our minds was to what extent the cases identified by authorities as being in trouble in consequence of, or in association with, drug use accurately reflected use on campus and actual difficulties as reported by students. During the study year we asked school officials to keep a record of all students in school known to them because of drug-related difficulties. We put the same request to medical personnel on those campuses maintaining a health facility. Kinds and numbers of cases were then reported to us (not by name). At the end of the year, we also asked all state and local law-enforcement agencies concerned with drug offenses whether they had identified any offenders as students from the five schools. The adequacy of all of these records as rendered to us depended on the excellence of the record systems in each office and school. We did not conduct a study of these record systems but presume, generalizing from our work in other agencies (Blum and Ezekiel, 1962), that official record keeping was usually not very good. We must assume that some students who were, in fact, identified officially failed to be recorded as such. The police records failed entirely to report identifications, which was not a fault of their record keeping but rather represented a failure on the part of the police-record systems to inquire about student status.

The schools differed considerably in the kind and detail of records kept on discipline, academic, and health problems. Here we shall attempt to compare, combine, and summarize the differing levels of information as best we can.

In School I, ninety-six disciplinary cases were officially processed. These represented 1.6 per cent of the undergraduate student body. Between six and ten of these cases involved drug use, although whether the drug was alcohol or an illicit substance was not specified in the records. The maximum of ten cases involving drugs and discipline reflected 0.07 per cent of the total undergraduate population. In School II there were fifty-two disciplinary cases representing 1.7 per cent of the undergraduate population. Among these fifty-two cases, thirty (58 per cent of the total) involved rule violations associated with alcohol use-abuse, seven involved both alcohol and other (illicit) drugs, and two involved illicit drugs only. The alcohol-only cases comprised approximately 1 per cent of the student body; the alcohol and illicit drug group were 0.2 per cent and the illicit drugs only 0.05 per cent. For School III we were not given total disciplinary cases but were informed that one student was referred for rule violation in association with illicit-drug use and that five to ten students were disciplined for alcohol-related incidents. These cases (taking the maximum of ten for alcohol) constituted 0.2 per cent and 0.02 per cent respectively. For School IV disciplinary data were not available. For School V we learned that 196 students, 1.4 per cent of the undergraduates, were found guilty of disciplinary violations. Among these, alcohol-related offenses constituted seventy-one cases (36 per cent of all those disciplined) or 0.5 per cent of the total student body. There were no cases involving illicit drugs.

Summarizing the discipline data, we find that official discipline cases apparently involve less than 2 per cent of the students in any school, that drug cases of any sort comprise from 5 per cent to 75 per cent of all disciplinary cases, and that alcohol-related violations exceed violations involving any other drugs by a factor of at least ten—that is, there are at least ten students identified as rule violators in cases involving alcohol use for every case involving another drug.

Arrest data were available for two schools only, and for these they were inadequate. In School I, two students, 0.03 per cent of the full-time student population, were known to have been arrested. In School II no arrests were known; for School III and School IV there were no data; and for School V there were five arrests, comprising 0.04 per cent of the undergraduate student body. Summarizing these data, we can report that not many student arrests are evidently known to school authorities or to reporting police agencies, although all concerned agree that student arrests are likely to have occurred which have not been identified as such.

In School I, 71 students were suspended or disqualified for academic reasons and another 240 were put on probation. Of these 311 cases constituting 5.3 per cent of the undergraduate population, 30 to 45 were identified by deans as students believed to have drug-use (not alcohol) problems. No evidence was available to deans as to the causal role of drugs in these cases which constituted (taking the maximum, forty-five) 19 per cent of all academic-performance problem cases and 0.7 per cent of the undergraduate student body. In School II, we were not given total academic-failure data but were informed that five academic cases were also identified as having alcohol problems. Each of these cases also appeared as a discipline violation. These represented 0.02 per cent of the students. Schools III and IV provided no data on academic problems. School V provided no data on total academic-performance problems, but did report that fifty-one students identified as users of illicit drugs by deans failed, were put on probation, or dropped out. These represented 0.4 per cent of the undergraduate student body. We conclude that a maximum of 1 per cent of the students, and usually far fewer, will be identified as drug-use problems associated with difficulties in academic performance.

School I has an active student-health service. During the study year it reported no adverse drug reactions during the acute period as cases. It did report that seven students with adverse drug reactions (LSD, DMT, and so on), coupled with broader personality disorder, did present themselves as cases as their acute reactions had passed. The health service also saw one student for the treatment of alcohol-precipitated distress. These cases represented about 1 per cent of all psychiatric visits to the health service and represented a rate of prevalence of drug-related disorders (including alcohol) among health-service cases as a proportion of the total student body of about 0.07 per cent (.00007).

School II had no adverse reactions to report. School III does not operate a health service, but at the beginning of the study year, it did provide a psychologist-counselor to see students with drug problems. There were fifteen to twenty self-referrals to that counselor during the first months of the school year, a group comprising 0.4 per cent of the student body. That counseling service was closed when the counselor was assigned other duties; there was also evidence at the time that students were becoming reluctant to make visits, some saying it was for fear of being reported to the police under the then-just-passed California felony law for LSD.

School IV reported 30,000 health visits or about 2.4 visits per student. Of these, 306 individual cases were seen by psychiatrists (2.5 per cent of the students) of whom 11 were LSD reactions (3.6 per cent of all psychiatric cases seen, 0.09 per cent of all students). School V showed 628 students seen by psychiatrists (4.5 per cent of all undergraduates), of whom 6 had adverse illicit-drug reactions and 8 had drug use as a feature of personality difficulty. The adverse reactions constitute 0.04 per cent of all students and about 1 per cent of the psychiatric cases seen. On the basis of these data, we conclude that adverse drug reactions as such constitute less than 4 per cent of all psychiatric cases seen and that fewer than one tenth of one per cent of the student body are identified by health services, on any campus, as having adverse reactions.

DATA AND STUDENT REPORTS

The official data allow prevalence counts for the year 1966–1967, whereas the student reports are by drug and cover lifetime prevalence and do not allow specification of year. Thus, any comparison is bedeviled by these different bases and can be, at best, only a very rough order comparison.

The simplest statement, given the considerable amount of use of the approved drugs—alcohol, sedatives, and so on—and the prevalence of physical ill effects described, is that few or none of the ill effects from sanctioned drugs come to the attention of health authorities.[1] Thus, while half of the total sample have experienced physical distress attendant upon alcohol use—and their drinking is continuing and common—no case of intoxication, hang-over, and so on is officially known. Only alcohol, of the approved drugs, ever leads to bad outcomes of any kind identified by school authorities.

To assess the relationship of official statistics to bad outcomes, it may be helpful to report these latter not as a percentage of students using a particular drug but as a proportion of the total population, since the official statistics use as their sample that total population. Consider that 58 per cent of *all* students in our sample report bad outcomes from drinking—that is, over half of all students on the five campuses have defined in themselves some ill effects following drinking. One presumes that many students have had repeated bad outcomes of diverse kinds. Consider further that 138/1,314 are worried about their own excessive use (which we take to be dependency fears —that is, awareness of compulsive drinking), that 143 have suffered loss of self-control, 65 have been in fights, 38 have alcohol-related study problems, 35 have had auto accidents, 35 acknowledge they have received school discipline, and 20 students (20/1,314) admit having gone to jail for alcohol-related offenses. Yet the highest school figure—that from School II with its excellent individual discipline records specifying drug problems—shows only 1 per cent of the total student body as having had drug troubles (alcohol included) during the study year. Some of the difficulties reported by students may have occurred in prior years but, as we shall see, bad outcomes for alcohol become more prevalent with increased age and school year (as drinking increases). This means that the chances for a bad outcome's having occurred during the student's tenure in the school—and during recent years especially—are quite great. As a general conclusion, then, we must state that even the most carefully kept school records represent only a fraction of the unpleasantness and distress which students experience in association with their use of the approved drug. Put

[1] We could not survey private physicians and hospitals.

another way, it can be assumed that students handle that distress either privately—gritting their teeth—or informally, getting assistance from friends or possibly—and we suspect rarely—family physicians. We have no way of knowing to what extent parents or family physicians (and keep in mind many students are away from home so they cannot consult the family doctor, and so their medical care should appear in health-service records) are aware of student difficulties in association with sanctioned drug use; for example, are the parents aware of the suicide attempts which two students said occurred during a drinking episode? We shall, in a study now planned, attempt to establish the amount of information held by parents and physicians about their children's and patients' level of drug use and drug difficulties.

The same problems which we infer to exist in relationship to alcohol use occur with the other approved drugs.[2] There the schools report no data, and student prevalence reports of difficulty are less than for alcohol, but, nevertheless, troubles do exist. For example, 268/1,314 students are worried about their tobacco habit and would presumably be open to assistance aimed at reducing their smoking, certainly a worthwhile endeavor, given our knowledge of cancer and heart disease associated with smoking. Similarly, twenty-two students are concerned about their own possible amphetamine dependency and twenty-five about sedative dependency. Who knows of their fear and who can help?

What about illicit drugs? Even though the approved drugs are used by more students, and alcohol has the highest prevalence of different ill effects reported for intensive users, the illicit drugs—with their less frequent employment (except in samples of extreme illicit-use groups, see Chapter Eight)—are not without bad outcomes. Consider, for example, that the hallucinogens among all of the drugs have the highest prevalence among less intensive users of bad outcomes, half again as great as alcohol. Consider, too, that one particular bad outcome is potential for each incidence of use of each of the illicit drugs—and that is arrest. Given our finding that almost none of the physical and psychological disturbances in association with use of the approved drugs become official cases, we would expect little official reporting of disapproved cases because of the problem of detec-

[2] Keep in mind that considerable amphetamine use is illicit but is classified here under the approved drugs.

tion, shame, and so on. On the other hand, anxiety about the use of these drugs must be predicated so that individual students suffering ill effects would be expected to be more anxious about them and thus conceivably propelled into treatment.

Again, to facilitate comparison of official total-population figures with bad outcome reporting, we present bad results for illicit drugs as a per cent of the total population of students rather than as a per cent of using students. According to that scheme, a number equivalent to 4 per cent of all students suffer headache/nausea attributable to marijuana, 1.4 per cent have undesirable hallucinations, and 2.8 per cent emotional disturbance attributed to marijuana. About 1 per cent are concerned about their own marijuana dependency. Among hallucinogen effects, about 1 per cent suffer emotional upset or undesirable hallucinations, four students are worried about dependency, and three (0.2 per cent) say they have suffered psychotic reactions (to be distinguished from psychotomimetic effects or the acute toxic period). It is the academic performance rather than discipline records which best identify student illicit-drug users; for example, never more than 0.07 per cent of the students at any school were identified, during the study year, as illicit-drug users involved in a discipline problem—academic reports showed ten times greater an incidence rate, up to 0.7 per cent—which is still less than 1 per cent. Health or counseling records, on the other hand, also never achieved identification of more than one tenth of one per cent as cases of adverse effects among illicit users.

If we consider that the average age for initiation of illicit use is between nineteen and twenty-one for all users, we must assume that most of the bad effects reported have occurred during the college years and that some of them will have occurred in the study year— especially since the average age for the total sample is twenty years. If we assume, conservatively, that 1 per cent of the sample did suffer at least one bad reaction during the study year and we compare that with official cases, we see that health and discipline records bear a relationship—if that is what it is—of never more than one identified case for every fourteen self-identified cases. On the other hand, academic performance estimates can be closer, for every case of a self-identified bad outcome—very few of which are ever reported in fact as study problems—the maximum official rate was 0.7. These figures are only an exercise based on assumptions easily—and quite wisely—challenged. With data of the sort available we can do no better.

PREVALENCE OF USE

We have concentrated on students' reports of bad outcomes in comparison with official statistics relating drug use to problem cases. The larger question is what relationship does knowledge based on official cases have to the prevalence of illicit-drug use on campus? One can also ask how accurate are the estimates of illicit use which are arrived at by means other than official case finding, as, for example, the estimates offered by students themselves?

We think it requires little further discussion to affirm that at the time this study was made and on the campuses where it was made, illicit-drug experience was widespread, although still confined to a minority of students. Chapter Eleven shows that during the year of the study—and in the following years while our data were being analyzed—there was an increase in use—that increase amounting, at our best guess, to a two- or three-fold jump in the number having marijuana experience, that is, up to an average 40 per cent to 60 per cent. What relationship officially identified cases of trouble—discipline, academic, arrest, or health—had to prevalence of experience is very clear indeed. Official identification, including all official measures, never achieved a rate of identification of over 1 per cent of the students as illicit-drug users. Official case identification was often far below 1 per cent. We conclude that official cases do not provide any estimate of actual illicit use on campus and that official cases as processed on these campuses—including arrest figures by police—ordinarily are underreported by a factor of from 1/20 to 1/1,000.

Official cases, of course, represent more extreme reports either of persons or of institutions. Most things are handled informally by institutions; most conduct is not officially noticed. This does not mean that people—whether deans, doctors, detectives, or students—are unaware of what is going on around them; they, too, are part of an ordinary unofficial world which provides daily evidence—albeit based on limited samples—of what is happening. So it is that people do make estimates of the prevalence of things; and one of the things they estimate is the prevalence of illicit-drug use. As we said in the introductory chapter, when comparing estimates made by the journalist Richard Goldstein (1966), those seat-of-the-pants figures can be rather good approximations. Because we are interested in the general accuracy of such estimates and particularly in the accuracy of illicit-drug users compared with non-users, we now turn—at a tangent for the moment—to a consideration of the accuracy of drug-use estimates by students themselves.

We expected that the more students themselves used illicit drugs, the higher would be their estimates of others' illicit use. The expectation was based on their selectivity in acquaintances, the fact that (Blum and Associates, 1964) drug users associate with each other more than with non-users and, also, that they can more easily identify—through their gossip channel—other users. We also expected they would want to believe there were many users because there is discomfort if one feels alone in being unlawful and deviant, a sentiment we think is linked to that proselytism which so characterizes illicit-drug users (Blum and Associates, 1964). For the sake of completeness, we shall not only compare estimates by intensive and less intensive users of illicit substances, compared with each other and with non-users, but we shall also note estimates by class of users of the other drugs.

First, applying the Kolmagorov-Smirnov Test, we learn that there are significant differences between the estimates of nonsmokers compared with lesser smokers, as well as between lesser smokers versus intensive smokers. The same significant differences both between non-users and users and between less intensive users compared with more intensive users obtain for alcohol and marijuana. Significant differences between non-users and either intensive users or less intensive users, or both, are found to hold for amphetamines, sedatives, tranquilizers, hallucinogens, and special substances.

Actual illicit experience varies by school. We can, at best, only estimate it since there is overlap by drug class and since the illicit use of amphetamines, except by first source, by 55 per cent does not allow us to estimate later illicit amphetamine use. It is also not possible for us to distinguish between purchase on the black market, a frankly illicit act, and informal uses which would not be prosecuted even if apprehended—as, for example, taking an amphetamine tablet from a roommate. Therefore, if we limit our base figure of illicit use simply to the per cent of students with reported marijuana use (since all but five hallucinogen users say they have used marijuana) plus a

5 per cent to 10 per cent arbitrary "safety" factor, we can then determine which groups classified by use of each drug make the best estimates on each campus of any illicit experience. A measure which is likely to be more sensitive to the mood of the students is one which uses as a base not estimates of persons with past illicit experience but one which estimates student intentions either to continue marijuana use or to begin it.

School I has actual marijuana experience of 21 per cent but shows that 32 per cent intend to begin or continue, with another 9 per cent unsure. In contrast, the student-body average estimate of illicit experience is in the range of 10 per cent to 19 per cent, which is low. Those who make estimates in what we take to be the correct range of actual experience, 20 per cent to 30 per cent and defined as the median estimate group, are low-intensity tranquilizer users, low-intensity amphetamine users, high-intensity marijuana users, high- and low-intensity hallucinogen users, high- and low-intensity opiate users, and high-intensity special-substance users. The groups sensitive to the intentions of the students (and this is the campus for which we have some evidence of considerable drug increase in the two years following the initial survey) are high-intensity amphetamine users and the few low-intensity opiate and special-substance users. It seems clear that on this campus, a large private university, the majority underestimates illicit-drug experience and that almost all groups underestimate the potentials for increased drug experience. Those who come closest to being accurate are illicit-drug users but even they underestimate the reserve of students ready to "turn on."

On Campus II, a Catholic university, marijuana experience is reported by 11 per cent. If we add our arbitrary safety factor for illicit use, it would remain in the range of 10 per cent to 20 per cent. Positive intentions to begin or continue use are expressed by 24 per cent, with another 1 per cent not sure. The average estimate by the total student body for illicit use on campus is between zero to less than 9 per cent in range, which is obviously low. Those groups correct in their experience estimates are the intense tranquilizer users, along with the less intensive marijuana users. No groups successfully estimate the mood of the campus when defined as the greater number who intend to continue using illicit drugs or to try them.

Campus III, the junior college, reports 21 per cent marijuana experience which, with the safety factor added, remains in the 20 per cent to 30 per cent range. Twenty-one per cent also intend to continue or begin, with an additional 11 per cent uncertain. For this campus we deem intention to remain within the 20 per cent to 30 per cent range. The average estimate by the total student body for the per cent of students experienced in illicit drugs is in the 10 per cent to 19 per cent range, although the modal estimate is in the 20 per cent to 30 per cent range. The student groups who make accurate estimates of experience and intentions are tobacco smokers, heavy drinkers, low-intensity amphetamine users, low-intensity sedative users, (all) tranquilizer users, and the few intensive special-substance users. On this campus we encounter overestimates, all of which are by marijuana and hallucinogen users.

Campus IV suffered, as noted in the introductory chapter, from poor sampling, so that our estimates of drug use here are very likely to be in error. Since sampling bias arose out of overpresentation of older upperclassmen, a group already shown to have greater drug use than others, the reported experience here must be assumed to be erroneously high, that is greater than the actual total-population experience. On this campus, marijuana experience is 33 per cent; our safety factor would raise that but keep it in the 30 per cent to 49 per cent range (the same range as used in coding estimates). Intentions to begin or continue marijuana use are expressed by 34 per cent, with another 9 per cent uncertain. We deem the range unchanged—30 per cent to 49 per cent. Actual estimates by the total student sample yield a mean of 20 per cent to 29 per cent, although the modal estimate is in the 30 per cent to 49 per cent range. If we are correct in describing the sample as biased toward illicit-drug experience, then the overall student average estimate would be correct. Student groups achieving estimates in the 20 per cent to 30 per cent range include nonsmokers and low-intensity tobacco smokers, light drinkers, non-users of amphetamines, sedatives, tranquilizers, marijuana, and the other illicit drugs, as well as less intensive sedative users. Those groups arriving at the higher figures, which are the ones reported by our sample, are heavy tobacco smokers, heavy drinkers, (all) amphetamine users, (all) hallucinogen users, (all) tranquilizer users, less intensive marijuana users, heavy sedative users, and less intensive special-substance users. Overestimates are given by intensive marijuana users, (all) opiate users, and heavy special-substance users.

Campus V, a large state university, reports actual marijuana experience by 10 per cent of the students. Intentions to begin or continue use are expressed by only 5 per cent of these users. In this school a coding error occurred with the result that no non-users were asked about their intentions, so that we cannot gauge their readiness to begin. If we assume that at least 6 per cent to 15 per cent are in that group, then the range for future users is 10 per cent to 20 per cent. The average sample estimate of experience is in the less than 0 to 9 per cent range. Groups correctly estimate actual experience and our assumed future-users group, both in the 10 per cent to 20 per cent range, when they are intensive marijuana users and less intensive hallucinogen users. No overestimating groups were found. On this campus there is a consistent trend to underestimate illicit-drug use slightly.

Estimates of how many students on campus use drugs illicitly are significantly associated with students' own use of all classes of drugs; the more the drug use, the generally higher the estimate. The accuracy of estimates varies from one campus to another and may be measured either in terms of figures derived from past experience or from statements of plans for use, which constitute, we believe, a greater sensitivity to the campus mood or readiness to take drugs illicitly. On the majority of our campuses, non-users of drugs and the student body as a whole are consistently low in their estimates; on two campuses only are overestimates of use in evidence; these were made by marijuana users primarily. No one student group, classified by its drug use, is accurate for all campuses. What stands out are (1) the general underestimates of past use and especially of readiness for future use and (2) the need not to discount the estimates by the illicit users which, though sounding high, may very well be correct.

CHARACTERISTICS OF BAD OUTCOMES

We now return from our tangential discussion of the estimation of illicit-drug use back to the primary concern of this chapter: bad effects. At this point we can ask whether there are any outstanding characteristics among drug users who report bad outcomes as compared with users who do not make such a report. As in earlier chapters, we shall report trends. At the outset, remember that we have already shown that for every drug class except the hallucinogens— and to a lesser extent the special substances—a greater number of diverse bad outcomes are reported by those who use drugs intensively than by less intensive users. Remember also from Chapter Six that intensive users are, for the most part, more extreme in their characteristics than less intensive users and are likely to be (although not always so) a mid-point on a theoretical continuum. We have already shown in Chapter Three that non-users of any drug are a group constituting the anchor of the continuum at the other extreme.

The characteristics of those reporting ill effects compared with those not reporting them are not nearly as consistent, either by characteristics in relation to general drug-use trends as we saw in Chapters Three and Four or in relation to intensive users vs. less intensive ones as reviewed in Chapters Five and Six. Part of the problem is the small N in some cells as one gets down to particulars, such as "those who are marijuana users who have used drugs for suicide efforts and who do report adverse drug effects." We suspect a larger problem is that, other than its demonstrated relationship to drug intensity, except for hallucinogens and special substances, the bad-effect variable is compounded of many features whose extent and ramifications are quite beyond the scope of the present endeavor. Bad effects, to be identified and reported, cover the gamut of social, psychological, and physiological processes. In spite of its inconsistencies and surprises, we present this limited material, which should be considered primarily as a basis for speculation and future research.

We limit ourselves to reactions to four drugs of interest: alcohol, amphetamines, marijuana, and hallucinogens. Our first observation is that the ill effects of alcohol are mostly reported by people with the same characteristics that predict drinking in general and heavier drinking in particular. One surprising feature is that the politically left-of-center students are more heavily represented among those having ill effects than would be expected from simple trend data on use or use intensity. Another surprising feature is that Jewish students—in spite of statistical overrepresentation on the left—have the lowest rate for any religious group of reported ill effects.

Notable among characteristics associated with amphetamine adverse effects or incidents is the low prevalence of bad outcomes among students from wealthier families, from Jewish families, among those politically active, among Republicans, among those recalling little parental concern over their health, and those dissatisfied with school and course work. If these characteristics serve to identify a special subgroup protected from ill effects, then others suggest those particularly vulnerable. We find that females, older students, those from unsettled families, those politically left of center and those with a history of dropping-out and planning to drop out remain proportionately more at risk of ill effects; we say "remain" since we recognize these characteristics as ones linked to drug experience and intensity.

Marijuana ill effects are notable primarily for the apparent reversals in characteristics ordinarily linked to use and intensity of use. At higher risk of adverse outcomes are females, younger students, lowerclassmen, those from poorer families, those in agreement with their fathers' politics, those whose parents did worry about their childhood health, and those who do find their studies related to how they want to live in the future. On the other hand, what may be another more familiar group "at risk" are those with childhood-illness advantages, those with incomplete grades, those who are school drop-outs, those who are pessimistic about doing what they want, and those using drugs for diverse functions.

With reference to hallucinogens, our data provide no insights into those experiencing adverse outcomes. One finds few notable reversals or dramatic trends. On an impressionistic basis, supported both by the evidence for no increase in ill effects with increases in hallucinogen use and by the hodgepodge of characteristics linked to it, we would propose that adverse hallucinogen effects—and these are, for the most part, LSD effects in the student sample—are less linked to psychological, social, or ideological variables identified in this study than are adverse effects from other drug classes. If such is the case, it would follow that other or "deeper" psychological variables are involved—as, for example, a prepsychotic personality—that the life situations of these LSD sufferers are so bizarre as to be ruled social variables outside of the ordinary ken, or that the outcomes noted are determined in part by biochemical idiosyncrasies not linked to the kinds of characteristics with which this study concerns itself. LSD bad outcomes are, we propose, a different kettle of fish.

SUMMARY

Examining the prevalence of kinds of bad outcomes reported by students from their drug use, as well as benefits claimed, we find that ill effects are described for all drugs used. The prevalence of ill effects as a proportion of those reporting them over the total population using the drugs is greatest for the opiates and for alcohol, followed by amphetamines and hallucinogens, and least for sedatives and tranquilizers. These rates do not imply incidence—that is, they do not say how many times a person has had ill effects or what the expected rate of ill effects per occasion of use may be. Since we assume that alcohol-use occasions are likely to be more frequent than any other while hallucinogen use is likely to be quite infrequent, we can surmise that the risk of ill effects per occasion of use is much greater for hallucinogens. As for benefits, these are claimed by the majority of users for most drugs; fewest benefits are claimed for opiates and the special substances. Kinds of ill effects vary by drug; physical distress, for example, is most often mentioned in regard to alcohol, as are accidents, fights, criminal offenses, and so forth. With amphetamines, emotional upset is the most common complaint; with marijuana and opiates, headache/nausea and discomfort over criticism from others rank foremost, and with hallucinogens, unpleasant hallucinations and emotional distress are foremost. Psychoses following use are noted with the hallucinogens more than any other drug.

Examination of official cases reveals that school records, whether academic, disciplinary, or medical, report far fewer cases of distress than students themselves report. Indeed, almost none of the ill effects from approved social or prescribed drugs appears to come to the attention of school authorities. Police records, which are not geared to identifying students as having ill effects, are not a source of student-arrest data. Discipline and health records never achieve a ratio of identification of bad outcomes greater than 1 to 14 as compared with population self-reports. However, careful examination of academic performance, including drop-outs and probations involving student illicit-drug use, can achieve an identification-rate estimate of students reporting drug *problems* which is only a little less than the actual rate of occurrence. That the number of students identified as having academic problems associated with illicit-drug use can approach self-reported prevalence rates for bad outcomes in no way gives an estimate of the incidence of bad outcomes or of the simple prevalence of students on campus with illicit-use experience. On the other hand, attention to estimates of use per se rather than bad outcomes leads us to conclude that most estimates made by most students are low; if one asks the estimates of use to encompass those intending to use drugs—many of whom, we believe, will become or have become users—the estimates are even less adequate. The exceptions tend to vary by campus but users of illicit drugs more often give better estimates than do non-users. On any campus overestimates of either use or of intentions to use are rare, even when those estimates are made by intensive users of illicit-exotic drugs.

Analysis of the characteristics of students reporting bad outcomes shows the expected link between the amount of use and the prevalence of bad outcomes. This leads to the inference that characteristics associated with intensive use are also the characteristics associated with the bad outcomes reported. The most important exception is in the case of hallucinogen use; here, infrequent one-time users report more ill effects than frequent users. Other exceptions include Jewish students, who are low in bad outcomes for alcohol and amphetamines. In one subgroup marijuana ill effects are apparently linked to special features not part of the ordinary intensive-user trend; specifically, females, younger students, lowerclassmen, poorer students, and those closer to family report more distress. Intensive users with the usual constellation of dissatisfaction, pessimism, and so on suffer equivalent ill effects. These characteristics which appear linked to outcomes are, for the most part, not striking. In the case of hallucinogens—where there is that unusual phenomenon of low use but high ill-effect prevalence—one senses a special case that can be accounted for by positing biochemical idiosyncrasy, individual psychopathology "setting off" acute reactions triggered by single drug use, progressive loss of critical faculties with increased use, or altered definitions of what constitutes an ill effect as use increases. Sheer sampling artifact and unwarranted inference on our part may also be occurring.

Students'
Drug Diaries

Richard H. Blum

X

We asked three subsamples of students to keep a diary of their drug use over a period of six months. This chapter reports on those diaries, which were set up to include a record of kinds of drug use, incidence, time of use or ingestion, people present, the purpose for taking a drug, the effects experienced, and the events associated with any important changes in regular drug-taking patterns—that is, with innovation or marked reduction in use.

In two schools, I and II, the subsamples selected to keep a drug diary were drawn at random (random-numbers table) from the larger sample constituting our study population at each school. In a third school, IV, panelists were not selected at random from the study population but, instead, were selected because they were found to use illicit-exotic drugs. We selected such a group because we wanted to know more about the day-to-day drug habits of illicit-exotic users as such. In School I we began with thirty-six students and ended up six months later with twenty-two in the panel; School II began with twenty-eight and also ended up with twenty-two. School IV began with thirty-six and at the end had only sixteen, and these for only five months instead of six. Panels in Schools I and II began recording in November of 1966 and completed work in April of 1967. The panel in School IV began in January of 1967 and completed work in May 1967.

To reduce the amount of recording required for students, we developed a modified diary which required that on only seven days each month would a record be kept. To avoid any systematic error due to recording the same week consistently in the month, we rotated the weeks—that is, students began recording with the first week of November, then with the second week of December, the third week of January, and so forth. In case anything special happened with regard to drug usage during any of the off-weeks, students also completed a monthly summary noting any remarkable changes in drug use or in drug effects. We kept in touch with the students during the panel period, encouraging them as best we could with reminders, thanks, pleas, and gifts of pens to keep at it. It was, for some, a tedious job, and we are much in debt to those who persisted.

DRUGS USED

Alcohol. Seventy-two per cent of the students at School I, 71 per cent at School II, and 42 per cent at School IV record having used alcohol on diary days. Results show the most common pattern of drinking to be between one and six times a week. Only one panelist records drinking on fifteen or more occasions within the same week. For the two schools whose panelists represent a subsample of the larger sample and thus have some claim to representativeness (that claim diminished by small sample size), drinking occasions are reported to occur about every four and a half days. In the School IV group with its smaller alcohol intake that average is raised to about once every week.

Not unexpectedly, the most popular time of day for drinking is evenings—at least in Schools I and II; afternoons rank first in School IV. In all schools alcohol consumption at mealtimes ranks second. School I shows five specific occasions of morning drinking, one in School II, and none in School IV. Drinking with close friends is the most prevalent pattern. In School II, the Catholic university, these family drinking occasions are proportionately much more common than in the other schools. Twenty-three occasions of drinking alone are recorded at School I, six at School II, and five at School IV. Compatible with the group setting, most drinking occasions are said to be shared group activities. As far as stating further purpose is possible, students report the most common is to achieve pleasure. On the other hand, on fifteen occasions in School I, fourteen in II, and four in IV, the students say their drinking was to relieve psychological distress.

With regard to marked changes in drinking habits, these are few. Their occurrence—specifically, in six instances—represents innovations in drinking among previous nondrinkers and are attributed in one case to group pressure, in four instances to curiosity, and in another to escape from tension. These same reasons in that same order are offered as explanations of increases in amounts consumed over ordinary practices; such increases are noted on fifty-seven occasions. In contrast, decreases recorded over ordinary drinking habits are indicated on only eleven occasions, most of these also attributable to social pressure. In two cases students gave up drinking entirely at some point in diary keeping, both of them giving as reasons social demands or pressures. These two terminations are in contrast to the eleven occasions marking the beginning of drinking. (These beginners may have had earlier alcohol experience, but presumably they have not had anything to drink recently.) These figures combined suggest that during the diary period more students began or increased their alcohol use than decreased it; on the other hand, for most students there appears to have been no great change.

Regarding alcohol outcomes, we find that the most prevalent is a positive effect as reported on more than half (54 per cent) of the drinking occasions. No effects are also common and are reported on 36 per cent of the occasions. Bad outcomes are reported on 13 per cent of the occasions.

Amphetamines. Eleven per cent of the panelists in School I, 5 per cent in School II, and 33 per cent in School IV record having taken amphetamines on diary-keeping days. Each amphetamine-taking student averages twenty-five amphetamine-taking occasions in School I, five occasions in School II, and 6.5 in School III. This means an average use in Schools I and II of amphetamines once every three and a half days to four days for those few students taking the drug. In School IV, the illicit-use panel, occasions occur on the average of once a week. The most common pattern in each school is to use amphetamines less than six times a week, although the few intensive users in School I are more likely, proportionately, to take them between seven and fourteen times per week; in fact, about one third of the occasions for use are concentrated in episodes seven to fourteen times per week in School I. Given such intensive use, then other periods must be slack, and we conclude periodicity or acute cycles for use rather than steady and regular use.

The time of day varies considerably by school. In School I the prevalent period is mornings; in School II it is mealtimes; in School III it is evenings. Most students deny any social use of amphetamines; the only exceptions are in School IV, where on three occasions use was a group drug experience. In School I intensive use is almost entirely the consequence of medical prescription; very few occasions are inspired by "mind-expansion" individual aims. In School II all use is medical; in School IV, where very little use is medical, psychedelic aims predominate along with individual interest in effects or in pleasure seeking per se.

During the panel period, initiation of amphetamine use (where it had not been in use previously or had been used long ago and was now resumed) took place most often in School IV. Here we find this innovation attributed to pleasure seeking and also to the availability of the drug. Illness, as such, accounts for its initial use only in School II. Escape motives appear only in School I. Increase in use (in contrast to initiation) is in School I linked to illness, whereas in School IV it occurs under group pressure, for pleasure, or when an amphetamine supply becomes available. There are no reports of diminished but continuing use, but in two schools termination did occur; one student in School I was unable to get a supply and one in School IV also quit after finding himself "oppressed" by methedrine.

Amphetamine effects are reported as positive on 88 per cent of the occasions, nil 7 per cent, and negative 5 per cent. Most negative effects are recorded in School IV (where social-hedonistic-psychedelic use is paramount); no ill effects are noted in School II, where use is entirely medical.

Sedatives.   Eleven per cent of the panelists in School I and none in either II or IV record having used sedatives on diary-keeping days. We find thirty-seven sedative-taking occasions among these ($N = 4$), nearly all of them occurring at a rate of frequency of six times or less per week. One diary period reports seven to fourteen sedative-taking occasions during one week. Most ingestion is in the morning; bedtime ranks second. Almost all use is medically prescribed, although one finds one instance of use because of curiosity and four occasions when the student medicated at home without a doctor's advice. Most occasions for drug taking, even though medically prescribed, are described as social ones—that is, others are present (roommates and so on) even though social motives are not involved. Half of those using sedatives record a decrease over the six-month period, decreases being attributed to the healing of illness and the reduction of tension. With regard to effects, most occasions (80 per cent) of use are said to lead to desired effects, a few to no effects at all (17 per cent), and 3 per cent to ill effects.

Tranquilizers. Eleven per cent ($N = 4$) of School I students, 4 per cent ($N = 1$) of School II, and 11 per cent ($N = 4$) of diary keepers from School IV report using tranquilizers on diary days. In actual numbers these amount to ninety-nine tranquilizer-taking occasions, the frequency of which are twice as great per person at School IV as at School II. The most prevalent pattern for tranquilizer use is in the range of one to seven times a week. Almost all use at School I is at bedtime; in contrast, at School IV, bedtime, morning, and afternoon use are about even. In School IV use is in a family setting; in School I students say they take the drugs when they are alone. Medical prescription is given as the paramount reason for tranquilizer use, although on a third of the occasions students say they self-administered tranquilizers because of psychological distress.

During the panel period three students report beginning tranquilizer use, each for reasons of tension or distress; during the same period, two say they stopped use, one as tension subsided and the other when what he considered an experiment was at an end. With reference to effects, the most common effect is stated as nil—this in 62 per cent of the cases. In 27 per cent of the cases, students report obtaining a desired effect, while in 11 per cent they record bad outcomes.

Other Drugs. In their diaries we asked students to record the use of other mild agents such as aspirin, Cope, and Endin, as well as prescribed drugs that are not psychoactive—or at least not designed to be that—which would include antibiotics, birth-control pills, and the like. We find 55 per cent of School I panel, 82 per cent of School II panel, and 67 per cent of School IV panel recording either prescription or over-the-counter analgesic or stimulant (No-Doze and so on) drug use. There are 896 reported occasions of such use on diary days for the sixty-seven students in the using group. The daily incidence of use approximates a rate of one occasion of use per student every third day. The most prevalent pattern indicates no more than six occasions for use during any one week, with only 7 per cent of the occasions involving use more than seven times per week. Drug taking is fairly evenly distributed during the day; mornings rank first, evenings second, mealtime third, afternoons fourth, and bedtime fifth. Drugs are reportedly consumed for the most part when the student is alone. Almost all use is self-prescribed; only 9 per cent of the occasions recorded for use appear based on medical advice and prescription.

In their use of common drugs, most students are continuing long-standing habits; those initiating the use of a new drug (or renewing an old one) do so primarily with the onset of illness or because of recommendations from friends or relatives; psychological distress is also a factor. The same factors account for increases in use over normal intake. Diaries indicate very little decrease in use during the panel span; two students diminished drug intake when their illness passed and one, in response to advice, stopped taking a drug entirely. The general picture which emerges is one of continuing or intermittent use of over-the-counter remedies by the majority of panelists. Medical prescriptions as such play a minor role in drug taking as do—we infer—clearly defined physical illnesses. With regard to effects, 62 per cent are reported as those desired, 34 per cent are reported as nil, and 4 per cent are reported as bad outcomes.

Marijuana. Seventeen per cent of the panelists in School I, 4 per cent in II, and 89 per cent in IV record having used marijuana on diary days. (Keep in mind that panelists in School IV were selected because of known high illicit-drug use.) In School I we find that use amounts to forty-eight occasions for six students on a total of about 250 diary days; average use by this 17 per cent amounts to once every fifth day. In School II, one student records having tried marijuana once. In School IV, the 412 occasions recorded mean, on the average, that users have taken marijuana on two to three days each week. The predominant pattern is of use less than six times a week, which suggests regularity rather than acute periodicity in use. In most cases marijuana is taken in the evenings, although in School

IV students report 8 per cent as morning occasions. In School I most use is alone whereas in IV 85 per cent of the use is social. The sociability of purpose, or the sharing of experience, is emphasized by students in School IV, although we should note that those using it in School I indicate having social factors in mind—the implication being that even when taken alone, marijuana is preparatory for some upcoming social event. Among individual functions for the drug, the pleasure-giving one is most often cited, although 14 per cent of the School IV panelists say they use the drug in an attempt to relieve psychological distress.

In the sample four students, as best we can determine, began marijuana use for the first time during the panel period. This number would represent 4 per cent of all panelists. Twelve per cent indicate having increased their consumption during the panel period, most of them because of pleasure seeking or increased availability of supplies. Thirteen record having decreased consumption at one time or another, some because of social pressures, some because of reduced availability, and some because their curiosity was satisfied. Three mention having quit use during the panel period, one because of social pressure (which includes awareness of risk or disapproval) and two because their "experiment" was complete.

With regard to effects, students view 90 per cent of the occasions as leading to benefits and 6 per cent to bad outcomes; 4 per cent of the students report no effects at all.

Hallucinogens. Three per cent ($N = 1$) in School I, none in School II, and 44 per cent in School IV record use of hallucinogens (mostly LSD). One student (3 per cent) in School I reports two occasions of use over the forty-two diary days, or use once every three weeks. In School IV, the selected high-illicit-use panel, students report using a hallucinogen, on the average, once every ten days. Evening use is recorded as the most common, followed by mornings and then afternoons. Most occasions are in the company of close friends; a few are with the family; a few are alone. Panelists emphasize the importance of the group's sharing the drug experience and, among individual goals, cite pleasure the most frequently, although mindexpansion, self-exploration, curiosity, and the like also figure.

A number of increases in hallucinogen use are recorded as having occurred during the panel period. Nine students in School IV report having tried LSD and three, DMT for the first time. The reasons for use are related primarily to individual interests and not to drug availability or social pressures. Four students remark on a diminished use which they attribute to social pressures or to the end of their experimentation. Three others speak of having quit during the period for these reasons and in one case apparently also because of worry over use and effects.

With regard to effects, 80 per cent recorded desirable effects, 3 per cent no effects, and 17 per cent bad outcomes. This proportion of bad outcomes is greater than for any other recorded drug.

Opiates.   We find no panel members mentioning illicit-opiate use in their diaries.

Special Substances.   Three students, two in School I and one in School IV, recorded using drugs classified as special substances—banana peel in one case at School IV and Cylert[1] for the two cases in School I. One student in School I reports using Cylert every day for a week without positive effects. The other student, again in School I, says he tried Cylert once as a study aid with positive effects. (He remained awake all night writing a term paper.) Interestingly, the student using banana peel—which we believe to be inactive pharmacologically—on a single occasion says he felt no ill effects. Use of Cylert was alone, while the use of banana was in a group; motives for using the latter were social as well as individual, while for the former, mental alertness was the stated desire. All students report beginning their use of these special substances during the diary keeping period.

COMMENT

Clear differences exist among the panelists in each school. Some reflect the obviously successful selection of students for their illicit-drug-use propensities in School IV, while others presumably reflect the variations in student and campus characteristics discussed in earlier chapters. In the two panels selected randomly—and thus, at least, moderately representative of undergraduates in Schools I and II—alcohol is said to be the most widely used single drug. Even so, during the study period more than a fourth of the students in Schools I and II report they did not drink at all. (We did not ask students to record tobacco use.) Some inkling of future alcohol problems exists in both schools among those students drinking with high frequency

[1] Cylert, magnesium pemoline, was at one time popularized as an aid to memory and learning (Spencer, 1966).

in order to relieve psychological distress. Ill effects from alcohol are also not uncommon, occurring as a response to 13 per cent of all drinking occasions.

Self-medication with mild analgesics and over-the-counter stimulants and tranquilizers accounts for the second most frequent kind of drug use, although, of course, many different substances are reported as involved. The pattern of use is rather frequent and chronic self-medication for a majority of students, with interschool differences again emerging.

Among the legitimate drugs, one finds few panelists using sedatives, tranquilizers, amphetamines, or nonpsychoactive prescriptions obtained from physicians. Most panelists using these drugs do not take them often, although one diary records intensive sedative use for one week and several show intensive amphetamine use over short periods.

Concerning illicit-drug use, we find even among the randomly selected panelists that marijuana is the most popular drug—one that they use more often than tranquilizers, for example. However, it is not used intensively in Schools I or II, and indeed in School II—noted in earlier chapters for its low rate of illicit-drug use—only one student reports having tried it and then only once. The sample selected because their early interviews revealed them to be high illicit users (School IV) shows a remarkably different pattern. There, twice as many panelists take marijuana as drink alcohol (at least on diary days) and they also use marijuana more often, two to three times a week compared with only once a week for liquor.

Hallucinogen use is the second most popular drug experience among the panelists of School IV. Almost half the students there average a hallucinogen, usually LSD, once every ten days. Illicit-amphetamine use is ranked third in popularity, occurring among one third of the panelists on the average of once a week.

The information about styles of use of amphetamines reflects on the uncertainty raised in earlier chapters about our arbitrary classification of these drugs—whether as approved or illicit. Recall from Chapter Seven that initial sources for amphetamine use were distributed almost equally among legitimate and illicit-informal sources (for example, doctors and parents vs. friends). We now see that the choice of styles of use varies by campus, just as drug experience itself varies. The distribution of amphetamine-use styles for our panelists is equally divided, with half of the occasions involving the use of amphetamines legitimately prescribed for a diagnosed disorder and the other half being used without medical prescription or approval and involving "mind-expansion," hedonism, or other private goals—or group understandings.

When we consider the reasons entered in the panelists' diaries for their illicit-drug use at the time of occurrence—or shortly after—we find that pleasure seeking is the overriding and self-identified private motive for marijuana use (75 per cent of all occasions) and the most frequent single "motive" offered for hallucinogen use (50 per cent of all occasions). For amphetamine use, pleasure seeking is the reason given for 18 per cent of the drug-use occasions. The relief of distress is important only for marijuana use and that on 14 per cent of the occasions. "Mind-expansion," as separate from pleasure, figures primarily in amphetamine use on 75 per cent of the occasions and on 16 per cent of the hallucinogen occasions. Although a variety of other reasons are also given, they are minor in terms of frequency and lead us to conclude that, whatever other reasons for illicit-drug use are offered and whatever secondary functions for drugs are noted—as we saw in earlier chapters—the pursuit of pleasure as an individual goal is paramount.

Two other considerations are brought to bear, however: one is the social setting for use and the second, outcomes. Most marijuana use is a group event described by panelists as important in its shared drug experience; hallucinogens are also primarily taken as part of a social experience, as are amphetamines when these are used without medical prescription. Thus, whatever private pleasure may be attributed to the users' goals, these cannot be divorced from the pleasures of a social experience as such or—if not all group experiences are "pleasant"—then not from the fact that these drugs are taken with other people whose presence is recorded as an important component in the reason for use.

When we speak of the reasons for drug taking, there is a presumption of a means-end relationship, or "reward" or "reinforcement" in the sense of motives and learning—that is, ordinarily one expects the actual effects to matter. It is important to observe that such is not always the case. The efficacy of drugs—defined here in terms of what panelists entered in their diaries as positive, negative, or no effects—vary considerably from class to class. For example, almost two thirds of the occasions of tranquilizer use are described as having no outcomes, and one third of the occasions of the use of alcohol and over-the-counter remedies as leading to no remarkable effects. Curiously, no effects as such are rarely recorded for the illicit drugs—even though other observers have noted how often initial marijuana use leads to few noticeable effects and also that at least some of the marijuana use in California is known to be (Hollister, 1968) inactive—that is, without identifiable tetrahydrocannabinol content. In any event, no effects as such are recorded for less than 5 per cent of the use occasions of the amphetamines, marijuana, and the hallucinogens. We wonder whether these drugs are really that good or whether, as we suspect, a student who has committed himself to an illicit—and quite possibly to himself—dramatic act wants to admit that it has all been for naught, at least pharmacologically speaking.

As we consider the high rate of no outcomes for the tranquilizers and for home-remedy drugs, we should make one observation. (Our guess is that the unfelt effects of alcohol require little discussion, given the social significance of most drinking occasions among students—parties, dates, festive meals, seminars over beer, and so forth.) This observation is that people who use drugs do not need the reinforcement of an always noticeable drug effect in order to continue their use. What this implies is that drug use will continue in many instances even if effects are not felt. We can speculate as to the reasons. (1) Intermittent perceived efficacy of drugs may, like variable schedules of reinforcement in instrumental conditioning, serve to produce learning and to sustain behavior. (2) Some effects may occur which lead to conditioning even if the effects are subliminal, autonomic, or simply denied. One has in mind autonomic conditioning as such and demonstrations of subliminal reinforcement as devices capable of producing and maintaining behavior. (3) As long as the expectations for effects are maintained, these orientations or "hopes" may serve to induce behavior even when outcomes are nil. As long as advertising, peers, parents, doctors, and others continue to communicate their expectations, one acts in ways that are compatible with what others expect—as a good patient, child, and so on. One may continue such behavior even in the absence of authorities and one may also continue in order to reinterpret effects occurring in interpersonal settings so as to teach himself to "notice" what he failed to notice before. Becker (1963) describes this well for marijuana-use learning. We have also seen it among LSD users (Blum and Associates, 1964). (4) Drug ingestion as such can be satisfying, just as the group experiences associated with symbolic drug use can be satisfying, without regard to pharmacological outcomes. The satisfactions of ritual expressions are associated with act and context and not with perceived later internal effects. Whether on the level of gratification of oral needs, of "taking care of oneself" as taught by one's parents, of "being a good sport" and trying something new, or of being "regular" as some laxative users desire, what one is told and tells himself about the meaning or utility of use can be quite a sufficient cause for use. There can, of course, be a more complex psychodynamics associated with ingestion, as is often found among those compulsively ingesting food or what-have-you. Further investigation of these effects are in order.

Regarding the negative effects reported, we see that these are most frequent for hallucinogens and less frequent for alcohol. Curiously, none of the reasons offered by those very few persons diminishing or stopping drug use refers to negative effects specifically, although one LSD user did stop because he was worried about the resulting post-trip depression and confusion. That negative effects can occur without deterring use is a common observation for psychoactive drugs. First experiences with alcohol, tobacco, heroin, opium, and LSD are often unpleasant but yet drug novitiates continue use. This is a poorly understood but important phenomenon deserving further investigation. Whether these negative outcomes that are part of continuing or even expanding use—with alcoholics or, for that matter, with others —may occur with simultaneous gratifications, as has been shown with acute LSD reactions (Katz, Waskow, and Olsson, 1968) or with the curious phenomenon of almost-achieving which we identified in those continuing LSD use (Blum and Associates, 1964), remains to be seen.

A final comment is in order with reference to the prevalence of marijuana use among panelists in the two "representative" panels. The 4 per cent using marijuana on diary days over six months in School II squares with the overall 11 per cent experience rate in that school and with the maximum rate of use[2] during any given year

_____

[2] This is a statistic we have not given in earlier chapters. For other major age groups in School II, the figures are 2 per cent use among eighteen year olds with no regular or considerable use, 4 per cent among nineteen year olds with less than 1 per cent regular use, 3 per cent among twenty year olds with no regular or greater use, 3 per cent among twenty-one year olds

(prevalence), which is, for twenty and twenty-one year olds, about 3 per cent. In School I the prevalence of marijuana use on diary days among 17 per cent of the sample is high in comparison with the overall sample experience rate of 21 per cent and in view of the maximum use reported for any one year, which is 11 per cent among twenty year olds. One explanation may lie in sampling error and a consequent error of estimate because of the small size of the panel subsample. While granting that possibility, we hasten to say that the trend is in conformity to other data that suggest the higher percentage be accepted. In the first place, at least one (3 per cent) of the panelists began marijuana use during the panel period, most of which was in point of time after the completion of the survey in School I (done in the autumn). Secondly, Chapter Eleven shows that by 1968 in School I a much higher prevalence of marijuana experience existed than during the early survey period of 1966. That increase in School I is

---

with no regular or considerable use, and 1 per cent among twenty-two year olds with no regular use or greater.

For School I the prevalence of use by age is as follows: 4 per cent among eighteen year olds with no regular use; 9 per cent among nineteen year olds with 1 per cent regular use; 11 per cent for twenty year olds with 1 per cent regular or considerable use; 7 per cent among twenty-one year olds with 1 per cent regular or considerable use; and 1 per cent use among those twenty-three and over, with less than 0.5 per cent using marijuana regularly.

For School III, prevalence among eighteen year olds is as follows: 9 per cent with 3 per cent regular or considerable use; 12 per cent among nineteen year olds with 2 per cent regular or considerable use; 6 per cent among twenty year olds with 3 per cent regular or more use; 4 per cent among twenty-one year olds with 2 per cent regular or considerable use; and 2 per cent among twenty-two year olds with 1 per cent regular or greater use. In the twenty-three-and-over group it is also 2 per cent with 1 per cent regular or considerable use.

For School IV the figures are as follows: eighteen year olds show 8 per cent with 2 per cent regular or considerable use; nineteen year olds show 11 per cent use with 7 per cent regular or considerable; twenty year olds show 14 per cent use with 8 per cent regular or considerable; twenty-one year olds show 16 per cent with 4 per cent regular or no considerable use; twenty-two year olds show 8 per cent use, 2 per cent of which is regular and none considerable; and in the range of the twenty-three to twenty-seven year olds there is 11 per cent use of which 4 per cent is regular or considerable.

In School V, prevalence of use among eighteen year olds is less than 1 per cent with no regular use; among nineteen year olds 3 per cent with no regular use; among twenty year olds 2 per cent and no regular use; twenty-one year olds show less than 1 per cent use. There is 1 per cent use among twenty-two year olds and again none regular, and there is 2 per cent among the group twenty-three and over, none of which is regular.

compatible with very great increases in rates of arrest for juvenile drug offenses for California as a whole—a 176 per cent increase from 1966 to 1967,[3] and supports a generalization from School I to other Western student populations as well. In further support of the inference of increase, we would note that Chapter Eleven data show no increase in LSD use, which remains, according to these later survey findings, at about 6 per cent and which, among panelists, occurred in only one case, or 3 per cent.

In light of the foregoing, we must warn that other such increases are likely to have occurred in the other schools between the time of the survey and the time of publication of this report. For this reason we would recommend caution in relying on these figures as related to prevalence of experience. We further suggest that as use increases so that what was unusual behavior becomes usual, then the differences between students who take marijuana and those who do not become less consequential. When large numbers of people engage in common behavior, individual differences are to be expected within the group. Thus, consideration of differences between marijuana smokers and nonsmokers, as derived from our material in earlier chapters, must also be muted because what one is dealing with is no longer an individual but, rather, a general social phenomenon, the greater number of determinants of which are to be sought in shared social-environmental experiences instead of in the idosyncratic psychological sphere.

[3] California Bureau of Criminal Statistics, April 1968 report.

A Follow-Up
Study

Richard H. Blum
Emily Garfield

XI

A sensation of rapid change in the prevalence and incidence of illicit-exotic drug use among students continued during the course of our work. It is very likely to continue after publication. As our survey progressed during 1967–1968, we received rumors and reports to the effect that during the year major shifts were occurring. We had one small test available, reported in Chapter Sixteen, which verified for two fraternity-house samples that this period was indeed a year of change, at least for School I, for in the fraternity houses use increased by a factor of 2½. These findings, the other reports, and continuing student interest prompted a series of student-conducted studies in School I in the winter and spring of 1968. Those studies, the emphasis of which is on prevalence of illicit-drug use, constitute the subject matter of this chapter.

Students in the Graduate School of Business in School I conducted a self-survey using a mail-return questionnaire that was sent to all business-school students. Sixty-five per cent, $N = 374$, were returned. No data are available on the characteristics of the 35 per cent not responding. Among these presumably "conservative" (business-oriented) graduate students, 31 per cent report having tried marijuana and 7 per cent LSD. Twenty per cent of the sample claim continuing marijuana use once a month or more; half say they "turned on" during the preceding or current school year. Such a rapid increase in illicit-drug initiation during 1967–1968 conforms to data in our two-fraternity study, reported in Chapter Sixteen. Apparently only a few of the students have sold marijuana for profit. When compared with non-users, the marijuana users estimate that more students are users than do the non-users; this is a statistically significant difference ($P < .01$). Marijuana users are younger, are less often married, and more often come from nontechnical undergraduate majors; each of these differences is statistically significant ($P < .05$). Ninety-seven per cent of all users have friends who are users, compared with 67 per cent of the non-users; users are 10 to 1 in favor of their friends' trying marijuana, but non-users are 3 to 1 against. Users are proselytizers and initiators, claiming among them sixty-one converts; however, only sixteen of the sample claim to have been introduced to use by friends in the school. Marijuana users are politically more liberal and are opposed to the Vietnam War, both differences significant beyond $P = .01$. Marijuana users report more use of alcohol.

Students residing in a dormitory complex conducted an anonymous questionnaire self-survey in the spring of 1968. Although sample bias was likely, its direction is unknown; only 50 per cent, $N = 285$, returned the questionnaire. Among those responding (49 per cent of the men and 57 per cent of the women), 41 per cent of the men and 65 per cent of the women report experience with marijuana; 6 per cent have taken LSD. Twenty-five per cent of the men and 5 per cent of the women describe themselves as currently using marijuana on a regular basis, none very frequently. Most men who have not smoked marijuana have had the opportunity to do so; half of the nonsmoking men also have access to supplies. Ten per cent of the using men and .3 per cent of the using women consider marijuana to have detrimental effects. Four per cent of the women and 20 per cent of the men say they have also sold marijuana.

One student in School I developed and distributed an anonymous questionnaire for use in his own fraternity house in the spring of 1968. Sixty-two of sixty-seven members, 92 per cent, returned the form, which inquired solely about marijuana use. Seventy-six per cent report experience with marijuana and 61 per cent express the intention of continuing its use. Most of the experienced fraternity brothers are upperclassmen; most of the inexperienced students are under-classmen. Indeed, as the student author of the questionnaire writes, "Only one senior exists in this never using group; if the trend persists, everyone in my fraternity eventually tries marijuana before gradua-tion." Most say they began use in their sophomore year, which is the first year in which they reside in the fraternity house—a finding com-patible with the role of peers and leaders as set forth in Chapter Six-teen. However, for the year 1968, 30 per cent of the freshman pledges report marijuana experience, double the early experience rate for any earlier class. The student investigator writes,

> The use of marijuana is becoming more accepted on this campus, a fact which would lead the younger students to try it sooner. Only two people ever tried it in high school, so it seemingly remains a college experience; I would guess more so for my fraternity brothers who come from more conservative upper-middle-class backgrounds than most students.

In this fraternity house, marijuana use is associated by self-ratings with being politically liberal, and use is least found among natural- and hard-science majors. Examining future plans, those who have never used it, mostly freshmen, are undecided about their majors but definite about going to graduate school (a paradox the investiga-tor remarks upon with gentle humor). Among those who have tried marijuana but are definite in saying that they would not use it again are found the highest proportion intending to go on to graduate school. Nearly all students say a supply is readily available; among users about half smoke only one cigarette (a "joint") a week, and the other half from one to five a week. An interesting report indicates that some students began use while in Europe at overseas campuses where "freedom along with hashish is the big thing . . . many of my frat brothers tell me that's where they originally tried it." One third of the continuing users say they have told their parents about their marijuana use.

For the continuing users, "blowing up" with others is preferred whereas those who used marijuana but stopped it more often pre-ferred solitary smoking. The student investigator links that preference to fear of detection and suggests solitary smoking may be predictive of those who will not continue. More than half of those who have smoked marijuana claim to have influenced others to use it as well, proselytizing being much more common in the continuing user than in the group of discontinued users. As for preferred mode of administration, smoking rates highest; the low interest in eating marijuana is attributed to unpredictability of drug action and to difficulty in preparation. Asked their reasons for use, students list curiosity, enjoyment, and relaxation as predominant, although the student investigator, who knows his fraternity brothers well, comments about stated motives thus: "The results give only superficial reasons . . . the truth about use and non-use is really very individual . . . a really close understanding of each respondent would be necessary to get the real reasons."

UNDERGRADUATE SAMPLE

In the spring of 1968, a random sample of a hundred undergraduates drawn from School I was interviewed by students taking a psychology seminar. There were no refusals or losses. Students were trained briefly in interviewing techniques and were counseled intensively in the requirement that respondents' anonymity be protected. Neither time nor funds allowed a sample of more than a hundred, the small size of which requires awareness of a probable error of estimate, which is maximally $\pm$ 12.88 when there is a 50/50 split (for example, when 50 per cent say they have used marijuana and 50 per cent say they have not, the actual distribution in the total population lies between 37 per cent and 63 per cent maximally) and $\pm$ 2.56 when there is a 99/1 split (for example, when 1 per cent say they have used heroin, the distribution in the total population is between zero plus $N = 1$ and 3.56). The instrument employed was a much shortened form of the interview schedule used in the five-college study.

Our emphasis in reporting is on experience prevalence, present use, and future plans with reference to the illicit drugs. As in our earlier studies, proportionately much greater illicit-exotic experience is indicated among students majoring in the arts and humanities and in the social sciences; unlike the 1966–1967 data, the year in school is no longer a discriminating factor; underclassmen as often as upperclassmen report drug use; similarly, females as often as males report use of one or more illicit-exotic drugs.

Amphetamines. Thirty-five per cent ($\pm$ 12.29) of all students report amphetamine use, most of them students who have used other illicit-exotic compounds. Most use is intermittent. Two per cent ($\pm$ 3.61) have used methamphetamine intravenously; of these two, one is a regular user and one an occasional user. Half of the amphetamine-experienced group intend to continue use; only 3 per cent of the non-users anticipate taking up amphetamine use. The source of most amphetamines is friends rather than a legitimate medical or parental authority; most use is said to be in connection with combating fatigue and as a study aid, but the two regular "mainlining" users indicate their intent is to get high. Two thirds of the users report some ill-effects, whereas only one fourth claim benefits. Neither of the two regular users is concerned over his own amphetamine use.

Cannabis. Fifty-seven per cent of the sample ($\pm$ 12.75, for example, between 44 per cent and 70 per cent of the total population) report experience with marijuana or hashish. Sixteen per cent indicate regular or considerable use, 14 per cent at the present time. For 9 per cent ($\pm$ 7.37) that regular or considerable use has extended for over a year. Nearly all students (53 per cent) with cannabis experience say they intend to continue using the drug; most non-users do not intend to begin, although 12 per cent of the latter group ($\pm$ 8.37) say that they too intend to try cannabis. Eight per cent ($\pm$ 6.99) indicate that they began use in high school, and by the end of the sophomore year in college, two thirds of the experienced students have begun cannabis use. Most users report benefits from use, although one quarter of the users, primarily those with only one or two exposures, claim no gains from the drug. Ill-effects are reported by two thirds of those taking cannabis, most of these reporting multiple bad results. Eight students (14 per cent of the user group) say they are worried about their own (over) use of cannabis; ten students say their friends and parents are worried about their use of it.

Hallucinogens. Seventeen per cent of the sample ($\pm$ 9.68 or between 7 per cent and 27 per cent) report hallucinogenic drug experience. All have also used cannabis. LSD is the most common drug, although the heavier users have also tried STP, DMT, DET, mescaline, peyote, and psilocybin. Regular or considerable use is rare, with only 3 per cent of the total sample (12 per cent of the users) saying they take these drugs on any regular basis; only two students (at the time of the survey) say they are regular users. Most (88 per cent) of those who have taken hallucinogens say they intend to take them again, whereas only one student in the non-using group (1 per cent of the total sample) is interested in beginning hallucinogen use. Two students began their use in high school and most of the others (12/17) during freshman or sophomore college years. No use after the age of twenty-one is reported. Most students using hallucinogens claim benefits and most likewise report bad results, the latter being multiple. Two students are worried about their own LSD use (at the time of the survey).

Opiates. Ten per cent of the sample (± 7.73 or between 2 per cent and 18 per cent of the total undergraduate population) report the use of opiates, all ten having used opium. Two of these students, the same two who have used amphetamines intravenously, have also taken heroin prior to their arrival on campus. All ten have also used cannabis. Three students, or 30 per cent of the user sample, indicate they have used opiates considerably over a period of time; one reports being a regular opium user (at the time of the survey). Half of this group intends to continue use, whereas none of the students in the non-using group expresses an interest in beginning opiate experimentation. Most opiate users claim benefits, only half reporting ill effects. Two students are concerned about their own opiate habits. One is concerned about his amphetamine use as well, the other about his marijuana use, while both express their family's worry over their drug involvement in general. For most students, opiate experience first began during the freshman or sophomore years.

Supplemental items. Repetition of a few of the inquiries made in the major survey reveals that students in this new sample who have experience with illicit-exotic drugs more often are dissatisfied with their course work, their teachers, and the school as a whole. There are more incomplete grades taken by the drug-using group and past or future plans for dropping-out also occur more often.

Hippie dress. On a newly incorporated rating item, the interviewers were asked to rate the appearance of respondents in terms of dress, haircut, and ornamentation as being either "straight" (conventional college attire) or "hip" (beards, beads, sandals, long hair, and so on). Among the students with no illicit-drug experience, only one (1/43 or 2 per cent) rates as a hip type, whereas among those with illicit-drug experience, seventeen (17/57 or 30 per cent) rate as hip types. This difference, which is statistically significant, $P < .05$, shows that drug use and hippie costume are linked on campus; however, what must not be overlooked is that most of the students with drug experience are not clad as hippies. Our presumption is that these students are less intensive users and that those who embrace the drug ideology, which includes intensive drug experience, will embrace the uniform of the ideologue as well.

SUMMARY AND COMMENT

Including the data in Chapter Sixteen we have information on six groups for School I, all collected after the initial survey of 1966–1967. One small random sample of undergraduates, one sample of graduate business students, three fraternity-house samples, and one of men and women in a coeducational dormitory complex all yielded results showing a considerable increase in prevalence of marijuana-hashish experience during 1967 and 1968. In the 1966–1967 survey, 21 per cent in School I had tried marijuana and only about 4 per cent had been regular users (although drug diaries yielded a higher rate of regular use, 17 per cent). By late spring 1968, between 44 per cent and 70 per cent had tried it, with actual experience varying by group classified upon type of residence unit and type of major. The best estimate for all undergraduate experience is 57 per cent, which is an increase by a factor of nearly three in eighteen months. Regular use also seems to have increased, so that among all undergraduates, between 5 per cent and 23 per cent say they are currently employing cannabis with a best estimate at 14 per cent, higher in certain residence and major-subject groups. With this rapid increase, the number saying they still intend to begin cannabis use has diminished from the 32 per cent considering it in 1966–1967 to only 12 per cent ($\pm$ 8.37) in late spring of 1968. It is worthy of emphasis that when one takes the 21 per cent experienced in the original survey and adds to it the 32 per cent who then expressed an interest in beginning marijuana use, one emerges with a figure of 53 per cent, which is quite close indeed to our actual estimate of 1968 use. On the presumption that we may believe the 12 per cent who say they intend to begin, the estimate for cannabis experience for late spring 1969 at School I will be somewhere around 70 per cent.

Hallucinogen experience seems to have changed less. Figures for the business students and dormitory residence show no shift from the earlier-survey prevalence of 6 per cent. The random sample yields a rate of prevalence of experience almost three times greater, 17 per cent vs. the original 6 per cent, but since error of prediction here is $\pm$ 9.68, the 17 per cent may well be too high. One thing is sure, hallucinogen use is not diminishing on campuses, judging by its rate of increase. As for opiates, the random sample yields an estimate of 10 per cent, a rise of more than a factor of ten in eighteen months. Again, we are faced with a high maximal error of estimate ($\pm$ 7.73); nevertheless, even accepting maximal error in overestimating, it is likely that some opiate-use increase has occurred. That the drug is opium rather than heroin is compatible with the sophistication of students who are informed about the greater addictive potential of heroin. They appear to discount opium's potential for producing dependency, a view most experts would hold as painfully overoptimistic, although not without some support in the literature (see Chapter Three in *Drugs I*).

With regard to the amphetamines, we find evidence for a slight increase over the 25 per cent experience reported in the original survey. The 35 per cent in the new random sampling is subject to an error of estimate of about 12 per cent, so we cannot be sure that any actual change took place. On the assumption that it did, the style of use for students in School I remains occasional and primarily as a study aid. Yet the appearance of even 2 per cent now shooting methamphetamine intravenously is cause for concern. Like the opium figure, it is unreliable due to estimate error; this should not lead us to overlook the fact of some intravenous use of methamphetamine or of narcotics experimentation, especially since most students in both groups using amphetamines and narcotics express the intention to continue. Since such use is also demonstrably linked to the use of a variety of other drugs and to commitment to a drug ideology, since many of the more intensive users are already concerned about dependency, and since reports of multiple ill effects are already made by some of these users, it would be foolhardy to ignore the likelihood that some students not previously exposed to health hazards via drug use are now—with the inauguration of opiate and intravenous methamphetamine—severely exposed to hazard. Aside from health hazards, there are the continuing threats to social adjustment as evidenced in the students' reports of sensitivity to criticism from friends and relatives (exactly as found in the normal population study in companion book) and, of course, of increasing threat of arrest as they rely on illicit channels for their drugs.

We cannot consider, because that study has yet to be done, the implications for student attitudes and values—let alone the jeopardy to their persons—associated with reliance on illicit suppliers for their drugs. As methamphetamine and especially opium become drugs of choice, the informal, illicit channels employed for marijuana distribution (Mandel, 1967) may be supplemented by more organized criminal ones. One *can* consider the implications of the data from the dormitory and business-school studies which show that some students —for example, up to one fifth of the pot-using men—now admit to selling drugs as well. In a society which provides heavy penalties for drug peddling—death in some states, for example—such behavior is risky indeed. Yet it is not to be divorced from drug use, for as we have described in *Utopiates* (Blum and Associates, 1964), missionary zeal is characteristic of illicit users, especially intensive users. All of our findings confirm the activity of users in influencing non-users to join the society of the illicit elect.

As for the correlates of drug use, we see continued support for earlier findings, even though a majority of students in School I are now in the experienced group. Liberal to radical political views, school drop-out history or intentions, course-work incompletes, and general dissatisfaction with school interpretable as low morale are all confirmed as correlates. What has changed markedly is the association between class standing and age, for now we find most students have been "turned on" in freshman and sophomore years and an increasing number have come to college with high school drug experience as well. This phenomenon was predicted on the basis of the high school studies reported later in Chapter Nineteen, on the basis of Blumer's (1967) youth sample, and on the basis of the trends over time in the direction both of a younger age of initiation and of a spreading social base (outward from university, artistic, and professional samples). At the upper end we see confirmation of the earlier reported decrease in use with older age and, especially, with graduate standing, marriage, and other conventional career commitments. However, as the business-school study suggests, the absolute and proportional numbers of graduates and older students either "turning on" or carrying undergraduate drug-use habits with them are increasing, so that we must expect that the "immunity" to continued illicit-drug use previously imposed by graduate plans and graduate status will diminish. We anticipate that the diminishing rate will be much slower in contrast to the rapid rate of onset of use occurring in high school and junior high levels. Thus, one can predict that most persons now over twenty-four will not become illicit-exotic drug users if they are not already; however, over the coming years as present youngsters grow older and carry illicit-drug use with them, especially cannabis use, then more university-trained people will grow old with cannabis for company.

Student Ideologies
Compared

Richard H. Blum

XII

*T*his chapter compares students espousing several different and important ideologies, the active use of illicit-exotic drugs being considered as one of these. The study rests upon a sample of students selected for their ideological engagement—a set of commitments to activities and beliefs much more than the simple acceptance of one idea or, as in the case of drugs, one activity.

When we talked to students in the period during which marijuana and LSD were first appearing among graduates and undergraduates on cosmopolitan campuses, we soon realized that those students who were becoming confirmed exotic-illicit drug users were involved in group activities which were strongly related to ideological issues (see Blum and Associates, 1964). No matter how much the interest of students was focused on seeking and talking about drug effects or how important their group activities were, we observed in all those committed to drug use a third less immediate and less concrete component: the sharing of ideas and viewpoints about the world. These, which we term "ideological," were shared by persons in differ-

195

ent drug-using groups and on different campuses and were so broadly distributed by age group as to embrace many older drug users—for example, the professional people we describe in *Utopiates*—along with a very few persons younger than college age.

What we heard either in group discussion or in individual conversations was not only the rights and wrongs of drug use, of what was safe or unsafe or potent or less so, but also a much larger brace of opinions covering politics, pacifism, sex, love, fun, individual rights, the nature of an ideal society, and so forth. Whatever justifications, rationalizations, or party line were detected in these discussions, it was obvious that important social values and special ways of looking at and experiencing the world were part of being a drug user. The beliefs expressed were also certainly more elaborate and sincere than simply being justifications of delinquency or of selfish pleasure seeking—charges often heard and, consequently, often strongly denied by that first wave of illicit-drug users.

The themes in such discussions were—like those we have seen of the valences of drug use in the survey chapters—positive, multifaceted, and interwoven with expectations of what human beings could be and what drugs could accomplish. In those days when drug use was new to campuses—and we would estimate that to be the period of 1962 to 1966—there was also a sense of discovery conveyed during the conversations. Young people had not only discovered illicit drugs and new in-groups but they believed they had also discovered new experiences, new freedoms and pleasures, new insights, and new world views. Nowadays, as drug use appears to be more and more common on campus and as students in urban high schools learn it so that they are "old hands" by the time of college, the feeling of discovery or of the special nature of the drug ideology is likely to be attenuated. On the other hand, since many schools of conservative bent or in rural areas are at the time of this writing just at the point where cosmopolitan liberal colleges were some years before, there are still many places where the avant-garde on campus can be seen in a fervor of drug-linked discovery. That is, of course, not a phenomenon limited to the drug ideology; most educators hope their students will enjoy the fervor of discovery—of ideas, ideals, and of life itself—as often as possible.

During that same period—let us say from 1962 and continuing through today—the most visibly "fervent" groups on campus have been the New Left, the student radicals whose protests, sit-ins, and other forms of political activity have stirred so much interest. Those in the left wing, some characteristics of which are noted in Chapter One, are now shown from our survey data to be the most likely students with illicit- and exotic-drug experience. We also see a tendency for the most intensive drug use to be associated even more with the politics of the radical-left student. This association is not by any means perfect; in our data some left students—Marxists for example—stand out as strongly opposed to illicit-drug use. In any event, with this more-often-than-chance coupling of left political ideologies and the drug-linked belief systems, a likely range of possible beliefs emerges within any student drug-using in-group. For one thing, they can be reasonably "pure" in the sense that they are vitally interested in drugs—which means interested in inner experience of various sorts and its correlated outward expressions such as communal living, sexual freedom, "love," "peace," and what-have-you. For another, they can have these drug interests plus a strong admixture of active left politics with its emphasis on power sharing (or grabbing), confrontations, and expanded individual freedom (or anarchy).

One would expect that students who embrace either of the "pure" radical involvements, left politics or drug use, would differ from one another not just by virtue of their current beliefs but by virtue of the assumption that those ideologies represent an outcome of what the individual himself has been prior to college—his background, development, and current personality. One could also expect—although without a longitudinal study it is not easy to prove—that these students differ in what they are becoming. The reason is not only that the ideologies they embrace commit them to one or another more probable sequence of opportunities but that they are, during these adolescent and postadolescent years, forming themselves out of the ideologies with which they are involved. This is not to say that as adults they will accept everything they believed when in college, but, rather, to suggest, like Erikson (1960, 1968), that adult personalities are partly developed out of a variety of youthful social experiments, each of which contributes something, and that ideologies and group involvements are part of these tests and tastes of life. Being a hippie, as Weakland (Chapter Fifteen, *Drugs I*) points out, can be one of these transitional and exploratory periods.

Since engagement in the left or drug ideologies, or in what appears from our data commonly to combine both, represents an apparent new development for most individuals, it can be conceived of in two ways. One would be a relatively easy or natural movement from family orientations and personal interests into a still consistent but more active and complex set of ideas and actions—an example being the socially aware child of liberal parents becoming a student radical. The other conception implies more tension and putting asunder—that is, a more dramatic shift away from parental values in the direction of disapproved behavior. We already know from the survey data that it is the illicit-drug users—compared with non-users—who more often report a shift away from parental values, opposition to parents, feeling on the "outs" with conventional people and values, and so forth. We also know that it is the total abstainers (no alcohol, tobacco, and so on) who report the closest relationships to parents and the most homogeneous—as well as conservative—family life. Without further evidence, one would expect that it would be the illicit-drug users on campus who do the most shifting from earlier to later years. One additional reason to expect this, of course, is that for students coming from middle- or upper-class homes (the case in most of our sample) and presumably without histories of serious delinquency (a set of inferences from correlated information on educational level, family income, and so on as related to visible delinquency), the move to illicit drugs is itself a rather significant renunciation of convention and of at least one kind of lawfulness. The radical students, of course, take similar action when engaging in "civil disobedience" through trespass, draft-card burning, and the like.

Over the recent years those who have been on campuses—or parents from their vantage points—have been able to watch the coming together of students into groups which have become the nuclei of drug use. Ethnocentric and avant-garde in the early years, proselytizing then and now, the illicit-drug set created a scene attractive to the new arrivals looking for adventure or something special. As young people joined the fringes—and some moved into the centers of these groups to become committed rather than simply experimental or playful users—one observed the changes in vocabulary, in dress, in prized activities, in the definition of who or what was friend or foe, and in explanations for what was wrong and right with the world. Although these were shared viewpoints, each person's own personality modified the group offerings, so that among campus drug users individual characteristics were certainly not submerged.

For most students the involvement in drug use was a slow enough process, one proceeding apace over college years with other liberalizing trends, other growths in confidence and exploration, and other tests of doctrine, pleasure, and action through immersions that were usually not total since the core of self was buoyant and the choice of friends or drugs was apparently not permanent. For a few students the involvement in drugs appeared quite sudden, whether through the accident of proximity to users in a residence unit or because the student himself was ready for something dramatic. Thus, it seemed in some that there was short hair one day and long the next—or as their parents must have felt of themselves, dark hair one day and grey the next! Although these sudden cases must also have been growing, groping, and learning along the way—with some clearly stumbling, regressing, and rebelling—the dramatic character of their engagement in new ways drew attention and for these few sustained the label "conversion." Yet one must grant that individual conversion, like social revolution, is but the final step in a long sequence of less extraordinary events which happen to have gone unnoticed. But, whether conversions or not—and most were not—those students who became heavily involved with drug users and almost inevitably with drug use had made important choices.

The presumption is that these choices were at least partly functional in the sense that they were directly satisfying, attractive to students who were ready for a move in that direction, and useful or instrumental in bringing students closer to other things they wanted. We would say of the drug-linked—or other—student ideology and beliefs that they are like the opinions of which Smith, Bruner, and White (1956) write in that they "reflect the deeper lying pattern of life. They are mediators between the inner demands of the person and the outer environment. . . ." These beliefs and opinions which are part of an ideology can serve a variety of functions, as, for example, in ordering or stereotyping the environment and in the social process facilitating ties between people or, conversely, channeling aggression and vanity so as to identify others as the enemy. As Lewin (1964) and Erikson (1960, 1968) have theorized, they can help people test life and build of themselves an elaborated—or possibly a restricted—personality. It is also the case, as Freud understood, that ideologies are strategies whereby feelings are expressed, defenses constructed, cognitions elaborated, and interpersonal mechanisms routinized. While these are functions of ideologies for individuals, the ideology is also functional for the larger society. Stable when societies are stable, ideologies grow and die rapidly under conditions of change and in doing so go beyond their individual functions to form groups and institutions and to create testing grounds where existing beliefs are challenged and where new social experiments, most of them doomed to failure, are tried. Toch (1965) suggests that social movements—which necessarily express their appeals and programs in an ideology—emerge to meet the needs of persons currently not being met by the social environment.

Ordinarily, as Apter (1964), Lane and Sears (1964), Toch, and others have discussed, ideologies are familial—that is, they are transmitted from parents to children in the home and, in stable societies, can be maintained over many generations. They are also modifiable—typically in America on a gradual basis and by exposure to important groups, such as friends, fellow workers, teachers, and so on. They are also modifiable intellectually and by exposure to mass media, although the latter process is usually mediated by influential persons. During college years, modification is not only expected but usually demanded by the university as horizons are broadened and gradual shifts away from parental views are encouraged. Ideologies can also shift suddenly, although that is not the college pattern. Conversion is an illustration, but this is a rare case and among those so engaged the presumption is of considerable pre-existing tension, of very great immediate pressure (whether under the sword of the conqueror or from the persuasive arguments of spouse or of laws) and often of unstable solutions—as one sees in the seekers and joiners moving from sect to sect. Buckner (1966), Dohrman (1964), Stark and Lofland (1965), Pratt (1924), and Wilson (1961) provide illustrative studies of the latter. Implicit in the understanding of who will shift in response to mediating environmental forces—especially involvement in group situations where others hold different views—is the idea that there are individual differences in conformity. These demonstrations have long been the business of social psychologists Asch (1952), Berg and Bass (1961), Cartwright and Zander (1953), Crutchfield (1963), Janis and Howland (1964), Kogan and Wallach (1964), Rokeach (1960), Sherif (1936), and Witkin *et al.* (1962), all of whom have made important contributions which show, in essence, that the size of the group, level of membership in it, importance of the issue, kind of communication, status of the person, and his personality (confident or not, flexible or not, neurotic or not) all play a part.

Since in this chapter and the next we are looking at students with three important styles of belief—political, religious, and drug oriented—it may be well to look briefly at where these ordinarily come from and how they change. There is some literature on the religious phenomenon and, as we saw in Chapter One, a very considerable literature on politics and student politics in particular. For the most part, the literature shows belief systems to be transmitted in the home and, if there are shifts, these to be in the direction of the collegiate milieu in America—teachers and older peers—who are usually liberal. Fichter, for example, cited in Carrier (1965), studying "model" Catholics finds that among very religious youth a shift to "negligence" occurred about age twenty and continued in many through age thirty-nine; beginning at age forty, a return to religious values was observed. That return is accentuated among older persons who have children (Telford and Reuss cited in Carrier). The importance of religion to youth varies with the intensity of their religious education during childhood, which is, in turn, a function of the importance of religion to the parents (Carrier). When religious disaffection occurs, it is likely to be in combination with other forms of dissassociation of the youth from his parents. Cohen and Hale (1967) concur that lack of religious interest on the part of parents is necessary before campus liberalizing pressures are effective in shifting student religious affiliations. Defection from religion as such tends to be a Protestant phenomenon (Allport cited in Carrier).

With regard to political shifts, the same factors appear to operate and have elsewhere been demonstrated. Lane (1962, 1959), for example, finds that there is a strong relationship between parental and offspring ideology; for example, Democratic preferences occurred among 82 per cent when both parents were Democrats and Republican preferences among 73 per cent when both parents were Republican (see Lane and Sears, 1964). Lane and Sears cite a study by Middleton and Putney (1963) showing that degree of parental closeness was the critical factor in rebellion against parental political stands; the less close a child felt, the more likely he was to change his politics, particularly if politics was an important area for the parents; thus, the student choice of politics as an area for rebellion was dictated by parental interests, this disagreement dictated by conflict. The investigators found that such rebellions generally involved mild shifts rather than the adoption of dramatically different positions. Lane and Sears have discussed how exposure to college leads to shifts in the liberal direction in regard to political stands.

Specific studies on left politics abound. Some of those focusing on students have already been cited in Chapter One. Others of note include Almond (1954), Howe and Coser (1957), and Krugman (1964), focusing on adult American Communists. Studies of the right wing are fewer but when linked with personality research include Adorno, Frenkel-Brunswik, Levinson, and Sanford (1950), Apter (1964), Bell (1963), Chesler and Schmuck (1963), McClosky and Scharr (1965), and Shils (1956). Although Apter's results do identify a very successful radical-right constituency, generally neither the social situations nor the personalities of either the extreme left or of the extreme right—or even of the less extreme right—are described as favorable.

As for our own sample, we at first sought converts since we had a special interest in ideological change—this because of our drug-use focus. However, after canvassing all of the campus ministers, we found few converts except to the more liberal or humanistic creeds, Unitarian, Congregational, or Quaker. With all respect to the churches based on such creeds (and the author is a member of one of them), we felt they were not good examples of religious conversion; to the contrary, they were illustrations of liberalization in college which were, if anything, in the direction toward reduced dogma and faith. Consequently, we were unable—on a campus of 11,558 students—to find sufficient religious *spiritual* converts to constitute the sample we desired. Abandoning the search for converts, we settled for devoutly religious students, of whom we were sure a sufficient number would exist from traditional families in spite of the data showing that Protestantism suffers most from religious defection; thus, School I draws its students from mostly Protestant homes.

As for the right, we did not go looking for converts, simply for confirmed believers. Following Apter's (1964) finding of a heavy concentration of upper-status, Protestant, and well-educated whites in California's radical right, we felt safe in assuming that enough of their children in School I would be true to the family spirit to comprise a sample. With reference to the left—and, in particular, the "pure" left

—we were unsure. There was no question that leftist agitation and interest on campus were generating the impression of multitudes—pro-Mao, pro-Castro, and pro-Che Guevara, among others. How many dedicated leftists there actually were we could not be sure—nor were we confident of their cooperation with a bourgeois or establishment venture such as ours. As for the drug users, we knew they were there because we knew many of them from other studies and other times. As for their ideological development, we expected them, by reason of the body of research findings, to show evidence of independence of and opposition to parents and authority and, because of the fact of illicit-drug use, to report shifts in beliefs in the direction of a drug ethic incorporating and supporting unconventional activity. On the other hand, we thought it unlikely that most of the involved drug-using students would have moved to positions dramatically different from those of their parents on matters of life interest or fundamental value. After all, if we concluded from the studies done that ideological movement is for most people only a matter of small shifts, the shortest distance to left-and-drug ideologies is from the liberal or radical, permissive, unconventional, and personal enrichment oriented home. There was another reason not to assume that even the unconventional students at School I would have moved dramatically far from home base. In spite of trappings of beards and beads or of mysticism and militancy, these students were from a well-nourished and privileged elite whose very presence in school testified to their intellectual capabilities, their social grace, their physical and mental health, and their sensitivity to the kind of an education that bodes best for later careers. We thought it unlikely that such a favored and realistic group would be about to destroy themselves, at least within the limits of their estimates of risk and gain, by any behavior so radical or so unconventional that it posed a genuine danger to safety, personal relationships, freedom, or career. Thus, we did not expect to find in School I, with its high standards for entrance and continuation, much in the way of disabling pathology and social deprivation of the sort that contributes to self-destructive and compulsive drug use such as that of heroin (Blum, 1967; Chein, Gerard, Lee, and Rosenfeld, 1964; and Robins, 1966).

On the other hand, the drugs in question, mostly LSD and marijuana, are illicit and even if by now experimentation is common, their use in School I in 1965 to 1966 was unusual enough to be taken as a sign that something was "wrong." It was reasonable to assume that the deviancy of the committed users of that time—and here, as throughout this section, we are not considering playful or conforming marijuana experimentation—would express itself in some aspect of their past—that is, something was unusual or "wrong" there, too. As the data from Keniston (1965), Middleton and Putney (1963), and Maccoby, Matthews, and Morton (1954) suggest—and as we have already seen from the survey data on student-parent conflict and dissatisfaction, that "something" was likely to be a family matter or, at least, partly a family matter. We shall see that it turned out to be so, that the intensively involved campus drug ideologist of 1965–1966, like the illicit-exotic student user of 1966–1967, was one who seemed to lack close relations with parents and appeared to suffer from unresolved family and interpersonal problems. These were the students who were often sensitive and visionary, relatively without structure, discipline, or genuine people-to-people warmth and who lacked enthusiasm for their community or careers.

COMMENT

Out of theory, others' findings, our earlier observations, and from sheer hunch, we developed a set of questions which constituted our inquiry to students in the several ideological groups. What would be the differences among students who came to the drug-oriented life style compared with those who chose (or, if one were to pretend to strict determinism, had no choice but to follow) other life styles equally available on campus, equally respectable in terms of having at least some campus support and no formal negative campus sanctions, and able to provide equal opportunities for being with friends, being active, and for developing a world view and fashioning out of oneself an identifiable person in the sense of having things to believe in, to be for, and to be against—in other words, having a cause? We chose (and thereby strongly deny strict determinism for ourselves!) four positions to contrast; as indicated, these were the involved illicit-exotic drug users, the radical left, the deeply religious, and the political right.

It was our intention to draw a sample of about twenty-five students representing heavy involvement in each of these ideologies. To recruit our samples, we asked students we knew to make nominations of persons on campus whom they considered to fall into each of these groups. Among students initially classified by us or others as demonstrating the ideologies which we sought, we asked for further nominations. In addition, we scanned the published membership list of the various political and religious organizations on campus. For the religious sample, in which we sought not simply affiliates of conventional churches but students who were deeply religious, we asked each of the campus ministers to nominate his most spiritual or devout student parishioners.

We accepted the nominees who were willing to participate in the study and who, after initial screening, appeared to fall within the ideologies of interest to us. We were, from the beginning, required to accept mixed rather than "pure" cases simply because we did not have the resources to conduct a more extensive search. Indeed, we had no assurance that twenty-five pure cases of single-minded investment in each of the four contrasting ways of life could be found in all of School I, even though our final classification scheme hardly required fanatics. Our definitions were as follows: a *drug user* was a student who had in the past taken one variety or more of the illicit-exotic drugs three times or more, who at present was still using these drugs, and who, in the future, intended to continue using them. A *religious student* must describe himself as "interested" in religion, as having an institutional religious affiliation or preference, and as never having changed from a strict to a liberal faith—for example, from being Methodist to being Unitarian. Further, on the self-rating item "Religion: being a religious person, having religious sentiments," he must rate as "very important" (the most extreme rating). The *left political student* had to meet the criteria for such descriptions as New Left, Social-Democrat, Marxist, Maoist, Communist, radical, Castroite, and so on. In response to an item asking whether his left direction had changed, if he answered "yes" he must have moved further left and, in the self-rating, he must describe as "very important" the item on politics, subdefined as "caring about who obtains power and public responsibility, how it is exercised, and what political ideologies hold sway." To be classified as *right politically*, the student must describe himself as conservative (not Republican), preferring Goldwater, Rousselot, and so on. When asked about political shifts, if answering "yes" he must have changed to the right and on the self-rating must rate as "very important" to himself the political item quoted above.

The final sample was composed of 105 students as follows:

I. Illicit-drug users who were not involved in religion or politics, N = 26

    II. Religious students who were not political (as defined above) and who were not drug users as defined above, N = 24

   III. Left-wing students who were also drug users as defined above, N = 17

   IV. Right-wing students who were not religious or drug users, N = 13

    V. Our screening failures who turned out not to be drug users, religious right, or left wing. We have tried to make ourselves feel better about this unwanted group by calling them "controls," N = 10

   VI. Left political students who were not involved in drug use and not religious, N = 5

  VII. Right political students who were also religious, N = 4

 VIII. Drug users who were also religious, N = 3

   IX. Students who were simultaneously left, religious, and drug users, N = 2

    X. One left student who was religious, N = 1

Only groups I, II, IV, and VI were pure in the sense we sought, with a combined N of 68. The remaining thirty-seven students were mixed as to ideologies. In response to these harsh realities, we set up two other analytical schemes. One classification combined all drug users into one group regardless of their other interests; thus, groups III, VII, VIII, and IX, all of whom included drug users, were contrasted to the nondrug-user groups I, II, IV, V, VI, and X.[1] A second comparison limited itself to the drug users and compared those with multiple-drug interests to those with restricted interests. The multiple-vs.-restricted scheme was derived from our pilot study of a normal adult population. (See Chapter Eleven in *Drugs I.*) Students were asked whether they had used any drugs on a list of 13 ranging from those we found often employed to those rarely employed. By classification, these were home remedies and medical painkillers, social drugs, prescribed psychoactive drugs, and the illicit-exotic drugs. The cutting point for dividing our drug-using students fell midway, so that those who reported use of six of these different drugs (or drug classes) or less became the restricted-drug group N = 24; those who reported use of seven or more of these drugs were classified as multiple-drug users, N = 22.

    The procedure we shall follow in the presentation of data is to identify those factors in student background, viewpoint, and activity

---

[1] On some early computer runs, the control group, group V, was excluded from comparisons.

which, following our inquiry, were found to differ from samples under comparison. Our criterion of "difference" here is that of statistical significance at the .05 level or beyond. So as not to overlook trends, we shall also report on differences which are not significant according to the .05 convention but which fall between .05 and .10 levels of probability. For each variable, three different runs were made, the first on all of the ideological subsamples, the second on drug users vs. nonusers, and the third on the multiple-vs.-restricted drug users. We shall see that the latter comparison but rarely yields differences, whereas the former two show consistent ones. As we discuss the differences among ideological groups, one should keep in mind that a significant Chi Square, which is the test used, tells us only that the differences in the overall table would not have occurred by chance any more than one time out of a hundred (or a thousand or ten thousand as the case may be), while not specifying what directions of difference are involved. We shall undertake in the discussion to indicate the direction the differences take. Any one such difference which we remark upon without further test against all others might not by itself prove significant but, as part of the distribution of the variable, does contribute to significance. At the end of the chapter, we shall consider those major items which we expected also to discriminate among groups but which failed to do so.

Life Style
Interviews

Richard H. Blum

XIII

*T*his chapter presents the results of intensive interviews with 105 students selected for their intensive involvement in drug, left-wing, right-wing, or religious ideologies. The interview items describe the students' background, interests, activities, viewpoints, and aspects of personal development.

BACKGROUND

Among the ideological subsamples, the year in school of students differs significantly at the .006 level. One finds that both the right-wing and the right-wing religious groups tend to be comprised of lowerclassmen, whereas the pure-left wing is made up entirely of graduate students. The drug users tend to be upperclassmen, but when drug users are combined and compared with non-users the differences are not significant. What this means is that the components which contribute to significant difference rest upon other than drug-use characteristics—that is, religious and political groupings. We should remark that our sample is skewed toward upperclass and graduate status, while only 30 per cent are lowerclassmen. This compares with the actual per cent of lowerclassmen in School I, which is 21 per cent of the matriculated students and 41 per cent of undergraduates.

Ideological groups differ significantly in the distribution of majors among them, significant at the .053 level. The highest concentration of drug and/or left-wing students is among the arts and humanities and also the social sciences. The religious students and, to a lesser extent, the right wingers have the greatest representation in technology and the hard sciences. When students are classified by drug use only, one finds non-users more often in technology and the hard sciences and users more often in the arts-humanities area, as indicated above. The difference is not significant; one reason is that arts-humanities and social-science majors comprise two thirds of the students in our sample. This is to be compared with the actual representation in School I of these majors, where they constitute 29 per cent of undergraduates and graduates.

Only four out of the 105 students are not American citizens. Of these four, three are extreme left in ideology. These differences emerge as significant beyond the .001 level (Chi Square = 32.92, 9 degrees of freedom).

Given the basis for our nomination and ideological-group classifications, one would expect religious interests per se, as expressed by students, to differ significantly among the ten subgroups. This is the case, significant beyond .001. Let us note that in spite of a lack of deep commitment to religion, some students classified thereby as nonreligious do say they are interested in religion. Classifying students by either use or non-use of illicit drugs, one finds those not involved in drugs are much more interested in religion, significant beyond .001. Among drug users, split by multiple or restricted use, there are no significant differences.

We conclude that expressed interests in religion are significantly different among ideological groups—a finding compatible with our use of deep religious interests as a classificatory device. One finds that those describing themselves as having any religious interests (apart from deep convictions) are much less likely to have interests in drugs.

Among ideological groups there are important differences in religious affiliation. Two categories encompass most of the students, Protestants (non-Fundamentalist) and the "no-religion" group. Students without religion fall heavily into the drug-using and left-politics-leaning ideological groups; religious students—whether Catholic, Protestant, or Jewish—fall, as one would expect, into the religious group. The differences are significant beyond .0001. The same trends occur when drug users are compared with non-users—Protestants, Catholics, and Jews all more often being non-users and the "no-religion" students, users. The differences are significant at the .001 level, but they are not significant when restricted-vs.-multiple users are contrasted to one another.

We expected that those becoming involved in drugs would move away from religion (we assumed a conventional childhood affiliation for these successful and privileged young people in School I), so that they would show more shifting of faiths than would the religious and right-wing groups. The left wing we also expected would move away from past religious sentiments as they espoused liberal-to-left causes. We were wrong. No significant differences appear in response to a question about changing religion when the ideological subgroups are compared. No significant differences appear for the drug users vs. non-users or for the restricted or multiple users, either. On the other hand, those admitting to religious changes do show shifts in expected directions; what we anticipated was that the drug users and the liberal-to-left political students would move from what we termed "strong" to "weak" religions.[1] The strong-to-weak shift is shown among drug and left-wing ideological groups (including the combined groups) compared with others, significant at .068. The same trend is shown when drug users are combined and compared with non-users, the differences significant at .07.

Although no significant differences obtain when ideological groups are compared for the congruity or homogeneity of religious faith within the home (student, mother, and father), the trend emerges when combined-drug users are compared with non-users, significant at .056. We may note clinically that the greatest homogeneity occurs among nondrug users but that more occasions occur among drug users when the student is lined up with either the father against the mother or against the combined father-mother religion. On the other hand,

---

[1] By "strong" we meant religions of dogma, faith, emotion, and doctrine; by "weak" we meant religions with more humanistic or intellectual but less compelling articles of faith; for example, Jewish, Methodist, and Catholic would be "strong" and Unitarians, Friends, and Congregationalists would be "weak." We recognize that these shifts might also be conceived in terms of upward class or professional mobility.

we do not see any trend where the drug-using student is lined up with the mother against the father as Keniston's (1967) findings might suggest. Multiple-drug users do show, on the other hand, more congruence than restricted users—not significantly so but enough to suggest that when the pattern is one of the use of socially sanctioned drugs, it may well be that the student is acting with rather than against parents (if religion can be taken as a "with" measure).

When compared, the ideological groups show significant differences (P = .016) in expressed interest in local and national politics. Religious and drug-only groups are least interested, while right-wing, right-and-religious, drug-and-left, and left-wing groups are more interested.

As one would expect from the definitions employed to create ideological groups, there are significant differences (P = .001) among students in terms of their political preferences or affiliations. Our right-wing students are conservatives, the drug-left are left, and so on. What is more striking and less expected is the lack of radical affiliation among the drug-only group, who are mostly Democrats or apolitical. All drug users combined emerge significantly (at .001) more left and the non-users either more conventional or right wing.

There is a trend, significant only at .10 for ideological groups, to differ on the congruence or homogeneity of father-mother-student on political affiliation. Religious and right-wing students describe their families more often as sharing political views; drug-using and left-wing students more often present themselves as standing opposed to the combined (congruent) parental views. Rarely are families described in which all persons differ; when so described, it is most often the drug-and-left students who do so.

When all drug users are compared with non-users, the trend becomes significant at the .002 level. We find that whole-family congruence on politics is the situation most often reported for nondrug-using students, while for drug-using ones the picture is one of the student set against the politics of mother-father. We also see the earlier trend, not significant, whereby multiple-drug users report more whole-family congruence than do restricted users. Again, we suggest that wide use of sanctioned drugs can be a with-family rather than against-family phenomenon.

We expected that drug users would report more childhood food problems (aversions, lack of appetite, and so forth) because of our anticipating that illicit-drug use is a form of deviant ingestion and, more dynamically, may imply oral preoccupations not adequately gratified by ordinary means. Unfortunately, the question was omitted from the schedule and asked, on the basis for an addendum, of only seventeen students. Ideological groups as such show no differences in such reporting, but when drug users are combined to be compared with non-users, the expected trend emerges, significant at the .067 level. Given the low N and the finding, it is clear that this inquiry area demands further exploration.

DRUG USE

We have seen that one classification is grouped according to multiple- vs. restricted-drug use based on inquiries as to experience with over-the-counter, prescription, social, and illicit drugs. It is not surprising that our groups differ on that experience; among ideological samples, the least variety of use is reported by religious-only students, left-only, and right-only students, and the greatest variety of use is reported among various drug-using students (significant at .001 level). All drug users combined, as expected, show significantly more variety of drugs employed than do non-users, significant at .001. The differences are not in the use of painkillers or sanctioned social drugs but in the prescription psychoactives and illicit-exotic substances.

Although no significant differences emerge between drug users and non-users in terms of named first source of painkillers and sanctioned social drugs (tobacco and alcohol), the two groups do differ significantly (.022) on their initial source of prescription psychoactives (stimulants—including amphetamines—sedatives, tranquilizers, antidepressants). Excluding from analysis the non-users who have not had any of these drugs, one finds among non-users of illicit-exotic drugs that parents, physicians, and the student himself (that is, he seeks out the drug on his own) are more often the first source, whereas among those who use illicit drugs, the first source of prescribed psychoactives is informal—illicit also, as they receive their drugs more often from friends, siblings, or from a variety of sources (which implies early, frequent use utilizing several sources, some of which are nonsanctioned). The implication is that users of the frankly illicit drugs also get prescription drugs in informal or illicit ways, which are geared to age-mates and are necessarily social and uncontrolled. Non-illicit users rely more heavily on authorities for their prescription drugs and use them in ways that are either controlled or private.

There is a significant relationship between a student's drug use and his family's. When total congruence scores for both use and non-use of all drugs inquired about are compared among ideological groups, one finds the greatest congruity among right-wing and religious students, the least among drug-only and drug-and-left-wing groups. The differences are significant beyond .001. The same trend appears when all drug users combined are contrasted to non-users; family congruence is higher for the non-using students, significant beyond the .001 level. What is implied is that there is a shared use of sanctioned drugs and a shared non-use of the illicit-exotic ones among non-illicit users, whereas among illicit-drug users congruence is low by virtue of their experience with illicit compounds, an experience their parents do not in any large measure share. When multiple users are compared with restricted users, we find, conversely, that there is greater family congruence among the former, significant at .056—a distribution which we have commented upon earlier.

Students offered reasons (sometimes several each) for their first use of illicit-exotic drugs. We find the following proposed as reasons by the majority of students who have used marijuana, LSD, and so on: 60 per cent say they first took an illicit-exotic drug out of curiosity or for adventure. This theme of novelty and excitement stands as the primary "motive" offered by students for their initial illicit-exotic drug behavior. Other reasons put forth less often are, for example, as follows: 25 per cent say they used such a drug because they were in a social situation where they were persuaded to try it or where the example of others using it led them to do so; 25 per cent deny they made any active decision or had any reason to try drugs and "it just happened"; 23 per cent say they took a drug on the basis of (intellectual) information describing drug effects; 15 per cent say their reason was because of personal goals of an aesthetic-sensory nature; 12 per cent for fun, kicks, or pleasure; 8 per cent because of personal goals of a religious-mystical nature; 8 per cent for self-exploration or enhanced self-perception; and 4 per cent out of rebellion against convention or the law (or parental wishes).

PARENTAL VALUES

Students were asked to describe the importance to their parents of several orientations to living: success in the world (money, prestige, possessions), being religious, caring about politics and power, understanding oneself, maintaining health and bodily strength, maintaining traditions and the status quo, adjustment in the sense of getting along with others and avoiding strife-anxiety, having a good time (drinking, eating well, socializing, pleasant leisure), and being with family and children (enjoying family life, emphasizing family over outside activities). Restricting ourselves to significant differences only, we find that parental values, as perceived and reported by the students, which emphasize success, religion, politics, traditions, and adjustment do show a discrimination among (at least some) groups beyond the .05 level. Parental values on family and good times show a discrimination at .10 or better. Specifically, political students—pure left and pure right— see their parents as emphasizing *success* (significant at .16), whereas non-users of drugs compared with users more often see their parents as valuing success—this significant at .002. Religious students describe their parents as emphasizing *religion*, while the drug-left group (and some right-wing students) say their parents do not consider religion important (significant at .001). Similarly, the drug users combined say their parents do not emphasize religion as a life orientation; non-users of drugs say their parents do, significant beyond .001. All political groups (right and left wing) see their parents as emphasizing *politics*, whereas the drug-only and pure-religious groups more often say their parents do not consider politics important, significant at .071. *Self-understanding* as a value does not emerge as a significant discriminator among any groups. *Health* as a value does not emerge as significant, although the trend is for non-users of drugs to report their parents as emphasizing it more ($P = .121$), than users; similarly, multiple-drug users more often say their parents emphasize health than do restricted-drug users, significant at .12. Emphasis on *traditions* reflects a difference among the parents (that is, as students perceive their parents), with the drug users saying their parents do not value tradition or the status quo, whereas both religious-and-right-wing students say their parents do, significant at .005. In the same way, non-users of drugs have parents who value traditions, whereas drug users do not, significant beyond .001. *Adjustment*, or getting along, is emphasized more— report the students—by parents of drug users and left-wing students than by parents of religious or right-wing students, significant at .01. Among all drug users, combined parents more often value getting along in contrast to non-users, significant beyond .001. *Having a good time* is not an important item, although religious students, in contrast to all others, more often say this is not valued by their parents, significant at .10. Emphasis on the *family* is said more often by nondrug users to characterize their parents than by users, significant at .068; similarly, multiple-drug users say their parents emphasize family more than restricted users, significant at .09.

We derive from these student views the conclusion that students do, in fact, see their parents as valuing general themes that are akin to the themes and ideologies which they themselves embrace. Going one step further, we presume that these differences are real, that their parents do differ, and that these differences are such that children do grow up in families whose orientations strongly influence what they as students come to value. Further, even when students see themselves as independent from or opposed to their parents—as we saw in earlier chapters is the case with drug-using and left-wing students—those differences must occur within rather narrow ideological limits, although differences as such may well reflect interpersonal (familial) conflict or distress. Consider, for example, how much of what constitutes the apparent values of extreme drug users—reduced emphasis on work, change-oriented status quo denying politics, irreligiousness, being distant from family, and getting along with others (the love ethic) are derived directly from parental values, even though perhaps expressed more extremely by committed drug users. We would also expect that the pleasure theme would more often characterize parents of drug users and are surprised it does not. As for the health theme, it is consistent that multiple-drug users do have parents emphasizing it more —an orientation compatible with the greater use of prescription drugs.

As for the other groups, there are no incompatibilities in the ideology of the religious or right-wing students compared with those of their parents—which they report to be much like their own. The pure left-wing students are too small a group to allow much inference; that their parents may emphasize success, politics, and getting along (we would stretch this to embrace a theme of social harmony and not tradition or religion) is a phenomenon at least compatible with the ambitious (and successful) radicalism of the left-wing leaders who comprise our sample.

We used a list of twenty specific issues, much like the items on issues in the student survey, and asked students to rate their parents individually and themselves as pro or con (for example, pacifism, socialism, segregation, getting out of Vietnam, using LSD, and so on).

What we call here "identification" was termed "family homogeneity" in earlier chapters; what we called "opposition" earlier we shall now term "independence." The former is simply the sum of issue agreements among student and parents and the latter issue, disagreements between the student and the combined parental position.

High scores, indicative of family homogeneity on issues and of inferred identification of student with parents, occur among right-wing, right-religious, and religious-and-left-wing students. The lower scores are found among drug users, including one subgroup of the drug-left group. The differences are significant at the .037 level. When drug users are combined and compared with all non-users, the same trend emerges; users report less family homogeneity and, we infer, less adequate identification with parents than do non-users, significant at .03.

Independence, inferred from a large number of issues on which the student says he differs from or is opposed to the combined position of both parents, does not differ significantly when all ideological groups are examined but does discriminate between drug users as such when compared with non-users. Drug users are more independent (or oppositional) than non-users, significant at .03.

WAYS OF LIFE

We asked students about crises, troubles, or sorrows they had experienced which had been a major influence on their lives. These were coded as to kind of crises, severity, and age at time of occurrence and were then compared group with group. Ideological groups, we find, do not differ among themselves, significantly, only on the frequency with which crises—any kind of crises—are reported; however, drug users when combined and compared with non-users do differ on the frequency of reporting family-relationship crises, with drug users more often perceiving family crises as having influenced their lives (significant at .042). Trends toward differences occur among ideological groups in regard to crises with age-mates (friends, lovers, spouses), significant at .078 (with left-wing and religious students reporting more).

Another question asked about disillusionments as such. A trend toward differences exists in the extent to which important *interpersonal* disillusionments are reported among ideological groups, right-wing students being those with fewest and drug users the most—significant at .07. Drug users combined and compared with non-users show the same trend; more students who have never been seriously disillusioned with other people are nondrug users, significant at .094. There is also a trend for ideological groups to differ (significant at .097) in the reporting of disillusionments with abstract ideals—including the law and their faiths—the left-wing-and-the-drug-plus-religion group reporting proportionately more idealistic disillusionments.

Students were asked about revelations, or other reorganizing experiences, which brought new solutions, joy, or understanding to their lives. Important differences show up among ideological groups, among whose members the majority report some kind of revelation or wonderfully reorganizing experience. Drug-induced revelations are reported by most of the drug users and by none of the pure-political students and only one pure-religious student. On the other hand, nondrug revelations are described by most of the pure-left students, most religious students, most drug-plus-left students, and half of the right-wing ones, as well. The overall differences are significant beyond .001. The same degree of significance obtains when drug users are compared with non-users—drug students reporting a preponderance of drug-induced revelations and non-users reporting a preponderance of other types of joyful or problem-solving reorganizing experiences. When the focus is on religious-mystical revelations, particularly significant differences among ideological groups emerge (.016), with religious students, left-wing ones, and right-religious students highest; however, drug-only users are low in such reporting. Sensory-induced revelations (sunsets, sex, music, and so on) also show differences by ideological group (significant overall at .035) and are most commonly described among the drug-plus-left and the drug-plus-religion groups. Drug users when compared with non-users show a significantly greater number of reports of sensory-induced, nondrug revelations, significant at the .011 level.

Ideological groups differ significantly (beyond the .001 level) on the expression of dissatisfaction with school. Proportionately high satisfaction is found among religious and right-wing students and proportionately low satisfaction among drug users and left-wing students. Drug users combined and compared with non-users also show significant differences (.019 level) in the same direction.

Students were asked about the extent to which they were now certain about their life and career goals and also whether or not their parents were in sympathy with these. We find that ideological groups differ significantly overall (.019 level) in respect to these. Among pure-right, pure-left, and religious groups, goals are clear and parents approve; among drug users and the drug-plus-left group, goals are much less clear *and* parents are perceived as disapproving. When all drug users are compared with non-users, the same trends are seen of uncertainty and perceived parental disapproval of the present status or the future plans among drug users, significant at .02.

Students were asked whether there were persons whom they would really want to be like—an admired model for themselves to become. Again, we find that significant differences emerge among ideological groups (at .016). Left-wing and drug groups least often describe another person as their model: the religious and right-wing groups most often did so. When all drug users are compared with all others, the same trend, albeit attenuated, emerges (significant at .099). When the models were identified and coded by us by type of occupation and by intimacy (known persons vs. distant or unknown persons), significant overall differences also obtain, although that statistic continues to reflect the high number of drug users and left-wing students without any model or idealized persons. We do see that the pure-left group chooses no personal models—that is, members do not want to be like anybody they actually know but, rather, select political or artistic people. Religious students emphasize persons known to them and, in addition, philosophers or religious figures. Drug users when they do have models usually select distant ones, often artists but occasionally philosophers, politicians, and the like. Right-wing students, like the pure-left ones, emphasize political figures when their idealized person is not someone they know. The kind of model is not found to be significant when drug users as a group are compared with non-users.

Students were asked to nominate five great persons living in the world today. Although analysis of replies for hero-rejection (that is, "There are no great men") and for distant-vs.-known persons shows no overall significant (level is .114) difference among ideological groups, the drug-only group has the highest proportion of hero-rejecting answers. When those nominating heroes are classified by type of hero chosen, significant differences emerge. Those nominating avant-garde artists, for example (such as James Baldwin, Joan Baez, and so on), select them at different rates (significant at .031) with drug-only users high and others low; the same trend appears when all users are combined to contrast to non-users, significant at the .027 level.

Here, too, multiple-drug users choose more avant-garde artists than restricted-drug users, significant at .034 level. The choice of other artists (traditional or modern but not avant-garde—for example, Steinbeck and Hesse) also differs significantly among ideological groups (at .028 level) with drug users and the left high on selecting them as heroes and religious and right-wing students less often nominating them. When drug users are combined, there is a significantly greater nomination by them of artists—at .003 level—than by nondrug users. Heroes with change-oriented ideologies (intellectuals but not politicians, such as Alan Watts, Leary, Fromm, and Sartre) are also nominated at significantly different rates (.002 level) by the ideological groups. The drug-plus-left group has the highest rate of such nominees; the drug-only group is also high; pure-right and pure-left political students are low. When drug users are compared with non-users, the same trend obtains, the level of significance being beyond .001. Heroes in positions of legitimized power (Mao, De Gaulle, Castro, Churchill, and so on) are differentially nominated (significant at .057 level), right and left political students nominating them at high rates and the drug-only students at lower rates. Drug users compared with non-users show the same trend, significant at .002. The choice of insurgent political leaders (power not legitimized) also varies significantly (.021 level); the drug-plus-left group most often chooses them, as does the pure left and, following in rank, the religious students. Drug-only students and the right wing do not choose heroes such as Che Guevara, Trotsky, Martin Luther King, and Gandhi (here, students clearly do not confine themselves to the living). In this comparison, drug users do not differ from non-users. Apolitical religious leaders (Tillich, the Pope, Billy Graham, Buber, and so on) are also chosen at different rates (significant at .01) with religious students doing so often and drug users doing so rarely—a trend repeated when drug users are compared with non-users (significant at .001).

PRINCIPLES REGARDING DRUGS

The same question asked in the general survey was asked of these ideologically select students. Differences in the valences of principles guiding conduct in regard to illicit drugs emerge as significant among groups beyond the .001 level. An all-negative approach is most often espoused by right-wing and religious students, followed in rank by the pure-left, whereas drug users present either an all-positive approach or a negative-positive mix. The same trend is seen, significant beyond .001, when drug users are compared with non-users. Specific differences occur—at levels of significance beyond .05—when drug users are compared with others in respect to the risk of physical harm they feel drugs may offer, the effect of drugs on the student's social status, social values, or conceptions of appropriate behavior, the presence of personal motives or desires for pleasure, and the extent to which there is no regard for rules. It may be as important to note principles which do not differentiate drug users from non-users here; these include expressed concerns of morality, worries of undesirable changes in self, risk of change in social relations, attitudes of friends, and the views of authorities—including laws themselves. Thus, the drug-resistant group, essentially, may have either fears of physical damage or an absence of personal interest in drug experiences including drug-induced euphoria, or may judge drugs as socially inappropriate. Morals and laws are not admitted, even among the religious and right-wing students (all of whom may conceive of themselves as "sophisticates" at School I), as deterrents to using marijuana and LSD.

Students were asked whether they had always had pretty much the same views on drugs, whether there had been a slow evolution in their ideas, or whether there had been some sudden shift, insight, or a crisis in belief which had led to a new and different position on drug taking. We find that differences in response characterize the ideological groups, their overall significance being beyond the .001 level. Right-wing students unanimously and most religious and pure-left students say they have not changed their views at any time; those religious students indicating a shift say it has been gradual. Only in the drug-only and drug-plus-left groups are there any number reporting sudden shifts in belief. In these groups, the majority report an evolution of views. When drug users are combined and compared with non-users, the same trend, significant beyond .001, occurs. We find that about four fifths of the users report a shift, one third of this latter group saying it has been sudden; on the other hand, among all non-users less than a fourth have changed their views at all.

Items similar to those in the general survey inquired as to which groups students thought were most dangerous in the country today. Among ideological groups overall significant differences in nominations occur. Those holding power (the Establishment) are nominated as enemies most often by the left-and-drug-using students, never by the pure right, and rarely by religious students (significant at .005 level). The same trend appears when drug users are compared with non-users, significant at .007 level. The left wing nominated as an enemy also differentiates the groups, significant overall at .001. The right-wing and religious students nominate the left as the menace; the left-wing and drug users do not. Drug users combined and compared with non-users show the same trend, significant at .001 level. Neither the middle-of-the-roaders nor the right wing as enemy achieve significance in different rates of nomination. This is because middle-of-the-roaders are mostly disregarded, whereas right wingers are nominated by some right-wing-and-religious students as dangerous.

As expected, drug users report significantly (at .009 level) that more of their friends are also drug users than do the non-users. All but 7 per cent of non-users deny any involvement in groups with drug interests as such and only one person says most of his friends are in such groups. In contrast, 86 per cent of the users say some or most of their friends are involved in drug-interested groups; 57 per cent of all users say most of their friends are in such groups.

Ideological groups differ significantly (.001 level) on reported membership in formal organizations. Only pure-drug students hold no memberships in formal clubs, associations, teams, and so forth; in contrast, right-wing students are involved with the largest number of clubs, while left students and religious students are also active. When drug users are combined and contrasted to all other students, the difference in organizational activity is significant beyond the .001 level.

The same list of thirteen groups or classes employed in the general survey to inquire about insider-outsider feelings was used here. We shall indicate only a few specific differences occurring and then consider total scores. For example, drug users more often report (significant at .056) feeling as outsiders with their own families and, at School I, in relationship to the student body (significant at .018). Overall, on the thirteen groups, drug users compared with others describe themselves as outsiders more often than non-users; specifically, more than half of the users feel outside of three or more groups; more than half of the non-users feel outside of two or fewer groups. The same score reveals differences among ideological groups, significant beyond .001. Noteworthy is the fact that the pure-religious and the religious-plus-right-wing students most often feel outside of none of the groups. Regarding a few other items, one finds, amusingly, that most religious students and many right wingers feel "in" with the campus hipsters or swingers, and all of these say they are "in" with the "student revolt" as well. Ironically, the drug users more often feel outside of the campus hipster group (swingers, "heads"). Most students feel "out" of the university power structure, but the feeling is more common among the left and drug segments; the same is true in regard to feeling "in" or "out" with the people who hold power in the country. (Worthy of special note and further irony is that during the time of a Democratic President [Johnson] more right wingers—and, to a lesser degree, religious students also—felt "in" among the national power holders than any other student group.) As far as "being an American" goes, this is something that most drug and left students feel on the outs about; the right-wing and religious students feel strongly "in." All of these items are drawn from tables where overall significance of differences among ideological groups are beyond the .05 level.

DIFFERENCES NOT OCCURRING

Age. Had our sample been like the random survey sample, we would have expected that drug users would be in the older group. We find, however, that over three fourths of this special sample are age twenty and over, which means that we have selected older students. Even so, the trend is in the expected direction; the right-wing and religious students are youngest, having median ages at eighteen and nineteen, whereas the drug-use-only group has a median age of twenty-one. Members of the pure-left wing are oldest and have a median age of twenty-four and above. The age differences are significant only at the .158 level. However, when drug users are compared with non-users, significance is achieved at the .074 level. One would note that the year in school is a more powerful factor than age in contributing to ideological position; this is a trend noticeable in the survey data as well and suggests that drug and left-wing ideologies especially develop with students' exposure to university life—or perhaps become visible as leaders in these groups develop. We have also seen earlier, in the survey data, that age and year in school have an effect on the marijuana group in that use begins to diminish as students get older.

Sex. The distribution of the eighty-four men and twenty-one women in our sample among the nine ideological groups plus the "controls" demonstrates no significant difference. This ratio of 4:1 males to females compares with the ratio in School I of 8,962 males to 2,596 females. It appears that our nomination and selection procedures did encompass more men as well as more older students. This is not surprising if nomination as an outstanding and ideologically committed student is seen to rest upon visibility, recognition on campus, and election to formal office or informal leadership—all of which probably rest upon sex, age, and school-year characteristics.

Father's occupation. It will be recalled from Chapter Two that School I has the wealthiest students. It is no surprise, then, that 75 per cent of the sample have fathers in executive or professional positions. Given this clustering in one occupation and income stratum, it is not surprising, either, that no significant differences emerge among ideological or drug-use groups when fathers are classified by occupation.

Parents alive. Both parents are alive in the case of 89 per cent of the sample. No significant differences obtain in the distribution of students with one or both parents dead.

Housing mobility. In the survey sample, housing mobility more often characterized drug users and their families. In our sample, one third of the students have lived in six houses or more by the time of high school graduation. There is no significant difference in the distribution of housing mobility by ideology or by drug-use status except that multiple-drug users have tended to move more than restricted users, significant at the .09 level.

School politics. There are no significant differences among subsamples in their interest in school politics.

Medical problems. We expected that drug users would differ in the kinds of medical problems they reported in a brief medical-life history; we also expected them to report more psychosomatic or "functional" disorders and to have medical problems at an earlier age. Generally, we expected them to report more illness. We find the data do not bear us out.

Age of onset of legitimate-drug use. We expected drug users to begin use of sanctioned drugs earlier, and in a life history we asked them for age of first use of medically and socially approved substances. We find no significant differences emerge.

Crises. We expected drug users and left wingers to be more sensitive to a variety of life crises and not only to report more of these but to report them in such a way that interviewers would rate them as more severe crises compared with those of other groups. Our data show that, except for the family crises which do emerge as expected, the groups do not differ in their reporting of their own health, health of others, or money and self-development crises. What is implied is that drug users at least do not see themselves as experiencing more trauma or setbacks in life—except within their families—than do other students.

Disillusionment. We expected drug users to report a wider variety of disillusioning experiences. Data show that interpersonal disillusionments do characterize the drug group and disillusionments in ideals, the left wing; nevertheless, these are not dramatic, and a variety of other coded kinds of disillusionment do not emerge. This finding supports the crisis data above in suggesting that drug users do not see themselves as suffering a variety of trauma but that they do feel they have suffered interpersonal—and especially family—trauma.

Hopes regarding goal achievement and changing the world. Unlike the survey or fraternity-house samples, the experimental samples of students here do not differ in their optimism or pessimism about life-goal achievements or their wishes to change the world. The direction is as expected, with drug users more pessimistic (level of probability .179) and less interested in changing the world (probability level .181).

Life expectations. Asked the same question as the survey sample about whether they found their present life better, worse, or the same as they had expected it, students followed the trend as predicted. Drug users more often say it is worse—but it is not significant at the .05 level (significant only at .109 level).

School performance. The survey findings indicated that illicit-drug users, for the most part, did not differ in grade-point averages from other students. We asked this sample not about grade points but about their being on the dean's list or having an academic scholarship; results indicate we have no differences to report. We also asked them about troubles in getting down to studying; again, we have no differences to report. Only on one variable is there a trend; drug users do say they find it harder to get their work in on time (significant at .09 level) compared with non-users. We believe that this report is linked to the lack of interest in conventional modes of achievement as exemplified in the high past and planned drop-out rates shown in the survey samples, along with the absence of clear plans as reported earlier in this chapter for the drug-using group. What emerges strongly from all the data so far is that students who use drugs, including committed users in school at the time of inquiry, do not perform less well on any academic measure applied. Illicit-drug users as such are neither better nor worse students than their peers. The implication is that drug use does not interfere with day-to-day academic performance. We have seen that such drug use is correlated with dropping-out as such and with dissatisfaction, but these are clearly not a consequence of intellectual incompetence. This is not to say that drugs may not, during an acute phase, interfere with studying; we have seen from the analysis of bad outcomes (Chapter Nine) that this may well occur, but legitimate drugs, as well as illicit ones, can contribute to functioning difficulties as part of either toxic or emotional reactions. Given the fact that some of the students in the survey panel and experimental samples have been using illicit drugs often and over time, we also conclude that no evidence exists for probable damage to intellectual functioning over a several-year period, at least among those students who stay in school.

CHANGES IN RELIGION AND POLITICS

It will be recalled that when asked about drug beliefs, drug users for the most part said they had undergone shifts in their beliefs about drug use, while others had not. Those differences were significant. Now, considering questions about changes in religion and politics, we find no significant differences exist among groups in the rate reporting such shifts. With regard to religion, about 30 per cent have changed religion (only 5 per cent of them moving from weak to strong religions). With reference to shifts in political ideology, 39 per cent of the sample report changes. Of these, 36 per cent of the total sample say they have moved in a liberal or left direction. About half of the students who are now left wing (and keep in mind our sample is comprised of committed left-wing students) are among those reporting such shifts. We conclude that the majority of our sample are now ideologically in the same place they started with regard to religion and politics, that original position presumably being in the bosom of each of their family's beliefs. An important minority, about one third, say they have shifted in important ways; when we examine these, we find that nearly all shifts are in a liberalizing direction—a direction which is quite predictable given the presumed intent of a university to open minds to new ideas and, in addition, School I's reputation for a liberal faculty. Thus, we propose that about 95 per cent of the student's broad ideological position is accounted for by family beliefs and being in a liberal university. The intensity of the shifts that do occur—that is, to left-wing views presumably beyond most faculty and parents' views, as well—is yet to be accounted for, although when we consider the student revolt, it is obviously "part of our times," whatever that phrase may imply. We think that the extremity component is not only culturally induced but individually as well.

In any event, what is rare in our sample is a reversal in any belief system in religion or politics—"reversal" being defined as moving into a dogma opposed by family and university surround. Just as Rokeach (1968) points out, when religious "conversions" occur, they are usually only one-step ones to the religion next door—that is, from Episcopal to Catholic, Congregational to Unitarian, and so on. When more marked conversions do take place, they are likely to be in response to very strong interpersonal pressures, as, for example, when marrying into a different faith or shifting into or becoming a member of a new class group and then changing religion to match the new surroundings. The drug changes, on the other hand, which appear to be more dramatic insofar as they are limited to drug users and presumably do not reflect official parental or university positions, may be of a different order. For the majority of users, the shifts are gradual; as we inspect data from Chapter Sixteen, we see how these are in part responses to the views and use habits of peers and leaders in residential units, and as we look over the life themes said by students to be important to their parents, we see that these are also compatible with the emergence of a drug ethic. Furthermore, from the studies of the New Left, described in Chapter One, and our own survey observations on the high economic status—and implied high educational level with its correlated liberalism—of drug-using students, we conclude that parents of drug users are more liberal than those of non-users. There is also the minor observation from the examination of drug histories that for almost all drugs the parents of users are more likely themselves to be users, although in the case of the illicit drugs such parental use is unusual. What these observations imply is that the general drug-use orientation (primarily for licit drugs) and the liberal atmosphere of such homes, with their emphasis on adjustment and disregard of tradition, are settings in which the development of children who come to be illicit-drug experimenters or users occurs. In the case of drugs, the development is more extreme than that of the parents, and we believe that this exaggeration over the family and university ethic rests on additional factors in the individual and his group. Some of those factors, implied by both the survey data and the comparison data of this chapter, may include the following: feelings of apartness from important groups; general dissatisfaction; pessimism about conventional means and ends; lack of involvement in countervailing belief systems such as traditional religion; exposure to peer groups already using drugs; personal interest in self-pleasures through drugs; the presence of curiosity and other self-centering goals; particular opposition to parental stands and the presence of unresolved crises in family relationships; and the actual effects of drugs which previous to the initial experimentation have been described as pleasurable, useful, and reorganizing experiences. Other specific test-derived inferences about drug-user personalities as also playing a role will be explored in the next chapter.

We conclude, to this point, that student drug use insofar as it reflects an ideology develops along lines similar to political or religious beliefs in that it derives from the values and practices in the home, is modified by contact with a liberal university atmosphere, and is solidified—or comes to flower—in the presence of peers in school. The committed drug user differs in his development of a drug-linked ideology in that, unlike the right or religious students, he selects a route not compatible with the conventions of the larger society and, unlike the left, his route emphasizes positive personal ends rather than social goals and experiences which can be achieved by pharmacological agents. The engaged student drug user also differs from other "pure" ideological students in that, more than they, he feels opposition or apartness from his parents and most of his peers. Furthermore, there are the personal factors of pessimism, dissatisfaction, childhood food problems, childhood use of illness for gratification, lack of close ties to others, and so on, which imply distress or, at least, frustration or disappointment and which are reflected in higher prevalence among the drug users. Again, there is implicit the belief that distress can be alleviated by psychoactive drugs, both licit and illicit ones. We also suggest that the association between the left and drug ideology is important and functional and that both ideologies, in their expressed idealism, change-orientation, antiauthority sentiments, and emphasis on personal freedom—if not ascendancy, reflect not only parental influence and personal predilections but also a responsiveness to actual forces within the society which make life painful and disappointing to young and old.

SUMMARY

In this chapter we have compared the reports of students—as gathered from an intensive interview—who engage in different ways of life. These life styles which we have chosen to call ideologies include left-wing, right-wing, religious, and drug-use commitments. The students chosen to represent these ideologies were nominated by their peers in School I as representing intense and active involvement along each of these lines. We found that exclusive (or single-minded or "pure") involvements were hard to find, for there was often an overlap between drug use and left-wing commitments. Nevertheless, some exclusively left-wing students could be found just as could many exclusively drug-using students. The exclusive drug users tend to be apolitical and inactive, whereas the left can be like the exclusive right, firmly opposed to drug use and committed to political action only. (The illicit, drug-using radical left commented to us that heavy involvement in drug use is irrelevant to their goals; they view heavy drug users as unable to perform effectively in radical politics because of their casual behavior, the presumed drug effects, and the risk of losing key personnel through arrests.)

On most of the items of inquiry, based on our original expectations about differences among the ideological groups and between drug users and non-users, findings are significant in the expected directions. In almost every case, these findings are compatible with those of the survey, panel, and fraternity samples as well. For example, drug users tend to be upperclassmen, arts-humanities or social-science majors, irreligious, and opposed to parents on many specific issues, including politics and religion. Drug users unlike non-users report more childhood food problems, more family crises, more interpersonal disillusionment, a greater variety of use of legitimate drugs—particularly the prescribed psychoactive drugs—and the use of informal-illicit sources to obtain these latter drugs. Among drug users there is least similarity of drug-use patterns with parents because these students engage in illicit use whereas most of the parents do not. The illicit users are guided by beliefs in the benevolence of illicit drugs and report as initial motivations curiosity and adventure seeking or the response to social pressures. Non-users, on the other hand, worry about physical damage, believe illicit use is inappropriate for themselves, and report an absence of interest in drug-induced euphoria or drug-induced self-focused experiences and effects. Importantly, few students either among users or non-users say they do not use illicit drugs because of reasons of morality, illegality, or the disapproval of authorities—whether parental, scientific, or what-have-you.

Students, in general, follow directly in their parents' footsteps or, when shifting away from parental ideologies, do so in the liberalizing direction offered by the university atmosphere and in response to the presence of peers who have already arrived at liberal positions. Drug users most often have friends who are also drug users. The drug-only user is unlike religious and politically committed students in that he is likely to have changed his views on drugs, although these changes are themselves compatible with the inferred liberality of his parents, their unconventionality and lack of political interest, and their use of sanctioned drugs. In the case of the committed drug-only user, something more is added that is associated with his shifts in beliefs about the use of illicit drugs. This "something more" is independence of, opposition to, or rebellion against parents and also emotional distance from most peers, as well as high personal dissatisfaction, pessimism, and so on. With regard to the selection of life models and ideological heroes, the drug-only users tend to have no models; in fact, they tend to reject heroes and, when choosing, nominate distant rather than personally known individuals. One also infers the importance of drug effects as such for drug users, those in the nature of providing not only pleasure but life-reorganizing experiences (revelations).

The religious, right-wing, and pure-left-wing students also differ in many ways from drug users, although the right-wing and religious students are often similar in reporting family cohesiveness, high satisfactions, and the like. Right wing and left wing are similar in their emphasis on political areas—although not in content—including the derivation of their ideologies from their families. As to particular characteristics of each of these groups compared with others, we need reiterate only the important feature that very few of the students in any group show marked shifts over their lifetimes toward beliefs that are in opposition to family or school settings, even though many do report important experiences that they believe have changed their lives. Sharp "conversions" and dramatic rebellion are the exception even among the committed drug users.

In all of this, however, we must remember that our committed drug users of 1966 were but a small group on campus. By now, things have changed and one must expect that the followers—and the sample contained many of the early leaders—by their very number will be less dramatic in their engagements and less intense in their differences from those who remain non-users or simply curious or derring-do experimenters.

Psychological
Tests

Richard H. Blum

XIV

This chapter continues the comparison of the ideological groups described in the previous chapter and of all drug users compared with non-users. We are abandoning comparisons of multiple-drug users with restricted-drug users, since that variable has been shown to relate primarily to family factors associated with prescription-drug use and to be correlated with illicit-drug use; otherwise, it sheds little light. Presented in this chapter are the results of the following psychological tests: the Allport-Vernon Scale of Values, Rokeach Dogmatism Scale, Ås Regressive Experience Scale, McClosky's Alienation Scale, Myers-Briggs Type Indicator, California Psychological Inventory, and Strong Vocational Interest Scale. We shall present significant differences (.05 or better) on subscales. Differences significant between the .05 and .10 level will also be presented as trend data.

A serious problem in our study was that a number of students did not complete their psychological tests; for example, 20 per cent did not complete the Rokeach, Myers-Briggs, and other relatively short and possibly amusing scales; the CPI, which is long, was not returned by 26 per cent. Those who failed to return the tests were more often drug users—for example, on the CPI, 33 per cent of all drug users failed to complete the tests compared with 14 per cent for the non-users. That high rate of noncompletion was quite in accord with the drug-using students' remarks (see previous chapter) about finding it difficult to get work in on time, their feelings of the pointlessness of much conventional academic and research activity, and their lack of interest in pleasing adults in positions of authority. A number of drug users told us—as we sought to cajole them into completion—that tests bored them and they refused to go through the exercise. Unfortunately for the study, among those who did not complete the tests were the most extreme drug users, measured either by drug histories, ideological intensity, or campus visibility. Our clinical impression was that the nonresponders were just the ones likely to score high on personality distress. This failure to complete tests, coupled with the reduction in N and especially in the drug-only and drug-plus-left groups, reduced the likelihood of significant differences being achieved.

Subscales on the *Allport-Vernon Scale of Values* test measure the interests and values of persons along theoretical, economic, aesthetic, social, political, and religious lines. Each student's score on each subscale was ranked so that values distributed by rank could be compared. The ideological groups differ among themselves (.013 level) on the aesthetic scale. Religious students most often receive their lowest scores on the aesthetic subscale, thus giving this the lowest ranking among the six subscales. Right-wing students have aesthetic values mid-way in rank, whereas the drug-only, pure-left, and drug-plus-left-wing groups have the majority of their members first ranked on aesthetic values. When drug users are compared with non-users, the same cluster of first-ranked aesthetic scores occurs among the former while among the latter much less emphasis is placed on aesthetic values, the difference being significant beyond the .001 level.

On political values the ideological groups differ among themselves, significant at the .016 level. Here, the concentration of first-rank scores are among right-wing students, with most other students receiving scores leading to a mid-way rank on political values; note, too, that the left-wing students are, for the most part, in that middle range. When drug users are compared with non-users, it is the non-users who more often are high ranked on political values, that difference being significant at the .02 level.

Religious values differ among ideological groups, being significant at the .002 level. As expected, the religious students most often receive scores which lead to religious values being ranked first for them; religious values of the right-wing students and drug users are ranked very low. Drug users compared with non-users are found to differ on the primacy of religious values (significant at .017), with non-users giving primacy to religious values more often.

The *Rokeach Dogmatism Scale,* which is related to the F Scale for measuring authoritarianism, describes dogmatism or closed-mindedness and is related to rigidity in thinking and perceiving the world (Rokeach, 1960). There is no statistically significant difference among ideological groups on score distribution, although the trend is for the greatest number of high dogmatism scores (140 and over) to be concentrated among the right-wing and the religious students. When all drug users combined are compared with non-users, differences significant at the .015 level emerge with high dogmatism more often occurring among the non-users.

The *Ås Regressive Experience Scale* is called the Experience Inquiry. This test has been shown by McGlothlin to be associated with interest in LSD. It measures regressive-mystical experiences (Fitzgerald, 1966) and is correlated with the ability to be hypnotized (Ås, 1963). Ideological groups differ on this scale, significant at the .03 level. The drug-only users have the highest scores on this test with the lowest scores being concentrated among religious and right-wing students. The left-wing-plus-drug group also has high scores. When all drug users are combined with non-users, the differences are significant beyond .001 with high regressive-experience scores being concentrated among drug users and low scores among non-users.

McClosky and Schaar (1965) have presented findings suggesting that their "anomie" scale, the *McClosky's Alienation Scale,* is an effective discriminator among samples of people with differing political persuasions and life experiences. We administered only the ten items of that scale (out of 500 in their global instrument), entitling it a "state-of-the-world" inquiry. No significant differences obtain among any group comparisons on this test.

McGlothlin, Cohen, and McGlothlin (1966) report finding that scales on the *Myers-Briggs Type Indicator,* a test derived from Jungian theory (Myers-Briggs, 1962), successfully distinguished among graduate students interested in taking LSD and marijuana and those not interested. On the extroversion-vs.-introversion subscale, there are no significant differences among our subgroups. On the sensing-vs.-intuition subscale, we do find differences among ideological subgroups, significant at the .01 level. Right-wing-and-religious students score low on intuition, while the drug-left group comprises the highest scorers, with the drug-only users also high scorers. When all drug users are compared with non-users, the difference is significant beyond the .001 level—again with drug users high on intuition sensing vs. intuition and non-users low (that is, high on sensing). On the thinking-vs.-feeling subscale, significant differences obtain among ideological groups (at .04 level). High scorers—those who emphasize feeling rather than thinking—are found both in the drug-only and in the pure-religious groups; the low scorers—that is, those emphasizing thinking modalities—are heavily concentrated among right-wing students. This dimension is not significant when drug users are compared with non-users (.177 level). On the judgment-vs.-perception subscale, which measures liking for structure compared with spontaneity, significant differences are found among ideological groups (at .028 level). Right-wing students emphasize judgment and prefer structure, as do religious students to a somewhat lesser extent; the drug-only and the drug-left students score high on "perception," implying the uncertain spontaneous modality. When drug users are compared with non-users, the difference is significant beyond .001.

The *California Psychological Inventory* (Gough, 1956) suffered the most from drug users' being unwilling to complete it. As noted, it was our clinical impression that those who refused were the more deviant students. An overall test of CPI sum scores shows no differences among ideological groups and only on the sociability scale, among eighteen subscales, do ideological groups differ at all—and there not markedly. When drug users are combined and compared with non-users, the results show that non-users have higher scores on socialization, significant at .002. These high scores imply honesty, sincerity, responsibility, conformity, and conscientiousness. The low-scoring drug users must, conversely, be characterized, according to the manual, as "defensive, demanding, opinionated, resentful, stubborn, headstrong, rebellious, and undependable; as being guileful and deceitful in dealing with others, and as given to excess, exhibition, and ostentation in their behavior."

Trend differences, significant between .05 and .10, are observable on the dominance subscale, with non-users being more dominant. Thus, drug users, according to the manual, are more likely to be indifferent, to avoid situations of tension and decision, and to lack self-confidence. On the other hand, there is also a trend for users to score higher on social presence, defined as clever, enthusiastic, spontaneous, active, and expressive. The contradiction in trends implies the presence of several subgroups in terms of personality constellation within ideological groups. Another trend difference is on "achievement by conformance"; here, drug users score lower. The characterization of users which follows is that they are aloof, awkward, insecure, opinionated, and easily disorganized under stress or pressures to conform; they are also pessimistic about their future careers. Non-users by implication are more cooperative, capable, organized, efficient, responsible, stable, persistent, and industrious.

The *Strong Vocational Interest Blank* test shows how closely a person's interests correspond to the interests of those in various occupations. In presenting results, we differentiate between males and females since two different forms of the test are used. On an overall sum of scores, there is a trend among male drug users to achieve mid-range scores that are indicative of rather low levels of interest as such. Among girls, the non-users score significantly higher on overall sum scores, indicating presumably greater intensity or level of job-related interests as such.

Specific occupational-interests scores found to be associated significantly with group membership are shown separately in the following table for males and females. Few significant differences can be expected among females given the N of 19.

SUMMARY AND COMMENT

A number of important differences occur among the ideological groups and between drug users and non-users on psychological tests. Even greater differences would have occurred had not many of the more extreme drug users refused to take the tests. On values measured by the Allport-Vernon Scale, one finds religious students low on aesthetics and high on religion. Left-wing students are high on aesthetics and mid-ranked on political interests. Right-wing students rank highest on political values and are low on religious ones. The combined drug users rank high on aesthetics, low on politics and power, and low on religion, with non-users the reverse. Other scales are not significant. On the Rokeach Dogmatism Scale, the highest dogmatism scores occur among right-wing and religious students and, when drug users are con-

Table 12

FOR MALES: (N 64) DIFFERENCES AMONG SUBGROUPS ON STRONG OCCUPATIONAL INTERESTS

Occupation	Sig. at Level	Ideological Groups with Similar Interests	Ideological Groups with Most Dissimilar Interests	Drug Users Vs. Non-Users: Which More Similar to Occupation	Sig. at Level
Artist	.011	Drug users, left wing	Right wing, religious	Drug users	.001
Psychologist	.027	Drug-left	Right wing	Drug users	.017
Architect	.005	Drug users, drug-left	Right wing	Drug users	.001
Physician	.034	Religious	Right wing	Non-users	.01
Psychiatrist	.021	Drug-left	Right wing	Drug users	.09
Osteopath	.005	Religious, left wing	Right wing, drug users	—	—
Engineer	.056	Religious	Right wing	—	—
Printer	.032	Religious	Right wing, drug, drug-left	—	—
Policeman	.032	Religious, right-religious	Drug users, drug-left, right wing	Non-users	.083
Business Education teacher	.003	Religious, left wing	Drug users, right wing	—	—
School superintendent	.100	Drug users, drug-left	Religious, right wing	Drug users	.019
Musician	—	—	—	Non-users	.028

Table 12—Cont.

Occupation	Sig. at Level	Ideological Groups with Similar Interests	Ideological Groups with Most Dissimilar Interests	Drug Users Vs. Non-Users: Which More Similar to Occupation	Sig. at Level
Certified public accountant and accountant	—	—	—	Non-users	.038
Purchasing agent	.038	Right wing	—	Non-users	.006
Mortician	—	—	Religious, left wing	—	—
Life-insurance salesman	.039	Drug users, drug-left, right wing	Religious	Drug users	.001
Advertising man	—	—	—	Drug users	.051
Lawyer	.051	Drug users, drug-left	Right wing	Drug users	.001

FOR FEMALES: (N 64) DIFFERENCES AMONG SUBGROUPS ON STRONG OCCUPATIONAL INTERESTS

Occupation	Sig. at Level	Ideological Groups with Similar Interests	Ideological Groups with Most Dissimilar Interests	Drug Users Vs. Non-Users: Which More Similar to Occupation	Sig. at Level
(1) Artist	—	—	—	Drug users	.031
(2) Author	—	—	—	Drug users	.031
(15) Housewife	—	—	—	Non-users	.047
(16) Elementary teacher	—	—	—	Non-users	.047

trasted to non-users, the users are significantly less dogmatic and more open-minded. On a scale of capacity for regressive experience, related to the ability to be hypnotized and possibly to mysticism, religious and right-wing students score low. Drug users score significantly higher than non-users, suggesting more "openness" to inner experience, to regression, to mystical phenomena, and to being hypnotized. On the Myers-Briggs, a Jungian typology indicator, right-wing students are low on intuition and high on sensing, low on feeling and high on thinking, and high on judgment and low on perception. The implication of these scores is that these students are practical, rely on experience, are logical, efficient, and decisive, attend to details, require organization and structure, are impersonal, and focus on facts. The religious students score high on sensing and low on intuition, high on feeling and low on thinking, and high on judgment and low on perception. The implication is that while they are like the right-wing students in some ways—that is, they are fact oriented, attend to details and require structure—they are more sympathetic and warm, and enjoy people. They are also more adaptable. The drug-left group is high on intuition and low on sensing and high on perception and low on judgment. The implication is of depth and concentration, spontaneity, adaptability, interest in insight and complexity, of having sympathy and adaptability and, conversely, of antagonism to organization, facts, structure, and practicality. The drug-only group, those students uncontaminated by strong interests in religion or politics, score high on feeling and low on thinking, high on perception and low on judgment. They differ from the drug-left on feeling as opposed to intuition as a modality. They would be characterized as lacking discipline and perseverence, as being open-minded, easy going, and tolerant, needing to find meaning in activities, disliking the irrelevant, and vulnerable to feelings of inadequacy. When all drug users are combined and compared with non-users, the former score significantly higher on intuition and lower on sensing, as well as higher on perception and lower on judgment. Such a constellation also characterizes the drug-left group as described above. On the Myers-Briggs, no significant differences in extroversion-introversion occur.

The California Psychological Inventory discriminates significantly between drug users and non-users on only one scale and shows trends (significant between .05 and .10) on three. These combined suggest that drug users more than non-users are undependable, guileful, rebellious, and exhibitionistic; they also seek to avoid tension, can be indifferent, lack self-confidence, and are spontaneous, expressive, active, clever, aloof, insecure, pessimistic, and disorganized under stress. Nonusers—in this sample right-wing, pure-left-wing, and religious students— are more honest, conforming, efficient, responsible, and sincere. On the Strong Vocational Interest Blank, a considerable variety of occupation-related differences are observed. The drug-left males score high as psychologists, psychiatrists, architects, school superintendents, lawyers, and advertising men. The drug-only users score high as artists, architects, salesmen, lawyers, and school superintendents. The pure-left wing emerges high on business education and osteopathy; the religious students are high as physicians, osteopaths, engineers, printers, policemen, and business educators; and the right-wing students are high as insurance salesmen and morticians. When all drug users are combined and compared with non-users, the same trends are found; in addition, non-users differ significantly in having more interests akin to musicians, accountants, and purchasing agents. Among females, the users differ significantly from non-users in scoring higher as artists and authors and lower as housewives and teachers.

It is difficult to draw together all of these findings—most of which provide a compatible but complex set of descriptions—into a few words. Each reader may have his own preference for either compact or global characterizations. At any rate, our characterizations are as follows: The right wingers are solid, practical, unimaginative, closed-minded fellows interested in facts, organization, and power. They see the world impersonally and handle it mechanically. The religious students are also solid, honest, dogmatic people who, though they want things organized, have considerably more interest in people; this interest is always moral as well as friendly and warm-hearted. The drug users without other interests and the drug users who are also actively left are much the same. They are artistic, interested in insights of the mind, are tolerant, spontaneous, and have less interest in reality or convention. They are also superficially sympathetic, are unable to withstand tension, are opposed to structure or order, are flamboyant, untrustworthy, and often feel inadequate. Because they are not as well "socialized," they are more "psychopathic," just as McGlothlin *et al.* (1966) found on the MMPI. Our pure-left wingers are too rare to benefit from as many significant comparative findings; we suspect them to be aesthetically interested but quite likely unimaginative, to be honest and sincere in terms of their new creed, insensitive to human relations, and interested in ideals, power, and manipulation.

Horatio Alger's Children: Case Studies

Eva M. Blum

XV

Ihis chapter presents two composite portraits of students with quite different drug-use behavior. Both portraits are of young men attending the same university, ones with similar ethnic, religious, and socioeconomic backgrounds. One prototypical young man is Jurgen, whom we have named after James Branch Cabell's hero who drank of every cup offered, thereby tasting many a sweet draught and many a poisonous one. Enchanted, he slew monsters, delivered princesses, loved sorceresses and queens, but in the end returned home to a nagging wife and humdrum job to live happily ever after. Our student Jurgen has also tasted many draughts, mostly of the mind-altering sort, for he is a drug user and has tried cough syrup laced with codeine, airplane glue sniffed from a paper bag, marijuana and hashish, LSD, psilocybin, STP, DMT, DET, opium and barbiturates, and methamphetamine. He has used heroin as well, that quite recently, but only a few times and, as he says, almost by accident. He also smokes tobacco and drinks alcohol, the latter to excess in the past but no longer. At the moment he is devoted to marijuana but is decreasing his previously intensive use of other exotic drugs. We shall see the reasons for that shortly.

Our other portrait is of Paul, named after the apostle who preached against the pleasures of the flesh; advocate of abstinence, he was the one who said, "It is good neither to eat flesh, nor to drink wine, nor anything whereby thy brother stumbleth, or is offended, or is made weak. . . . Happy is he that condemneth not himself in that thing which he alloweth. And he that doubteth is damned if he eat, because he eateth not of faith; for whatsoever is not of faith is sin (Romans 14:21–23)." Our Paul has had a few sips of wine and a taste of beer. He does not smoke and is glad of it, for tobacco would be bad for his health and would impair his athletic prowess—a matter on which his varsity coach is firm. Furthermore, his parents do not smoke, and he likes neither the taste nor the smell of tobacco. Paul uses medicine rarely and is reluctant to take aspirin unless it is prescribed by the family physician—a rare event since he is a healthy young fellow. He considers marijuana and the exotic-illicit drugs to be "artificial" in their effects and undesirable. He has acquaintances but no close friends who use them.

As Greek peasants are wont to say, "Everything is real; everything is unreal." So it is that our Jurgen and our Paul are real and unreal. Composite portraits are not real people no matter how many true-to-life elements are blended in the painting. Yet they are real insofar as conceptions and generalizations can be so and the component parts out of which the portraits are derived do exist. In the case of Jurgen and Paul, each portrait is derived from information gathered from three to four hours of interviews with a group of students representing, within the limits we imposed of sameness of background, two extremes: the campus "heads" nominated by their student peers and the abstainers also identified and sent to us by students whom we know. The essence of the composite is blending, and so it is that the originals, Jurgen #1, Jurgen #2, Jurgen #3, and so forth, may have differed politically, one being an anarchist, another a member of the New Left, a third an independent radical, whereas our Jurgen is a compromise which resulted from our judgment of the most representative political affiliation among all the Jurgens. This was easier to do for Jurgen than for Paul, since among the abstainers we encountered a greater variety of moral stances; for example, one group was made up of individual Gospel fanatics and, simultaneously, right-wing extremists; another, strict sectarians reared in the abstinence tradition; whereas a third subgroup was not so specialized religiously or politically but was, instead, athletic, solid, and nature-loving. Rather than to try to blend from among these, we elected to create our Paul out of the latter subgroup—a group, in any event, whose members came closest in being like Jurgen in religious and socioeconomic background. As it turned out, the two groups of students who sat as models for these portraits were from very similar backgrounds indeed. Furthermore, they sometimes had the same majors and classes, sometimes were interested in the same sports, and were all alike in being bright, able, personable, healthy, wealthy, and a pleasure to come to know. Their choice of the university and its choice of them assured other similarities, for their interest in its high status, lyrical setting, and excellent facilities and amenities implied an appreciation in them of the good things in life as conventionally defined. The university's choice of them by means of rigorous selection procedures implied, in turn, qualities of leadership, outstanding academic records in high school, wide extracurricular interests, and athletic prowess.

The families of both our Jurgen and Paul are well-off. In the case of the several "original" Jurgens, the range of family income was from $50,000 to $200,000 per year; and in the case of our subgroup of Pauls, from $20,000 to $40,000. Our composite boys are both WASPs—that is, White Anglo-Saxon Protestants, all of whose parents and grandparents are—or were—native-born Americans. Each has siblings (in the subgroups never more than three). Family stability is the pattern, marred neither by divorce nor by frequent moving from place to place. All of the parents are moderates by their own lights, although Paul's are much more likely to be on the right. Both boys have been and are veering toward more liberal views, as one would expect of students attending a liberal university. Jurgen is further left than Paul, although he has traveled no more steps than Paul in his political changing, since his parents are the more liberal.

The fathers of both young men share a remarkable number of characteristics. Both came from poor but hard-working backgrounds; both struggled to achieve their present positions of income, security, and community respect—and in the case of Jurgen's parents, national fame. Both are self-made men who worked days to support school at night or, when a bit more was saved, combined work and schooling. Both are practical men who measure the world and their sons in concrete terms and who gauge others in terms of the work ethic and success, on the one hand, and the humane and Christian virtues, on the other. The fathers of Jurgen and Paul are fulfillments of the American dream; they are the embodiments of the culture hero Horatio Alger and subscribe themselves to that mythology. Paul and Jurgen are Horatio Alger's children. They understand their fathers better than the older men their sons. Both Jurgen and Paul admire and respect their fathers' character, ability, stamina, and, last but not least, their success. They appreciate their fathers' values of work, of doing everything for oneself, of honesty, of exploring all the possibilities and not taking anything for granted, and of optimism (that effort will be rewarded). Jurgen even explains his experimentation with illicit drugs in terms of his father's ideals for him—that is, his father has always taught him to do for himself, to question, and to be curious. Consequently, Jurgen is trying out quite a different type of life for himself, which includes exotic drugs, feeling that he is basically following his father's precepts to their ultimate conclusion. Jurgen and Paul both sympathize with what they describe as their fathers' dawning awareness of nihilism in sectors of the country and which they feel bound to combat. Of the same cloth as their fathers, these young men hardly regret the reserve which holds them at a distance from them; they admit that it is easier to talk to their mothers, who, unlike their fathers, are able actually to make them feel bad, who can, in turn, be made to cry, and who can be asked to give them what they would like to have. They think of their mothers as emotional, sensitive, and volatile in contrast to their well-controlled, formidable fathers. In spite of the professed warmth of feeling attributed to their mothers, neither Paul nor Jurgen can give many instances in which this has manifested itself. Demonstrativeness is clearly not part of either family's style; and if it ever has been, the sons seem to have forgotten it as quickly as possible. In their youth the mothers of both Jurgen and Paul were the fine, strong, energetic, outgoing, community leaders or college graduates one would have expected to make a suitable match for the men who were to become models of the American dream come true.

Paul and Jurgen reflect in themselves the happy outcome of the union between such vital personalities and of the advantageous family circumstances. They are good-looking chaps, well mannered, confident of themselves and their future even though both are in the midst of a transitional period, aware of inner changes and of ambiguities, but welcoming these in a mood of adventure as a widening of their horizons and the opening of doors onto sights that will be pleasing. They are athletes, achieve a good grade average although the competition is quite fierce, and they carry a heavy academic load. Their parents support them at the university (although Jurgen's parents do not approve of his drug use and therefore pay only his tuition and a basic allowance for food and essentials—by design not enough for his two motorcycles, his living outside the dormitory in a commune, and certainly not for the illicit drugs).

In one sense one can say that Jurgen stumbled into his drug career by following his elder brother's footsteps. Like him, he became an athlete and was a member of the school football team; also like his older brother, he became a discipline problem in junior high school and was picked up by the police, together with some friends, for drinking beer in a car. His parents did not discipline him harshly for his continued alcoholic binges, for apparently they had found punishment ineffective with the elder son (who did not go on to the use of exotic drugs, however). Jurgen and his friends found their fun and excitement in drinking themselves into a stupor and, on occasion, driving around in stolen cars. Jurgen also smoked to excess in company with his "elite" friends, all sons of the wealthy. His drug career gained momentum in high school, where he drank more frequently and heavily. At the same time, he gave up smoking as he made the varsity team and tried to live up to its code. This did not last for long. He became increasingly bored—though he mentions that his boredom had already started in kindergarten—but at the time he did not know how to label that discontent. The more bored he became, the more he was moved to copy his friends who were already trying pep pills, codeine cough medicine, and phenobarbital. About then it dawned on him that he (and his group) was different from the rest of the students who liked school. In conversation he does not say much about his growing awareness of alienation; he does not dwell on the rise of his sense of difference and discontent, but he does say that he was upset enough to try to "drink his problem away." That only aggravated the situation. His parents then transferred him to a private military prep school. He was able to embrace its strict code for a while until once again he became "intolerably bored" and, together with new friends, passed the time by taking phenobarbital stolen from a fellow student who had obtained the drug from his physician father. Jurgen dates his real involvement with exotic drugs from that time. It was at the military academy that he made friends with student activists (albeit covert rebels then), who smoked marijuana at their bull sessions. He was soon deeply involved. Later on, during vacation, he did not return home but instead lived with his friends in an apartment where they systematically tried all the pills and drugs any of them could obtain. He says that one of their suppliers ". . . used to motorcycle to the apartment with a shoebox. He would hold open the shoebox, which was filled with pills, and say, 'Take all you want, but don't mix the colors.' " In the fall Jurgen returned to school, where he joined his activist friends and continued to smoke marijuana heavily but intermittently. He was then seventeen. To combat the boredom of dormitory life, he "buried himself in literature." This failed and he returned to marijuana. He contends that he and his friends managed to "function quite well while stoned" (on from two to six "joints" a day); but, nevertheless, they were discovered. A few were expelled; the rest were disciplined. Jurgen was put on probation and was allowed to graduate at the end of the year. He spent the first week after graduation camping with his friends in the woods near home, smoking a mixture of marijuana and cocaine most of the time, and trying out LSD. LSD produced a "tremendous revelation" which started him on his current adventure with oriental philosophy and existentialism. The rest of the summer he spent in communal living with a group of about twenty to twenty-five young men and women, all of them constantly "high on acid." (He states they "dropped acid every two or three days.") For a week they tried heroin. They took methedrine ("speed"), used "pot" constantly, and went to shows and jazz concerts "stoned out of their minds," giving drugs to the doormen to get in free. Jurgen and his friends then began dealing in illicit drugs. His income from peddling reached $1,000 one month. When he came to the university in the fall, he once again joined the activist students, with whom he continued to smoke marijuana socially. He also pursued his LSD interests and hopes to try mescaline soon. The other mind-altering drugs have palled on him as these are not in vogue at the university. When he is in the mood for them, he goes to a nearby campus where he finds friends with whom to "shoot speed, heroin, and Demerol." Paradoxically, he does not find these to his taste. His experiences with LSD continue to stimulate interest in matters transcendental and have led him to the writings of oriental mystics and to try out Yoga and Tantric meditation. He has also visited one of the local Buddhist chantresses, and found that her recital of the mantras put him into a trance state that surpassed the visions he had had under LSD. In spite of this, he has no intention of visiting her again but plans to continue his use of marijuana. He is dropping to more potent substances. He admits that he has to be cautious, because he has been arrested for narcotics possession and sale and is now out on bail. The arrest upset him so that upon release he went to his room and proceeded to take five bumper-to-bumper trips on "acid" in order to think the whole matter over. After his arrest he also had a violent scene with his father. Both parents were deeply shocked. Jurgen believes that the shock has been a good thing for their relationship. He claims that his parents now consider him more of a person in his own right, one living his own life independently from theirs. It may also be that the emotional tumult which followed the discussion about his drug use convinced Jurgen that his father, usually calm and rational, actually did care for him very much since that imperturbable fellow so lost control that he wept. Jurgen was pleased to see he had "gotten through" to his father. In the past it had been only his mother who would get upset over him. His father talked things over logically, not only with Jurgen but also with his mother; and, incidentally, he was able to bring her to tears with the invincible correctness of his argumentation. Ever since the arrest and explosion, Jurgen considers his relation to his parents as "groovy."

Paul, on the other hand, needs no such proofs of love. He has always been able to get his parents shouting mad. Furthermore, his father and mother were always home when he was growing up, while Jurgen's father's business required prolonged trips and his mother's charitable and committee work took her outside the home. Later, of course, Jurgen himself was sent off to private school. Even now, Jurgen is farther from home than is Paul, whose family lives close by, visits him every other week, and lends him the family car for the weekends. Paul goes home about once a month; Jurgen only for some holidays. One senses that there is a more intense attachment between Paul and his parents than there is in the case of Jurgen, even though the latter reports far less friction—with one major exception—between himself and his family.

Paul says that his father's main interest is to put his children through good colleges and to see that they have an easier life than he had when he was making his Horatio Alger climb. Jurgen's father, on the other hand, is too absorbed in business, too "tiredly energetic" to dedicate himself to his children's lives. Nevertheless, Jurgen describes an idyllic family life and a perfect family much in the same manner that he describes his friends as members of an "elite" or otherwise superior group. Jurgen's picture of himself depends very much on his belief in the excellence of his associates. There is another aspect as well: the only time that Jurgen "lost his cool" during our conversations was when he was asked to discuss family troubles. He had graciously assured us that he would talk about anything and that there were no problem areas. Yet he was mildly annoyed and politely sarcastic when we touched upon the distasteful business of his allowance from home and of how his father acted in a superior manner to his mother. Anyone talking to Jurgen must be impressed with how he shows himself and his associates in the best possible light, with his social grace, cooperativeness, capacity as a raconteur, and his charm and warmth. Given these, and what the researchers (Seeley, Sim, and Loosley, 1956) in *Crestwood Heights* consider general to upper-middle-class suburbia—namely, the formation in childhood of a salable self-image, a persona which becomes a commodity[1] for the social market place— one can readily see the reason for Jurgen's resistance whenever he is invited to discuss tensions that mar this picture.[2]

Paul makes no effort to prove how groovy his family is. For one thing, he is in the process of differentiating himself from his parents so that, by now, their personal goodness or badness is their own and no reflection on him. For another, he is not interested in what or who he is or in putting only his best foot forward. Furthermore, he really enjoys his family and has grown up in a setting where his parents were home evenings, weekends, and vacations. His father also organized the Little League and taught all the kids how to pitch, while his mother kept score; she was also the neighborhood den mother for Cub Scouts. Paul says his mother understands children because she

[1] Stein (1960) in a critique concludes that Seeley *et al.* show clearly that "Children manipulate their personalities according to the latest theories which they pick up almost as quickly as their parents. They know the importance of appearing 'well-balanced' in order to sell themselves to the primal customers, their parents, as well as to their peers and teachers (p. 214)."

[2] The importance of maintaining one's "cool" may be taken as more than noninvolvement and as a frank acceptance of a naive mental-health doctrine which values tension-free states combining with the rational-emotional void deemed necessary for the interchange of people as parts in a technological apparatus.

has always been with them so much. Jurgen's family was certainly less child centered and less cohesively organized as well, at least from a child's eye view. Yet both childhoods, to hear the reports, were equally happy. Jurgen's account is of a cloudless sky in a radiant childhood without memory of sadness, fear, or disappointment; he had a family without harsh discipline and sleep without nightmares. All Jurgen remembers, in terms of clear events, are items such as his putting on the golf course or beating his father in a game while his mother practiced tennis. He also remembers, with some pride in his mother's strength and devotion, how she used to carry him in her arms, walking him up and down for a long time when he was very small and could not settle down to sleep. Of punishment meted out, of disharmony and anger, he can call but little to a reluctant mind. On occasion, his parents talked over his minor infringements of rules; of course, later, when he engaged in more serious misdemeanors (stealing cars, drunk driving without a license, doing badly in school), his parents would attempt to control his behavior, but not harshly; and, to be sure, they did not succeed.

Paul's parents were, in his eyes, rather intolerant and overcontrolling. They did not respect his opinions, nor did they trust him very far, insisting that he be home at certain hours, inform them where he went and with whom, and tell them exactly what he had done. If he had not done his homework, his outside activities were restricted and he was not allowed to use the family car. He recalls spankings and adds, ruefully, that it was not only his father who took a hand in disciplining the children. Once, as a little tyke, he made off with a piece of candy and had to endure a long lecture from his father, which he has not yet forgotten. That was his last delinquency. He considers his childhood a happy one, full of small worms and snails to be collected and examined, with wilderness outings with his parents on weekends and summer camping trips with much fishing and hiking, swimming and sailing.

Nowadays, he finds himself in some disharmony with his family, for he tries out his newly acquired perspectives on them and finds them falling on deaf ears. Paul feels that his father has not given the burning issues of today enough consideration, that he gives only lip service to the ideals of equality and integration. However, he thinks of his father as an honorable man who acts according to his conscience. One senses that Paul does have to work rather hard at finding fault with his father's point of view since they both are rather staunch middle-of-the-roaders; yet the son is more optimistic about the possibilities of reform.

We have mentioned in passing that both Paul and Jurgen admire their fathers. Although Paul speaks of disagreements between himself and his father, his own goals have been for a long time exactly those that his father had for himself when he was a young man and dreamt of becoming a marine biologist. Paul's father was not able to realize his dreams because of his early struggles to make a living.

With Jurgen, matters may be fundamentally no different, but on the surface, at least, there does appear to be a divergence between his and his father's aspirations. Jurgen will admit that he may—a long time from now when he is old, over thirty, that is—return to the fold to become a businessman as his father would have him be. Meanwhile, his life and he himself are the diametric opposite of his parent's. Typically, he is interested in "soft-headed," subjective enterprises foreign to his father's interests: drugs, meditation, jazz music, trance states. He surprised his patriotic brother, who is serving in Vietnam, by turning in his draft card; he also participates in activist sit-ins occasionally, as the spirit or his friends move him, and goes on selected protest marches. In school he tries to take only those subjects which fit in with his immediate concerns. He can be found in classes of oriental philosophy, film making (which may become his major), and creative writing. He speaks with disdain of required courses which do not touch him in a subjective, emotional way; the current term of derogation for them is that they are "irrelevant."

Jurgen is unusually bright; studying has always been easy for him. When he applies himself, he is able to make very good grades; but subject matter outside his prevailing range of interest has always been neglected. Teachers with whom he does not have a personal relationship cannot get him to do the work. He may cut classes, arrive "stoned out of his mind" on marijuana, or if he does any work at all, he may substitute for the assignment a topic that happens to touch him personally—a discussion on why Socrates should have disobeyed unjust laws instead of allowing justice to take its own course, for example, when instead his comments should have been on the relationship between Socrates and the sophists. When Jurgen does become involved with a given subject matter, he is capable of turning out a respectable piece of work, not necessarily in the spirit in which his professors would have him go about it, but with his own, always distinctive, and sometimes even distinguished, idiosyncratic interpretation. His grades in individual courses reflect this, whereas his grade-point average, which is slightly above the norm, does not. Had Jurgen been sent to progressive schools in which the emphasis is to bring out creative and original abilities in students, centering the teaching around their own areas of interest, he would have been outstanding. As it is, his career through conventional high and prep schools and now in the university follows an up-and-down course, with so many hair's-breadth escapes among the steep precipices he skirts that one is surprised to find him still in college.

Without question he has a number of genuine intellectual interests and in the university his voyage of discovery includes philosophy, poetry, and literature. He has come to admire Hermann Hesse, Newman, Marcuse, Sartre, and Ginsburg. Closer to home, he admires a film professor, himself a fine artist, who knows how to get the best out of his most erratic students. Depending on his other professor's tolerance, Jurgen may also get a high grade for his quite unconventional essay on oriental thought. He will need all the good grades he can collect to offset the incompletes he is amassing. Another plus in Jurgen's life is that since he has come to the university, some of his poetry has been published in the school paper as well as in one of the little magazines. His English professor may include one of his short stories in a publication of student writings. In spite of all this, Jurgen is seriously considering dropping out of school, at least for a little while "to see where his nose will lead him." Perhaps he'll start on his voyage this summer and return for the fall term; perhaps, he'll stay away longer. Who knows? Meanwhile, as we have seen, he is doing well enough in the extremely competitive and demanding university he attends.

Like Jurgen, Paul is doing well, even if not brilliantly. He is a *B* student. Like Jurgen, Paul is also critical of some of his classes; however, his objections are that the subject matter is either poorly taught or is unnecessary for his career plans. Unlike Jurgen, he has chosen "hard-headed" science classes which will allow him to become a marine biologist—a career combining his enthusiasm for various swimming and crawling creatures with his enjoyment of outdoor activities. Paul was on the high school swimming team and is still in training. Exploration of the inner space, or world, does not fascinate him as it does Jurgen, who prefers the tale of *Steppenwolf* to the tale of *Seawolf*. Yet Jurgen is a good athlete too; but sports take a very secondary place in his life, far behind his search for meanings, for esthetic and sensual pleasures, and his religious and political concerns.

For both young men the past has been benign—it is true that Jurgen has skirted disaster from time to time, but so far he has escaped unscathed. It appears he will even beat the narcotics charges now against him. Let us see how the two of them tackle the business of fashioning their future lives. Paul knows exactly where he is going, what steps will lead there, and enjoys the prospects of a profession that will bring him status, respect, money, and interesting work. The hours will be arduous and the program of studies required will be hard, but as it is in line with his natural bent for science, he looks forward to it.

Jurgen enjoys the anticipation of going into the unknown, for he has no definite plans other than to let himself be carried along the stream of events wherever it takes him. Anxiety as well as pride can be detected over this ambiguous adventure, so different from the serious business of ascending the straight-and-narrow path to success his father chose, with goals firmly in view and no deviations allowed.

Perhaps Jurgen feels there is no challenge in traveling the same path, especially since it stretches out so smoothly before him. The security it offers is unbearably boring. How can there be conquest when someone else has laid the garlands of victory at one's feet? Too, that earlier victor, his father, though he may be followed, cannot be surpassed. Jurgen can never be Horatio Alger and achieve his father's national reputation, for birth prevents him from beginning at the bottom. Still, there is a way to be someone special, not by competing or by copying, but by being different. He need not follow the path, in the Christian metaphor, of active seeker but can let the river of life carry him, in the oriental metaphor. Yet, a Western child after all, he casts himself into the river, but once there looks forward to uncharted experiences, to new discoveries. In his eyes he is also a pioneer, an explorer now of inner experience and of the immediate present; he considers himself in his way as vigorous an explorer as his striving father before him, who, in his youth, also could not know where his journey would lead even though the goal itself was certain.

For Jurgen there is danger on the frontiers of the mind and psychopharmacology and in the optimistic belief that one can expand consciousness or find a chemical nirvana. The danger is that achievement may be the illusion of vanity or drug-induced euphoria. It would

not be his first illusion, for he has long been led into mischief and intoxication with only visions as guides. Even now, it is illusion which
shapes his view of his own life, for we do not believe the harmony of
his childhood. Unnoticed by him, two themes recur in his story which
sound discordant notes. One is his preoccupation with achieving for-
getfulness; the other is his fight against boredom. It is remarkable how
little Jurgen does recall; and he complains about his memory. Considerable repression must be at work when one so bright, so capable,
and so creative has so little to report of his childhood, which, after
all, was not so very long ago. Had Jurgen chosen to mislead us deliberately, he would have found it very easy to regale us with an interesting and dramatic account. We believe that he is genuinely amnesic for
most of what was significant in his past.

One of his stated aims in taking drugs is to help him *concentrate* on a single emotion or experience, to blot out all extraneous stimuli, feelings, and thoughts. Quite often he ends up stoned, totally unconscious, together with his friends. In fact, one of the few problems
which he has mentioned is the inability to *concentrate,* to shut out un-
wanted problems, seemingly irrelevant remembrances, and emotions.
His drug use, whatever else it represents, is an ally in his struggle to
keep his consciousness focused on one single content, a struggle which
entails attempts to abandon much that belongs to the past. One infers
that bygone unpleasant events and painful conflicts have indeed occurred which are better forgotten.

From the clinical point of view, not too much credence can
be given to the one-dimensional family- and self-portrait Jurgen has
conjured. We may speculate, calling to our aid the second theme which
recurs in Jurgen's life: boredom. Recall that he said that nursery school
must have been "intolerably boring" but that he did not know what
boredom was at the time. Certainly by junior high, boredom had become a recognized and unwelcome guest. The state is one in which he
"feels nothing," in which he has "lost touch with things." Boredom
happens to him when he is "doing things that mean nothing"—for
example, some of the required courses produce boredom when they
"don't mean anything to me as a person."

We mentioned that in junior high he and his friends stole cars
for a lark. As Jurgen describes it, there was more in this for him, something of a cure for his boredom, for "It was at least feeling something."
Football, too, was thrilling for the same reason; he says once again,

"It was feeling something." He looks on his riding a motorcycle in the same light, considers it to be dangerous, and therefore "forces you to be more aware, and especially when the traffic is dense, there is the thrill of danger. Interesting for a while. To maintain attention against death, one must be aware of everything. It's a kind of meditation." During meditation, he says, he is flooded with experiences and feelings. That is not boring. Nor is taking drugs boring. He explains that it is "a synthetic way of creating something to feel, like taking methedrine." Jurgen thinks that bad experiences during meditation or "bad trips" are good in the sense that "that is the way it should be." He adds, "Now the thrill of danger is transferred to realizing that everything is good and bad." By that he means his life is satisfactory when he feels the heights of pain and joy and intolerable when everything is smooth. Right now he describes his life as going extremely well and badly at the same time—it is "as it should be."

The notion of extremes of feelings is romantic; it has been beautifully described by Goethe: "Jubilant to the heavens, despondent unto death, such is the heart of one in love." Most Americans, however, seem content without this Dionysian exaltation. Why does Jurgen continue to yearn so many years for intensity of experience to the point of actually risking his health and life—not to mention his invitation of other disasters, as he walks the tightrope of being almost expelled from school and almost being sent to prison?

Jurgen has not told us much that would explain these feelings and actions. We shall therefore present our own speculation, not with a claim to truth but as a working hypothesis. What Jurgen describes as boredom would be labeled by a clinician as subacute depression, a dysphoric state which apparently began when Jurgen was quite young. He can overcome it temporarily by drugs, either by being stoned out of his mind or by the opposite effect of intense concentration. The latter state he can also achieve by meditation or by placing himself in imminent danger. He has recently obtained longer-lasting relief by the intense emotional interaction between himself and his family, as when the outburst between father and son over the drug issue took place. It appears that the cure for Jurgen's dysphoria consists in (1) forgetting and (2) emotional intensity, or more specifically, emotional intensity between himself and his father. Turning the puzzle around, we deduce that the origins of his dysphoria lie in Jurgen's relation to his father. We find further support for this notion in the two childhood memories

Jurgen has been able to dredge up. Both are early scenes depicting parental concern over him. One is of his parents waiting for many hours with him at the pediatrician's office when he had been slightly injured; the other is of his mother patiently walking up and down with baby Jurgen in her arms to help him go to sleep.

If one were to probe more deeply than we have been able to in our conversations with Jurgen, we would explore the possibility with him that he is suffering from a "loss of object cathexis," as the psycho-analysts would put it. In ordinary language, the inference would be— to be verified later by Jurgen himself through many additional talks— that, indifferent though he may seem to his mother and father and unbeknownst to himself, he actually suffers from a sense of loss in the absence of a flow of emotions between himself and his parents, espe-cially his father. He feels as though they were quasi-dead. He is mourn-ing their nonexistence, though, of course, they are alive. What Jurgen indicates is that their relationship to him has not been as alive as he needs it to be, except on those occasions when he manages to provoke them into an emotional storm.

Why is it his relationship to his father which Jurgen feels to be especially blighted? He has told us that when he was little his father was at home in the evenings and helped bring up the children. It was only later, when Jurgen was about seven or eight, that his father began to absent himself for long periods, sometimes for three months at a time. Weekends and evenings were spent on business. Is it not likely that Jurgen felt this absence as a loss? His father was absent not only physically but in other, more subtle ways as well; for in his self-con-trolled, unemotional, and rational approach to his family, it was hard for Jurgen to discern any warmth. He thought of his father as a dis-tant, uninvolved figure. In a word, he believed that his father "felt nothing" for him; and now to "feel nothing" is the very state of bore-dom Jurgen finds so "intolerable" and combats in the various ways we have described. We cease our speculation at this point as we cannot go beyond it to gain a more profound perspective, nor do we have any way of validating it from the conversations we had with Jurgen. We believe we have presented a heuristic interpretation, limited though it be, of Jurgen's past—mostly forgotten—and the present. What about the future?

We have already discussed Jurgen's predilection for charting an indeterminate course, for uncertainty, and for leaving all the doors unlocked in case a kind wind of fate would blow one of them open to some unforeseen enchantment. In a sense, the future does not exist any more than does the past. Jurgen lives not for the moment but *in* the moment. His time perspective and definition of selfhood are those of Sartre, in whose philosophy, expressed in its most extreme and allegorical form, man in his manner of dying determines whether he is a hero or a coward. So Cicero, inviting death fearlessly, thereby placed heroism as the indelible stamp upon the whole rest of his previously hesitant and vacillating conduct, according to Sartre's doctrine. With each engagement, with each new encounter, a new man emerges. Jurgen thus feels himself free to become at will what he chooses to be from instant to unconnected instant. Another illusion? Perhaps. Yet, without the conception, without the dream, the impossible will never be a reality. Jurgen is trying to create what the conventional world holds impossible: the phoenix ever renewed, all roads open.

Jurgen subscribes to the New Left, occasionally actively, but more often as a critical sympathizer. He is neither leader nor permanent cadre. He subscribes to Mao's doctrine of "permanent revolution"; and one can see, given his attention to the immediate and his faith in himself as phoenix ever renewed, that he is consistent in so doing. He is convinced of the need for constant change, rebirth, purification, not just as social policy but as a personal demand. Why? Perhaps to avoid stagnation, to avoid becoming part of that which has just been denounced, to prevent being bypassed and outdated by a younger generation following but a very few years behind, and to avoid the depression of an inescapable course which contains the trap of empty material success, that illusion which Jurgen, like Siddharta, readily diagnoses. Perhaps, too, Jurgen's absorption in the moment is a passive adaptation to the accelerating speed of social and technological change to which his generation is exposed. Life may be, after all, what his friends imply: a series of unrelated, uncontrollable, and unpredictable "happenings" arising from revolutionary transformations in his surroundings. Perhaps by making their own tiny "happenings," his friends maintain the illusion of control, but at a deeper level their choice of entertainment terms betrays their uncertainty.

In Jurgen's writings—and he has considered a career as a serious writer—one gains a feeling for his immediacy and for his attempt to dissolve the ordinary categories of space and time. Let us quote, with his permission, from the first page of a novel he has begun. It is about himself.

> . . . everything is always spinning so many times faster than life. So many recordable incidents are falling into my conscious awareness and then slipping out again just as simply as they had come. People drift in and out of their everyday noday things . . . Here I sit confusing life with my life . . . Through all the confusion our cheshire cat keeps reminding us that "We're all Mad" . . . Meanwhile back in insanity, we all try to keep our sanity, which we never seem to really want anyway . . . Constantly . . . the record player spins on our lives. Which brings me back where this whole insane thing began. Now where did it all begin . . . ?
> I never have been able to remember . . . and I'm always smoking a cigarette. Funny how cigarettes last forever . . . but they're always there. Just burning down. Things have a different meaning now. Maturity's eyes have-have-have changed my perspective. It's all your point of view. But view of what? And that brings me back. Music—it's always . . . It's always.

From a historical perspective, Jurgen's attitudes and ideals are by no means without antecedents. Although relating the new to the old is not an act of which Jurgen would approve—with him history begins with his own birth and is made only by his private experiences— we think it is of value. Jurgen's nihilism, for example, including his one-dimensional concept of time and his denial of past and future, aspires to the breaking of form which Nietzsche's Zarathustra preaches and which the German existentialist Heidegger propounds in his theme of the "negation of negation." That theme is in vogue today on many fronts, the arts especially, where artists experiment with the destruction of forms, which, instead of leading to new forms, moves on then to destroy the earlier product which itself was in the destruction of form— that is, the destruction of destruction. (See Kahler, 1968.) Jurgen as artist, as well as Jurgen as philosopher and Jurgen as experiencing man, is seeking the negation of negation. Insofar as what he is doing is derived from Nietzsche, Heidegger, and artists who have gone before, it is, ironically, a *form* of approach which he has learned. With his optimistic nihilism, Jurgen hopes to bypass the conventional categories of sensing and responding so as to overcome the limits of time and space and destroy the ordinarily perceived and logically categorized barriers between beholder and that beheld, between the adorer and

God, between madness and sanity, or reality and dream. Such aspirations are supremely individualistic, for they assume that a man, one man, because he wishes to, may do and become what other, ordinary men have tried and failed.

Kant in his lifetime dealt at length with seeking final truths through metaphysical speculations by means of the use of a mental apparatus fit for processing empirical data. He concluded that man's machinery is not adequate for the task, which is best abandoned. Later philosophers disregarded the Kantian warnings and sought superhuman understanding, as in Zarathustra, for example. Paradox enters, for these understandings are to be found in the destruction of reason itself. Jurgen feels himself to be superman during hallucinogenic experiences when he is one and the same as God, when the supreme power of feeling and understanding illuminates him. It is an experience not found through intellect or even by means of the ordinary mystical seeking—the latter depending on concentration, discipline, control, and other qualities much like work. Jurgen accepts that his metaphysical attainments depend on the negation of forms and, insofar as form impedes and rules are expressions of impeding forms, he must be anarchic. Without rules or a hierarchy of values imposed from without —whether from the wisdom of culture or simply from the power of the Establishment—he must denounce such rules. Simultaneously, faced with the fact that he shall, as a living creature, act, he must select among acts or justify those acts taken. The existential solution, which has arisen partly from a counterreaction to Kant, is accepted by Jurgen. There are no external values which dictate what to do, no "categorical imperatives." Simply to choose any "engagement" is sufficient—that is, an act justifies itself. For example, one of Sartre's heroes is approved for drowning some kittens. Jurgen also wants to be "engaged" and prides himself on belonging to the New Left, whose other members join with him in espousing the destruction of forms. There is an important difference between his activism and that of Mao, whom he admires. With Marxists the ends justify the means, whereas for Jurgen the means are the ends themselves.

One of Jurgen's acts of engagement was to join an antiwar march. The marchers were attacked by a motorcycle gang, one of whom rode his cycle straight at Jurgen. He would have been badly hurt except for the intervention of the police, who protected him. He does not recall being afraid, but he remembers wanting, furiously, to kill the cyclist. After that, Jurgen decided he was not nonviolent and, furthermore, that he wanted no part in dangerous engagements. He, nevertheless, turned in his draft card to symbolize his protest against the war in Vietnam. His next political steps are uncertain. He thinks of leaving the country to avoid a prison sentence, should he refuse induction; yet he realizes to do so would make him a permanent expatriate, a role he does not want. He is also unhappy about looming punishment on the drug-sale count. He finds, ironically, that even though he has wanted to remain "uncommitted," his actions have led him into very serious predicaments which jeopardize rather than maximize his freedom.

Paul has no such paradoxes to resolve. Under the impact of his university experiences, new friends, new ideas, exposure to activism, and the freeing effect of being away from direct parental supervision, he feels himself gradually evolving from a moderate conservative toward being a liberal Democrat. He does not consider going as far as the activists, nor does he count any of them among his friends, but he would like to see an end to segregation and is sympathetic to the Black Student Union on the campuses.

Comparing the attitudes of the two young men, one senses that Paul is really trying to think matters politic out for himself without particularly trying to annoy his parents. In Jurgen's case, one has the impression that he is not only working through various possibilities of improving the world but also by his actions is satirizing his parents' liberalism. To paraphrase him, "We are putting into action what our parents were preaching in the Thirties." "Preaching" is the word he underlines to show his disdain for their lip-service principles. Such overtones are absent in what Paul says about his political growth in relation to his parents.

Implicit in Jurgen's position is that he and his friends are very different from—and superior to—their parents in the ideological-philosophical sphere. He accepts the generation gap as a phenomenon and would deem it desirable. The novel, the young, the innocent, and the idealistic are the wave of the future capable, perhaps, of unsullying the tawdry machinations of a generation of money-making, war-instigating hypocrites. Although Jurgen did not say it, we believe he thinks of history as a sequence of ever more monstrous errors. To escape the inherited calamities, the sins of the father, the generation gap must be a chasm across which misery and ugliness cannot pass. On the young side of the gap, new history will be created and it will honor gentleness, love, and beauty, not as form but as experience. Yet, as we sense it—albeit from the corrupted side of the crevasse—there is in Jurgen a nostalgia for things that *were* rather than for things that will be. Consider his appearance when he is not required to look square: his long hair, colorful shirts, and other finery suggestive of the dandy, nineteenth-century style.

His interest in literature and music—not to say the films—gives him a poetic stance, one, we believe, that is derived in part from the radical romantic revolution which evolved in England during the late part of the eighteenth century. Briefly, that spirit insisted upon the rights of man; furthermore, it insisted that government exists only to protect those rights, and that—after Rousseau—man is born noble and can be corrupted only by unnatural institutions. Men are brothers, and authority which destroys equality is intolerable. Thomas Paine said, ". . . a great part of what is called government is mere imposition." Godwin concluded in 1793 that all man-made institutions are shackles to be discarded. Shelley looked forward to the abolition of the tyrannies of religion, custom, and government. Coleridge, in the fashioning of a concept of mind itself made in God's image, denied Kant and embraced metaphysics and, in his poetry, sought to dim the line between the real and unreal. His "Kubla Khan," perhaps inspired by an opium-induced dream, is the essence of that romanticism. These poets strove for mystic ecstasy, too. Wordsworth's rapture is an example. The romantic poets were, furthermore, interested in mind itself—in its analysis and in confessions. That interest led some—for example, De Quincy in England, Baudelaire in France—to explore the mind with drugs—opium and hashish—out of which literary creations grew. This is not to ignore the immense importance of alcohol for most Englishmen after the mid-1700's. There was also a fascination with other states of consciousness, such as the excitement over hypnosis demonstrated by enthusiasts from Mesmer to Janet to Freud. The excitement over mind in all its various states of consciousness and in experience for its own sake was an aspect of the romantic period.

We propose that Jurgen is, in part, a romantic poet without history to tell him from whence his poesy came. This same ahistorical stance also requires him not to know that his nostalgia is for causes already espoused and in some ways irretrievably lost. Wordsworth and Coleridge adored the French Revolution, but after the Terror they became conservatives. Hypnotism was exciting, but Mesmer proved a fraud. Opium and hashish were delights, but not for long, whereas alcohol, commoners' blessing, proved commoners' curse as well. As for the dissolution of enslaving government, Marx and Lenin conceived how with Communism the state would wither and die—an advocacy to which the USSR cannot in good faith testify. As for the syndicalists and anarchists who emerged later in the 1800's, their myths have also grown to weeds. Jurgen, not knowing these things, is not simply an old-fashioned boy but one who, having set himself the task of reinventing civilization, will have little time left to advance it.

As one would expect, Paul and Jurgen occupy their leisure in quite different styles. Jurgen is busy earning money to support his drug use, which costs him from $25 to $50 a month. Since his parents refuse to support it, he gets money from selling drugs to students and by working in one of the university laboratories. He carries a full academic load as well, which means his leisure is limited. What he does is to enjoy being with his friends in the small "commune" in which he lives, where music, marijuana, sex, talk, and parties are ways of having fun. Paul's leisure life is centered around his residence as well, but he lives in on-campus quarters. In addition, sports are very important to him. He dates girls, but he feels a bit uneasy about boy-girl matters. He recalls that his parents were so restrictive—quizzing him closely about each date as to where he had been and what he had done and insisting on a midnight return throughout his high school years—that he never brought a girl home for his family to meet for fear they might embarrass him and her. His parents were afraid he "might do something" with girls, not that they talked directly to him about sex or ever taught him the facts of life. He did not "do anything" and while in high school considered intercourse immoral. Now he is not so sure, although still in conflict: "If I really liked a girl, it (sex) wouldn't seem important, for you can love a girl without it; but if I see a girl crossing the street, cute and neat . . . that's what I want to do. When I know and like her, it goes down in value to me."

Jurgen, more sophisticated, is living with Jennifer, with whom he has been sleeping for some months. He is fond of her, and they share money and marijuana. He says they usually do not make love when smoking marijuana since one's prevailing mood can make sex with pot much worse, as well as much better. Jennifer is not the first girl Jurgen has had intercourse with, although his first sexual encounters were "disastrous." In high school among his friends on the football team, the prevailing code was "for all the rods to screw every chick." Jurgen went along—"It had to be done"—but he could never quite bring himself to complete the act. Somewhere in the middle of it, he was struck with the absurdity of it all and "everything kind of dropped off." The girls could not understand why, but they seemed not to mind his failure since they were scared, too. His parents, like Paul's, had not told him anything about the facts of life; sex was never discussed at home. However, his parents made no fuss about undressing; and everybody was casual about nudity. His grade school friends saw to the rest, telling him "horrendous things." He cannot remember conversations about sex in prep school. He does not consider that his lack of detailed knowledge has ever hampered his life, nor is he concerned about it.

He found his first intercourse "enlightening," for it taught him that sex could be both ugly as well as beautiful. He felt guilty for not caring about the girl herself—"what was inside the chick's head"—and found it unsatisfactory to just use her to "let out his sexual desires." Nothing ever came of their meeting; he has not seen her since. Before he came to the university, Jurgen had lived with a girl for a few months. This was a far better experience for both. They did not rush into sex, had been living in the same room, sleeping in the same bed, and smoking marijuana together for some time before they had intercourse.

Jurgen had one nightmarish sexual adventure during a school vacation; it was a descent into the underworld, perhaps a dream—although he tells it as an actual event. This happened during an earlier experiment in communal living, on an afternoon when everybody in the apartment had left and he was alone. He had not tried heroin yet and decided this was the opportune moment. By mistake he "snorted" a whole package, thinking it was a very small dose, and passed out. Three hours later, he opened his eyes to find someone sitting on his lap. It was a black girl. She commanded him to "ball her." He followed suit as best he could in his semi-drugged state, feeling degraded and disgusted: "It was just purely the physical thing . . . the miserable, horrendous, weak situation." When he was fully conscious again, his friends assured him that it had not been a dream, that the whole thing had really happened. This was his last venture into casual sex relations.

When he came to the university, he eschewed the usual form of dating around. By this time he had gotten away from his football team's "playboy" attitude and was looking instead for someone with whom he could "function as a person" and be friends with over a period of time. In Jennifer he found a girl who would go to movies with him on the spur of the moment, study with him, have a beer or smoke marijuana, or walk to the library with him if they happened to meet. No advance notice was needed. It was not dating in the usual sense. In this spontaneous manner, they drifted into an intimacy.

One brief mention must be made about homosexuality. Paul has never considered this as a possibility. Jurgen has a more tolerant view of it by now than he did when a high school student. Many of his friends are homosexuals and have often tried to seduce him. Jurgen says the prospect does not appeal to him.

With regard to religion, the parents of both young men are Protestants. Both sons have only a philosophical interest in the Protestant religion; yet Jurgen is much more concerned with religious issues than is Paul. He reads books on Eastern meditation and is currently practicing Yoga and Tantrism. He attends courses at the Free University which deal with religion. Jurgen also has experienced mystic hallucinations. Not surprisingly, he thinks of himself as profoundly religious. Indeed, he claims he may give up the use of most drugs soon in favor of trance-induced mystic states. Paul, on the other hand, neither probes nor poses religious mysteries. A lukewarm Protestant, he has moved as far from his parents in religion—for they are reasonably strict observers—as he has in politics. It is no rebellion, but simply a loosening of ties compatible with the liberal irreligiosity of many of his student friends.

What about the future? There is no question that Jurgen's is at risk, at least as viewed in conventional terms. Expatriation, a prison sentence, drug dependency, a fall over the academic precipice should he encounter too many "irrelevant" courses: all are possibilities. Yet we have also seen his strengths, which are many. It is his drifting and "going with it" which make prediction uneasy. So, too, does the shallowness which we detect in his relations to friends and causes, for that is the essence of his "cool," his non-commitment. Yet in that same shallowness we detect a masquerade. Because he has not put his heart into it, because he does not take it too seriously himself, his emphasis on immediacy allows a different interpretation, for it may mean that *right now* simply does not count. Erikson (1968) suggests that adolescents endure a moratorium before taking on adult roles. Indeed, the very notion of the university provides for much exploration before settling into one channel of life. Jurgen himself tells you, sheepishly, that when he receives his large inheritance, he does not plan to give it to the worthy causes his ideological beliefs recommend. He then adds that he will come into a large trust fund next year, which he knows he should give away. But he will not because some day he "might" have a family, and it is wise to plan for that. Listening carefully, watching closely, one detects a subtlety in his maneuvers which, while inviting risks, seek to avoid self-destruction. He is, after all, a suave and deceptive young man. Heroin is dangerous: he agrees that he will not use it again. The drug charges? Well, the family lawyer is working on it, and the chances are excellent that . . . . The draft card? Well, he has not really decided yet. . . . And so it goes.

Other Jurgens we have known are not so protected by their personal strengths, by superior social skills learned during the course of growing up in a social elite, or by a family which is in our Jurgen's case—and in spite of parental uncertainties and outside interests— stable, cohesive, respected, responsible, and at least moderately affectionate. Those other Jurgens—for example, the pallid nightcrawlers, sick and unkempt, on the Haight-Ashbury scene, the still struggling students who are personally disorganized and without claim to stronger resources, or simply the young and foolish—are more likely to be victims of their own game.

As for Paul, we have given him less attention simply because he is the more solid and simple of the two, *if* it is "simple" to be a good citizen in good health moving along confidently without giving or receiving undue pain from his fellow man. Repression? Yes. Limitations? To be sure. A future too certain to be exciting? Quite likely. One may protest that Paul is dull at a party or even wish, when he is a student in class, that he might be more imaginative. But these are small complaints and most societies are pleased to have a solid core of citizens who, with good hearts, are pleased to work and to be alive.

In retrospect, what clinical inferences are to be drawn? First, and contrary to surface appearances, we propose that it is Paul who is the more independent. Paul was reared so closely to his family that peers have never exerted great pressures on him. Certainly they have not dictated his morals, his values, or his directions of experience. It is no accident that he has chosen friends whose codes are similar to those of his parents. That was partly his parents' supervision and partly, too, because he is a whole creature a-building. He does not need to be contrary or, more psychodynamically, to choose a social setting consonant with superego demands, or the demands of his conscience derived from parental teaching. Repression of undesirable impulses, clearly seen to be at work, has been reinforced, rather than challenged, by his peers. One here thinks of a total, balanced integration, not just of the intrapsychic structures of self, family, and surroundings. In any event, as Paul matures in school and tests life slowly, as he continues to differentiate himself from his parents without rancor or compulsive opposition, he is free to fashion standards and styles that fit him best. He is not and never has been a slave to conflicting or competing standards from peers, nor has he been dog-at-the-knee for their approval. One says "free to fashion" with strong qualification. His freedom will be limited by a strong superego and by a commitment to family, institutional, and cultural values, which he cannot and probably would not wish to escape.

Not so Jurgen on any count. With his mother and father often away, he was not closely supervised at home, nor did his parents have the energy or even the conviction that would have allowed them to mold him in directions deemed important or to stand against undesirable outside influences. They had not that simplicity, certainty, and firmness which Paul's parents had. Recall that Jurgen said his parents had given up disciplining him strictly after they sensed the failure of punishment to bring results with his heavy-drinking, then-delinquent, older brother. That brother is now a military officer with no illicit-drug use, sympathy for political anarchy, or present delinquency. Or so Jurgen reports. For Jurgen the rules were never as clearly defined or enforced as they were for his own brother—or for Paul. Yet Jurgen, too, in growing has had to act and in acting has developed guides, beliefs, and conceptions of value. But much of Jurgen's acting and orientation has been with and toward his peers, who then and now have helped him to constitute an idea of self and to provide him with his sense of worth. His parents, of course, have played such a role as well; but their distance and uncertainty have made his own response to them more uncertain and, as we have seen, a matter of anger and amnesia as well as of admiration. As Jurgen has grown away from them, much more fitfully than Paul and in a legal-social sense perhaps even dangerously, he has come to depend more and more on peers. Denouncing organization and rigidity, he has, nevertheless, required structures of a sort; and his definitions of what life and experience and being a person are all about have come from companions. Thus, distance from parents has meant more leaning on confreres, which, unadmitted by Jurgen, confines him to their shared postadolescent fashions, condemns him to discomfort from the ambiguity of standards none can acknowledge as "right," and may also have engaged him in specific dependencies on psychoactive drugs as such.

There is, in this regard, an additional variable which has contributed to Jurgen's vulnerability to nonfamily influences. It is pleasure. Recall that in Paul's case it was his parents who not only arranged for but also participated in the fun and leisure of his free time after school, on weekends, and on holidays. There was only one car in the family and Paul depended upon it—and his mother's driving—for outings and later, with his family's permission, for dates when he could drive himself. Even now his parents come to the university to bring him the car for his own weekend use. Since they could easily afford to get him a car, one sees in this a continuing control, as well as an opportunity for giving and receiving and for getting together as a family. Consequently, throughout most of his life Paul has looked for his primary source of gratification from his parents. Even now he does not expect his peer group to fill the void as Jurgen does.

Jurgen's situation was different. He attended private schools when quite young, and although his family got together—and still does—to celebrate major festivals and occasionally to have a party, their leisure-time activity was not an interdependent affair. It was rather a side-by-side arrangement, as well illustrated by the incident Jurgen recalls when he practiced his game while his mother practiced her own, and different one. So it came about that Jurgen shifted for himself—that is, he turned to his peer group as the primary source of pleasure. It is no wonder that for a long time now he has been dependent upon his friends for fun, derives his self-esteem from association with them, and is therefore doubly bound to their rules. Expressed in psychological language, it is the peer group which controls his libidinal and narcissistic supplies and is thus in a position to play a superego function. It determines what conduct will be experienced by him as pleasurable and as inviting derogation. His friends decide what is good and what is bad. Jurgen's peer group has arrogated to itself the traditional parental and authorial roles relinquished by his mother and father and other authorities dealing with him.

Jurgen's tale is replete with recollections of how he tried out first one and then another kind of conduct—however difficult or uncongenial—in accordance with the different groups he belonged to because "it was the thing to do." He and his friends got together to engage in this or that form of illegal pleasure, because the group wanted to.

We have noted that he does not have to struggle to emancipate himself from his parents as Paul does, for Jurgen was never much influenced by them. Jurgen, however, would have a more arduous task to free himself from peer-group codes; it would be difficult because the pressures are more diffuse and insidious and because they change depending on the group with which he is associated. Recall how he once followed the football team's credo and then abandoned it when he discovered that it was not as satisfactory as the activist's code. For a while it was the prep school spirit that inspired his performance, but not for long. Presently, he follows the lead of artists in the communications courses in which he is intensely interested. We here underline the fact that Jurgen's drug use, starting with cigarettes and alcohol, was initiated by his friends. It was as a group that they smoked secretly and drove about drunk in stolen automobiles. It was as a group that later they stole barbiturates and smoked marijuana and cocaine. It is with groups that he now uses and peddles illicit drugs.

Let us extrapolate from the Jurgens and the Pauls we have known. We suggest that the type of education which draws heavily on the notion of equals teaching equals, which rewards teamwork in play and work, and which frowns on solitary or individual enterprises from nursery school onward cannot but fail. "Failure" is defined here as the inability of education to transmit the history or value systems of our culture as such, the stewardship of which is vested in people who are older, more powerful, and different from the young. What parents, teachers, judges, doctors, policemen, or the rest of the bearers of tradition teach cannot be the same as that which a child's peers will value and teach him when they are left to their own enterprises.

The implications are many. Foremost, with regard to the use of dangerous or illicit drugs, it follows that if one does not wish one's children—or other people's children—to follow the expanding fashions which find the young playing with their brains as with a basement chemistry set, then one must see to it that one takes the trouble to tie children to the immediate family group by controlling the sources of pleasure as well as using the family as a vehicle for transmitting values and common sense. Common sense about drugs includes, at the very least, concern about taking risks, about pretending to be invulnerable, or about acting as if there were no tomorrow or tomorrow were not worth the trouble. It is also evident, we believe, that the family must consistently control behavior through the application of negative as well as positive sanctions. Furthermore, the parents themselves must serve as models to whom there are affectionate as well as simply proximate ties. As models, parents must teach sensible drug behavior through concrete personal example. From other data, reported here and elsewhere, we know that alcoholic parents put children in danger of alcoholism; tobacco-smoking parents teach their children to smoke; and marijuana-smoking parents are more likely to have children who smoke marijuana heavily; and finally, as Robins (1966) shows, sociopathic fathers produce sociopathic children. Clearly, then, the bad habits are easily transmitted. To get the good habits across means effort and non-abdication by parents to the tyranny of youthful peers.

We think one reason for the abdication of many parents, teachers, and other elders is that in this youth-worshipping, change-oriented society the elders doubt themselves. They are ambivalent about holding or exercising authority and have placed an optimistic, admiring, and benevolent faith in the young, hoping that the clear-eyed innocent will do a better job. Certainly in a culture which changes daily it is imperative that youth be flexible, be prepared to adjust, be critical of that which no longer works or never did, be inventive, and avoid blind ties to styles of life which are either inappropriate or downright destructive. Granting the inevitability of new ways, one must not conclude that all of the old ways are expendable, that the great heritage of our civilization is without strength or merit, or that every social experiment will work simply because it is both new and idealized. To the contrary, most social experiments, like most evolutionary mutations or most laboratory experiments, will fail. If we are lucky, we know this in advance and prepare to learn rather than perish from the failures. Caryl Haskins (1968), president of the Carnegie Institution, has recently written:

> As in biological evolution, effective social evolution must be at once radical and conservative, freely embracing the new yet scrupulously preserving basic and well-tested elements that have had high survival value in the past and which remain relevant to the present.

. . . In embracing new and experimental courses with the ardor that we must, we must not discard long-tested values and long-tried adaptive courses which, if they are lost, will only have, one day, to be re-won—and probably at enormous cost. . . . Successful adaptive evolution within any society can only be accomplished in the presence of as complete a nexus of communication among all parts of the social structure as can possibly be secured (p. 181).

The elders—and we speak now of everyone with responsibility to the young—must not allow the young to stumble or to perish because of their ignorance of their history of either man or other evolving creatures. This means that communication between young and old must be enhanced, not restricted. We believe that teaching is one of those vital forms of communication. Necessarily, the teacher himself must have insight and wisdom and must not, through his teaching, simply perpetuate or even magnify error. Thus, the requirement for the elders is that they do have wisdom, which means, at the very least, insight, reflection, humility, and the capacity to recognize vanity and error in their own lives. Teaching itself is more than telling and certainly more than mechanical programs of instructions. It is human guiding; and guiding is more than recommending. It is seeing that the conditions for learning, for maturing, and for directed development exist.

What the personal histories of Paul and Jurgen teach is that children as well as nature abhor vacuums. If well-meaning but otherwise ineffective elders do not shape the child, then the child will seek his molding elsewhere. Should his random search not yield a mold, that child will be chaotic. We were talking to a hippie mother the other day, a girl just back from a "happening" for children in the Haight-Ashbury. There had been lollipops and soft drinks, and then a puppet show as the big event. The little ones had run wild, had thrown bottles at one another, had trampled on the lollipops and used them as spears, and in a grand finale had launched a cannibal attack on the puppets, tearing off their arms and legs. The mother was appalled by the savagery; it was not what her genuine gentleness had intended.

If fewer savages and fewer Jurgens—to avoid the risk of disaster—are to be produced, some major changes in education and child rearing are in order. We propose the following be considered:

That parents provide and control the majority of the pleasures for their children throughout childhood and the adolescent years. Thus, in addition to supervision, there must be conjoint fun in which the parents are pleasure-givers and not simply observers. The provision of pleasures becomes a sanction capable of being withheld so that, with punishment available as well, parental control is enhanced. This intense involvement also provides a deep source of affective ties. By parents we mean both parents, the implication of which is that the American father reconstitute his role as head of the family, director of activities, model for his sons, and partner in recreation and meaningful age-appropriate work with his children, not as a peer but as a leader.

That peer-group domination be reduced rather than increased and special efforts should be made to protect the child from the requirement that he adapt to each and every age-mate group. If peers provide fewer pleasures for one another acting as isolated groups but, rather, act more often as children integrated with other age levels and with institutional structures as well, it will be easier for the child to avoid peer domination and chameleon shifts in conduct. It would be in order that the separatist and centrifugal aspects of adolescent subcultures be countered at all levels, from the mass media to the intimate family.

That elders continue to dedicate themselves to teaching to the young the cultural wisdom they have learned. In the drug arena this means teaching the young that which is known about the safe uses of drugs, beginning at an early age. It should begin, for example, with prohibitions against access to the medicine chest and careful instruction in the dangers of aspirin, chocolate laxatives, and other remedies. The goal is to produce a generalized awareness that any drug which produces benefit is also likely to produce damage and that decisions to use such substances are not simply private choices but are also social acts subject to authoritative control during childhood and, then, during adulthood, to concern for the welfare of others as well as self-health. One sees the evidence for such teaching of drug use in the success of ethnic groups such as Italians and Jews, who learn early to use alcohol unemotionally and in integrated and controlled settings.

That the family be reconstituted by creating parents with confidence in their own knowledge and in their right to exercise authority as well as to grant freedoms—rather than further fragmentation of family responsibility through reliance on specialized agencies for taking over family functions (schools, welfare departments, mental-health organizations, recreation departments). We suggest that the competent child-rearing or child-supervising specialist in these many fine programs serve as consultants to families rather than as surrogate parents to other people's children. What are needed are programs of teaching, training, and confidence-building—many of which might also be psychotherapeutic—directed to parents themselves. In the drug arena one envisions course offerings and parent meetings sponsored by schools and PTA's, health and medical associations, women's and fraternal clubs, and other interested organizations, which can assist parents to expand their own capabilities for rearing children in this increasingly complex society. One envisions programs designed specifically (1) to help parents themselves become safe drug users through the control of their own addictions to tobacco, alcohol, tranquilizers, and the like; (2) to give parents information about drugs and the effects of various styles of use along with guidance on how to communicate that knowledge to children at various age levels; and (3) to support parents morally and emotionally as they approach their children to achieve safe rather than unsafe drug use. The perspective required is a matter-of-fact one which does not rely on romanticism, demonology (see Chapter Fourteen in *Drugs I*) or on lies to transmit data about drugs, personal hygiene, and social responsibility. A further perspective requires that parents and others realize that many of the problems in drug use which worry us —drug *abuse* per se—are best conceived as social and psychological difficulties centering about the circumstances of use and the particular individuals who are using drugs. Thus, the prevention of drug abuse requires the application of the same principles of social and mental hygiene which are to be applied to the prevention of other personal or interpersonal distress.

Predicting Who Will Turn On

Richard H. Blum
Bruce Ferguson

XVI

This chapter reports an exploratory effort to predict which students will begin illicit-drug use during the academic year. It is based upon the premise that among the many variables related to initiation of drug use, those which will operate as influences are past drug-taking experiences, expressed willingness to take drugs, the past illicit-exotic drug-taking experiences of one's chosen friends and admired peers (leaders), and the willingness to take drugs expressed by friends and leaders.

Subjects were asked to rate their willingness to take drugs under two conditions: a medical-research experiment to evaluate the effects of the drug, and a social situation where the drug is available without cost from a friend or an acquaintance. Willingness was to be rated on a scale of five from definitely unwilling through neutral to definitely willing. Eighteen drugs were listed. These included as follows: three hallucinogens, psilocybin, LSD, and peyote; two sedative-hypnotics, phenobarbital and seconal; three narcotic painkillers, Demerol, heroin, and codeine; one tranquilizer, Miltown (Equanil); two cannabis preparations, marijuana and hashish; two accepted social drugs, alcohol and tobacco; three stimulants, benzedrine, dexedrine, and methedrine; and two fictitious drugs, ergathol and TM-15. The list indicated the classification of each drug except marijuana, tobacco, and alcohol. The fictitious drugs were described as having "varied effects." To develop a score, the sum of willingness scores for all drugs under each condition was summed and averaged. When there was an interest in willingness by type of drug, for example, hallucinogens, the average willingness score for drugs in this class was obtained. In cases where a subject failed to indicate willingness, the willingness scored was based on the average of ratings given.

For each of the eighteen drugs, subjects were asked to indicate the approximate number of times they had taken the drug, including medical and nonmedical uses. When exact figures were unlikely to be known, as, for instance, in the case of alcohol or tobacco, frequency in terms of guesses or estimates was requested.

An attempt was made to validate the willingness scale, although it might just as well be considered a measure of consistency or reliability. An accomplice was selected from among male students[1] living together in a dormitory, all of them enrolled in the same summer language program. The accomplice named seven fellow residents with whom he could speak frankly about drugs. Each of these seven plus the accomplice was independently approached by the experimenter and told he had been selected at random to take the willingness scale. In the week following, the accomplice approached each of the other students and initiated a drug discussion in which he individually asked them about their willingness to take marijuana, benzedrine, and phenobarbital at a get-together where the drugs would be available. In the hypothetical situation posed, each subject was asked whether he would take such drugs if someone present proposed doing so to get "high." After these discussions, or "invitations," the accomplice rated each subject on the willingness scale. The twenty-one ratings (seven subjects, three ratings each) were compared with the corresponding self-expressions of willingness originally obtained. The association between the friend's rating and the subject's self-rating yielded $r = .78$, $t = 29.5$ ($P < .01$), which shows a positive correlation between stated willing-

---

[1] We have reason to believe that females would show a lower correlation—our observations indicate they respond more in terms of who the offering person is and what their relationship to him is.

ness expressed in a formal setting ("tested" by an unknown student researcher) and willingness rated by a friend after a discussion of drug taking in a setting which implied an invitation to take drugs.

Several expectations about the relationship of stated willingness to other variables were set forth and tested on a student sample. The sample was casually drawn from students going through registration at a junior college. The experimenter, himself long-haired and casually dressed (in hippie garb, according to some), asked each of seventy-five students (consecutive) to participate. Thirteen refused, eight failed to complete the questionnaire, and fifty-four remained, of whom thirty were male and twenty-four female.

The range of possible scores on the Social Willingness Scale is 18 to 90. Actual scores obtained ranged from 18 to 86 with a median of 31. The first expectation tested was that social willingness would increase the more the related experience; thus, there would be least social willingness to take drugs not previously taken (Wn), more willingness to take those previously administered by a physician (Wd), and most willingness to take ones already previously used socially (Ws) —that is, procured through a friend or acquaintance. The scores, obtained by analyzing and then matching each subject's willingness and one-time-or-more experience with scale items, support the expectation. The average social willingness for Wn drugs is 1.82, for Wd drugs is 2.45, and for Ws drugs is 3.07. Note that this latter score is only a bit above neutral, which indicates that social willingness is not predictable solely from past social use of the same drugs.

Illustrative of the factors contributing to differential willingness are differences by drugs and by amount of experience. For example, among those who have never taken marijuana (N = 32/54), Ws is 1.2; for those who have smoked it once (N = 6), Ws is 3.2; whereas for those who have smoked it more than once, Ws is 4.1. For benzedrine, on the other hand, those who have not used it average Ws of 1.4 and both one-time and more-than-one-time users average 3.3. LSD willingness (Ws) for inexperienced subjects (N = 46) is 1.7, whereas for those six subjects who have had LSD—and all have taken it at least three times—Ws is 4.5. For alcohol those who have taken it rarely (ten times or fewer) average Ws of 2.0, whereas more experienced drinkers express an average willingness of 3.9. Note that the range of scores is greatest for the two illicit-exotic drugs, ranging from relatively strong unwillingness among inexperienced persons to strong willingness among more experienced ones, whereas with the more acceptable drugs (even though alcohol is illegal in this under-twenty-one age group and benzedrine can only be legally obtained by prescription) lesser ranges of average willingness are obtained. One wonders whether, under conditions of broader sampling, the moderate-vs.-the-extreme range of social-willingness scores might not parallel the moral-attitudinal intensity surrounding particular drugs.

The range of possible scores on experimental willingness is also 18 to 90 and actual scores range from 18 to 87 with a median of 38 —a median higher than that obtained for social willingness. We would expect that social willingness and experimental willingness would be related and when tested this is found to be the case, r = .73 significant beyond P < .01. Controlling for past experience by excluding all drugs previously taken, one finds that a relationship still obtains, r = .60 (significant at P < .01), which means that there is a relationship between one's willingness to take a new drug socially and one's willingness to take it experimentally. The occurrence of that relationship should not let us overlook the large amount of variance for which we cannot account.

The questionnaire contained a number of other items which we thought would be associated with varying degrees of expressed willingness to take drugs. These covered the number of friends who have used tobacco, alcohol, marijuana, LSD, or other drugs for kicks, family use of medicines and drugs, involvement in typical social commitments, rejection of parents' values, rejection of society's values, general interest and curiosity, and orientation to life. We find significant correlations to obtain between the number of friends using the drugs listed and social willingness, r = .53, and between expressed interest and curiosity[2] and social willingness, r = .42. No significant relations are found between social willingness and the other factors as measured here.

A special inquiry was made into orientation to life, defined in terms of the ranked importance of the following themes: success, religion, politics, self-understanding, health, tradition, adjustment, having a good time, and family and children. (These same themes were the

[2] There were six questions asking about interests in seeing new places, meeting new people, trying new foods or cooking, participating in psychology experiments, in medical research experiments, and experiments to evaluate new drugs. Thus, one component of the curiosity scale was itself a drug-willingness item.

foci of ratings of parent-subject agreement on values and of society-subject agreement or disagreement on values.) Subjects with low, intermediate, and high social willingness were compared as to the frequency with which each theme was rated as "very," "slight," or "not important." A theme score for each Ws group was derived by subtracting the "slight" and "not-important" ratings from the number of "very-important" ratings. Among subjects with low social-willingness scores, health and adjustment rank higher than among the intermediate Ws group, which, in turn, ranks these higher than the high Ws group. Conversely, "having a good time" is ranked low by the low social-willingness group, whereas both intermediate and high Ws subjects rank it high. It is of interest that the themes of religion and tradition are uniformly ranked low by all groups.

From the foregoing data it appeared that the factors—among those examined—most likely to predict who would, in fact, "turn on" to illicit-drug use were expressed social and experimental willingness, past drug experience, illicit-exotic drug use among one's friends and, secondly, admired peers, and expressed willingness to take drugs socially on the part of those same friends and group leaders.[3] We did not expect that these would be the only variables related to turning on, far from it, since drug access, personality variables, unusual social pressures, accident, and a host of other factors are likely to play a role. On the other hand, we expected that, given a situation in which drug use on campus was increasing, experience, willingness, and friendship patterns ought to play a detectable role.

The original plan called for enlisting the support of all members in two residential (Greek-letter) fraternities, one high in illicit-exotic use, according to campus opinion, and one low. At the time the study began, the highest-use house selected was bathed in the unflattering light of various investigations of drug use by deans and other administrators, so that its officer, sensitive to further explosions, declined to cooperate. Two presumably low-use houses were willing to cooperate. The plan called for the experimenter to explain the study and to distribute and collect questionnaires at the beginning of the fall quarter and again at the end of spring quarter. Resistance in both houses to an outsider's playing a role meant inaugurating a new procedure, one in which a student resident in each house was enlisted to "manage"

---

[3] The interest-curiosity variable which also correlated was discarded because of the overlap between it and experimental willingness items.

the work in each house. No direct supervision of him was possible since there was insistence on absolute anonymity of respondents and of freedom for nonresponse. A further sampling problem arose from the fact that in both houses some students were at overseas campuses in the fall while others were overseas in the spring. A further limitation arose when students completing both questionnaires selected as friends or leaders men who did not complete the initial questionnaire. Since the predictions rested upon knowing the drug experiences and willingness to take drugs of all those designated by a subject as friends or leaders, any missing questionnaire might be a needed one. In any event, twenty men in House A and twenty-six men in House B completed both questionnaires and designated two or more persons who had also completed the initial questionnaire. These numbers represented not only about half of the student residents in the house during the year but also about three quarters of those not going to an overseas campus during the year.

RESULTS

Because the samples were small we combined both houses for all predictions and analysis. Three groups were distinguished on the basis of the drug-use information given on the first and second round of questionnaires. One group, comprised of twenty-one students and, designated as the 00 (zero-zero) group, reports no use of any illicit-exotic substance either at the beginning of the school year or at the end of the year. The second group reports no illicit-exotic drug use at the beginning of the year but by year's end says members began drug use, usually marijuana but possibly LSD, peyote, and so on. There were fifteen students in that group which we designated as the 0+ or zero-plus group. The third group of ten students, designated as the ++ or plus-plus group, reports on the first round of questionnaires that members have had experience with illicit-exotic drugs and so necessarily have had experience on the second round as well. In October at the beginning of the year only 22 per cent of the students in the two houses had had experience with illicit-exotic drugs (a figure that corresponds quite closely to our overall sample of the same university taken during the fall quarter) but that by June 55 per cent had had such experience. It is in the comparison of the group of fifteen (33 per cent) who turned on with those twenty-one (45 per cent) who did not begin use that we are primarily concerned. We shall also present the findings on the plus-plus group in the expectation that as experienced users their scores on willingness and so on would be highest.

One assumes that what people say they are willing to do has something to do with what they in fact do. So it was that we expected that those who had turned on during the year would have had a greater expressed willingness to use drugs when asked at the beginning of the year than would those who had not turned on. Recall that our willingness scale was divided into two components, experimental and social; we expected that social willingness—which is the kind ordinarily involved in the taking of illicit-exotic drugs—would be more relevant than experimental willingness. The individual willingness score used was the average score (minimal 1, maximal 5) on each of the eighteen drugs on the scale (including the two fictitious drugs).

We find that the zero-zero group received an average experimental-willingness score of 2.13 and an average social-willingness score of 1.54. The zero-plus group received an average experimental-willingness score of 2.75 and a social-willingness score of 2.04. In contrast, the plus-plus group received an average experimental-willingness score of 3.22 and a social-willingness score of 2.34. Because the groups are small, these differences are not statistically significant; they are, however, in the predicted direction in that members of the zero-zero group consistently show the lowest willingness scores, both experimental and social, members of the zero-plus group show higher scores, and those of the plus-plus group show the highest scores. Note, however, that social willingness does not differ from experimental willingness. The willingness score of even the experienced subjects is itself moderate in the sense that an average score of 3 represents a self-rating as "neutral" on taking drugs, whereas an average score of 2 represents slight unwillingness. On the other hand, to gain an average score much higher than 3, subjects would have had to express high willingness to take drugs with known characteristics productive of physical dependency. It appears that overall willingness is too broad a measure to pick up eagerness to take particular drugs.

One can, for this reason, focus on willingness as expressed in regard to those drugs on the list that were exclusively illicit: psilocybin, marijuana, LSD, heroin, hashish, and peyote. There we find that the zero-zero group has an average experimental willingness of 2.3 and a social willingness of 1.4; the zero-plus group has an average experimental willingness of 2.6 and social willingness of 1.8, whereas the plus-plus group has an average experimental willingness of 3.4 and a social willingness of 2.7. Once again, the results are not significant although they are, as one would anticipate, in the expected direction. What stands out is that social willingness does not differ from experimental willingness in terms of discriminating among the groups and also that willingness limited to illicit-exotic drugs is no better a measure than the overall willingness scale.

We expected that students who turned on would have, at year's beginning, more friends who were themselves experienced drug users than those who did not. Our assumption was that the choice of friends experienced in illicit drugs was itself an indicator of acceptance if not interest in that kind of conduct and, secondly, that there would be more opportunity for drugs and social pressure to use them from such friends. The questionnaire called for subjects to estimate the number of drug-using friends they had on a four-point scale ranging from "none" (value = 0) through "very many" (value = 3) for each of three drugs: marijuana, LSD, and "other drug or medicine for kicks, to get high." The maximum score for any subject (very many friends using each) would be 9, the minimum 0 (no friends using any).

One finds that the zero-zero group has an average score for estimated friends' use of illicit drugs of 1.6, the zero-plus group has a score of 2.9, and the plus-plus group a score of 5. These differences are clear-cut and in the predicted direction, although again our small N means that they are not statistically significant.

We expected that the attitudes of each subject's own friends and leaders in the fraternity house would also be associated with his turning on or not. We assumed that when the friends and leaders nominated by him (the sociometric nomination called for them to name the five best friends within the living group and, separately, the five most respected individuals) were themselves more willing to take drugs, then these attitudes would support or encourage the subject to do so. Such attitudes were not likely to be separate from the drug experience of these friends and leaders. Our measure of attitudes here was the willingness score of those nominated as friends and respected leaders.

One finds that the zero-zero group nominate friends with average experimental willingness of 2.5 and social willingness of 1.8; the zero-plus students nominate friends with scores of 2.3 and 2.1; the plus-plus group nominate friends with scores of 2.8 and 2.1. With reference to respected leaders, the zero-zero group nominate students whose average social willingness is 2.5 and whose experimental willingness is 1.7; the zero-plus group nominate leaders with average scores of 2.7 and 1.9; the plus-plus students nominate leaders with average experimental-willingness scores of 2.8 and social-willingness scores of 2.0. Slight trends notwithstanding, it is clear that the willingness of selected friends and leaders, as reported by those friends and leaders, little distinguishes the students who are drug experienced, those who turn on, and those who stay aloof from illicit experimentation.

Subjects were asked for each of the eighteen drugs on the test list whether they had used it and, if so, how often. Replies were grouped with a range of scores from 1 for little use to a maximum of 4 for considerable (ten or more times) use. Total scores were for the sixteen real drugs on the list. We expected that students in the zero-plus group would have higher past-experience scores than those in the zero-zero group.

One finds that the average total scores for the zero-zero group are 4.5, for the zero-plus group, 6.9, and for the plus-plus group, 11.5. These are in the anticipated direction although, once again, they cannot achieve statistical significance.

If one excludes alcohol and tobacco, one finds that the average past-experience score for the zero-zero group is 1.1, for the zero-plus group, 2.0, and for the plus-plus group, 4.9. If one further excludes illicit-exotic experience, which can affect only the plus-plus group, the average score of that group drops to 1.8.

It is of interest to see what happens to these groups on the end-of-year retest. At that time the average past-experience score (excluding alcohol and tobacco) for the zero-zero group rises slightly to 1.2, for the zero-plus group it rises to 2.9, and for the plus-plus group it nearly doubles to 7.3. Clearly, the year of observation (or conceivable retest effects) has been an active one during which all students increased their drug experience. The already experienced students increased it most, followed by the newly turned-on students in second place. The implication is that once begun, use of illicit-exotic drugs among these fraternity students led to considerably more such use.

Illicit-exotic drugs can be obtained only through informal channels. We expected that the students in the turned-on group would have more experience using friends and acquaintances as drug (informal) sources than would the students not turning on. For the purpose of this comparison, sources were limited only to those drugs (phenobarbital, benzedrine, seconal, Demerol, dexedrine, Miltown/Equanil, codeine, methedrine, and also alcohol and tobacco) which could be obtained either from doctors or from informal sources. We find the zero-zero group averages 1.8 drugs from informal sources and 1.2 from doctors; the zero-plus group averages 1.9 from informal sources and 1.7 from doctors; and the plus-plus group averages 2.7 drugs from informal sources and 1.1 from physicians; this latter group has an elevated informal-sources score because of members' experience with illicit-exotic drugs. The trend is as anticipated but is hardly dramatic.

Each student was asked six questions which touched upon his future plans, and these were condensed in scoring to specificity of plans with reference to future activities, relevance of present schooling, and family plans (marriage and children). We expected that the zero-zero group would show the greatest certainty in planning and the zero-plus group less.

We find, after assigning scores, that the zero-zero group averages 4.9 for future-activity planning compared with 4.1 (lower scores mean less certainty or specificity) for the zero-plus group, and 4.5 for the plus-plus group. Scores on school relevance for future activities are 4.8 for the zero-zero group, 3.8 for the zero-plus group, and 4.2 for the plus-plus group. Family-planning scores are 3.0 for the zero-zero group, 2.6 for the zero-plus group, and 2.8 for the plus-plus group. These are in the anticipated direction for the two prediction groups, although the slightly greater certainty scores for the students with high drug experience is not what we expected.

There was also an open-ended question under plans which asked what the student expected to be doing in five years if he followed the trends and interests of his present life. Replies were categorized into three groups: those with utopian or idealistic themes; those still "in process" or continued moratorium as, for example, staying in school or in military service; and those with settled Establishment expectations. We expected the zero-zero group to have the most certain and conventional plans. We find that in the zero-zero group half of the replies anticipate being settled in Establishment activities in five years, among the zero-plus group one third anticipate being settled in regular jobs, and among the plus-plus group only one tenth expect such routines. "Don't know" accounts for only 5 per cent of the zero-zero replies but for one third of the zero-plus replies and for one fifth of the plus-plus group. Idealistic-utopian expectations appear, in round one, most often in the plus-plus group.

Interestingly enough, on the second-round inquiry, at the end of the school year, shifts one might have expected did not materialize —that is, the zero-plus group had not become more idealistic-utopian. Indeed, the greatest shift had occurred among the zero-zero group, where three students (3/21) became more uncertain and, dropping their expectations of Establishment routine, entered the "don't-know" group while one in the "moratorium" group moved to an idealistic plan. What this suggests is that career uncertainty can increase during a school year without being associated with the onset of drug use. Even so, by the end of the year, both drug-using groups remained highest in career uncertainty and in moratorium-type expectations, although by year's end the zero-zero group was highest in plans for an idealistic career.

We find that among the fifteen expectations advanced, fourteen have proven to be in the anticipated direction with regard to the differences in the beginning of the year between those students who later begin to use drugs illicitly and those not initiating such drug use. The only exception is a very slight reversal in the experimental willingness to take drugs on the part of nominated friends. In all fifteen cases, the plus-plus group have scores in the predicted direction vis-à-vis the zero-zero group, and in eleven cases these scores are also more extreme, as anticipated, than those of the zero-plus group. Individual tests of these differences fail to achieve significance because of the small N and the narrow range of scores involved; however, the probability of fourteen out of fifteen findings being in the predicted direction or, more extreme, of twenty-nine out of thirty using the plus-plus group as well, is significant—that is $P < .05$.

A prediction table: Aside from the small satisfaction in seeing that trends in scores were as expected, we wondered what our maximum success would have been in individual prediction if we had employed each of the major measures to construct a prediction table. To construct that table we did three things: first, we selected nine major variables to include; secondly, we revised scoring procedures so that the range of scores on each was about the same—that is, scores ranged from 0 to 5; and third, we summed each individual score on each of the nine variables and averaged them for each drug-use group. These scores were given equal weight and an optimal cutting point was established.

If a cutting point is established at between the average score of 2.2 and 2.3, we find that sixteen students in the zero-zero group are below it as are four students in the zero-plus group (and none in the plus-plus group). This means that if, at the beginning of the year, we had used these scores and predicted that all students with a score of 2.2 or less would not turn on and that all students with a score of 2.3 or more would either be turned on (or already be turned on) during that coming year, we would have had four false negatives and five false positives along with twenty-seven predictions. All told there would have been twenty-seven successes and nine errors compared with a chance expectancy—had we but flipped a coin—of 18/18. Our success rate of three out of four capitalizes on hindsight and on the remarkable set of natural events which led nearly half of the non-drug users in the house to become drug initiates during the year of observation.

The prediction table demonstrates that within homogeneous groups subject to similar environments, one can predict illicit-drug use with some accuracy simply by knowing the subjects' past drug experiences, past drug sources, reported willingness to take drugs, subjects' estimates of friends' use of illicit drugs, and willingness of nominated friends and leaders within the same living group to take drugs. By adding to drug use another variable, future plans, and constructing a new prediction table, it is possible to further increase this after-the-fact "prediction." The new cutting point appears between those with average scores of 2.4 and 2.5. Seventeen of the zero-zero group fall below the cutting point and three above; four zero-plus students fall below and twelve above. Furthermore, all plus-plus students fall above the 2.4 point. Thus, we would have twenty-nine successes and seven errors or a rate of success of 81 per cent compared with the chance expectation of 50 per cent.

The foregoing indicates what the next step would be, which would require the use of the same scales at the beginning of a study in a similar setting. Even were one lucky enough—if one calls it "lucky" to be on a campus where marijuana use doubles in a year— to have some students turn on and others not, it would be unrealistic to expect the same table to yield a rate of success of prediction of 81 per cent or the even higher rate of success which emerges if one wants the table simply to identify all those who by year's end will be illicit users. Taking the latter tack, which requires the plus-plus group be included in the prediction, leads to correct identifications of student drug use in 85 per cent of the cases. The reason that cross-validation efforts will show lesser success rests essentially on one's having maximized success after-the-fact on one sample; the next sample will be bound to differ in some ways even if it is drawn from similar environments. That sample will also be exposed to altered environmental forces as the expanding attraction of drugs affects campuses. The statistical problems in prediction and cross-validation were long ago discussed by Horst (1948).

SUMMARY

An exploratory study has shown that, as measured by a scale among (male) students, stated willingness to take drugs is significantly correlated with their response to social invitations to use illicit drugs. Two components, willingness to take drugs in experimental settings and willingness to take them in social settings, are also found to be significantly related, even when all drugs taken in the past are excluded from the scales. Other correlations achieving significance are between social willingness and the number of friends estimated to be illicit-drug users and between general curiosity and social willingness.

Using the willingness scale, and an inquiry into future plans, plus sociometric ratings of friends and leaders, observations were then conducted in two fraternity houses over the course of the 1966–1967 school year. All residents were tested at the beginning of the year and again in late spring. They were classified at year's end as having used illicit drugs from the beginning of the year, as having turned on for the first time during that year, or as having never turned on to illicit drugs. At the beginning of the year, 22 per cent had had illicit-drug experience; by the end of the year 55 per cent had had such experience. Findings show that on fourteen out of fifteen variables based on the scales administered (willingness, experience, drug sources, friends' and leaders' actual use, and friends' and leaders' willingness and future plans) the group not turning on received lower scores than the group turning on; furthermore, on all fifteen variables, the group already experienced with illicit drugs received higher scores than the group not turning on, and on eleven variables received average scores higher than those turning on during the year of observation. Constructing a prediction table based on the average scores on these variables, we found that those turning on had higher scores on the average than those not doing so—to such an extent that, after the fact, there was a success rate of 81 per cent in identifying students as having turned on or not. Although future studies utilizing the same prediction table among similar samples cannot be expected to achieve the same success as an after-the-fact construction, we do conclude that among homogeneous student populations the prediction of who will turn on can be accomplished at a better-than-chance level by attending to the variables of drug experience and willingness among students and their friends.

Psychiatric
Problems

James Paulsen

XVII

*A*mbrose Bierce, America's Civil War iconoclast, describes the mind as ". . . a mysterious form of matter secreted by the brain. Its chief activity consists in the endeavor to ascertain its own nature, the futility of the attempt being due to the fact that it has nothing but itself to know itself with." Bierce could not foresee scientific developments of the twentieth century: gradual elucidation of unconscious mental processes, knowledge of molecular protein metabolism in the brain, and neurophysiologic discoveries which make the phenomena of consciousness almost fathomable. Concurrent with these advances, psychedelic drugs emerged from the laboratory. Whether derived from plant life (marijuana, peyote, psilocybin, and morning-glory seeds) or created in the laboratory (LSD, dimethyltryptamine—DMT—and amphetamines), these drugs can markedly affect and possibly even alter the human brain, that supreme masterpiece of evolution.

Psychiatric problems associated with drug use are comparable with the kinds of problems which plague students who avoid drugs: (1) disturbances of intellectual functioning (thinking); anxiety, phobic, panic, or depressive episodes (feelings); and (3) behavioral disturbances (action). Most problems involve elements of all three, vary in degree from mild to severe, and tend to be *acute* (of short duration) or chronic (enduring and prolonged). They are also ubiquitous. Of the tens of millions of students in the United States (six million in colleges and universities), 10 per cent endure emotional problems which need professional attention and treatment. Most students with psychiatric problems do not receive appropriate treatment. Some seek help from peers and important adults in their environment. Many assume the role of doctor and "prescribe" drugs for themselves and friends. To relieve anxiety, a nervous high school student snitches a few pills from her mother's supply of tranquilizers. In response to academic pressures, a college freshman smokes marijuana to induce relaxation. A depressed sophomore takes LSD, hoping to rid himself of despair. In order to hide her gnawing disillusionment with college life, a dateless coed furtively sips vodka. These kinds of self-treatment frequently produce erratic results, distort an already complicated situation, and aggravate a glaring societal problem which is now dominated by marijuana and LSD.

At the University of California at Los Angeles, until September of 1965, one patient, usually a student, was seen monthly because of complications following ingestion of LSD. During subsequent months, five to twenty individuals were seen each month at the Neuropsychiatric Institute (Ungerleider, Fisher, Fuller, and Caldwell, 1968).

College and community-health centers have observed similar increases. In a well-intentioned but futile effort to "control" the predicament, society has enacted hasty legislation. Instead of being controlled, drug use has merely been driven underground. In spite of prohibitive regulations at schools and punitive laws created by state and federal lawmakers, students are using illicit drugs to an extent far greater than most people are able, or willing, to admit. Some students claim that these drugs create the "real scene." The scene is now almost bizarre. A student rushes to a hospital because he has "freaked out" after eating peyote. Another student complains of taking 300μg of LSD and getting no reaction. Still another, who has used no drugs for months, experiences a "flashback" of a previous psychedelic episode, but now it is a "bad trip."

Illogical? Of course. Bizarre? Probably. However, equally strange and inexplicable manifestations occur during psychology re-

search. A fascinating experiment, conducted by Hebb (1961) at Mc-
Gill University will illustrate:

> Let us take a young, vigorous, healthy male, a college student, and
> deprive him simply of the perceptions that are part of ordinary life,
> which we take so for granted. Make him comfortable, feed him on
> request, but cut off that bombardment of sensory informations to
> which, normally, we are all exposed all the time except when asleep.
> We turn him in on himself, leave him to his thoughts. For some
> hours, this presents him with no great difficulty . . . but after a
> time a malaise appears, concerning the very center of the subject's
> being. The subject becomes restless and somewhat unhappy, but
> more significant is the report that he can no longer follow a con-
> nected train of thought. Some of our subjects entered the experi-
> ment thinking to review their studies or plan their research in the
> atmosphere of peace and meditation to be found inside the experi-
> mental cubicle. They were badly disappointed. Not only was serious
> thinking interfered with, but there was a repeated complaint that
> it was impossible to do any connected thinking of any kind. Tests
> of intelligence showed changes occurring by about the second day,
> and after the subjects had come out of isolation there were marked
> disturbances of ordinary motivation and work habits lasting 24 to
> 36 hours . . . a good many had elaborate visual hallucinations, but
> these did not seem to involve the subject's own personal identity.
> More significant in the present context is the occurrence, in about
> 8% of the subjects, of sudden sharp emotional breaks, taking dif-
> ferent forms, e.g., something like a temper tantrum, or an attack of
> claustrophobia, which put a sudden end to the experiment as far
> as these subjects were concerned; or in another group, alternatively,
> disturbances of the self-concept, in which the subject might feel
> that he had two bodies, that his head had parted company from
> his neck, or that he had become the immaterial mind wandering
> about space wholly detached from his body (p. 45).

This, without drugs; no wonder that adverse reactions are
common in psychedelic-drug use. Such reactions are conveniently classified as mild, moderate, or severe. Mild reactions predominate, usually appear abruptly, and consist of feelings of uneasiness and tension
or of being physically uncomfortable and restless. Specific physical
symptoms commonly occur: sweating, increased heart rate, and nausea
(more frequent with peyote and LSD). However, in a mild reaction,
the individual is able to tolerate and talk about what is happening.
Although there may be some concern or fear that the anxiety and discomfort may increase, panic does not develop and behavior remains

controlled. The "episode" may last but a few minutes, rarely an hour. Reassurance provided by a pleasant environment and supportive friends is usually sufficient. A male undergraduate reports the following:

> Last quarter a friend brought some marijuana to my apartment and I smoked too much of it—went into a half-hour "panic"—was really bad—after that it got good, ecstasy and all that, and I went to sleep eventually. The week-end before finals I got depressed about things and *it* happened again without any drugs—my girl friend brought me to the Health Center and a doctor gave me tranquilizers and I stayed in the infirmary overnight—was OK the next day. Two days later I got the "shakes" again, felt tense, anxious and afraid—reminded me of the first pot incident—like being sucked into a void and losing my identity. I was put on tranquilizers again and things got much better. Then last night the medicine didn't work and I got to trembling—wasn't afraid, though. I decided I should come in again.

During the interview he discussed at some length his guilt about recent sexual activities with his girl friend and the relevance of this to family problems which have bothered him for years. He said his girl friend has a relaxed attitude about sex and it bothers him that he doesn't. Since any medical treatment would have been at best perfunctory, he was referred for continuous outpatient psychotherapy. Drugs, for him, ceased to be a problem.

Drug complications of a moderate degree tend to occur in (more or less) chronic users. Panic episodes, depersonalization, moderately severe depressions, and the "apathy syndrome" are examples of what is possible. Here are several cases.

During her ninth acid trip, a twenty-year-old coed "freaked out" while at a fraternity party. She dashed into the hills, got lost, and finally returned exhausted to be "confronted" by a dog which "terrified" her. She stumbled into the house and was "talked down" by the fellows, who also provided some Librium capsules. She told her therapist that prior to this trip she was depressed, yet aware that depression preceding drug intake makes a bad trip more possible. A nineteen-year-old male took 500μg of LSD in divided doses, an hour apart. Prior to the second "installment," he played the guitar to "relax." Soon he

> . . . began to get shaky and nervous—looked up at the ceiling and visual images distorted the color and design in the ceiling. My mind

seemed to detach itself (depersonalization) from my body and it seemed that I was looking at myself. The room seemed to assume a soft, warm shape—it would be anything I wanted it to be—then I got worried that I might think about something negative and that it would expand and terrify me. I kept worrying about this. I wanted to go to sleep but I couldn't. It seemed that I was always being promised something, either a great insight or a great horror. I went to the bathroom, looked in the mirror and my face was distorted: big eyes, lips sinking. I tried to use the urinal but seemed to sink so I sat on the commode and urinated, then returned to the room. My friend had been asleep for several hours. It got to be dawn and I got worried about not sleeping. He got up and walked me to the campus—I still felt detached. We passed the church and I thought that if I prayed to God, He would help me—I got inside but looked up at the stained glass windows and they turned into a horrible psychedelic color and seemed to move. I ran outside and we went to the cafeteria. The doughnut I tried to eat looked weird; I got scared and asked my friend to take me to a doctor for help.

A phenothiazine spansule helped give him a fourteen-hour sleep; he hadn't slept more than five hours any night during the past week. In the morning he appeared rested, felt transformed. He told of family members who suffer from insomnia. He also mentioned that he didn't like to be "high" on anything, even beer, because he needed to be in control of himself. He said he took the LSD because he was dissatisfied with school, wanted to change, and that he had an "irresistible impulse." An interview five days later showed full recovery.

Another male, also nineteen, reported that he obtained a mediocre average during the first quarter of his freshman year. He enlivened the second quarter by taking LSD every second or third day, for a total of thirty trips. He lost interest in studying, dropped a course, and ended the quarter on academic probation. After registration for the third quarter, he abandoned LSD, but drank beer excessively. A disastrous third quarter terminated, quite appropriately, in a medical leave. He related that before he ever took LSD he once smoked four "joints" within fifteen minutes and it "zonked me completely—I was reduced to a nonfunctional stage of vegetable mass—mind clicking like a computer machine. I ended up in bed in the fetal position still going strong. It was over in an hour but I felt mentally 'hung-over.' " During summer vacation, in spite of a promise to himself, he couldn't resist trying acid again:

I took 500µg about five o'clock in the afternoon while in a depressed mood, and got a little frightened about taking so much. I went for a walk after eating and things were starting to get out of hand. I was sitting in the park and it went out of control—the visual effect. I looked at the geraniums and it seemed to me that I couldn't get out. I ripped myself away and started to walk home. It seemed an eternity. Each block seemed miles but I fixed my eyes on the sidewalk and finally got home. It was about eleven and I went to bed. The map on the wall seemed to be playing with me like the water scene in Disney's *Sorcerer's Apprentice*—I began to be preoccupied with killing myself. I advanced my mind to the point that suicide was necessary to decrease the paranoid horror— to stop the map and walls from overwhelming me—I reached the state where it had complete control of me. About two-thirty I went to sleep, but didn't go to work the next day. I went to our minister and did get some help from him. I kind of returned to a placid acceptance of things and decided that I'd never go near acid again.

After returning to the university, he did *B−* work, which he believes will be improved in subsequent quarters. When asked how he now felt about the bad trip, he said,

Unfortunately, I've read too much of the odd-ball literature stuff —cellular consciousness and all that—I wonder about the possible validity of metaphysical concepts, extrasensory perception and the supernatural. I won't go around and say that because I've taken some pills I now see the light.

He subsequently involved himself in psychotherapy and is doing well academically.

Janowitz (1967), director of Mental Health Services at the University of Massachusetts, tells of a series of students coming in because they were not able to come down off a "high" induced by marijuana. Feelings of estrangement, poor reality testing, and strange body concepts have continued even weeks and months after the last marijuana episodes. He reports that all but one of these students responded well to medication.

Barbato (1967), director of University Health Services at the University of Denver, writes of a student who was picked up by the police in town at about two A.M. The student was wandering aimlessly and obviously under the influence of some drug, but created no disturbance and was brought to the Health Service by the officer, who did not book him. By late morning he was able to leave on his own. He admitted having smoked marijuana and said it was prompted by curiosity.

Prolonged use of potent psychedelic drugs can exert a gradual and insidious effect on some individuals who fervently maintain that they have developed insight into themselves and that they can be objective toward their involvements with the drugs. Ungerleider *et al.* (1968), at UCLA, describe chronic side effects as a

. . . dramatic shift in one's value system. Many persons after using LSD are no longer interested in working or playing what they call "ego games of society." LSD users often leave their families and become quite withdrawn, devoting most of their time to thinking, writing and talking about LSD, and what they would term "perceptual distortion." This refers to a subjective feeling of improvement concomitant with an objective loss of functioning.

It is to be expected that the incidence of such side effects will increase. Ungerleider *et al.* report that at the UCLA Neuropsychiatric Institute prior to September 1965, one problem case associated with LSD ingestion was seen approximately every two months. Beginning at that time, the incidence increased gradually from five to twenty cases a month. In addition, phone calls from people in trouble were coming in at the rate of twenty-five to a hundred per month.

One male graduate student at Stanford felt that LSD gave him powers of observation and reasoning which excelled those of the faculty. His professors disagreed. Until he "revised" his style of thinking, he was in danger of being asked to pursue his originality elsewhere. Without drugs, such grandiosity in thinking would suggest a paranoid disorder. The probable effect of LSD in the student suggests aggravation of latent paranoid tendencies.

It is perfectly understandable that troubled and emotionally unstable individuals are frequently those most attracted to psychedelic drugs. Essential to part of this motivation is a wish that these problems will magically diminish or disappear. Professionally trained researchers and much of the "lay" literature report dramatic improvement or even "cure" (an awkward word to use in psychiatry) for individuals "treated" with LSD. These reports are poorly substantiated and constitute fervency rather than science. The same is true of hysterical scare articles, in many newspapers, which violently condemn psychedelic drugs, even marijuana.

Not only troubled individuals seek these drugs. As described by Lipinski and Lipinski (1967), various motivations prompt drug use in students, who seek change and improvement in personality style and function. The opposite may occur. Walters (1967) asserts that "the hallucinogenic drugs are dangerous . . . their result is narcissism and their penalty is emptiness and decreased self-esteem." Farnsworth (1966), director of Health Services at Harvard University, warns of the abuse of psychedelic drugs in young adults. He feels that these drugs inhibit academic function, creativity, and interpersonal relationships.

In severe adverse reactions, panic, psychotic episodes, or suicide may occur. Panic reactions are symptoms of a complex (usually intense) emotional build-up, often accompanied by paranoid thoughts of a persecutory nature, seeking expression in erratic, impulsive action. If appropriate emergency treatment is readily available, hospitalization is not necessary. At the Haight-Ashbury Free Medical Clinic in San Francisco, "bummers" are "talked down" by volunteer workers, who are most frequently nonprofessional individuals personally experienced with drugs. David Smith, director of the clinic, feels that nonprofessionals do a better job of handling a panic reaction than a psychiatrist, who may complicate matters by focusing on negative symptoms instead of providing reassurance and support. So-called "antidote" drugs (phenothiazines and sedatives) are rarely used or needed at the Free Clinic. Drug synergy in the form of the atropine effect of DMT added to the atropine effect of a phenothiazine is thereby avoided, since many drug users do not always know which drug or drugs they have ingested. Such a synergistic effect can produce death, as can happen when an individual who is drunk takes a nonlethal but excessive amount of barbiturates.

Psychotic episodes are short-lived or prolonged, involve thought distortions (called delusions), fear, illusions, and unusual if not bizarre behavior. Frequently, due to the abrupt onset, the episode startles. A twenty-year-old male had this experience:

> About six weeks ago I went to Vietnam on a ten-week civilian volunteer program, but was sent home because I was using drugs: the Eastern type of marijuana and a small amount of LSD. I didn't accomplish what I wanted to do. For six weeks I used drugs, immersing myself in them and in teaching. I was caught by a government official and three days later was on a plane returning home. My parents and friends were surprised and a little amazed at my personality change—I understand it as a type of schizophrenia—I'm very ambitious—want to talk to the *New York Times* about covering the situation in Vietnam—want to bring my Vietnamese girl

friend back here and marry her—she could go to college—she's bright.

He was confused, moderately dissociated, and depressed. He asked whether I thought he should take any more drugs. I strongly advised that he let his doctor prescribe any drugs he might need, and helped with a referral for treatment. That evening, at home, he took 500μg of LSD, became floridly psychotic, and on an emergency basis was hospitalized.

Another case involves a twenty-one-year-old male and some marijuana.

> I had some kind of emotional crisis or breakdown which was pre-cipitated by a break-up with my girl. Then I took some marijuana and went off the deep end. Suddenly I left school and went to see my mother, who wanted me to stay at home. I didn't, and started driving back to school. I began hallucinating, thought I was chas-ing around trying to find my girl friend and a fraternity brother. I was driving like a mad man, once on the wrong side of the free-way. Then I stopped the car and climbed down the embankment. I dug into the soil trying to find my girl friend and fraternity brother. My fingers started bleeding. I took off all my clothes and ran through a field to a house where a woman lived alone. After opening the door, she panicked and ran screaming out of the house to a neighbor's. The three of them tried to calm me. About five minutes later the police arrived and took me into custody, where a doctor gave me first aid. In jail I tried to commit suicide—had lots of religious thoughts. They booked me on a vagrancy charge. I pled guilty. Then they took me to a mental hospital.

Extensive in-patient psychiatric treatment resulted in improvement. Marijuana, at best, played an incidental role. Psychotic reactions last-ing months or years occur in those individuals who possess a predilec-tion for such a reaction, either by being a "borderline individual" (pre-psychotic) or because of "malvaria." According to Hoffer (1965), a malvarian is an individual who excretes in his urine a mauve factor, identifiable qualitatively by a laboratory litmus-paper test. It is believed that some of these individuals possess a (greater than average) latency for schizophrenia, possibly due to familial biogenetic predisposition. Hoffer contends that malvarians are more likely to endure prolonged adverse reactions to psychoactive agents, especially LSD. Further re-search is necessary to investigate the possibility of this suspected clinical entity.

Suicide is an uncomfortable reality in America. In college students, the suicide rate of about 1/10,000 per year is higher than the suicide rate of the nonstudent population of the same age. In the total population, one third of all suicides occur in individuals who use drugs obtained from, or prescribed by, a physician (Brophy, 1967). This would include those who beg or steal drugs from relatives and friends. Conventional suicide (drug ingestion such as that of barbiturates, leaping from heights, and *some* car "accidents") cannot match the sensationalism evoked when LSD is incriminated.

In Southern California, a twenty-three-year-old student took LSD three times within four months. He developed the delusion that he had *all* the answers to the work in his academic program and went to discuss this with his professor, who referred him to the outpatient psychiatric clinic. He was evaluated as schizoid and severely depressed and was hospitalized. A month later he left the hospital against medical advice, saying he was going to return to his work. Police were notified, but he couldn't be located. Two days later he committed suicide by inhaling carbon monoxide.

Another male student, age twenty, took LSD eight or nine times, came to the outpatient psychiatric clinic because of being "out of contact with reality" intermittently. While waiting for the psychiatrist on emergency call to interview him, he impetuously fled from the building, ran into the parking lot, and rammed himself against a parked car, breaking his neck. As a quadriplegic in the hospital, he displayed no emotion but told of "feeling that I was fused with the car —that we were one." Death occurred in two weeks.

The last case brings up a vital point: an individual who remains *aware* that the bizarre effects of LSD intoxication are due to the influence of the drug which he has taken will tend not to *act* in a bizarre manner. He who "forgets" what is happening sacrifices reality orientation, permitting terror to be followed by impulsive, life-endangering behavior. Apathy can also be life endangering, though not in the *physical* sense. It endangers mental and emotional stability. The "apathy syndrome" is a risk invited by the chronic LSD user.

A twenty-year-old male undergraduate voluntarily came to the student health center. He spoke slowly, deliberately, and his voice contained no discernible emotion. He hadn't shaved or changed clothes for a week. During the past year, he had taken LSD more than forty times, gradually withdrew from his friends, and lived alone. He said,

"I want to go away somewhere and be alone. I'm tired of school. Someone said that I could get a medical leave and not get *F's* in all my courses. I haven't been to classes in six weeks." He appeared dejected and disillusioned. Hospitalization was refused; he declined any medication. A medical leave was arranged and he left the office. Three years have passed; he remains on medical leave. Of course, one sees analogous cases in students who eschew drugs.

A specter waits. It is called amphetamine, a chemically uncomplicated mime capable of several beguiling roles. Usually, for students, it is prescribed for those individuals who desire to lose weight or for procrastinators needing to grind out term papers or indulge in exam-cramming. Its most vicious role is manifest when amphetamines are injected intravenously. Thus, a person "shoots speed" to "blow his mind." Users proclaim that this sledgehammer effect has no equal. Doubtless. The undesired medical and psychiatric complications are also not to be doubted. They include: abscesses, septicemia, and hepatitis, due to needle contamination. An in-house drug administered with out-house sanitation.

The psychic effects? Wow! One gets cerebral "flashes," intense stimulation and wakefulness, hallucinations, loss of appetite, insomnia, mental exhaustion, and possibly convulsions preceding death. Tolerance to the drug is rapidly developed; therefore, increasingly larger amounts of the drug are necessary to obtain and maintain the "desired" effects. The average dose of an amphetamine prescribed by a physician is five milligrams; a devotee shooting "crystal" (methedrine) requires five, ten, or even twenty times that amount.

Serious complications following methedrine use are a common occurrence in the Haight-Ashbury district, and surely are also seen in all major cities. Physicians and staff at college health services are uneasy about the insidious but recognized increase in the use of amphetamines. One university in the South reported six amphetamine-induced psychoses in the past year. Recently, three students using amphetamine intravenously have come to our attention, two because hepatitis required their hospitalization. They recovered. The third student admitted to using heroin occasionally. The "hard stuff" is rare on college campuses.

Accurate statistics on trends of drug use among students are not obtained easily. The consensus of college mental-health personnel is, in 1968, that LSD usage is decreasing, while marijuana usage is increasing. Good news for botanists; bad news for amateur chemists. Unfortunately, marijuana is not totally innocuous. Keeler (1967) reports eleven cases of adverse reactions in a student population, including symptoms of panic, gross confusion, depersonalization, depression, and paranoia. He further comments that "all but two of the eleven individuals considered the benefits to far outweigh the unfortunate aspects and planned to continue use of the drug."

Reports of chromosomal damage and congenital birth defects, though not as yet scientifically documented, probably play a relative role in LSD's becoming less popular. More likely, the fact that the drug doesn't *do* much for students has an infinitely greater negative effect. In general, college students are better informed about drugs than older generations. But some can be incredibly naive. They are also gullible, particularly in regard to peer and "in-group" influences. These enticements and pressures are exerted on both emotionally disturbed and well-functioning students.

McGlothlin, Cohen, and McGlothlin (1967), studying the effects of LSD on normal human beings, find that ". . . persons who place strong emphasis on structure and control generally have no taste for the experience and tend to respond minimally if exposed. Those who respond intensely tend to prefer a more unstructured, spontaneous, inward-turning (though not socially introverted) life, and score somewhat higher on tests of aesthetic sensitivity and imaginativeness. They also tend to be less aggressive, less competitive, and less conforming."

Great literature provides marvelous characters who were aesthetically sensitive and by experimentation were "transformed." Dante invaded Hell by means of fantasy. Faust beckoned Mephistopheles to transform his body and soul. Dr. Jekyll ingested a foaming chemical to create Mr. Hyde; but what would have happened if Dante had chewed peyote, Faust had smoked pot, and Dr. Jekyll had become an acid head? Would the stories of Dante, Goethe, and Stevenson have been different? Imagine Kaffka on a "trip," Anton Bruckner "blowing his mind," El Greco "stoned."

The promise of transfiguration is inherent in psychedelic-drug use. But there isn't an erg of work, a microgram of love, a measure of creativity, or a degree of motivation in all the psychoactive agents that exist. These qualities exist in people, not in drugs. It is true that some individuals are stimulated or affected by drugs to perform work, love, and to be motivated toward function and productivity. Others may be negatively "stimulated."

In summary it can be said that psychedelic drugs *make evident* what already exists within the human mind, whether it be suicide or creation, hate or love, apathy or productivity. It is imperative that these drugs (use and abuse, as well as research, which *must* be continued) be controlled and utilized, if appropriate, by professionally trained and competent individuals. The crude laboratory, indiscriminate "prescribing," and persecution by misguided laws and authorities can play no effective role in a society which professes to be rational.

As in the Faustian dilemma, life must contain viable opposites and degrees of mystery. Albert Einstein, perhaps the most aesthetically sensitive scientist of our century, said, "The most beautiful experience we can have is the mysterious. It is the fundamental emotion which stands at the cradle of true art and true science."

Drugs and Catholic Students

Jack H. Curtis

XVIII

*W*hat we wish to consider in this chapter is a contrast which may throw light on some of the features of the campus social environment conducive to marijuana use or to nonuse. Think, if you will, of a random sampling of students in a metropolitan Catholic university which reveals that only 11 per cent have had any experience at all with marijuana and that, of these, less than a half could be described as having been, at any time, regular users of "pot"—that is, even once or twice a month! Imagine musing about this finding while standing in front of a window in a research lab which overlooks the Haight-Ashbury District in a valley less than a mile from the hill on which this university stands.

Before "Haight-Ashbury hippies" became a cliché, the Urban Life Institute had openly courted the then-new "community" with daylong conferences, cooperation with the Diggers, police-harassment studies, Haight-Ashbury Town Hall meetings, and other neighborhood activities. Several commune dwellers had developed into cooperative and sympathetic interpreters of the hip culture to the "straight" researchers of the Urban Life Institute. Two of the facts which they communicated to us, long before they became public knowledge, were (1) that the hippie culture was a drug culture—the use of marijuana was a *sine qua non* of being hip and (2) that most of the new community came from middle-class families. Although we were never able, because of the high mobility of the hippies, to get any exact proportions of Catholic-family backgrounds during the time period we are considering, I can recall that I made a habit of asking this question and being surprised, in answer, at the number of Catholics reported. Ex-seminarians, especially, were greatly overrepresented among the hippies in comparison with the composition of other neighborhoods in San Francisco. At any rate—and regardless of the per cent of the total number of hippies that had Catholic backgrounds—it suffices to note that there were large numbers of them in the Haight-Ashbury using pot, while up here on the hill the predominantly Catholic student body of the university did not. There are many "obvious" answers to the question "Why the difference?" Those in the Haight-Ashbury had left the Church while those at the university had not, for example. Yet the fact is that the Church has no position on the smoking of marijuana. Catholics can smoke marijuana and remain in the Church.

There was one question-answering procedure that was easiest for a middle-class researcher in his late forties to follow—this was certainly not participant observation in the youthful hippie movement but, rather, keeping one eye on that movement through student and hippie reports, and doing an intensive analysis of the student population at the university. There were two questions that ordered our analysis of student use of marijuana—"Why?" and "Why not?" The "why" question was, of course, why did the small percentage of marijuana users engage in the practice in a milieu which they shared with the vast majority of students who did not engage in the act even once? "Why not?" is the obvious question with regard to this majority.

The Catholic university studied was in the process of responding to the general pressure for an updating of the Church. Administrators, resident assistants, faculty members, and students were anxious that an objective look at the university be taken—one with no punitive action against the real or suspected illicit-drug users who might be identified. In a pilot, naturalistic inquiry, fifteen LSD users who had also smoked pot and more than thirty-five students who had had experience with marijuana only were found to be extremely vocal about their experiences and viewpoints. Some of these same students were also drawn in the random survey sample where they became doubly voluble, since, on the one hand, they could serve as critics—providing information on what the survey questionnaire schedule did and did not uncover about the university scene—and since, on the other hand, they could serve as contributors and provide valuable data about drug use itself.

It was our naturalistic or intensive-observation sample that told us about off-campus students. "Dormies" vs. "day-hops" have differing exposure to marijuana use. The "day-hops" have a higher incidence and prevalence of the practice. "Day-hops" living at home are not as prone to marijuana smoking as those who share quarters with other students off campus. These latter are not as prone to illicit-exotic drug use as those who share quarters with nonstudents or students at other universities. Very few students live alone. Our interview data supported these crucial distinctions made by our intensive sample of fifty.

Even more importantly, our fifty informants—the anthropological term seems to fit them best—were able to provide information which made it possible to characterize the nature of the milieu of this Catholic university, to give us leads to the subterranean social networks of pot users, and to tell us the reasons why marijuana use there was not a widespread practice. They showed us how the family backgrounds of the students, the selection factors which brought them to this university, the school's social system and its control mechanisms, and the nature of parent-youth relations were all crucial social variables to consider. Peer-group relationships shed light on the question only in the context of these other factors.

The students voiced much of the same self-criticism that Catholic educators had advanced in the past decade regarding the American Catholic "mentality." Monsignor Ellis (1966) ascribes these Catholic attitudes to lower-class backgrounds, the nonintellectual traditions of immigrant American Catholics, and the moral and pragmatic orientations of their ecclesiastical leaders. O'Dea (1958) asserts that the Catholic mentality suffers from "the basic characteristics of the American Catholic milieu" which inhibits the development of mature intellectual activity: formalism, clericalism, moralism, authoritarianism, and defensiveness. Hassenger (1966) posits that Catholic universities "founded to serve a self-conscious minority" reflect an isolationist stance which emphasizes external devotion, strict sexual morality, and other protections from the lax new-world morality.

Our Catholic university here serves that clientele so vigorously criticized. The ethnic backgrounds of the students who dominate the university are Irish-American and Italian-American. The lower-middle and middle-class standing of so many of the students' families is a testimony to their persistence in striving for upward social mobility, for many can ill-afford the tuition. Bureaucratic more than entrepreneurial in orientation, students' families are well integrated in society in positions of responsibility and economic security considerably above those of their families of a generation or two ago. Respectability is prized and it is extremely threatening when a member of the family appears to be "throwing it all away."

Most of the students here are raised in Catholic homes which do not reflect so much a Catholic isolation as a solidarity with and a conformity to those values which, ironically, have been associated with the Protestant ethic. For instance, no student interviewed described his marijuana trip as a mystical experience. It seems paradoxical that illicit-exotic drug users and students at a religiously oriented university are almost unanimous in rejecting any notion of mysticism attached to their drug practices, whereas other students (see Section I) do seek religious meanings through drugs. The answer to the paradox lies in their socialization into a modified "Protestant ethic" by their Catholic parents and supportive Catholic institutions. Weber (1963) describes the predominant "givens" in the Western world as

> . . . inner worldly asceticism; rationalism; a sober and dominant bureaucracy; the ideal of alertness and self-control; the exaltation of commerce and vocations with a power distribution to maintain them and military force to protect and facilitate them; the proliferation of the apparatus of the state; indifference to religious feeling (*in the present context this would have to be interpreted as indifference to emotional or expressive religious behavior in contrast to rational and formalistic religious participation*) and the emphasis on institutional religious forms accompanied by suspicion of the independent religious seeker; the rejection of personal ethics and personal loyalties as dictating modes of economic and bureaucratic intercourse; and success in business as the proof of salvation and as the finest fruit of a rational way of living (p. 220).

The Protestant ethic of the parents as reported by their children and the usual characterization of American Catholics as "bureaucratic" are not inconsistent. *These* Catholic families, as stated earlier, are highly selective and not representative of all Catholic families in America. They have managed an amalgam of both the entrepreneurial and the bureaucratic mentalities. Helmut Wagner (1954) seems to describe it well:

> The main economic ambitions of the American middle classes, in contrast to the Protestant ethic and spirit of capitalism, is to gain and spend what one can, and to spend part of future earnings as well. Hard work to increase income, by way of advancing one's occupational career in the corporate setting, becomes the key to an increase in possessions which increases the material comfort of one's family.
>
> This ambition is not "materialistic." It represents an intangible value: that of demonstrating, asserting, or improving one's social status in a community which has changed the cherished price of competitive effort from economic independence combined with the "inner-directed" self-satisfaction of "rugged individualism" to status dependence combined with the "other-directed" satisfactions of a mobile conformism (p. 38).

While it would be an oversimplification to equate this "Protestant-ethic-in-a-bureaucratic-social-context" with the world view of these students' families, nevertheless, students fell back on reasons such as these when asked how their parents view people who use drugs. Their parents characterize marijuana as deadly and dangerous and lump it together with addictive drugs such as morphine and heroin. This is not so important for the questions we are pursuing here as the reasons which parents give these students for not using exotic drugs. In the main, they view people who use drugs as threats to the social order. When there is a good society to live in and a God to pray to, when one's needs are met by family protection and solidarity, when there is approval and prestige to strive for, and when, if one needs it, there is an acceptable drug—alcohol—available, experimentation with the social forms and psychological adaptations which characterize the image of marijuana users is viewed with suspicion and hostility. Marijuana use is a threat to the good, the given, and the hoped-for.

The successful family makes of its young both good Catholics and successful men and women. The symmetry of male-female socialization is disrupted in the middle-class Catholic family. It is not uncommon for more affluent Catholics to follow the Kennedy pattern of providing a first-class secular education for their sons and routing their daughters to Catholic colleges for protection. Despite its proximity to the university, few students frequent the Haight-Ashbury. Many coeds at the university have not been over to this area of the city because "their families would be upset." The curiosity that young people from a different background might have is not expressed. Family authoritarianism—which dictates "proper" conduct—is reinforced religiously (in both senses of the word) in Catholic elementary and high schools. Data from the Office of Admissions reveal that approximately 75 per cent of the students have twelve years in such institutions. Students from such a background have a strong influence on the general atmosphere of the university. Although a few parents have criticized this university as wicked because of stories they have heard or because of some of the public utterances of the faculty, the social milieu of the university comes close to being precisely what the family would like it to be.

Whether or not the views imputed to their parents by the students are accurate and, if so, how characteristic these parents are of the American Catholic family are not as relevant as the point that these are the views upon which the students *act* both in relation to the university and to their parents. Secondly, of course, the students at this university are highly selected and the selective processes are intricately interwoven to bring a type of person from a type of family to a type of university, and finally, to keep him there.

The Catholic women's "choice" of a college is simply an extension of their prior attendance at parochial elementary and high schools. It seems likely, in view of the high percentage of men at this university who have attended parochial high schools, that the same holds true for them. The cost of tuition fees and books and room and board and allowances are such at this university that only parents of higher socioeconomic status would seem to be able to afford them, but from data on parental income it can be inferred that many families make extraordinary sacrifices to send their children here. They want to give their children opportunities; for many it is a further upward social step beyond what they as parents had. When their children come here, it symbolizes the parental aspiration for their offspring's socioeconomic success. It also demonstrates that the parents themselves are "arriving." No wonder students report that they are under great family and self-imposed pressure to make good.

Another selective factor is the admission standard. Both a high grade average in secondary school and high scholastic aptitude-test score are required. This seems to work in two directions. It is probably the successful middle-class which can produce the acceptable student for this university. Middle-class parents value the child's development of internalized standards of conduct, and he tends to be trained primarily for attitudinal conformity. Expectations of attitudinal conformity in this socioeconomic class are directed at the very identity of the child, at his whole personality. *All* of his being must conform. Arnold Green (1946) has called this "personality absorption." The admission requirement selectively brings a more "motivated" student to the university and this has great consequences for his behavior while here and his readiness to accept the parental authority of priests and other faculty members. Obviously, other schools with high standards *do* have higher rates of marijuana use. Presumably, their selection is of less convention-abiding youth. The Catholic orientation here suggests that the conformity of our students is to a specifically Catholic as well as middle-class convention. About 90 per cent of the students accepted to the university are Catholic and approximately 70 per cent are from Catholic high schools. It seems likely that only families bent on preserving their Catholic heritage through exposure to Catholic philosophy and theology (and to potential Catholic mates) are willing to make the financial sacrifices involved and to dedicate their children to these same ideals.

There are selective factors of a more subtle nature which affect the student body. There is a high attrition rate at the university. Those who have been sifted out are, of course, no longer available for study. The juniors and seniors remaining, despite frequent complaining, are the ones who have survived the classroom competition for grades and the continued demands for behavioral control imposed by the college social system. Those who don't like it, who want a more casual scene, drop out, fall out, or transfer. One pot-LSD user who was both in the random sample and who served as an informant in the intensive-study group, illustrates this point: coming from a rural state, he has a great desire to be "where the action is."

> I have always thought the bohemian life was what I wanted. I had visions of a mattress on the floor with a hot-plate and books surrounding it. Marijuana didn't enter the fantasy at all, though I vaguely knew it was there. Until reading about the drug, I was con-

vinced I would never use it, for I thought it was addictive. LSD
had interested me since I had first heard about it. At first, I was
sure I wouldn't use it either, but as I read more about it I decided
it would be safe under a doctor's care.

He was easily able to get marijuana, and for two-and-a-half months
he smoked pot. "I spent thirty-five dollars on grass during this time,
and I'm convinced it led to my downfall in school. It seemed to make
me indifferent toward my studies so I simply quit attending classes.
By the time I caught myself and tried to salvage the semester it was
too late." Despite a bad LSD trip, which took him to a psychiatric
ward, and swearing off drugs to placate his parents, and to remain in
school, his poor grade average finally got him disqualified. He now
lives in the Haight-Ashbury.

Since a goodly number of the hippies using exotic drugs and residing in the nearby hippie area report that they have a Catholic family background, it is interesting to find that they describe it in much
the same way that university students do. Although there is little interaction between the university students and the hippies, many hippies are drop-outs from Catholic families of the same socioeconomic
stratum as the university students. *What the students want to conform
to, the hippies want to get away from.*

Why most students at a Catholic university do conform and
do not use marijuana and why a handful of students plus the Catholic
hippies do not conform to middle-class conventions and *do* use marijuana requires further consideration. Our data show *some* tendency
for broken homes to be related to marijuana use and some tendency
for parochial-school background to be related to non-use, but a much
more revealing comparison is made possible by taking an approach
bolder than the use of statistics.

The Catholic students (who have smoked pot) *unanimously
reject the idea that marijuana or any psychedelic drug can have any
effect upon a life philosophy or a mystical approach to life or the supernatural.* Anyone familiar with the original hippie movement knows
that this is a direct violation of the hippie dogma that "turning on"
is an absolute requisite to discovering one's self, one's relations to
others, and one's relations to God or the All. These contradictory beliefs, I feel, bring us closer to the "why?" and to the "why not?" answers that we seek. As a sociologist, I have no quarrel with the notions
of Protestant and Catholic ethic, of the importance of socioeconomic

class positions and family background as they relate to behavior. These social factors, however, are the external, observable phenomena which we can measure. In our preoccupation with the positivistic approach, we suffer the disadvantage of diverting our gaze from an area that tells us more than all of the questionnaire responses and statistical data that we have gathered. In this instance I suggest that we need to look at the inner-life of the Catholic student and the ex-Catholic hippie. We are looking for values, cathected and made a part of the individual's most important motivations—those which move him to the "good life" and which govern his conception of the "good man."

We were extremely fortunate to have such a tantalizing difference in conceptions of the inner life emerge right under our noses. The situation had all the makings of a crucial experiment. Yet problems of methodology made it difficult for us to be as precise as we should have liked. We were forced, as is all too common in social epidemiology, to take the retrospective approach to an experimental design. We have two groups of students which are—or were—in many ways alike and yet sufficiently different as to invite our curiosity. When we imitate the form called experimental design, we imagine a point in history when the difference did not exist. Finally we attempt, by inference, to reconstruct what happened developmentally and/or situationally to the Catholic hippie vs. the Catholic university student to explain the difference. Do you not share with me the sense that such hindsights are contrived and artificial even if sophisticated by the dodge of correlation chasing? I prefer to rely on conceptions of the inner man instead. There are three paths to these.

One conception is that the exotic drugs, including marijuana, do have genuine religious functions. This is the "psychedelic" assumption. It is held that the drug experience can be either directly one of revelation or a series of gradual expansions of the inner awareness until a full-fledged mystical union of man with God occurs. A corollary conception is that the drug may not have within it any compelling force which leads man to the mysteries, but that the drug—whether LSD, amanitas, marijuana, and so on—does work to reveal to a man his inner self and that it does this by peeling away the successive layers of preconscious material, of restraint and defense and so forth (Masters and Houston, 1966). When a person sees within himself, understands his structure and feeling, he is then free to accept himself, free to experience, and free to see the world as it is. Necessarily, such a process would lead a religious man directly to God. In either case the conception is of the exotic drug as a tool to open the inner self and to set up conditions whereby a man may have a mystical experience therein to sense the nature and the glory of the Lord.

In our samples we had only one student who found a psychedelic (mind-expanding) drug an aid to what could be called a mystic experience. The fact was that he originally had used marijuana as part of a gesture of independence from the "paternalistic atmosphere" of the university. He found it relaxed him. He made elaborate preparations for an LSD trip and taped his comments during the trip. He volunteered us the tape for transcription. During his trip he kept repeating that now he knew what it was to be in the darkness and to walk into the light of Christ. He mentioned frequently that it was all as Father X had said it would be when he could see the light of Christ for himself. When he was reinterviewed, he said that he thought he could have come close to the same realization without LSD. He said that he was very much under the influence of Father X and that it would only have been a matter of time before he had such a revelation. He continued the sporadic use of marijuana, for relaxation, and discontinued using LSD. Months after he left the university for civil-rights work in the South, he made special reference in a letter to his LSD experiences and commented that he was now receiving the sacraments regularly, whereas before, he had been quite lax in his religious practices. He was the only student among twenty whom we knew as LSD users who even remotely related his psychedelic experiences to mysticism.

Another conception, a sociological one, has two aspects. On the one side is social control which has already been discussed. There are external prohibitions on illicit-drug use. The family, the faculty, and the university administration are against it. Local religious and political authority is also against it—and that authority is also very much part of the local Catholic world since the mayor and police chief are also Catholics who represent official positions that back up the negative sanctions of family and school. Thus, there are no institutions in the sociological sense which allow—let alone induce—the student to try marijuana. On the other hand, students as adolescents have been living in a cosmopolitan center where marijuana use is widespread and where most youth share the folklore or informal pharmacology pertaining to its effects. The effects most discussed in the teen-age groups in which students earlier participated were of pleasure. Before they ever had access to a supply or perhaps even to a real pothead, students had learned what marijuana was supposed to do. The success or failure of pot smoking rested, then, simply on whether it produced—when finally the individual did try it—a "high." Almost all of our informants agreed that such was the case. Those who did try it, in spite of negative social sanctions, in spite of their own interests in being good students doing the conforming things that they themselves had come to value, were doing it simply for fun. There was no underground community among them which provided justifications on more far-reaching grounds of personal or social value, no set of justifications which created them as a group opposed to or superior to the square and terrible world against which the hippies inveigh. Adolescent fun-seekers did not become a separate community, did not develop an ideology of their own. When they did use marijuana, they knew it was for fun and they knew it was wrong and they disagreed with neither tenet. If marijuana then failed to give pleasure, which is very often the case with early use (Becker, 1963), there was no reason at all to continue.

A third consideration is philosophical. Bergson's (1935) two sources of morality and religion, pressure and aspiration, are involved. The advantages of extending the analysis beyond the psychedelic and sociological models are several. The way remains open for our regarding mystical experience as genuine without positing successive layers of the unconscious to be probed by drugs or reduced to the determinism of individual conduct by social forces which are abstractions. Secondly, by widening the concept of biology, we say that all morality is in essence biological, another Bergson concept. By this we mean that life is a vital impulse which struggles through matter and is not reducible to it. Briefly, it is a rejection of mechanism as anything more than a heuristic model and one that has little heuristic value in analyzing mysticism. One's confidence in that approach is strengthened by the fact that William James passed this way before us. He successfully avoided reductionism in his *Varieties of Religious Experience*. Though he intended to translate Bergson into English, death prevented him from it.

In the foregoing we have the ingredients of our conclusion. The students on our hill who have used pot deny its utility for mystical experience. The hippies in the valley have an ideology which affirms its variety of uses, among which are journeys into the mystical realm.

The students, on the other hand, are living in a community characterized by a social system depending on more or less deeply rooted *habits*, habits of obedience to parents, parent-surrogates at parochial schools, and now to professors, priests, and residence assistants. From the student body itself there emanates a vaguely perceived impersonal imperative. There is a pressure to be accepted socially, to succeed in classes. There is an order which is experienced by the student as a social imperative. He is conscious of this pressure. He complains about it, too, and may imagine how fine it would be to transfer to a more glamorous campus, an exotic one with more excitement. Sometimes the student complains that the campus social order is a police state; yet it is quite evident that the student wants this social solidarity of shared obligation and goals. The greater part of his strength, his social self, is invested in his campus life and to responding to its demands which his presence here legitimizes. Through the university he gets the greatest returns for his activity. Most students, even those who forecast darkly that theirs is "the last generation of Catholics," are attached by their own engagements to the obligation of the community. External constraints are secondary. Religion sustains and reinforces the claims of the social order at the university.

There is moral distress when there is too great a gap between the social self and the individual self. Catholic mysticism has had many rapturous and ecstatic practitioners in the past, but the variety of mysticism generally advocated at the university aims at restoring the personal self to tranquility and peace. True, sermons in the university church are often designed to motivate the student to share Christ with others. From time to time, there are movements to *do* something for the poor, the handicapped, or the oppressed. Almost every student participates at some time or another in a social-action program. There is a strong theological motivation in such work.

Yet, most significantly for our analysis, the appeals to fulfill one's obligations in the university community and to extend one's activities into the larger society outside the university are based on reason. Morality and religion are based on rational norms. Proofs for the existence of God, for necessity of moral order and for personal sanctity are offered as morally imperative. "You should . . . ." is applied as a pressure or a propulsive force. Faith means "the Faith" which is defended by rational arguments.

This is the context in which Christ is presented to the university students. The Ten Commandments are considered valid, but negatively stated.

> Which Commandment is the first of all? Jesus answered, "The first is: Hear, O Israel, the Lord Our God, the Lord is one; and you shall love the Lord your God with all your heart, and with all your soul, and with all your mind, and with all your strength. The second is this, 'You shall love your neighbor as yourself.' There is no other commandment greater than these." (Mark 11:29–31)

Thus, the emotion introduced by Christianity in the virtue of charity and in identification with Christ—the charisma—leads to behavior and a doctrine is developed to regulate the behavior. "But [says Bergson] neither has its metaphysics enforced the moral practice, nor the moral practice induced a disposition to its metaphysics." The two forces of pressure and aspiration blend into a system of obligation, become rationalized into norms which can be appealed to by reason. But the role of emotion—in this case, the charisma of Christ—is primary in the motivation to behavior.

Thus, students who face a crisis of faith are often led back into an even greater faith than before by a priest (ordinarily) who, charismatic himself, is able to guide the student from the dark into the light of Christ. Other waverers may decide that they are "in too deep" with their parents and the university—graduation is not too far off—and they effect some accommodation between their personal selves and their social selves and make-do until they graduate. Ventilating one's emotions to intimate friends provides some relief for the person whose faith is, at best, formant. For the accepting student and for many of those with a crisis of faith, marijuana smoking is a pleasant relief-giving lark, much on the order of other less forbidden fruit, such as liquor and girls. But this is not so with the student whose crisis of conscience leads him to leave the university.

It is extremely significant that the main source of marijuana and LSD for campus students—at the time I speak—was the drop-out who came back to turn on his former classmates and friends. Regrettably, most of the information I have on this point is second-hand, but of the six drop-outs I was able to reach personally and from the second-hand information I received from the students (eleven others), it can be said that these former students were all impressed with the idea of love as personal union with fellow man and with God. Some of them were described as being fanatical in their zeal to turn on to

this mystic trip. Students remaining at the university failed to compre-
hend them although they spoke of them favorably.

Enough of the students at the university who set the tone of the
campus consider marijuana smoking as unacceptably deviant—alien to
the obligation system of the student body. Those who have smoked
marijuana did so as a lark—perhaps as a sophisticated one. They were
seeking pleasure; they did so surreptitiously and precisely for the reason
which they gave. Most users really could not explain their behavior
except to say that they were "looking for something."

Q. "Something religious?"

A. "No. Catholics have their trip. I admire Him more than anyone else who ever lived. He was on a trip all of his life."

The Catholic mystic (and there are some on campus) imitates Christ
and achieves a spiritual union, a more or less complete identification.
He is absorbed into the system of obligation with the emotional warmth
of his love of God and his fellow men. In his external appearance, at
least, he is Apollonian. Marijuana is not his "bag," for his is a philosophical rather than pharmacological orientation.

Just as there are some Catholic students who—apparently less
interested in religion and more interested in the secular world—drop
out or fall out of the university, there are also religious men who do so.
It is sometimes difficult to assess the grounds for departure, whether
it is a crisis of faith which is so resolved or whether it is simply lack of
interest. For those who leave because of faith and conflict, the aban-
donment can only be false since, in Bergson's terms, what are abandoned are obligations, metaphysics, and a set of ethical conceptions
but what cannot be left behind are the essence and the cause. These
are the emotional aspirations and the spiritual inspirations of Christianity. Those who do leave, shedding the pressures of obligation but remaining mystically oriented, are the ones most likely, it seems to me,
who will not only open themselves to a variety of worldly experiences
—and disappointments—but to the psychedelic drugs. Having failed
their mission, failed to satisfy their hunger within the traditional environment, would they not be the seekers most ready to believe the
psychedelic arguments? Whether or not in turning on they find their
goal, we cannot say. We would assume that their effort involves an
extension of their being into new grounds, an attempt to remythologize
in terms more universal than Catholic.

In any event, both the psychedelic argument itself and the more worldly myths come from outside the Catholic environment. Thus, I propose that the Catholic student who becomes a hippie is moved initially by a crisis of faith, is attracted by the apparent opportunity to evade the community and its mysteries of obligation, and is then exposed in his wanderings to the alternative conception whereby a religious solution is offered which is pharmacological and universal—that is, he must learn the new myths outside of a strongly Catholic milieu. Upon accepting those myths, which necessarily implies that he is considerably involved with others who are non-Catholics or ex-Catholics, he embarks on a new path which, however odd its trappings, finds him bound by the same dimensions of the religious absolute that defined his seeking when it was conducted within a more conventional world.

It may be that, as Bergson suggests, there is a mystic within each of us. Perhaps, that essence can be called forth by pharmacological means. Certainly we know it can be exalted by the more traditional ones known to the saints and the prophets. If it is to be a pharmacological route to mysticism, let us be sure of its effectiveness. Let it not be that "diabolical mysticism" of the delusional and paranoid experience, the dangers of which William James saw so clearly. And let us by all means seek the ways by which each of us can meditate on the prophets of Israel, on the visions of Christ, on the emanations of God, and on those other mysteries perceptible by those blessed with vision and understanding.

Drugs and
High School Students

Richard H. Blum, Jean Aron,
Thomas Tutko, Sanford Feinglass, Joel Fort

XIX

This chapter offers the results of questionnaire surveys of 5,480 students in four San Francisco Bay Area high schools. The organization of the chapter reflects the development of the study itself. The first round consisted of a pretest questionnaire to about 2,000 students in several schools. Difficulties in questionnaire administration, which biased the sample, and inadequacies in question phrasing led to revisions in procedure and also account for the fact that results of the pretest are not reported here. The second round, which is reported, consisted of the administration of the revised questionnaire to all students (N = 1,614) in one high school in an upper-middle class suburban area (average family income $12,000), a town adjacent to one of the colleges included in the study. The high school survey was conducted during the same year that the college study was being done. The findings from this high school are reported by Blum (with Bausek) in the first section of the chapter. The second section of the chapter represents the next step, which was a further modification of the questionnaire. This version was administered to 2,221 students in two high schools that

321

were both within twenty miles of the first. One was in a middle-class neighborhood in a suburban town; the other was in a lower-middle-class-working class neighborhood in one of the Bay Area cities. The data in the second section were gathered and are reported by Aron and Tutko. The third section of the chapter sets forth the results of a town-wide school survey using a similar instrument, administered to 1,645 students in a middle-class senior high school. The results are reported by Feinglass.

The several sections are bound together by common inquiries into reported student use of tobacco, alcohol, marijuana, hallucinogens, heroin, stimulants, volatile intoxicants (glue, gasoline, and so forth), and other substances. Common inquiry is also made into parental drug habits, drug use of peers, illicit-drug-taking opportunities, beliefs about drug effects, and information needs about the drugs in question.

UPPER-MIDDLE-CLASS HIGH SCHOOL

Tobacco. Thirty per cent of the boys and one fourth (27 per cent) of the girls report that most of their friends smoke. About three fourths (72 per cent) of all students say they themselves have tried smoking, and three fifths say their parents smoke. Eighteen per cent of the boys and 14 per cent of the girls say they themselves smoke regularly. Asked whether there is anything bad about smoking, 84 per cent of the students say "yes"; asked whether there is anything good, 34 per cent say "yes." Asked with whom they were when they first tried tobacco, they most frequently reply "friends of their own age"; this is five times more common than being with "older friends or parents." About 10 per cent say they were alone when they tried their first cigarette.

Analysis of the replies to open-ended questions asking what is good and bad about tobacco and what more information they want about it leads to the impression that they are informed about cancer dangers, although smokers' comments indicate that they do not appear to care. They accept smoking as a social practice and are taught about tobacco in a course on social living; they are not curious about it and few want any further information. Some students make comments which suggest an undercurrent of disbelief or distrust in what they are taught, asking "Is it *really* habit forming?" and "Does it *really* cause cancer?" Some are explicit in wanting facts, not opinions, and in disapproving of "scare" lectures. Some also speak of being uncertain because of disagreement among authorities: sometimes they remark that such disagreement leads them to doubt all authorities. A number of interesting individual observations were made in response to a question about differences between students who smoke and those who do not; some students are quite sophisticated in terms of psychological notions; others are careful observers.

However much teaching these students have had in regard to tobacco, they have not been given a sufficient orientation which allows them to expect and live with uncertainty or to think in terms of probabilities and an unfolding world of new but always tentative knowledge. Thus, the emphasis on "science" in health education appears to have been in terms of absolutes and possible moralizing—quite unlike the philosophy and proper uses of science itself. One sees how concrete and simplistic presentations, however much their ease and short-term appeal, lead to long-term educational failures. Here the problem becomes one of teaching teachers before teaching students.

There is also indication that high school health education—if it is to be called that, even though in this school "social living" may well be a course in conventional morality—must come to grips with the same problems facing adult health education regarding tobacco use. These problems include how to handle the anxiety, the primitive sense of invulnerability, and the denial of drug dependency which lead confirmed smokers intellectually to accept information on tobacco leading to disease but to disregard it in their conduct. An alternative reaction of discounting that information on various pseudo-intellectual grounds is also found to occur among students. It would be well, indeed, to find out which styles of presentation of what information to which students actually work best to reduce smoking.

Some few students are quite profound observers. It is likely that a teaching program utilizing their awareness might well help shape group norms. One also wonders, given the relationship between parental smoking and children's smoking (also noted by students here), about a double-barreled education program in prevention simultaneously involving parents and students. Could one not offer meetings once a week of evening groups for parents about treatment principles, in the hopes that as they reduce smoking (as some do), their youngsters might be more responsive to pressures to stop smoking or not to begin? In any event it is heartening that less than one fifth of the stu-

dents report themselves to be regular smokers. Any endeavor to learn
how that low rate came about (assuming it is correct) and how it can
be maintained is worth while.

Alcohol. More boys (43 per cent) than girls (35 per cent)
say that the majority of their friends drink, but slightly more girls than
boys (88 per cent vs. 84 per cent) state that they themselves have tried
alcohol. About the same number of boys and girls (88 per cent) say
their parents drink. Regular drinking is limited, 14 per cent of the boys
and 11 per cent of the girls reporting they do so. Three fifths of the
total sample acknowledge something wrong with persons their age
drinking whereas one fourth also state that there are good things about
persons their age drinking. Most students report that their first drink
was taken in the presence of their parents; this setting occurs almost
twice as often as being with friends their own age. Almost 10 per cent
of the girls report their first drink was on a date; about 3 per cent of
the students first tried alcohol when alone. Asked what was the largest
number of drinks consumed on any one occasion, students (almost a
third of those answering) most frequently say "one," with the next
most frequent number being six or more (for almost one quarter).

Analysis of replies to open-ended questions gives the impression
that drinking is accepted although more so for boys than for girls. Alcoholism emerges as an issue about which there is considerable confusion
and anxiety-producing misinformation; for example, "If you start
drinking at fourteen, will you become an alcoholic by age eighteen?"
Taught about alcohol in a social-living course, they are not avidly curious but those commenting do want information about its physical effects, about what constitutes sensible drinking, and about what alcoholism is and how it can best be avoided. An apparent exposure to
"scare" lectures leads them to stress extreme physical results such as
brain damage, cirrhosis, and kidney disease.

What the students have themselves requested by way of information appears to be a good basis for alcohol education: physical effects, how to drink safely, what alcoholism is, and how it can be recognized and prevented. In addition, one would propose using students
as "case finders" so that they not only learn something about how alcoholism can be treated, and where, but how they themselves can be
useful in guiding persons they know who may be pre-alcoholic or alcoholic into treatment. Such a positive program would reduce stress upon
dangers unlikely to occur in most of them and would accent their own

role as preventive and treatment agents. This should not only prove flattering and occasionally useful but should provide an acceptable vehicle whereby information might be conveyed. As with any drug-education program, the teacher becomes the critical agent. How to train teachers to teach about alcoholism (and tobacco and other drugs) in an informed and acceptable way constitutes a major area of endeavor. Of considerable interest is the extreme bimodal distribution of drinking frequency, with one large group being quite moderate, the other ingesting enough to become drunk. One wonders what further research would demonstrate about the drug-abuse potentials of these two strikingly different groups.

Marijuana. More than half of the students (57 per cent) know someone who smokes marijuana and one quarter have had the opportunity to smoke it. Sixteen per cent of the boys replying to the question say they have tried it, as have 10 per cent of the girls. On this item, unlike the others where "no-answer" or "don't-know" categories usually run about 3 per cent, there is a very high per cent of nonresponse, with 31 per cent of the sample not answering the query. Asked about present use, 5 per cent of the boys and 3 per cent of the girls say they are currently using marijuana; nonresponse to this item drops to 6 per cent. Seventy-seven per cent of the boys and 84 per cent of the girls indicate there are bad aspects to marijuana smoking, whereas 25 per cent of the boys and 23 per cent of the girls signify there are good features as well (primarily giving pleasure). Asked to describe the people they know who smoke marijuana, students (about two thirds) most frequently refer to casual acquaintances; one third have good friends who smoke. Almost 10 per cent say they have relatives who use marijuana. Many have older friends using it as well. (This is a double-coded item.)

The open-ended question replies reveal less information and more moralizing about marijuana than about tobacco or alcohol. Many believe marijuana use leads to other drugs, to dependency (physical or psychological), and so on. Some are concerned about the uncertainty of knowledge about effects or about differences among the experts. There is evidence that many would like to be better informed.

The remarkable number of "no-answer" reactions to the inquiry about marijuana experimentation as compared with the high response rates to tobacco and alcohol questions and to other marijuana questions raises the strong possibility that other students—possibly up

to the 25 per cent reporting opportunities—have tried the drug but are
afraid to admit it. Such anxiety is compatible with the angry explosive-
ness found in many spontaneous remarks scribbled on questionnaires
and accusing the survey administrators of a variety of sins of authority,
such as being policemen, being stupid, not understanding, and a series
of unflattering vulgarities. In any event, experimentation rather than
use appears to be the preferred pattern among those attributing value
to marijuana. Misinformation about the drug exists and students would
welcome an unbiased educational program.

    Hallucinogens. Almost half of the students (44 per cent)
know people who have used LSD, peyote, mescaline, morning-glory
seeds, or other hallucinogens. Seventeen per cent themselves have had
opportunities to try these substances, and 10 per cent of the boys and
5 per cent of the girls replying to the question say they themselves
have tried a hallucinogen. The "no-answer" category is again high,
with 34 per cent refusing to describe their own experience. On the
other hand, only 6 per cent refuse to comment on their current practices, and here one learns that 7 per cent of the boys and 1.5 per cent
of the girls are presently using hallucinogens (or 4 per cent of the total
student body). Most students (85 per cent) acknowledge bad aspects
of hallucinogen use but many, 41 per cent of those replying, also believe there are good things about such use (for example, medical and
mind-expanding uses). On this latter question, the "no-answer" rate
rises to 12 per cent. Some students volunteer that they are using datura
(Jimson weed); others that they are using Asthemador. Describing
the people they know who use hallucinogens, students (about three
fourths so reporting) most often cite the casual acquaintance; about
a third equally note good friends and older friends. Five per cent have
relatives using hallucinogens. (The user-description item is double-
coded.)

    Replies to the open-ended questions give the impression that
LSD is considered a dangerous drug on the grounds of brain damage
and chromosomal changes; psychological effects such as suicide and
the uninvited return "trip" are also known—sometimes almost directly
quoted from newspaper accounts. Several students from the school
have apparently been hospitalized following LSD use—events which
have shaped the views of the student body. There is considerable positive curiosity about what a trip is like and about the risks therein.
They are uninformed about hallucinogens other than LSD and would

like to know more about how it is used experimentally in medical work. Student comments indicate that some are involved in the hippie community of the Haight-Ashbury in San Francisco, and some acknowledge getting their LSD there. Others go to Big Sur for their supplies. Several report bad reactions to the hallucinogens they have taken.

More so than with conventional drugs, students do differentiate between hallucinogen users and non-users. In practice the marijuana and LSD users are grouped together by non-users and described as comprising the brightest *and* the dumbest students, also the richest and the poorest, and are further characterized as "loners" and eccentrics ("oddballs," and so on). Users, on the other hand, less often emphasize the differences between themselves and other students.

Proportionately the greatest sex differences in drug use occur in regard to LSD with four times more boys than girls using it. It is interesting that more students report current use of LSD than of marijuana, although a greater number of them have experimented with the latter. The "no-answer" rate raises the possibility that more have tried it than admit it, although the upper limit of experimentation is set (assuming that lie responses are minimal or balance each other) by the 17 per cent reporting any access or opportunity to use hallucinogens. It is also striking that the hallucinogens have a better image, defined as the number of students—approaching 50 per cent if nonresponse is extrapolated—saying there are good things about LSD use. This image is a general one: "Everything is beautiful under LSD" emerges as the most common kind of statement. The notion of a trip also has great appeal. One is referred to Weakland's chapter in *Drugs I* for a discussion of its significance. Unlike studies of adult LSD users (Blum and Associates, 1964) who were found to be more conscious of in-groups than matched non-using peers, students in this high school who are LSD (and pot) users discount their differences from other students, although we may assume they accentuate their differences from the "over-thirty" group. This finding is compatible with one social function of being a hippie (again see the Weakland chapter), which is to set oneself off against adults, not against peers. It is also compatible with the findings of our normal-population study (see companion volume) that illicit-exotic drug users are quite sensitive to disapproval from their age-mates and do what they can to minimize that discomfort.

Pep pills and goof balls. Fifteen per cent of the boys and 24 per cent of the girls say they know people using pep pills or goof balls, but only 4 per cent of the students say they themselves have tried them. On the other hand, most do not know what pep pills or goof balls are, and since their terminology is different, the low rate may partially reflect misunderstanding and the poverty of our inquiry item. Their terms "yellow jackets," "Christmas trees," "red devils," and other labels are descriptive of the pills themselves. Others report using No-Doze, Tirenol, benzedrine, dexedrine, and amphetamines without classifying these as pep pills. Cylert is also used to gain a stimulant effect.

Sniffing glue, gasoline, and other intoxicants. Twenty-two per cent of all students say they know people who sniff intoxicants to become high; 7 per cent of the boys and 2.5 per cent of the girls have themselves tried it. Many want to know more about the effects of sniffing; others volunteer that they have sniffed other things, for example, Johnson's Paste Wax, nitrous oxide from "Reddi-Whip" cans allowed to stand in the refrigerator after which contents are squirted into the mouth, and so forth.

Sleeping pills and tranquilizers. Sixteen per cent of the boys and 19 per cent of the girls say they know people using sedatives and/or tranquilizers without the knowledge of parents or physicians. Four per cent of the boys and 6 per cent of the girls say they themselves have tried such drugs without parental or medical approval.

Heroin. Four per cent of the students say they know people who are using heroin and five boys (5/1,560 responding or 0.3 per cent) say they themselves have tried it. The "no-answer" rate here is the average 3 per cent but may conceal a few additional heroin experimenters. One student volunteers that he is using codeine terpin hydrate in 80 per cent alcohol solution. Because of our interest in the use of heroin in such a favored-environment high school, we made further informal inquiries among students. Perhaps as many as 10 per cent of the students seem to know where it is available if they want it. The characteristics of high school suppliers appear to differ considerably from college drug sources. The latter tend to be students themselves or other professionals—for example, biochemists making LSD (see Blum and Associates, *Utopiates,* 1964)—whereas the high school students, although sometimes receiving supplies from their older college friends or siblings—especially for LSD or marijuana—report their heroin and stimulant sources to be lower-class adults. These poor males are said often to be Negro, living in near-by towns, who are habitual criminals even if not "professional" in the sense of career success. They obtain their supplies in the Tenderloin and Mission Districts of San Francisco and profitably resell to the curious high school market. College suppliers who were interviewed look down on the high school "peddlers," whom they describe as having criminal records, being vulnerable to "busts" (arrests), being unreliable, and not being "in"–members of any sophisticated drug-oriented group—that is, not hippies or swingers. Three high school suppliers were identified as once having been purveyors to the college trade, but not having made the grade socially, they slipped down to the high school sales department.

The questionnaire asked students whether they had ever felt "on the spot" because of group pressures to drink or take drugs. They were also asked how people responded to such pressures, how students reacted to being told *not* to drink, try marijuana, and so forth, and they were asked what they would tell their own high school-age children about using such drugs.

The replies to these open-ended items give the impression that students are aware of their own role in *choosing* groups or getting into situations where drug pressures are generated. Relatively few (16 per cent) complain of being under pressure but, instead, many propose that one ought to know what his associates are like or what situations are going to become before getting involved. Certainly, as students comment on drug-using situations, there is no feeling of the innocent's being seduced or of the naive's being misled. (The student doctrine of self-determination is in contrast to some adult conceptions of drug use as being initiated by means of victimizing the innocent; on the other hand, adults are well aware that youngsters may overestimate their capacity for evaluating friends and situations or for handling trouble.) The majority (57 per cent) do say they resent being *told* not to use a drug.

In considering their own role as potential parents, boys and girls differ, the girls being more conventional and moralistic in their comments whereas the boys are less systematic but, at the same time, less dogmatic. Younger students differ from older ones in their idea of what they would tell their own children; older students (seventeen, eighteen) are less directive and punitive and more likely to give information and leave the final choice to children. They are explicitly aware of the risk of a rebellious embracing of drug taking if parents insist on its not being done without giving grounds in fact. All students, however, fail to be aware of the role of psychological or group factors in considering either differential access or use of drugs or of risks of bad drug outcomes. A number propose that drug taking be done under parental or medical supervision; some are unaware that illicit drugs cannot be prescribed by physicians. A curious feature is that some students who are marijuana and/or LSD users themselves say they would not want their own children even to experiment with these substances, let alone use them chronically. (Note that similar child-protecting or alter-ego purifying responses may be elicited from habitual alcoholics or heroin addicts when asked about their wishes for their children.)

The replies to open-ended questions were coded for each age and sex group. Impressions derived from these replies are as follows:

Fourteen-year-old girls:
> Not well informed about drug use, not sympathetic to use of any drug except alcohol. Conceive of psychological abnormality as "causing" drug use; not particularly interested in learning more. Emphasis as mothers would be to scare their own children.

Fifteen-year-old girls:
> Much like fourteen-year-olds but becoming more perceptive and aware of shades of distinction in categorizing drug users and effects. A beginning reluctance to dictate drug conduct to their own children, but scaring remains the most common control device.

Sixteen-year-old girls:
> Increased sophistication about tobacco and alcohol with emphasis on the acceptability of "moderate" use. Increased concern with drug use as a rebellious response to injunctions and its symptomatic use to gain attention, or as an aspect of insecurity or emotional deficiency. They begin to accent the importance of good family-child relations as a way to avoid drug-use problems and imply that the drug issue will not arise in a well-knit family. Many girls accompany these remarks with conventional intolerance for drug use, except alcohol and tobacco, and for any excesses with these latter. Child influence by scaring is still common but being replaced by giving the child biased facts as a part of a rational (?) education.

Seventeen-year-old girls:
> Like sixteen-year-olds with reduced prejudice toward drug users, an increased tendency to blame parents if children become drug users, and in some cases the emergence of a tolerance for drug experimentation, preferably with parental knowledge (that is, with their

own knowledge as they play the parental role). Drinking and smoking are quite acceptable although there is more awareness of community dangers, as, for example, traffic accidents due to alcohol. Most are intolerant of drug use as a life style.

Eighteen-year-old girls:

This group speaks more of the diverse motivation of drug users and the need to examine motives instead of accepting simple explanations. As a group they are the most perceptive and thoughtful in considering individual drug use, and while they disapprove, they are least rejecting and punitive. Impartial explanations are preferred over biased information giving. More are now willing to let their children decide for themselves. In other ways they resemble the seventeen-year-olds.

Fourteen-year-old males:

Data lost.

Fifteen-year-old males:

Data lost.

Sixteen-year-old males:

Much like the sixteen-year-old girls except that differentiation between smokers and nonsmokers emphasizes the need for athletes to abstain from tobacco. They are sooner and more aware than girls of the dangers of driving after drinking. Theirs is a nonpunitive approach to drug users even though many disapprove of such use. They are unable to formulate what they would tell their own children, unlike girls who have obviously given their role of mothers considerable advance thought.

Seventeen-year-old males:

Marked differences between boys and seventeen-year-old girls emerge. They are much less perceptive or willing to think in terms of either individual motives or "psychology" or of group settings as playing any role in drug use or behavior. Nevertheless, they are more broad-minded, less punitive, even if they themselves would not use drugs. Condemnation of the comfortable moral sort found in the girls is rarer. They are also more likely to say they don't know about causes and effects and to suspend judgment as to rights and wrongs. This occurs even though they seem better informed as to the facts themselves. They remain unable to say what their disposition would be as parents guiding their own children in regard to drug use.

Eighteen-year-old males:

Much like the eighteen-year-old girls. A new difference which emerges between them and the girls is an emphasis on laws and on facts as factors to be considered in evaluating drug use and users. The laws themselves may become an object of interest and evaluation.

Students were asked their career goals and were classified by a job-classification scheme. Students sharing one or another career preference were then compared on their evaluations of marijuana smokers and on hazards and benefits from marijuana and hallucinogens. This attempt to link career interests to drug views was done on a subsample and because of the small numbers emerging into view—occupation subcategories cross tabulations—provide little information. The largest difference emerging is that students who contend that marijuana users are superior to non-users are more likely to express no career preference (40 per cent) than students seeing no differences between users and non-users or than those seeing non-users as superior; among these latter only 30 per cent express no career choice.

MIDDLE-CLASS AND LOWER-MIDDLE-CLASS HIGH SCHOOLS

Although there are inaccurate statistics throughout the drug world, there is, perhaps, no greater inaccuracy than on the high school level. One of the primary reasons is that the school officials who are responsible for drug education have a tendency to deny or discount any type of drug usage on their campuses. As a result, we have the ostrich effect—that is, most officials would prefer to bury their heads in the sand and not admit to drug usage until the problem becomes glaring. When it is no longer possible to do this, then the reverse seems to occur: there is intense fear that the problem is out of hand.

The present study grew out of such a situation. A number of schools denied any student illicit use until police arrived on campuses to make arrests. Then administrators became interested. After that—and in order to have as many schools involved as possible—we invited, on behalf of our Local Counsel on Drug Abuse, thirty-three superintendents to discuss the problem and the arrangements for a survey of prevalence. These superintendents represented an estimated 102,766 students. Of those invited, thirty-one responded positively and said they would attend a meeting. Only seventeen showed up for the meeting. Of these, five actually expressed some interest in finding out what their students were doing and thinking about drugs. In the final analysis only two schools cooperated, although two others did sponsor a drug-education program arising out of our discussions.

Either surveys or educational endeavors dealing with illicit drugs are faced with a number of problems other than the superintendents' and principals' fears or lack of interest, for often a great deal of reluctance and anxiety exist on the part of the instructors. Many are ill equipped for a drug-education program and do not know how to handle one. Often their knowledge is slight and biased, and they find it difficult to answer questions. Further, they are unable to handle many of the problems that might arise in the classroom as a result of a discussion of drugs. The techniques of use of drugs or the jargon employed by users are difficult for the teacher to understand. Moreover, the problem of confidentiality arises should the teacher allow the student to talk. If the student should open up and begin to discuss the drug scene, he becomes vulnerable to hostile or punitive action.

Another major factor is the student's attitude toward taking a survey concerning drugs. The users particularly are hesitant to reveal information because it may expose them and get them into trouble with the law. As a result, they hold back information. Our effort to alleviate underreporting led us to guarantee that the surveys be totally anonymous. As a further factor to facilitate frankness, the survey was administered and collected by outsiders, who were class students from a local college, and the materials were processed anonymously. In spite of this, there were a number of students who were still somewhat suspicious. Here is an example of their comments on their questionnaires reflecting this suspiciousness: "This better not be a God Damned bust. P.S. If it is all my answers are bull shit. P.P.S. You should really show us the conclusions of this corny test." A general distrust of older persons commonly appeared as part of lengthy paragraphs.

The senior high schools in Santa Clara County used in this study represent, with some expected overlapping, two different socioeconomic populations. School A, situated near a large university, is very much like the upper-middle-class high school reported in the first section of this chapter. School B, located some miles away in a large metropolitan area, has students from middle- and lower-middle-class families. The broad class difference is important since the use of drugs by adolescents has become an upwardly mobile social phenomenon no longer related to only the traditional juvenile delinquent coming primarily from the lower socioeconomic classes.

A few general comments are in order prior to consideration of the data. First, in 1967, when the study was conducted, the use by adolescents of methamphetamine hydrochloride ("meth," "speed," "crystal," "crank") in both injectable and oral forms was not evident. Our strong impression is that by 1968 the scene had changed dramatically. Consequently, the survey is inadequate, for it provides no inkling of that amphetamine trend. Second, it was impossible to prevent underreporting or overreporting; informal conversations with students made it more evident that some had lied. We do not know how many did so. A non-user can say "yes" to be "in"; a user can say "no" for fear of detection. From our standpoint the most valuable information yielded reveals attitudes toward drugs, reasons for use or non-use, and the student's eye-view of what's happening.

Tobacco. At School A, N = 839 out of 1,130 (middle, upper-middle class), a statistically greater percentage of boys smoke than do girls (52 per cent vs. 47 per cent). This difference is also true for the boys (47 per cent) and the girls (35 per cent) at School B, N = 1,382 out of 1,822 (middle, lower-middle class). Comparison of the reported smoking behavior of students at each school shows that School A has a significantly greater percentage of smokers than does School B. It would seem that the influence of friends cannot be discounted, for students reflect the same intraschool- and interschool-difference trends in response to queries as to whether their friends smoke. However, there is an interesting reversal when boys and girls at both schools, in answer to a question, describe the smoking habits of their parents. At School B, a greater percentage of both mothers and fathers are said to smoke than at School A, even though more students, both sexes, smoke at School A. It is difficult to say just what might lie behind this. There are several comments made by School A students that smokers are more mature and that smoking is very acceptable despite the dangers associated with it. One might speculate about differences in the kind of education about tobacco at the two schools and the willingness to accept factual information, for a greater percentage of both boys and girls at School B regard tobacco as "bad." The differences in sex-related trends noted before still hold true for both schools.

The replies to the open-ended questions differ not at all from those reported earlier in this chapter. Only a handful of students at both schools request further information about tobacco; apparently, the school course is seen as adequate. A frequently occurring comment from School A expresses the belief that the vast amount of money spent each year advertising tobacco would be better spent in research on other drugs about which little is known. In general, smokers' replies tend to justify their behavior; nonsmokers either do not reply or give examination-type answers displaying their knowledge about the dangers of tobacco. Responses to the question about differences between smokers and nonsmokers are most intriguing. The nonsmokers' comments "put down" the smokers by calling them stupid, immature, and dependent, and stating that they give in to group pressure, try to be "in," and just aren't concerned about their health or the state of their breath. Smokers, on the other hand, again either do not reply, say what they do is their business, confess to a "habit," or express some doubt that the dangers are real.

Alcohol. Student drinking at both schools fellows the same percentage patterns that are shown for smoking. The vast majority of students have a drink only occasionally, the most frequent setting being on a date or with their family. A very small number of students report heavy drinking (over six drinks at one time). The percentage of boys who take a drink is greater at both Schools A and B (78 per cent vs. 72 per cent; girls 69 per cent vs. 66 per cent). The sex difference is significant within the schools. More boys (86 per cent vs. 76 per cent) than girls (74 per cent vs. 70 per cent) at both schools state that the majority of their friends drink. Over a half (56 per cent) of all students at School A say that there is something bad about people their age drinking. A higher percentage of all students (65 per cent) at School B feel the same way. Responses to questions about parents' drinking habits reveal no differences between the schools, the most frequent response being "drink occasionally." However, even though the percentages are small, more students at School B describe their fathers' drinking as heavy.

Again, the replies to the open-ended questions seem to follow closely those reported earlier. Contrary to the results for tobacco, many students want more specific information about alcohol, primarily as to what constitutes alcoholism and how many drinks one must take before any physical damage occurs. Given the acceptance of alcohol in our culture, the latter question would seem to point up the need for education for sensible drinking rather than "scare" lectures stressing damage, to which only a small portion of students might fall prey. Since several students inquired about help for alcoholic parents, educators would be wise to consider the student as a potential prevention and treatment agent. Education about tobacco and alcohol should, in addition to offering factual material about each drug, consider drug taking in general in more depth, what factors are involved in dependency (potential for dependency), what the abuse potential for different drugs is, and how the individual can arrive at a sensible personal decision regarding drugs in a drug-oriented society.

Marijuana. A far greater percentage of boys (77 per cent) and girls (85 per cent) at School A know someone using marijuana than do boys (45 per cent) and girls (57 per cent) at School B. Asked to describe the people they know who use marijuana to any degree, three fourths of the students at both schools distributed their answers equally between good friends and casual friends. Four per cent of all boys and girls report that their older relatives or siblings smoke marijuana. At School A, 46 per cent of the boys and 45 per cent of the girls say they have had the chance to try marijuana. Twenty-three per cent of the boys and 19 per cent of the girls at School B have had the same opportunity. Curiosity about the effect of the drug is the most frequent reason given for trying it, which—coupled with its availability—logically accounts for the percentage difference between the schools. One can infer that few students actively seek marijuana but rather run across it in a relatively casual manner. At School A, 31 per cent of the boys have tried marijuana as have 28 per cent of the girls. The percentages are lower at School B: boys 13 per cent, girls 7 per cent. Asked to describe their present use of marijuana ("occasionally" to "regularly"), 24 per cent of the boys and 19 per cent of the girls at School A so characterize themselves. The figures for School B are boys, 7 per cent, and girls, 4 per cent. Less than 1 per cent at either school describe themselves as being heavy users. The gross relationship between availability and use of a drug is still evident. Only 22 per cent of the boys and 21 per cent of the girls at School A see marijuana as "good." For the students at School B, 6 per cent of the boys and 10 per cent of the girls have the same attitude. Approximately 13 per cent of all students at A and 5 per cent of all students at B have either no opinion or think marijuana is neither good nor bad.

Replies to open-ended questions indicate a strong desire on the part of the students for more factual information—minus moralizing—coupled with an opportunity to engage in honest discussion about the pros and cons of marijuana. Many students feel that marijuana should be legalized (and alcohol outlawed) or at least the penalties reduced. Angry comments were made concerning the unwillingness of both teachers and parents to engage in meaningful dialogue with young people about the physiological, psychological, moral, and social aspects of not only marijuana but all mind- and mood-altering drugs. Asked to describe differences between users and non-users of marijuana, students dichotomize users as being generally either "neat, groovy, turned on, and aware types" or "stupid, slobby, hippie types." More students at A give elaborate answers to the question. Students at B were more inclined to say "no difference," "don't know," or do not answer at all. Non-users are most frequently described as "smart," although the number of responses to this part of the question dropped significantly. Apparently it is the user who gets the lion's share of the attention. Could we not be overlooking a valuable resource in not spending more time exploring the characteristics of adolescent non-users of drugs to help identify a population at risk (potential users/abusers)?

LSD. As in the preceding sections, the nonresponse rate to questions remains low. Percentage differences between schools are still all statistically significant.

Of the students at School A, 81 per cent of the boys and 65 per cent of the girls know someone who uses or has used LSD. The figures for B are boys, 37 per cent, and girls, 50 per cent. At A, almost equal percentages are either good or casual friends; 10 per cent of the students report that older relatives or siblings have had experience with the drug. Students at B say that most of the people they know of are just casual friends. Only two students at B name older relatives and no students report siblings in this category. Thirty-two per cent of the boys and 29 per cent of the girls at A have had an opportunity to try LSD, while only 17 per cent of the boys and 18 per cent of the girls at School B have been similarly exposed to the hallucinogen. Since LSD is apparently a "higher-class" drug (see Blum and Associates, *Utopiates*) it is at this juncture that a class difference between the two schools might be seen as relevant. Of the students at A who have had the chance to try LSD, 14 per cent of the boys have experimented as have 13 per cent of the girls. Nine per cent of both sexes say they have gone on to use LSD occasionally to regularly. One wonders whether or not these students comprise an identifiable "in"-group at this school. Of the stu-

dents at School B, only 5 per cent of the boys and 4 per cent of the girls
have tried LSD. Three per cent of the boys and 27 per cent of the girls
trying the drug have gone on to some degree of use.

LSD is generally seen as "less good" than marijuana, with approximately 15 per cent of both boys and girls at A saying that LSD
is good and 5 per cent of each sex at B so classifying the drug. Less
than 5 per cent of all students either give no answer or reply "neither
good nor bad."

Replies to the open-ended questions about LSD are the most
interesting *and* disturbing, for it is about LSD that the greatest body of
misinformation exists. It is the authors' feeling that a young person
who "puts down" LSD on the basis of distorted knowledge is more
vulnerable to a change of heart at a later date than is one who decides
against use on more accurate information. "LSD melts your brain";
"You'll probably kill your friends"; "It makes you a blind cripple."
How much more rational is a decision based on "It's too unpredictable
for me to take a chance." The majority of students at both schools,
when asked whether they want more information about LSD, say
"yes." Many of these people go on to ask specific questions such as the
following: "Is it addictive?" "Does it help people to know themselves
better?" "Will it make you insane?" "Can I see God?" Asked about
differences between users and non-users, the non-users either don't reply or characterize users as hippie types, people who can't cope with
life, or lonely ones who are looking for "something." Few of the non-
users feel that LSD has much to recommend it at the present time, but
many say that research might show it to have medical value in the
future. On the other hand, users of LSD are, by and large, enthusiastic
about it, with only a handful of students reporting what was apparently
a bad personal experience with the drug. One of the students, who describes himself as a heavy user, invited us to join him on a "trip," for
he says that he sees us as "good people who could learn about love and
beauty with acid." The majority of the users feel that they have grown
by the use of LSD, but a few are apparently interested primarily in the
"kick" and attempting, as one user puts it, "to remove the stupid world
from life."

Other drug use. The illicit use of amphetamines, barbiturates,
tranquilizers, volatile inhalants, and related chemicals were not tabu-
lated as percentages. Simple observation of the raw data gives the
impression that many of the students know of someone using these

substances without medical sanction, but that few of the students themselves are illicit users. Pep pills, glue, and tranquilizers belong to the apparent descending order of drugs used. Ten per cent of the students at both schools say that they know of someone using heroin but do not say that they themselves have tried it. The majority of the students have been offered a variety of drugs other than marijuana or LSD at one time or another.

It is encouraging to note that only 22 per cent of all students at both schools subjectively feel "on the spot" about drugs, saying that they have resisted or would resist whatever was offered. Group pressure is only one factor in the decision-making process. Guided by the quality of questions, one can infer that users would be amenable to being changed from use to non-use through honest, open education and gut-level discussion. This hypothesis is supported by the observation that the use of LSD has declined in recent months, many former users reporting that they have decided against LSD on the basis of recent medical findings. It is the authors' observations that some of the older adolescent former users have matured out of LSD and have found means by which they can turn on naturally (music, meditation, Nature, and so on). This observation is a case in point for education about drugs to discuss not only drugs per se but to explore with students alternative methods for achieving legitimate goals often sought by drugs.

Students were asked whom they would consult regarding a friend in trouble with drugs and where *they* would turn for help with a personal problem. Over 50 per cent of all students at both schools indicate that parents are their first choice. School counselors, teachers, doctors, religious leaders, and friends fare about equally well over the remainder of student choices.

Despite the fact that many adolescents say that they have friends who will give them drugs free, money is a factor in drug use. Thirty-seven per cent of all students at School A have less than five dollars a week to spend; 33 per cent have from five to ten dollars a week to spend (income from jobs plus any allowance). The remainder (30 per cent) have from ten to forty dollars per week. At School B, the majority of students (56 per cent) have less than five dollars per week, 27 per cent have up to ten dollars, and the remaining 17 per cent may have as much as forty dollars per week. The percentages cited previously for the incidence of drug use at both schools—School

A having the greater percentage of use—would indicate that the means to purchase drugs is a variable that cannot be discounted.

Objective data provide one means of assessing the extent of drug usage. However, structured questions enable the student to mark objectively the extent of usage but do not give him an opportunity to express his attitude toward drugs in general. In order to get a closer view of the drug scene, we used open-ended questions, which provided invaluable information about inside reasons for drug usage. It has been common to determine *what* has been happening on the drug scene; the question *why* it has been happening poses an even more ominous problem. The comments provided by the students give clues as to the reason why students would wish to take drugs. Although specific questions were not asked as to why, the "free" remarks made by students seem to make their points quite well.

In a closer look at the open-ended data, it would appear that the responses can be classified into several categories. Listed below are the most common reasons stated by students in an indirect manner.

Rebellion-hostility.   One common way of expressing rebellion toward society is to break all of its rules. Drugs provide a convenient way of doing just that. In many of these cases, the students manage to get caught as well, only making the problem a more obvious one. Consider this response by a high school junior female:

> There is so much attention placed on drugs today! It doesn't help the situation when you have people telling you: No, No, No. You shouldn't smoke or drink or take drugs because it is bad for you or against the law. That only makes people want to take it or try it more. Just give the pro's and con's of doing it and leave the "you can't do it because there is a law" out of it. Many kids already smoke and drink so why have a law? I myself smoke once in a while and am very tempted to try grass—but not LSD, because practically nothing is known about it. They (adults) drink and smoke and in a way they are taking drugs. They smoke and drink and turn around and tell you it's wrong for you to do it. Hell! What kind of hypocrisy is this? You can't but I can.

Another type of hostility expressed in the questionnaire is reflected in this response:

> When I took this they said that there was no way of tracing anybody by this given information. If I am questioned, I am going to raise Hell. So how does this grab you, *Fuck Head!!*

Pressure-escape. There seems to be some reaction to the pressure the student faces as reflected in this response:

> Many of us need an escape hatch from the pressures of this damn Establishment—grades, money, status, college. Pressures upon pressures—you need to escape, in fact, I am getting so that I have to escape somehow or else I might have a breakdown! With all of the pressures and everything around us, can you blame us? You started this and we have to clean and fix-up everything you messed up in the world. Now, if that isn't a good reason for wanting to escape—I don't know what gives. Freedom now!

Self-exploration. Several of the responses appear to indicate that "finding oneself" or self-exploration is at the bottom of student drug usage. For example:

> Most people would be better off (know themselves better) if they used it a few times.

> Drop acid and find out where it's at. Do it wisely and carefully and you will see what nature is really like.

> Before having grass, I hated my parents and home, but after, I began to see that parents have to have some authority and now I don't mind my home—I'm quite happy.

Religion. Several comments seem to indicate that students seem to find a type of religion because of the profound effects by the drug. For example:

> It [LSD use] is, in my opinion, a religious sacrament and should be treated as such. I would like to understand the prejudice against it.

> There is a new church forming in this school based on morning-glory worship and light and color which we use in service and worship.

Curiosity. The desire to try something new and exciting is mentioned as one of the reasons for trying drugs as reflected in the following statement:

> I feel that most people will try something once—perhaps once would be too much. I have tried smoking once and didn't like it—never again. The same with alcohol. As far as drugs are concerned, I would never even want to try them. I am not involved with drugs; neither are any of my friends. If any one else wants to smoke, drink, or take drugs—that's their business and until my relatives or close friends get in trouble with it, I could care less about it.

Conformity. Going along with the crowd is another factor mentioned as a reason for drug usage. For example:

Most people who take drugs and continue to do so are insecure and start out by thinking it's the "in" thing to do. By the time they realize what a mess they're in, it is too late and they are addicted.

I think a lot of people take drugs just to go along with their buddies even though they may not want to take it.

Kicks. One of the more frequently used phrases is that drugs provide "kicks." These kicks are often not seen as the central idea but as related to other aspects of drug usage.

When people use it [marijuana] for kicks and not for any other useful purpose, the situation may become out of hand. Especially the teenyboppers of thirteen and fourteen, who get really screwed up and have no right to use it.

Creativity. The use of drugs as a means of becoming more creative and more mentally expansive is mentioned on several of the questionnaires.

Drugs give you a chance to see nature very differently, in a really beautiful artistic way. Gives you a chance to be very creative.

Obviously, students are not using drugs for one single reason alone. Some responses on the questionnaires include several of the statements listed above. The single most prominent emotion that appears to emerge from the questionnaire is hostility—direct or indirect. Swearing is quite common. Sometimes, the anger takes the form of attacking the persons conducting the survey.

I am afraid most people will take this fucking thing as a joke but my answers are correct. You fucking people who read these God damned things can't really use this shit for fact or God damned statistics for a brainwashing campaign to put people down. Get them down.

I'm frankly sick and tired of these confounded surveys of drugs and alcohol. I really don't think it is going to do any good to quiz students on these things when the real problem lies in the fact that marijuana is too easy to get hold of. Great quantities of it have been seized but there is still a lot around. Why don't you look for it rather than take time and money to make this stupid questionnaire?

I get the impression that this survey was made up by a crew of old ladies who teach kindergarten.

I think this committee on Drug Abuse (the group conducting the survey) is a last-ditch effort by the liberal Establishment (and in their best tradition) to patch up a hopelessly perverted society, and I think you should all drop acid and see where it's at.

At other times the hostility takes the form of an attack on society.

I hope that our generation isn't going to make Huxley's book, *Brave New World,* come true.

I believe in freedom. This country is not as free as most people say or as it could be. I believe that if someone wanted to take drugs and is mature enough to pay for them without stealing, he should be able to do so. There are many people in this country who are against things or ideas that they have never experienced. I believe that those who should judge should be the ones who know by experience. I am very open minded but I don't believe in things that make no sense. In our country we could have machines do most of the work, but still my parents and most people over twenty-five say work all your life. FUCK. I don't trust you either.

A common form of expressing hostility is to attack the injustices in the society, particularly regarding the drug laws.

I feel that drug use is on a very large scale now and instead of arresting kids for use of marijuana something else should be done as punishment. Pot is very harmless compared to alcohol and when a kid is caught for alcohol, nothing happens. When someone is arrested for pot, it ruins their whole life and socially, it puts the kids' parents back also.

Pot doesn't ruin your lungs or eat away your kidneys like smoking and alcohol do. If someone wishes to smoke pot, I think he should be allowed to take it like alcohol (same requirements for buying as alcoholic beverages). When he is twenty-one and mature enough to realize the potential dangers of drugs he *will quit!*

I think this questionnaire should be used all over to clear up some of the misunderstandings about statistics. How in the hell can people say so many kids take drugs when they don't know? Parents should also be aware of *correct* statistics. Newspaper estimates and the public exaggerate. Somehow, statistics should be as close to correct as possible. Radicals and "long-haired kooks" are blamed for a lot of drug use and sales—BULL SHIT. Someone ought to find out the *truth*.

When the Revolution comes, grass will be legalized. Long live the Revolution!

I believe most drugs to be harmful and addictive. However,

marijuana seems to be just like tobacco with the exception that it *is* nonaddictive and seems to be a good way to find some "kicks."

One of the surprises of the survey is the number of bizarre comments written on the questionnaire. These may have been the result of some emotional disturbances or could be the result of students' attempting to make the survey appear as a ridiculous venture. The following are some examples:

> Just make sure your feet aren't in the water.
>
> I like you and your head is full of things to eat and drink which are good or bad. If you think about them, you too can enjoy grass and acid and glory and such good things as these.
>
> My God! Could you explain your everyday thoughts and your own being in a sentence? Write me a letter.
>
> In your reality, can you picture me or am I just in a world of fantasy? Liberty and justice for all.

It is our conclusion that the students have a great deal to say and to ask about drugs. If given an opportunity in an encouraging setting, they are willing to discuss the drug scene freely. Such a protected environment does not seem to exist for the young people and, partly in consequence, the drug scene is underground. As long as it stays underground, we will have neither accurate incidence data nor adequate understanding of high school-student motives, feelings, or troubles associated with disapproved drug use. The students themselves, we believe, in spite of all the talk of distrusting those over thirty—the well-known generation gap—*want* to communicate. As one student puts it, "I sure hope this is used for the purposes stated. I wasn't going to answer honestly because I don't trust any of the teachers or counsilors [sic] around here, but then. . . ."

SUBURBAN HIGH SCHOOL

The fourth high school survey took place in the spring of 1968, using a modified form of the original (Blum) instrument.[1] The high school serves a suburban community with a student-body population (N = 1,645) resembling the two middle-class high schools already described in this chapter. As will be seen, the results show that, a year

[1] See also the prevalence data for the county-wide 1968 study reported: Chapter I, pp. 41-a and 41-b, using a short questionnaire. Its results, like those shown here, imply rapidly expanding illicit-drug use during the high school years.

and a half later, prevalence rates for illicit-exotic drug experience are from double to quadruple the earlier rates. There is also a much greater prevalence of continuing drug use, especially of marijuana. It may be that these rates reflect sampling among populations which are different, after all, or display a shift in bias from underreporting to overreporting. It may also be, as we believe, that the more recent survey reflects a considerable actual increase in exposure to, experimentation with, and regular use of illicit-exotic drugs among middle-class high school students in the Bay Area.

We find the following with regard to particular drugs. About one fourth say they are regular *tobacco* smokers, 13 per cent have not smoked, and 75 per cent have parents who are smokers. There are more smokers in the upper than in the lower high school years. Health hazards are emphasized as "bad" about smoking, and tension relief is cited most often as the benefit. Little interest is shown in additional information about tobacco.

Fourteen per cent of the boys and 9 per cent of the girls report regular *alcohol* use; 7 per cent of all students have not tried drinking. Eighty-seven per cent of all parents are described as drinkers, but most peers (61 per cent) are said to be nondrinkers. Drinking occurs more often in the higher grade levels. The majority deny any "wrong" in drinking by youth of high school age, but simultaneously say there is nothing good about it either. Health hazards are most often cited as dangers, and the majority point to recreational-social uses as benefits. There appears to be little interest in further information about alcohol.

Almost all students know *marijuana* users and three quarters have themselves had opportunities to obtain that drug. One third say they did not avail themselves; thus, about 55 per cent of the total student population say they have had marijuana experience. Among these, less than one third have discontinued use, so that we find 41 per cent of the boys and 37 per cent of the girls describing themselves as continuing marijuana users. The greatest amount of marijuana use is reported in the twelfth grade (49 per cent) and, by age group, among eighteen-year-olds, 63 per cent of whom have had experience. Less than one third of the students stipulate that anything is "wrong" about marijuana use; among those who identify something as being wrong, legal and mental hazards are equally important. Recreational uses and tension relief are seen as benefits by the more than two thirds of the students reporting positive aspects to its use. Few students express any desire, in response to a question, for additional information about marijuana.

Two per cent of the boys and girls report regular *amphetamine* use, whereas 11 per cent of the students believe that their friends are using these drugs. Eighteen per cent report they have experimented with amphetamines; 4 per cent say their parents have used them. No differences by age or school year are found for prevalence of amphetamine experience. Remarkably, almost none of the students (4 per cent) see anything bad about their use, but simultaneously most (84 per cent) see nothing good either. Among the 16 per cent expressing positive aspects, feeling good (euphoria) and the ability to do more (performance enhancement) are most often cited.

About two thirds of the students say they have had the chance to try *hallucinogens;* one fifth (20 per cent) say they have tried them. Repeated use is reported by 12 per cent of the girls and 10 per cent of the boys. Most students know of others using hallucinogens. Least use is among freshmen; the greatest use is among higher grades and older students. Half of the students say there is nothing bad about the hallucinogens; more than two thirds say there is nothing good. Those citing bad effects mention mental hazards and chromosomal damage. Among the nearly one third reporting benefits, personal and social insight or understanding is emphasized.

Glue and *gasoline sniffing* is reported by 9 per cent of the students, *goof balls* and *pep pills* by 13 per cent. For the volatile intoxicants there is a definite decrease by age group in those reporting (current) use. The nonmedical employment of *sleeping pills, tranquilizers,* and the like is admitted by 11 per cent. Twenty-nine per cent say they have had the chance to take *heroin,* 25 per cent say they know someone using it, and 2 per cent say they themselves have tried it.

A number of items inquired about *drug education and information.* From these one learns that most students affirm they do not like to be told *not* to try drugs—including illicit ones—that most rate the dangers of drugs as we presume average adults would—calling heroin and speed (methamphetamine) the most dangerous. Unlike the hypothetical average adult, they consider tobacco more dangerous than marijuana—an opinion many health scientists might share. It is clear that the students want no more conventional drug education. When asked to select the most reliable information sources, they say they consider teachers and police least well informed; physicians and ex-drug addicts they rate as best informed. The rejection of teachers and the expressed lack of interest in further information should not be taken as completely genuine, for when asked whether they would welcome informal information giving and assistance with drug decisions or problems, 94 per cent said that they would. Comments of students clearly imply distrust of most experts unless they themselves decide the authority is credible. Credibility seems to be enhanced if the teacher is informed about the drug-use scene as the students perceive it. For the most part, conventional teaching authorities are viewed as biased, moralizing, and Establishment-sustaining; they are not considered objective, scientific, or open to radical innovation. Particular hostility is directed toward law-enforcement personnel. The complaints are that police officers giving drug information are either ignorant or are lying to students, that they arrest disproportionately more juveniles than adults or pushers for drug offenses as part of a "war on kids," that they exercise undue influence on the educational establishment itself ("If someone tells us the truth, the cops see to it that he's fired"), and that law enforcement people have an unexposed self-interest in dramatizing the drug problem ("They overrate drugs so they can keep their jobs").

The impression from replies and spontaneous comments is that students prefer as teaching material illustrative cases and situations rather than broad general statements and that they prefer nonsensational, balanced presentations by qualified persons of issues involved in drug use. Although there is a vein of laissez-faire, the majority of students, in response to a question asking whether people should be allowed to use whatever drugs they want, favor controls over drug distribution and individual use.

With reference to *drug availability*, a scale derived from an index item shows tobacco as the most readily available (scale value 4.7), followed by alcohol (scale value 2.7), marijuana (scale value 2.4), LSD (scale value 1.5), methamphetamine (scale value 1.3), and heroin (scale value 0.9). Alcohol and marijuana are said by the students to be about equally available to them. Regarding *source*, alcohol is the only substance not first obtained primarily from peers. Rather, parents are the leading initiators. The presumption must be that parents approve of drinking, as opposed to smoking, and teach it early in the home—a practice approved by most modern health educators interested in teaching controlled or culturally integrated nonescapist drinking. Tobacco, which some students describe as a filthy habit, is most often tried first among friends of the same age, whereas marijuana may be first taken in the company of casual acquaintances, friends of the same age, or older acquaintances. Older siblings also introduce marijuana. One inference is that marijuana use is extensive throughout the teen-age social world. The amphetamines, like tobacco, are most often first tried in the company of friends of the same age. A fourth of the students say they have been "put on the spot" in a social group when offered a drug they didn't want to take; for the majority, initiation into tobacco and illicit-exotic drug use is not in response to felt social pressures—that is, no strain or compulsion is admitted. Our interview impressions are that this is the case, that little duress is involved, although clearly there are strong social forces at work which lead high school students (and younger ones as well!) to influence and respond to one another as vectors in the rapidly spreading use of psychoactive drugs—*all* of which are illicit in this state under the age of sixteen and the use of all except tobacco is illicit under age twenty-one.

As a final comment, all of us cooperating in the very limited high school surveys reported here would emphasize the apparent rapidity of the spread of illicit-exotic drug use, marijuana especially, but now including LSD and the amphetamines and soon, perhaps, the opiates as well. Our results do not account for the phenomenon, although the data on college students reported elsewhere in this book identify many of the variables operating. We strongly suspect that the expansion will continue geographically, downward by age, diffusing by social class, and extending to more regular use—as opposed to simply casual experimentation—for many of the illicit substances. The challenges and questions posed thereby to parents, educators, law-enforcement personnel, health workers, and the citizen at large are immense and dare not be ignored.

Overview
for Administrators

Helen Nowlis

XX

Ihe use of drugs by students and society's response to this use confront the college administrator and the educational institution which he represents with a multitude of problems—educational, ethical, legal, and professional. His dilemma, perhaps greater than that of any other individual, highlights the difficult conflicts of values inherent in the problem—ones often ignored by the legislator, the law-enforcement officer, and such professionals as the physician, the research scientist, the psychologist, and the sociologist, as they look at the phenomenon from their own special interest or point of view. Our overview will examine these conflicts, not, unfortunately, from the vantage point of systematic, empirical research but rather on the basis of our own experience in exploring the problems created by student drug use with administrators in a variety of institutions across the country, as well as on the basis of an on-going survey of drug policies and drug programs in still other institutions.

The thoughtful administrator recognizes that the institution's response to the use of drugs by students has serious implications for

351

every aspect of that institution's relationship to society and to the student. It would be most convenient if the problem were simple and decisions about it could be made in a vacuum. To most adults, including some educators, the answer to the problem seems to be as simple as stating that the institution is a law-abiding corporate member of society and that it will not tolerate the breaking of the law by members of its community. Implicit in this position are the assumptions that this approach will eliminate the use of drugs and that existing law-enforcement methods are the most effective way to accomplish this end. But a careful consideration of this position also requires an evaluation both of the means for achieving its objectives and the implications of these measures for fulfilling the overall educational function of the institution. Are there negative consequences from this simple answer? What is the price of adopting this position?

The answers to these questions will depend on the nature of the particular institution and its perception of its role as an institution of higher education. For a university with a commitment to freedom of inquiry, to research, and to education as opposed to training, the price may be extremely high both to the institution and to society. To the college dedicated to promoting maximum intellectual and social growth and developing young people both inside and outside the classroom—in contrast to mere training in classroom and laboratory—the impact of police methods, externally or internally imposed, destroys the campus climate for learning. To the predominantly residential college with its tradition of in loco parentis, even as this role is being redefined (Nowlis, 1966), it may be at the price of abandoning whatever constructive remnants of such a role remain. Just as we ask students to consider the utility-risk ratio in their drug use, the administrator must consider the utility-risk ratio and engage in a cost-benefit analysis.

Being faced with crisis and dilemma is nothing new for institutions of higher education. However, certain aspects of this particular crisis are unique: society's response to it is excessive and simplistic; the nature of the drug behavior labeled criminal is so private that detection of it requires informers, undercover agents, and the invasion of privacy; and such methods drive the whole problem underground, so that those students who do or may get into difficulty as a result of their drug use cannot be reached and helped until they are really in desperate trouble—or in jail.

Our cost-benefit analysis will explore the impact of the institution's posture with respect to student drug use on its relationships both to society and its students.

Since the establishment of the land-grant college, society has been increasingly of two minds about higher education. It has demanded that higher education serve a dual role. First, it is expected to serve the existing order, this service being defined by some primarily in terms of the economy or the maintenance of currently prevalent attitudes and values. It is also expected, by a seemingly diminishing consensus, to examine and question the status quo and existing knowledge and belief. Few object when this questioning leads to developments which support advances in technology, but objection increases when the same process leads to analyzing, criticizing, and advocating changes in the current laws and mores. There is little recognition or acceptance of the fact that the conditions which foster innovation and creativity in science and technology cannot be confined to that domain. Man cannot be free to develop knowledge and critical understanding in one area if he is not free to do the same in all areas.

Freedom in inquiry is essential to the very existence of the university. On balance, this freedom has served society well throughout the centuries. The attempts of society, not just to criticize but to impose on the university its own methods for dealing with the drug issue— methods which violate the structure and the atmosphere essential to its very existence—go far beyond concern over student use of drugs. Such use in defiance of laws which are increasingly being questioned has become a focal point, a chink in the armor through which certain groups are attacking the intellectual and the academic community. The wheeling and dealing involved in trying to force educational institutions to adopt current methods of responding to behavior of which society does not approve adds to the dilemma of an already hardpressed institution. Insistence on the part of many that a problem is being ignored if it is not being dealt with in a specified manner—in this case, police methods—no matter what the price, is unfair and shortsighted.

Fred Hechinger, of the *New York Times*, in evaluating the aftermath of the Stony Brook incident, wrote: "Having created a university, the state can also destroy what it has built but in doing so, the state diminishes and may destroy itself. The universities' part in preventing this is to maintain order in their communities, thereby making it easier to defend with all their might the 'no trespassing' sign that must guard their academic freedom." The university must be free to use methods which are appropriate to its structure and its spirit and to show that order can be maintained even when the status quo is examined and questioned.

The administrator—particularly if he is one whose responsibility is the general health and welfare of the student—must constantly be aware of the total climate of the campus as it affects all aspects of the student's growth and development. He, perhaps more than any other person, is continually impressed with the fact that there is no typical student, that each student is an individual with talents, abilities, experience, and ways of life which are unique. He is aware that students have already had almost two decades of living and learning when they enter college and bring to it a great diversity of attitudes, values, and goals. He knows that all students who show a given type of behavior cannot be treated in the same way, that failure, rebellion, depression, exploring the self, relieving boredom, facilitating social interaction, preparing for stress, and shutting out the world are not the same for everyone, and that uniform treatment of a specific type of behavior such as drug use has little or no meaning.

The administrator also knows that students other than those who engage in drug use may have many of the same problems, although they may show other types of symptomatic behavior. His only hope of helping students depends on searching out the reasons, the basic causes of the presenting behavior for each individual. Even if a given institution does not include in its goals the personal and social growth of the individual—and an increasing number do not—its modes of administrative handling of problem behavior will affect its total relationship with its students and the atmosphere in which its instructional activities occur. If the administrator's institution is concerned with learning outside the formal curriculum, if it is concerned with all of the factors which may interfere with formal instruction, there must be an atmosphere of trust, respect, open discussion, and free inquiry. If a student cannot seek counsel, either from a professional or from a faculty member, without threat of serious reprisals for both student and adviser, education in its broadest sense cannot occur. Recent events in New York State as a result of the Stony Brook incident have seriously threatened the ability of both faculty and administrators to influence constructively the growth and development of all students, not just the minority who may be either casually or seriously involved in drug use. It would seem that we may have reached the stage where even a faculty member must talk to students only from the lectern. Otherwise, he may have to make the decision that he is willing to face contempt charges and go to jail before daring to help or counsel a student who might mention drug use in discussing his problem. To engender suspicion and mistrust in one particular area may affect all areas.

It is clear, as reported in several preceding chapters, that drug use may attract some who are troubled and emotionally unstable. These of all drug users need help with their basic problems, not punishment of its symptoms. Laws which label such symptoms criminal effectively shut these individuals off from professional help and leave them to the ministrations of those of their peers who fortunately care. Even among the majority of students who do not use drugs, the whole range of motivations mentioned above may occur. The manifestations of these problems may happen to fall within behaviors which society, though not approving, does not consider criminal. Some of these students fail through no lack of ability, some sleep as much as eighteen hours a day, some drop out either literally or figuratively, and some resort to excessive eating or drinking. Some do what their elders do—what they are continually exhorted to do via TV and the mass media—and seek a chemical solution to their unhappiness and misery through legal chemicals, not the least of which is alcohol.

It is also clear from data presented in earlier chapters that most drug users and experimenters are not emotionally unstable or psychologically sick. Many of them are simply bored, unchallenged, disillusioned, and have a feeling of hopelessness and helplessness as they see society failing to deal with urgent problems arising from man's inhumanity to man. Some of them are bright enough and well-enough organized and disciplined to combine a high level of responsibility and achievement in their academic work with occasional to fairly regular drug use. As we have also pointed out throughout this book, no marked dichotomy exists between those who use drugs and those who do not, between those who experiment and those who use drugs with some degree of regularity—certainly not to the degree that all drug use deserves to bear the brunt of our wrath and our preachments. In the national preoccupation with drugs per se and in the persistent belief that drugs *cause* behavior, we have lost sight completely of the fact that the initial use of drugs is often only one manifestation of a disposition or decision to engage in new types of behavior. It is becoming increasingly evident that drug use does not cause but, rather, is caused by much of the behavior attributed to it and that drug use is only one manifestation of some fairly pervasive and basic problems which merit the attention of higher education. In focusing on a single symptom as manifested by only a minority of students, we may be neglecting, if not hampering, efforts to cope with basic problems which affect far more students than simply those who use drugs.

We pay a price for a simplistic and legalistic approach to the problems associated with drug use by forcing them underground, where they are not accessible to study and possible solution. We pay a price in terms of impairment of effectiveness in dealing constructively with a wide variety of student problems in the majority of non-users as well as users. We may fail to solve this problem, as well as others both current and future, by giving too little attention to the identification and solution of the basic problems of which this and other difficulties are merely symptoms.

Efforts at education on drugs and drug use are seriously hampered by current societal demands and by some institutional policies. Educators are in the uncomfortable position of knowing that most prevalent methods of drug education are ineffective and in many cases contribute to the very problem they seek to control. Most students simply will not accept as facts statements which are selected or reinterpreted to support a particular position. They reject moralizing and less-than-honest discussion. One needs only to listen to students who use drugs or who defend the right of others to do so to realize that neither preaching nor scare techniques work. Students do not accept the proposition that the effects of prolonged use or excessive amounts of a drug are "the effects" of any use of that drug. They know that millions of people use alcohol and that only a relatively small percentage become alcoholic. The use of marijuana has spread to the extent that they know of hundreds of people who use it with pleasure, with only a very small percentage showing any signs of the bizarre and horrible fate that is held before them. To follow this kind of educational approach leads only to being labeled as stupid or hypocritical. Neither label helps in efforts to deal with other less controversial problems.

An important part of any drug-education program must be accurate descriptions of the legal risks involved in drug use and of the legal penalties attached to violation of drug laws. The fact that, judged by the penalties prescribed, the sharing of marijuana with one's friends is designated by our society as one of the most heinous crimes a person can commit—a crime as bad as or even worse than murder, rape, embezzlement, and burglary—can lead to some most interesting discussions. Laws so harsh that no lawyer wants to prosecute, no jury wants to convict, and no judge wants to sentence are a travesty on the function of criminal sanctions in our society. Such laws, particularly when it is almost impossible to enforce them, are an ideal target of rebellion, if what one wants is to rebel. Any effort to justify such laws is fruitless and leads only to further loss of credibility and integrity.

Even the better methods of drug education are often misdirected to the symptom rather than the cause. If a student really wants to get "high," there are more things with which he can accomplish this than we can possibly legislate against, even after we have identified them. Alcohol is still the major vehicle. In the long run, the need and not the vehicle is the appropriate target of study and action. Except for possible legal consequences, there are far more potentially devastating vehicles than marijuana.

The hostile and bitter responses and attitudes toward "education" reported for high school students in the preceding chapter are also found in college students. They, too, want factual information minus moralizing and an honest discussion of pros and cons. They, too, want to communicate, not only about drug use but about their thoughts, feelings, disappointments, hopes and dreams and doubts as well as their joys and small victories, and, indeed, about their inability to communicate with parents and teachers.

The administrator, as the representative of an institution, by the kind of response he makes to the problems surrounding drug use— the policies, both written and unwritten, and the educational programs, both supported and unsupported—has an important impact on the institution's relationship both with its students and its community. Dishonesty in this area weakens credibility in all areas; hypocrisy generates wide distrust; reliance on external control and authoritative pronouncement weakens the development of internal controls and learning to make informed decisions. But the parents, the neighbors, the donors, the legislative committees must be kept happy. It could be that they need the educating.

Society seems to be asking that the administrator become an extension of civil authority; if he does, he loses his effectiveness as a counselor on serious intellectual and personal issues. Society asks that he, at the very least, force any drug user into compulsory therapy, even though he and his psychiatric colleagues have long since agreed that therapy should never be used as a disciplinary tool, primarily because no real therapy is possible under edict. Society demands that he support the party line on drugs and drug effects; if he does, his students will consider him either ignorant or hypocritical and neither label will increase his effectiveness as a teacher and a counselor. Society demands that he establish policies consistent with public policies; if he does, he drives users underground and loses all opportunity to educate, to counsel, to help, and to reduce risks for those who cannot be dissuaded. Society asks that he set up a system of detecting drug use; to use any of the means open to him or to introduce new agents would immediately dry up those channels through which he becomes aware of individual problems early enough to intervene. More than one tragedy has been averted because concerned individuals felt free to come to him in trust, confident that he, too, would be concerned and would see that appropriate help was found.

Perhaps the most worrisome aspect of the whole problem of student drug use is the increasing polarity which has developed in response to it. If one questions the appropriateness of accepted methods of dealing with a problem, he is automatically and falsely charged with condoning the behavior involved. What the educational institution asks is that it be allowed to deal with student drug use as it deals with any other problem and with methods that do not violate its very existence and do not prevent it from serving its main function.

Epilogue: Students and Drugs

Richard H. Blum

XXI

We saw at the time of our 1966–1967 survey and related studies that a goodly minority of students in the colleges studied had experimented with illicit drugs, primarily marijuana. We also saw from the four subsidiary follow-up studies conducted in 1968 on one of those campuses that a remarkable increase in use had occurred, an increase very much in line with the statements in the earlier year by students who expressed their intention to begin illicit-drug use. The concurrent high school studies suggest this same expansion of interest and use, and document, as do our other data, the continued lowering of the age for the initial use of illicit drugs, again primarily marijuana. We also learned that the pool of potential recruits for illicit-drug experimentation is by no means exhausted; the 1968 data show not only that a majority of the students have had illicit-drug experience but that there are still some who have not yet had that experience but who intend to begin. Experimentation, of course, is not the same as regular use, but while the former has increased, so has the latter; in School I—at least at the time of the repeat surveys—about 14 per cent report being regu-

361

lar users of marijuana. For the 1968 high school studies, the figures range between 18 per cent and 39 per cent. We also saw that once illicit-exotic drug use is initiated, it may well broaden to include a variety of illicit substances. Those using drugs tend to use a variety of them. We must anticipate an increasing willingness among illicit users and especially among the regular users to expand their drug repertoire to embrace new hallucinogens as they come on the market and to play with narcotics—opium at the moment but, perhaps one day soon, more heroin as well. Methamphetamine, of course, is included, and in time the new compounds linked in action and structure to the amphetamines and the hallucinogens will be more in use.

What is happening now, in 1968–1969, is what has been happening over the last fifteen years, ever since the "drug movement" (or craze) began with the introduction of mescaline (Huxley, 1954) and of LSD into the intellectual, artistic, and professional communities and spread to the student populations in metropolitan centers. What we see now is a rapidly increasing tempo. While it took approximately ten years, by our estimate, for experimentation and use to shift from the older intellectual-artistic groups to graduate students, it took only an estimated five years to catch on among undergraduates, only two or three years to move to a significant number of high school students, and, then, within no more than two years, to move to upper elementary grades—although we have no sound data as yet on the numbers involved in elementary schools. This progression is apparent only for metropolitan centers such as the San Francisco Bay Area, Los Angeles, Boston, and New York. We assume that each area, as with each neighborhood, will have its variations on the theme. Nevertheless, one may reasonably expect that the phenomenon everywhere demonstrates the rapidly lowering age for initial use and the interest in a variety of drugs, with the most potent ones being least used and marijuana being the most popular. As the base number of marijuana-experienced students expands, so does the proportion willing to risk LSD, DMT, STP, opium, heroin, methamphetamine, and the like.

With the continued increase in the number of students experimenting with illicit drugs, we have also seen an increased number of official cases, although it is our conclusion (based on the data in Chapter Nine) that official cases—whether arrest, physical or mental ill health, or school problems—register very few among drug-experienced youngsters, perhaps only one in a thousand. These official statistics (when the records are adequate enough to produce statistics, which is rare) reflect a lag to such a considerable extent that the curve of either health or arrest cases rises much more slowly than the curve of experimentation and regular use. This impression, if correct, suggests an interesting area of inquiry for drug epidemiology. At the very least, the lag represents the response time of society—and its official agencies—in becoming aware of a problem and in marshaling forces to handle it. The lag, no doubt, also reflects the development of discretion among adults and students as they engage in illicit behavior. It is quite possible, too, that the lag in official cases and the underreporting of them —whether cases of use or of bad results—reflects an uncertainty on the part of the community as to the kind of "problem" definition to be made, that definition, in turn, determining official response. Most adults are not eager for massive police action to invest campuses so that hundreds of thousands of their sons and daughters would be arrested. Most universities must ignore discrete illicit-drug use on campus or be forced into painful policing of the sort which would arouse new antagonism between students and authorities and which would, if it were to result in arrest of all students actually using such drugs, cut campus populations—at least in some areas—in half. The absence of official medical cases is another matter, one which may be taken either to demonstrate the relative nonseverity of most bad reactions—a reasonable conclusion—or to indicate the reluctance of students to expose themselves to identification by authorities by appearing for help. The latter problem is well known to college health authorities and has in some cases resulted in policy statements guaranteeing confidentiality for student drug users, in spite of the demands of other governmental agencies that no such confidentiality be accorded. One thing does seem clear—whether we discuss LSD bad trips or simply alcohol-induced illness—most students endure their ill effects and have devised informal procedures—including the nonmedical administration of drug antagonists or other relieving agents—so that, as in other folk medical practice, they take care of themselves and one another without calling for a physician. We would expect that such sophistication is related to maturity and social class; as illicit-drug use continues to extend to high school or elementary school students, these students will be less able to care for their own bad reactions and less able, as well, to seek competent professional help on their own. Furthermore, one anticipates, although at present without evidence, that younger students will subject themselves to greater risk because of not having sophisticated guidelines to use in choosing drugs with which to experiment or in selecting drug sources of reasonable reliability. There is also the strong possibility that younger students as a group will be less able to handle the emotional concomitants of strong psychoactive drugs, whether those emotions are direct drug effects or are reactions to the organic changes so induced—including, of course, emotions of guilt and anxiety which are likely to surround their involvement in behavior that is illicit and novel and may be associated with taboo impulse release. What we are suggesting is that as illicit-drug use becomes more common at high, junior high, and elementary school levels and as marijuana experimentation is replaced with trials of stronger substances such as LSD, STP, heroin and the like, the number of cases coming to official attention will increase. Anticipating this, health professionals and school administrative and counseling personnel would be well advised to be ready with modes of response. The police and the courts have the same problem and while, at the moment, drug cases are being processed routinely, it is evident that if arrests increase still further, both the courts and the correctional facilities will be taxed beyond their capacities. Police narcotic squads are already in this position, although they are in a better position to control their work loads.

A number of reactions to expanded youthful drug use and to added official case loads are occurring. They are paradoxical ones for, simultaneously, loosening and tightening, harshness and gentleness are under way. Proposals for changes in the federal law, for example, include adding felony penalties for possession of dangerous drugs, such as LSD and the like. At the same time, proposals in various states (California, Colorado) have been made for making punishments, especially marijuana penalties, considerably lighter and allowing judges more discretion in sentencing. Another widespread reaction has been in the field of education, where programs designed to reduce the amount of drug use have begun. One approach emphasizes scare tactics and biased information; another, free and open fact giving. In neither case does one know whether student behavior will be affected and, if so, in what direction. The reaction of health professionals seems to be more consistent and has been primarily in the direction of establishing new centers or facilities for treating drug users not only for bad trips as such but for both underlying psychiatric disorders and physical illnesses which may attend their life styles. Even here, response is not uniform, for one finds some public- or school-health authorities responding with heavy disapproval and recommendations for punitive action rather than health care. The latter is more desirable when evaluated by humane standards; however, one must confess that the evidence is wanting which would show that current programs for treating drug abuse medically or psychologically do in fact help, and there is even doubt whether the treatment of acute physical illness among persons continually re-exposing themselves to such illness (venereal disease, hepatitis, injection infections, upper respiratory ailments, nutritional deficit, and so on) is the most efficient health endeavor, although none challenges the goodness of a healing effort as such.

The drug use at which we have been looking is a middle- and upper-class practice. For the most part, the high school data reported here have also been drawn from middle- or upper-class schools. Although lower-class heroin use among youngsters is described in other excellent studies (Chein, Gerard, Lee, and Rosenfeld, 1964; Robins, 1966; Gordon, Short, Cartwright, and Strodtbeck, 1963, etc.; see Chapter One), we are unaware—with the possible exception of the Blumer study (1967), which does not specify neighborhood or class variables —of the changes occurring among lower-class elementary and high school students in their drug use. Investigators in New York City are gathering data, as are a number of others in East Coast centers. There have been preliminary reports of slum users' opposition to LSD—for example, that it is not their kind of drug; on the other hand, with the difficulty in obtaining good-quality heroin, the publicity for hallucinogens, and the increasing illicit traffic in methamphetamine especially, one anticipates that lower-class use will gradually alter itself by expanding to meet these new "opportunities." Simultaneously, we see the growth of heroin interest in the middle and upper class, as well as among hippies—despite initial denial of interest in drugs with a bad reputation—so that a certain homogeneity in the diversity of use is to be expected in the coming years. The old accepted drugs, of course, will stay in the picture (alcohol, tobacco, barbiturates, and the like), although one notes—and we shall come to this again shortly—an apparent lack of interest among many college students in tobacco use. Recall that over half of the total student population do not intend to smoke tobacco (Chapter Seven).

Beginning with our LSD studies as reported in *Utopiates* (Blum and Associates, 1964) and continuing with the college studies reported

here, we have found that the "pioneers" or leaders in introducing the
middle and upper classes to the exotic drugs have been intellectuals,
artists, and professionals, especially those in the sciences of the mind.
At the student level, their counterparts who initiate drug use have been
primarily those students who, like the adults studied in *Utopiates,* are
secure by reason of wealth, are white Anglo-Saxon, have Protestant
backgrounds, and are also more free of convention and attentive to
matters of adjustment, mind, aesthetics, and social philosophy—these
latter quite probably part of a heritage of elite family values. These
individuals are friends and teachers to the other students.

Socioeconomic position and vocational interest, along with family background, are obviously important characteristics or preconditions
for belonging to that class of students from which the drug explorers
are drawn. So, too, is individual personality, for as was shown in Chapter Fourteen, the more mind-interested, feeling-oriented, aesthetic, and
adventuresome students—who have less regard for rules or the feelings
or rights of others—are the most drawn to the kind of illicit-drug use
taking place on campus. In addition, we infer from the clinical data
that historical within-family differences contribute a great deal; families with greater divergency of opinion, more distant relationships to
the children, and more unresolved parent-child interpersonal crises
seem to be those which generate the drug explorers. However, social
background, personality, and within-family styles of parent-child interaction are not the only important contributors to the drug-exploring
student; this constellation can be supplemented by a long list of other
life-history behavior items—as set forth in earlier chapters—each one
of which can become a predictor of illicit-drug use. Recall just a few of
the consistent items: family mobility, disagreement with parents on
topical issues, dissatisfaction with school, career pessimism, drop-out
history, early gratifications from being ill, and early eating problems.
Yet, for actual drug use to occur, still other conditions must be met.
The initiate must ordinarily be informed enough about a drug to believe it to be safe and worth while—that is, his expectations about a
positive outcome must outweigh the risk of a negative one, although
the element of risk is itself attractive to adventuresome young people.
The initiate must feel reasonably secure about the situation in which
he takes a drug; indeed, part of the teaching of use is to give assurances
about freedom from risk of arrest and to show how discretion may be
used. That information may, of course, be incorrect, but our student

informants stress that they do not begin use unless they believe they are safe. Such teaching of expectations about drugs is offered daily by the mass media as these arouse interest in the various illicit-exotic compounds; however, probably much more specific teaching is conducted in those small groups which form and become the nexus required for social drug use. At this point we see that a necessary situational condition is the presence of others who, by example or persuasion, show how it is done and why it should be done. These others must also provide the *sine qua non*—that is, the supply of drugs to be taken and, if use is to continue, instruction in where further drugs may be procured.

The critical importance of exposure to such initiators introduces the role which accident can play. Even if we presume that people do tend to seek out others with similar interests and that these interests then draw them closer together—as, for example, humanities majors meeting each other in classes and clubs which facilitate drug learning among the newcomers—we also believe that accidental contact plays a role. Our students tell us how—as they moved from one university residence unit to another—they came in contact for the first time with users, how simple proximity allowed them to see marijuana use and learn it was safe, and how they then sought acceptance or were sought after by proselytizers until their own initiation took place. We have also seen (see Chapter Sixteen) how the drug habits of friends and respected campus leaders contribute to the likelihood of a student's using or not using drugs. We do not argue that friendship choices are without psychological significance in themselves. Our point is that the pre-existing drug scene within a residence unit may make a difference to a newcomer in whether or not he learns about drug use from people whose opinions, esteem, and conduct do matter to him.

As we have tried to emphasize throughout, as an unusual form of conduct is adopted by more and more people, one must expect that the unusual characteristics which describe the pioneers and explorers will no longer discriminate between users and non-users. In the case of metropolitan campuses, where we now have evidence that in some schools the majority have tried marijuana, the label of "unusual" falls more and more on the non-user. As we have observed among our abstainers (Chapter Three), such aloofness in a predominantly drug-using culture is hard to maintain, so that over the college years, the abstainers become at least users of approved drugs. Now that marijuana has become an "approved" drug by the standards of the majority of students (and an unknown but probably large portion of some faculties as well), one must expect that even the upright will succumb to social pressures and personal titillation, so that someday most students in most places will have had marijuana experience. We shall not make such a prediction for the more potent drugs of worse repute; while more students are trying them, it is our impression that widespread knowledge of dangers and risks does make a difference and that most students at the college level will refrain from the use of LSD, heroin, and methamphetamine. We are less sanguine about the high school level.

We may conceive of the foregoing circumstances that contribute to illicit-drug use as a set of vectors such as proposed in the scheme below.

The scheme below leaves out a very important set of variables, those associated with drug effects themselves. Conceivably, the use of a placebo could take place in response to these vectors; indeed, analysis of some of the materials taken by students in the belief that they were psychoactive shows that sometimes they *have* been taking placebos being sold as marijuana or LSD. Yet we cannot assume that the mind so lacks reflection on internal states or that experience sustains itself on symbols alone; thus, one must look to the drugs themselves and, in their administration, to the felt consequences. This is not the place to offer a discussion of the range of effects of the various classes of psychoactive drugs—or of the difficulties in discriminating between specific and nonspecific effects. However, it is the place to remind ourselves that whatever the symbolic value of various protest drugs, the effects are real and it is the effects that are sought upon repeated administration. One is not to assume that the effects of a single drug are the same on different people or that they are the same on one person given their use over time; differences in effects must especially be anticipated when dosage differs, when the mental and physical conditions of persons differ, when other drugs are present or absent in the body, when the intervals between use differ, or when the means of taking the drug differ. Even so, it has been amply demonstrated that at least some people receive a drug and say they like it sufficiently to want to take it again. "Liking" is an ambiguous term often enough and we would not wish to become involved in the painful psychological arguments about reward, reinforcement, or even pleasure. What-

PARENT-CHILD INTERACTION STYLES: Permissive; close to mother; disagreements within family on values; not child- or family-centered life styles; father-child aloofness; intellectual-ideals of relationship not put in practice; parent's teaching of drug use.

SCHOOL MILIEU: Liberal urban campus; intellectual emphasis; nondenominational; close ties with drug sources in metropolitan areas; faculty sympathy with student quests and challenges.

MASS MEDIA WITH INFORMATION ON DRUG USE: Specialized literature on drug effects; sensationalism; appeals through publicity to exhibitionistic drug use.

CULTURE: A drug-using society optimistic about effects of drugs in controlling mind and tolerant of insulated adolescent cultism and faddishness.

DRUG SUPPLY AND

A SETTING FOR USE

PERCEIVED AS SAFE

STUDENTS EXPERIMENTING

WITH ILLICIT DRUGS

SOCIAL CLASS AND FAMILY BACKGROUND: Wealth; liberal Protestant or Jew; mobile; values stress adjustment; independence; nontraditional life.

PERSONALITY AND INTERESTS, INCLUDING EARLY-LIFE EXPERIENCES: Interests in aesthetics, in the mind; shows regressive experience and feelings; is open-minded, intuitive, undisciplined, rebellious, insecure, spontaneous, guileful, sympathetic, unreliable, nonconforming, flamboyant.

PEER GROUPS ON CAMPUS: Friends who use illicit drugs; respected older students who show and teach drug use.

369

Figure 1. Presentation of Vectors Contributing to Illicit-Drug Use by Students

ever is going on, the person says he likes the drug effect and he acts as though that was the case by going on to take more. But we know that in the case of the illicit-exotic drugs—at least to date—most of the students who experiment with them do not become regular users. This brings us to a concern with differences between those who continue to use drugs and those who stop using them. In our earlier study of LSD users (Blum and Associates, 1964), it was apparent that matters of personality and of life orientation contributed to this discrimination when age, sex, and occupational status were controlled. In the present study when intensive and less intensive users were compared, we had no personality data; there we could see that a variety of factors were in operation, including parental drug-use habits, student ideology and dissatisfactions, and the like. Again, these are external descriptors and do not tell us how different students experienced the drugs taken either in terms of specific effects or in nonspecific ones, including the meanings attached to the experience. Why, for example, do half of those who have tried tranquilizers and a minority of those who use narcotics not intend to use these drugs again, whereas the majority who have used alcohol and marijuana intend to do so? Beecher (1959) gives strong clues for one drug, morphine: most normal individuals given this narcotic do not enjoy it; only 10 per cent of his population reported euphoria instead of dysphoria.

In the case of marijuana, which is the most popular of the psychoactive illicit drugs on campus, we make some presumptions about popularity that are linked to the drug's effects. For one thing, we believe most students when they say that they expected it to be fun; even if it led to nothing on the first round or two, some had been "taught" to continue use until they were convinced either that it was "groovy" or that, for them, it was nothing. For many students marijuana apparently works—that is, they experience a state which they say they like and want to repeat. This in itself accounts only in part for its popularity. Consider how it is used. Only marijuana among the illicit drugs is smoked (excluding opium, which is gaining in popularity). When tobacco smoking was introduced into Europe, it became epidemic and within a hundred years or so almost every society around the world had adopted it (see Chapter Five in *Drugs I*). Smoking was something special, and while tobacco was highly desired and today remains probably the most popular addiction in the world, other drugs could be substituted for it. Opium, hashish, and datura, for example, were put in the pipe or in cigarette papers and smoked—a habit continuing to this day. The values of smoking are several. For one thing, absorption of the drug is immediate and effects are felt rapidly. Dosage is visibly controllable; one can inspect the contents and be reasonably sure what they are (notwithstanding naive students who smoke field grass or oregano instead); one can choose to smoke as much as one wants; and for the mild drugs, such as tobacco and today's collegiate marijuana, the effects are not long enduring. Contrast that to the invisible contents of a pill, which, once ingested, cannot be retrieved and whose effects—whether sedative or hallucinogenic—may be felt for many hours. In our conversations with students, they have emphasized how important it is to be able to control dosage in this fashion. Smoking has another strong attraction, although it is difficult to identify in terms explicit enough for the meticulous. "Oral gratification" is what the psychoanalysts say; it means that people enjoy putting things into their mouths and—from nipples to fingers to chewing gum and cigarettes— mouthing them, sucking them, and returning for more. We believe that the oral-gratification component of marijuana smoking is one of its appeals.

For anyone who has smoked tobacco, it is easy to transfer the smoking habit to marijuana; once a method for administering one drug is learned, substitution of another drug easily follows. In our survey data, we have no test for the easy hypothesis that tobacco smoking is a helpful precondition for marijuana use. The data support such an inference, but not critically. On shakier but, in some ways, more satisfying impressionist grounds, we have interviewed nonsmokers who have volunteered that they hesitated to begin marijuana smoking because they did not like smoking as such. We have also interviewed students who were nonsmokers and who rejected marijuana on these grounds until someone came along to tell them that marijuana, or hashish, can be cooked and ingested—the famous recipe for brownies then being put to use. One girl, relating how she had done this, complained about the disadvantages; not knowing the dosage, she had ground up "a lot" of hashish, cooked, and eaten it and, in consequence, said she was "high" and sometimes hallucinating for five hours and had but the dimmest memories of the twenty-four hours following this episode, a fitful period in which she had slept and wandered about.

The substitution of marijuana for tobacco is not only easy, but there are strong reasons for doing this, or so the students say. For the last five or ten years, there has been a strong campaign to educate the public to the dangers of cigarette smoking. Students know it is linked to cancer and they know it is an addictive drug. The students have grown up amidst public health warnings announcing that danger. We believe they have responded. Consider, for example, data from Chapter Seven showing that fewer students than their parents are smoking or intend to smoke. Students can respond to warnings about specific drugs if, as a critical audience, they believe these are scientifically sound. Yet if we grant a culture of smoking around them, their own early experience with parents who smoke, and the satisfactions to be derived from oral gratification, then we must expect a strong set of forces to be contributing to the desire to smoke. Presto, tobacco is eliminated because it is unsafe, and a new drug, marijuana, believed not to be addictive and not to cause cancer, is substituted, with the additional advantages that its dosage can be controlled by smoking and its effects can be realized immediately by this method. Grant further that marijuana does, in fact, please many of the persons who try it and that, indeed, for some it is a very pleasant drug, then a compelling set of reasons for use are present.

There are two other sets of reasons to be considered as well. One has to do with alcohol, whose benefits are well documented (Leake and Silverman, 1966) if the reader needs such literature for proof. The students say alcohol has three disadvantages: its effects are long lasting, it is expensive, and it produces a hang-over. Marijuana, they say, is quicker acting, even at illicit prices costs less to produce equivalent effects, and, best of all, provides no hang-over. The arguments are set forth with conviction. They do not mention the faddish feature that alcohol is "old hat," while pot is associated with the exclusive modernity belonging to youth.

The other set of reasons concern the symbolic value of marijuana or any other illicit substance. We shall not dwell at length on this point simply because so many public discussions have done so. Briefly, the proposition is that marijuana, LSD, or other substances can serve as symbols which help make groups cohesive. When the groups are composed of youngsters simultaneously thumbing their noses at authority and eager to have their own way while, at the same time, planning, for the most part, to join the Establishment to work for a living, then the action must be concealed to avoid painful criminal sentences. We (Blum and Associates, 1964) earlier called it the "cool rebellion." As events from 1964 to date have shown, the student rebellion is not as cool as it was before; simultaneously, drug use is not only more extensive but it is more visible. We take it that these two phenomena are not unrelated and that secret nose thumbing is being replaced, at least by the anarchists and activists, by active disobedience to a variety of rules and laws—those violations reflecting anything from moral fervor and the doctrine of civil disobedience to provocations to violent revolution. Whatever the ideological component, we may be sure that diverse individual feelings and needs are being expressed. In any event, the climate of civil disobedience, the availability of a set of moral justifications for active violation of law, and the apparent inequities of present drug penalties, which provide up to the death penalty for marijuana offenses, combine to give a sense of righteousness to the drug user on campus. Yet with all the provocation and violation of law, we must not overlook that illicit-drug use on campus is not only attractive—for the foregoing reasons and probably many more besides—*but is safe*. Recall from Chapter Nine that few had enduring ill effects, that even fewer were disciplined by school authorities, and that still fewer suffered arrest. For all the inadequacy of police and school records, it is clear, for example, that of an estimated five thousand students at School I who have tried marijuana, no more than ten have been arrested for it and probably no more than five. To our knowledge none of these has served time, all having been released on probation or having managed to get their cases off the docket. What this implies is that for all the audacity, derring-do, and provocation that illicit-drug use signifies, the practice is not one designed to produce martyrs; rather, the students make realistic estimates of risk and enjoy nearly complete safety in the process of being unlawful. What additional psychological functions such controlled risk may have, beyond adventure and bon-vivant conspiracy, we leave to others for speculation.

At this point any further explorations into motives—beyond those already given by students or deduced by the many scholars writing in the field—are not fruitful. We believe that the social and epidemiological data, combined with psychological test data and observations, have been consistent over a variety of studies and speak for themselves. We should now, therefore, like to comment on points which we believe have been underemphasized so far, either because the inferences have not been made clearly enough from our data or because our statistics speak too strongly and require qualification.

With regard to the latter, there are two areas of inference which have been stressed within the preceding chapters and which, nevertheless, leave us with a sense of worry or dissatisfaction. The first concerns the characteristics of students in the illicit drug-using groups, especially in the intensive-using groups. Throughout, we have seen that the drug innovators and the intensive student users in the sample have appeared not only as change oriented and more removed from family closeness but more dissatisfied and pessimistic. These latter attributes require qualification, for the dissatisfaction and pessimism we have seen is not, except in rare cases, of the depressed and aimless variety that characterized Keniston's (1965) uncommitted, alienated clinical sample; rather, their expressed dissatisfaction indicates, we believe, an awareness of discrepancy between ideals and reality, between what they personally want to enjoy and what they must put up with, and perhaps, too, a need to gripe, which is fashionable for their age and station. There are a dozen ways to interpret what the student dissatisfaction may imply: restlessness and impatience; self-indulgence, vanity, and intolerance; hope and dedicated activity; and so forth. These terms reflect the prejudices and orientation to youth and life of the observer as much as the traits of the students. In any event, the drug users in our sample should not be viewed as people in despair or as undergoing acute psychological distress; their own words expressing dissatisfaction can hint at appreciation of much that is good and gratifying about the world—only they want more or better—whereas their pessimism can conceal much confidence about themselves, their own safety and sense, and the righteousness of their standards and deeds.

Perhaps the above can best be demonstrated by letting one drug-using student speak for himself. We have quoted but little from the students and now in doing so, we do not contend that a single student speaks for all who embrace the drug ideology. Nevertheless, we consider the following remarks—written as a term paper in response to our question to a seminar—as illuminating of one important point of view.

> "Why must students use drugs?" says the blinder-wearing public, barely aware of its own hideous hypocrisy. For a people who embrace not only alcohol but war, the Holy Profit, and social

injustice (and all in the name of some higher good) such moral indignation is ludicrous. Disgust at society's "phoniness" may encourage the use of drugs not only as a protest, but as an affirmation that there is a "better way," and that drugs can indeed be beneficial in helping society attain its ideals. The student becomes quietly (or violently) outraged when he realizes how leaders misuse America's potential. The harsh juxtaposition of an iniquitous society led by leaders of "menopausal mentality" . . . the System's evinced inhumanity—its failure to recognize people as human beings—is the prime enemy of the student and the bloodclot in the lifestream of America that he hopes and thinks can be dissolved through the constructive use of drugs. Expectantly, there is a tumultuous din from the vested interests who profit from that inhumanity and who sense that their reins might slip from their hands.

As society tumbles blindly from one day to the next, its college campuses are becoming testing grounds for the use of drugs and their effects on personal and personality development. Students are now experimenting with drugs the same way they are experimenting with life: they are looking for personal truth through their own experience. Students are interested mostly in hallucinogenic drugs and are wary of the dangers of drug abuse. Significantly, while hedonism may be connected with some drug use, there is little campus use of drugs to eliminate consciousness or to stay in a state of oblivion, both very asocial, "anti-life" (and therefore highly disesteemed) acts.

For me, as for many others, the primary cause for "turning on" is a curiosity that encompasses a longing for knowledge of an idealized "other world," (and thus a romantic escapism), and the sheer intellectual desire to experience and know new things. This insatiable curiosity for knowledge and experience, the type of curiosity that all good universities ideally hope to instill, is fired by reports of experimenting friends, and by the relentless drive to seek and establish a satisfactory identity, as well as to find meaning in the world. Hallucinogens, for example, offer one new experiences that can be valuable in a search for Existential Truth, and Ultimate Meaning.

The search for Meaning is extremely salient for the probing student. The student may be proud of his secure feelings of superiority and of joining the ranks of Nietzsche, Socrates, and other "liberated" men. But he might also feel a terrible emptiness because he now sees no easy "Answer" to replace the ersatz security previously provided by the smothering, mothering blankets of culture and religion. He is thus launched on his Existential Search and may resort to grass and other hallucinogens to see what they have to offer.

On another level, after one's initial curiosity about grass is satisfied, grass then takes on the role of being the social medium that provides an initial common bond among a group. Further, grass replaces alcohol and accordingly changes the very nature of social events. People's awareness of themselves, their roles, and other people is increased and the common conscious perception of that increased awareness becomes the basic tenet regulating intergroup action and communication. Thus, more maturity of thought and action is demanded, as opposed to the lessened need for maturity in the mind-dulling atmosphere of alcohol gatherings. This, then, becomes the major appeal of grass among sensitive students—grass effects a situation that is commensurate to the state of "honesty" and "naturalness" (i.e. facadelessness) that such students think appropriate to engender meaningful dialogue. Hypocrisy and phoniness become very obvious, and as people recognize these faults in themselves as well as in others, they succeed in gaining greater self-knowledge and self-mastery.

Continued use of grass and hallucinogens increases this self-knowledge and can lead to an overall greater maturity. As a person knows more about himself he is better able to decide what to do with his life and how to do it. His drug experience also has given him an increased knowledge and enjoyment of his natural as well as his social environment. He can now appreciate things more than ever before because having seen everything from a different perspective under the influence of drugs, he acquires a new sensitivity for the "realness" and "wonderfulness" of things. He is less dulled to the world. He is also less dulled to other people and recognizes them as noble creatures no less real than himself.

Students see hallucinogenic drugs, in their ability to lead one to serious introspection of himself and of his relationship to other human beings, as one elixir that may return sanity to the world, and effectively "humanize" the Establishment by causing the rearrangement of national priorities. This is the hope and the noble enterprise that is pursued and esteemed by today's idealistic, sensitive, and curious college youth. Society, then, need not be completely distraught over their experimenting students. A greater understanding of what it is to be a human being is the best "minor" any student can take out of a university, and that greater understanding has substantial influence in the youthful push for social renovation and revolution.

In appraising these students, we find that a curious scientific problem arises, for the interests of the liberal students who are the drug explorers and innovators are close in kind to the interests of many social scientists, psychiatrists, and school administrators. That correspondence of views is not derived simply from the Strong Test scores of Chapter Sixteen but is also apparent when values are compared.

The importance of adjustment, of curiosity, of social criticism, and of "progressive" sociopolitical doctrine, as well as an emphasis on aesthetics, on finding one's "identity," on spontaneity in relationships, and on being antagonistic toward traditional authority, are likely to be found in the social sciences and mind-studying trades, or espoused by their members, as well as by the liberal students. Consequently, when these scientists and clinicians undertake to evaluate today's left and/or drug-using students, they are often looking at people much like themselves. Indeed, if we recall the early attraction of exotic drugs for some of these professionals—a few of whom became leaders in the drug movement of the early 1960's—we see that drug interests as well as general orientation may be held in common. We recall from *Utopiates* that our interviewers, themselves psychologists for the most part, rated LSD users as being more likeable than the matched controls. The interviewers said the professionals who were LSD aficionados were more relaxed, appeared warmer and more open-minded, and enjoyed the interview and its mind explorations more. These "liking" reactions probably reflect preferences for people acting more as these interviewers thought people ought to act. Now, as scholars approach students, one wonders whether the same process may not be repeating itself: investigators seeking out subjects whose values are attractive and enjoying their company because they do appear warm, thoughtful, questioning, and exciting. The danger is that the evaluation may be positive only because of the charm of the young people without the investigators' recognizing the grounds for their reactions and without coming to grips with either fundaments or implications of student behavior. We are posing the problem of investigator identification with his subjects, of "countertransference," in which it may be—as some of the students contend—that the young are admired because they act out the fantasies of their frustrated elders. The corollary danger is also acute and is commonplace. When conservative people offer their more negative evaluations of the pot-smoking or radical students, many university and professionally based people reject outright what the "reactionaries" have to say. These two sets of bias, with their concomitant rejections of each side by the other, set the stage for the kind of nonconstructive, noncommunicating emotional standoffs that we saw in the views of narcotics officers and intellectuals contrasted in *Utopiates*, between liberal and conservative legislators examined in Chapter Thirteen in *Drugs I*, and in the contradictory directions of responses in legislation, education, and health care commented upon in an early paragraph.

Another point on which we feel dissatisfied and which is derived from our data concerns reports of ill effects from drug use. It is clear from Chapter Nine that a variety of unpleasant outcomes can occur but one gets the impression that very few suffer anything damaging over the long run. Thus, one can conclude, as we do, that anything but acute toxic ill effects are unlikely and that illicit-exotic drugs when used as students are now doing, for the most part, do not seem to pose serious hazards to school performance or to health. What hazards of drug dependency as such are incurred are unknown. We must not forget that in each sample of intensive users (including alcohol and to-bacco!) there were students who were really worried about their be-coming or being drug dependent. (See a similar finding in our normal-population study in Chapter Eleven in *Drugs I*.) Whether they were simply anxious or realistically at risk, we do not know; we fear it was the latter. What must be stressed is that the students in our sample were those still in school after taking drugs, so that not only are they a selected group of persevering young people but the ones still function-ing well. We have no idea how many have suffered ill effects and have left school; we have no idea about long-range bad results of the grad-ual sort that alter personality adversely or produce dependency yet are not recognized by students in their self-reporting as undesirable. We faced the same problem in *Utopiates* when continued users said of themselves that they were better people than ever and felt just fine, whereas for 10 per cent of these users family, employers, or friends said they had gone downhill. Not only are our standards for judging long-term personality and social change unclear and themselves emo-tionally laden but the methods of this present study have not allowed any assessment of adverse effects not recognized and reported by stu-dents. Paulsen's (see Chapter Seventeen) psychiatric observations are an exception. At this point, we feel very uncomfortable with what we know about long-range ill effects.

As to points underemphasized, the first is that the etiology of drug use appears to be in no way unique as far as the development of human social behavior is concerned. Davies (1963), in an excellent synthesis of the literature, reviews the forces that contribute to the development of political beliefs. Drug use shares with political beliefs— and, no doubt, with many other aspects of opinion and conduct—an etiology well known to social scientists. Our schematic diagram could be, with a few word substitutions, applied to a host of belief and conduct systems in mankind. Culture, family, institutional exposures, primary-group membership, personal idiosyncrasies, accident of birth and place—these are the typical abstractions for the sets of forces which influence human beings. Now that student drug use is becoming a common activity, it too can be seen to be shaped by common determinants. On the other hand, as with other special ideologies or unusual conduct forms, the outward similarities that people share conceal private meanings. Common social pathways are always utilized for individual—including psychopathological—needs. Illicit student drug use appears to be a remarkable phenomenon simply because it is a novel one, and while it is important to individuals engaging in it because it does have significance in their lives, yet—viewed either socially or pharmacologically—many of the events involved are ones well known in science—or in common sense—and the determinants are also found to be of an ordinary order of magnitude.

Not only can we identify student drug use as but one of the many things human beings do which have classes of determinants in common—none of which are bizarre—but we can point out that student drug use is intertwined with other aspects of his life and person. We tried to make that clear in our introductory chapter and again in the ideologies discussion, but fear the point was understated. The student who is using drugs is not ordinarily engaged in a random act or in one which is out of keeping with his character and circumstances. Drug initiation and use, however "strange" they seem to outsiders or "not like him" to parents, is very much like him after all, for it is in keeping with his social, psychological, and physiological apparatus. If it doesn't "fit" him, he will stop; otherwise, we may presume that his continued drug use serves a variety of functions at many levels. The more daring the deed in terms of social attitudes and the more daring the drug in terms of biochemical effects, the more significance it is likely to have both as symptom and as sign; however, the more common drug use becomes, the less significance it will have to students and the less it will stand out as an item which discriminates between classes of persons. Whether exotic-drug use remains noticeable for that large portion of society residing off campus will depend on how we respond as a society to the phenomenon facing us. That social response depends on a variety of emotional, political, and practical considerations.

Certainly, there are some major influences on the response of society to expanded exotic-drug use which have yet to come into play—and cannot come into play until an assessment is made of the impact which the new ideology has on interpersonal relations and until the longer-range specific effects on persons of a variety of new psychoactive agents are better known. Until that time, most of us place our bets on generalizing from principles we already accept but which we cannot yet be sure apply to what is happening now.

Implicit in much that we have said is the prediction that student drug use will continue to expand and that as these students grow older, many forms of drug use now considered deviant or dangerous will become part of what otherwise-respectable adults do. Whether or not marijuana and LSD use remains illegal or as severely punishable will make quite a difference in how these adults use their drugs—in secrecy or openly. It will also make a difference in the absolute number of young recruits and in the number of aging students willing to spend the effort involved in illicit procurement and discreet use as they continue into mature years, where many other demands are made on energy and where illicit conduct loses some of its romance and adventure. This prediction assumes that the illicit-drug users on campus today are the generators of new ideas and the adopters of new ways of life and that they will serve as leaders in a change-oriented society which is constantly looking for adjustment, pleasure, and personal enrichment. Unless a very considerable political reaction of a conservative sort takes place, it is very unlikely that this ordinary American process of seeking and changing, which emanates from universities and the centers of power to which university graduates go, would be impeded. The gradualist assumption is that laws and law enforcement will be liberalized to accommodate the new social reality. The agnostic alternative is that traditional forces will not give way, especially because of the link between student drug use, on the one hand, and left-wing politics, on the other. If that proves to be the case, one must expect an intensification of conflict between the left and the right, an exaggeration of repression and rebellion, in which drugs would be but a small issue compared with the overwhelming intensity of conflict between associated social and political forces. The American scene today clearly reveals these antagonistic forces. The pessimists on either side will predict that the opposition—whether left or right—will triumph and ruin will reign. Those in the larger American tradition—

which we interpret as one of gradual change through compromise and of conflict fragmented by interest groups rather than as being consolidated into monolithic confrontation—will be optimistic. They will trust that sufficient rationality and self-interest exist to allow individuals to rule out for themselves drugs whose effects are damaging. They will trust that sufficient orderliness remains so that the community—including the government—will continue to exercise control over the distribution of drugs with demonstrable damaging potentials and control over persons either suffering or visiting damage in association with psychoactive-drug use. They will trust that sufficient respect for freedom and humanism will prevail to allow individuals to go their own ways pursuing whatever conduct they will as long as it brings little harm, even if it brings little gain. They will remain tolerant of human diversity and sanguine about youthful resilience and will not hurry to condemn or to praise that which appears on the surface as long as they do not know what lies beneath or is signified in the future. Finally, they will, when in doubt and even if in anguish, take time to respect one another and to talk things over in order to come to common solutions, acting in concert rather than in opposition whenever possible. These are the things the optimists will do. If there are enough optimists in America, the fear and the fighting about student drug use will happily diminish in the coming years.

Bibliography

ABERLE, D. F. *The Peyote Religion among the Navajo.* Chicago: Aldine, 1966.

ADAMS, J. B. *Contributions to the Understanding of Adolescence.* Boston: Allyn and Bacon, 1967.

ADORNO, T. W., FRENKEL-BRUNSWIK, E., LEVINSON, D. J., and SANFORD, R. N. *The Authoritarian Personality.* New York: Harper, 1950.

ALMOND, G. *The Appeals of Communism.* Princeton: Princeton University Press, 1954.

APTER, D. (Ed.) *Ideology and Discontent.* New York: Free Press, 1964.

AS, A. "Hypnotizability as a Function of Non-Hypnotic Experiences." *Journal of Abnormal and Social Psychology,* 1963, *66* (2), 142–150.

ASCH, S. E. *Social Psychology.* New York: Prentice-Hall, 1952.

BARBATO, L. Personal communication, 1967.

BARKER, E. N. "Authoritarianism of the Political Right, Center, and Left." *Journal of Social Issues,* 1963, *19,* 63–74.

BARTLETT, M. S. *Essays in Probability and Statistics.* London: Methuen, 1962.

BAY, C. "Political and Apolitical Students: Facts in Search of Theory." *Journal of Social Issues,* 1967, *23,* 76–91.

BECKER, H. S. *Outsiders: Studies in the Sociology of Deviance.* New York: Free Press, 1963.

BEECHER, H. K. *Measurement of Subjective Responses.* New York: Oxford, 1959.

BELL, D. (Ed.) *The Radical Right.* New York: Doubleday, 1963.

383

BERG, I. A., and BASS, B. M. (Eds.) *Conformity and Deviation.* New York: Harper, 1961.

BERGER, B. M. "Hippie Morality, More Old than New." *Trans-Action,* 1967, *5,* 19–23.

BERGSON, H. *The Two Sources of Morality and Religion.* New York: Anchor Books, 1935.

BLOCK, J., HAAN, N., and SMITH, M. "Activism and Apathy in Contemporary Adolescence," in Adams, J. F. (Ed.) *Contributions to the Understanding of Adolescence.* Boston: Allyn and Bacon, 1967.

BLUM, R. H. *A Commonsense Guide to Doctors, Hospitals, and Medical Care.* New York: Macmillan, 1964.

BLUM, R. H. *Task Force Report: Narcotics and Drug Abuse.* The President's Commission on Law Enforcement and the Administration of Justice. Washington, D.C.: U.S. Government Printing Office, 1967.

BLUM, R. H., and Associates. *Utopiates: The Use and Users of LSD-25.* New York: Atherton, 1964.

BLUM, R. H., and Associates. *Society and Drugs.* San Francisco: Jossey-Bass, 1969.

BLUM, R. H. (with J. EZEKIEL). *Clinical Records for Mental Health Services.* Springfield, Ill.: Thomas, 1962.

BLUMER, H. "The World of Youthful Drug Use," in *Addiction Center Project Final Report.* Berkeley: School of Criminology, University of California, 1967. (Mimeograph.)

BOYD, W. J. "Today's Activist, Tomorrow's Alumnus." Speech before the American Alumni Council, 1967.

BREHM, M. L., and BACK, K. W. "Self Image and Attitudes toward Drugs." *Journal of Personality,* 1968, *36* (2), 299–314.

BRIGGS, I. M. *The Myers-Briggs Type Indicator.* Princeton: Educational Testing Service, 1962.

BROPHY, J. T. "Suicide Attempts with Therapeutic Drugs." *Archives of General Psychiatry,* 1967, *17,* 652–657.

BUCKNER, H. T. "Flying Saucers Are for People." *Trans-Action,* 1966, *3* (4), 10–13.

BUCKNER, H. T. *San Francisco Chronicle,* June 19, 1967.

BUTZ, O. (Ed.) *To Make a Difference: A Look at America, Its Values, Its Society, and Its Systems of Education.* New York: Harper, 1964.

"Cal Tech Student Survey." *Palo Alto Times,* April 21, 1967.

CARRIER, J. *The Sociology of Religious Belonging.* New York: Herder, 1965.

CARTWRIGHT, D., and ZANDER, A. *Group Dynamics.* Evanston, Ill.: Row, Peterson, 1953.

CHEIN, I., GERARD, D. L., LEE, R. S., and ROSENFELD, E. *The Road to H: Narcotics, Delinquency, and Social Policy.* New York: Basic Books, 1964.

CHESLER, M., and SHMUCK, R. "Participant Observation in a Super-Patriot Discussion Group." *Journal of Social Issues,* 1963, *19* (2), 18–30.

CISIN, I. H., and CAHALAN, D. "American Drinking Practices." Social Research Project, George Washington University. Presented at the Symposium on the Drug Takers at the University of California at Los Angeles, June 12, 1966.

City of New York, Mayor's Committee on Marijuana. "The Problem of Marijuana in the City of New York." Report made to the Mayor in 1940. (Usually referred to as *The La Guardia Report.*)

COHEN, M., and HALE, D. (Eds.) *The New Student Left: An Anthology.* Boston: Beacon, 1967.

CONANT, J. B. *The American High School Today.* New York: McGraw-Hill, 1959.

County of San Mateo, California, Juvenile Justice Commission (Landis Weaver, Chairman). *Report,* 1967.

CRUTCHFIELD, R. S. "Independent Thought in a Conformist World," in Farber, S. M., and Wilson, H. L. (Eds.) *Conflict and Creativity: Control of the Mind.* Part II. New York: McGraw-Hill, 1963.

DAVIES, J. C. *Human Nature in Politics.* New York: Wiley, 1963.

DAVIS, F. "Why All of Us May Be Hippies Someday." *Trans-Action,* 1967, 5, 10–18.

DEMOS, G. D., and SHAINLINE, J. W. "Drug Use on the College Campus: A Pilot-Study Survey." Prepared for the Committee for the Study of Drugs at California State College at Long Beach, 1967. (Mimeograph.)

DEVONSHIRE, C. M. Associated Press report, 1967.

DOHRMAN, H. T. *California Cult: The Story of Mankind United.* Boston: Beacon, 1964.

DOUVAN, E., and ADELSON, J. *The Adolescent Experience.* New York: Wiley, 1966.

DRAPER, H. *Berkeley: The New Student Revolt.* New York: Grove Press, 1965.

EELLS, K. "A Survey of Student Practices and Attitudes with Respect to Marijuana and LSD." A report from the California Institute of Technology. Unpublished, 1967.

ELLIS, J. T. *American Catholics and Intellectual Life.* Chicago: Heritage Foundation, 1966.

ERIKSON, E. H. "The Problem of Ego Identity," in Stein, M. R., Vidich, A., and White, D. M. (Eds.) *Identity and Anxiety.* New York: Free Press, 1960.

ERIKSON, E. H. *Youth: Change and Challenge.* New York: Basic Books, 1963.

ERIKSON, E. H. (Ed.) *Identity, Youth and Crisis.* New York: Norton, 1968.

FARNSWORTH, D. L. "Drugs: Their Use and Abuse by College Students," in *Psychiatry, Education, and the Young Adult.* Springfield, Ill.: Thomas, 1966.

FELDMAN, K. A., and NEWCOMB, T. M. *The Impact of College on Students.* San Francisco: Jossey-Bass, 1969.

"15% Princetonians Use Marijuana, LSD." *San Francisco Chronicle,* April 9, 1967.

FINESTONE, H. "Cars, Kicks, and Color," in Stein, M. R., Vidich, A., and White, M. (Eds.) *Identity and Anxiety.* New York: Free Press, 1960.

FISHMAN, J. R., and SOLOMON, F. "Youth and Social Action," *Journal of Social Issues,* 1964, 20 (4), 1–27.

FITZGERALD, E. T. "The Measurement of Openness to Experience: A Study of Regression in the Service of the Ego." Unpublished doctoral dissertation, University of California at Berkeley, Department of Psychology, 1966.

FLACKS, R. "The Liberated Generation: An Exploration of the Roots of Student Protest." *Journal of Social Issues,* 1967, 23, 52–75.

FREEDMAN, M. B. *The College Experience.* San Francisco: Jossey-Bass, 1967.

FUNKHOUSER BALBAKY, M. L. "Observations on Student Drug Users." Unpublished manuscript, 1966.

GOLDSEN, R., ROSENBERG, M., WILLIAMS, R. M., and SUCHMAN, E. A. *What College Students Think.* Princeton: Van Nostrand, 1960.

GOLDSTEIN, R. *1 in 7: Drugs on Campus.* New York: Walker, 1966.

GORDON, R. A. "Social Level, Social Disability, and Gang Interaction." *American Journal of Sociology,* 1967, *73* (1), 42–62.

GORDON, R. A., SHORT, J. A., CARTWRIGHT, D. S., and STRODTBECK, F. L. "Values and Gang Delinquency: A Study of Street-Corner Groups." *American Journal of Sociology,* 1963, *69* (2), 109–128.

GOUGH, H. G. *California Psychological Inventory.* Palo Alto: Consulting Psychologists Press, 1956.

GREEN, A. W. "The Middle-Class Male Child and Neurosis." *American Sociological Review,* 1946, *11,* 31.

HARRISON, G. H. "A Shocker on Use of Drugs at S.F. State." *San Francisco Chronicle,* May 29, 1965.

HASKINS, C. "Science Advances in 1967." *American Scientist,* 1968, *56,* 165–181.

HASSENGER, R. "Catholic College Impact on Religious Orientations." *Sociological Analysis,* 1966, *27,* 2.

HEBB, D. O. "The Role of Experience," in Farber, S. M., and Wilson, R. H. L. (Eds.) *Control of the Mind.* New York: McGraw-Hill, 1961.

HECHINGER, F. M. "To Keep Politicians Off the Campus." *New York Times,* March 3, 1968.

HENSALA, J., EPSTEIN, L., and BLACKER, K. "LSD in Psychiatric In-Patients." *Archives of General Psychiatry,* 1967, *16,* 554–560.

HERULF, B. Personal communication transmitted by M. Kihlbom, 1967.

HOFFER, A. "D-Lysergic Acid Diethylamide (LSD): A Review of Its Present Status." *Clinical Pharmacology and Therapeutics,* 1965, *6,* 183–255.

HOLLISTER, L. *Chemical Psychoses, LSD and Related Drugs.* Springfield, Ill.: Thomas, 1968.

HORST, P. "The Prediction of Personal Adjustment." *Social Science Research Council Bulletin #48,* 1948, 403–447.

HOWE, I., and COSER, L. *The American Communist Party.* Boston: Beacon, 1957.

HUXLEY, A. *The Doors of Perception.* New York: Harper, 1954.

IRWIN, S. "A National Framework for the Development, Evaluation, and Use of Psychoactive Drugs." *American Journal of Psychiatry,* Drug Therapy Supplement, 1968, *124,* 1–19.

JACOB, P. E. *Changing Values in College.* New York: Harper, 1957.

JACOBS, P., and LANDAU, S. *The New Radicals: A Report with Documents.* New York: Random House, 1966.

JAMES, W. *The Varieties of Religious Experience.* New York: Modern Library, 1929.

JANIS, I. L., and HOWLAND, C. I. *Personality and Persuasibility.* New Haven: Yale University Press, 1964.

JANOWITZ, J. F. Personal communication, 1967.

KAHLER, E. *The Disintegration of Form in the Arts.* New York: Braziller, 1968.

KATZ, J. *The Student Activists: Rights, Needs, and Powers of Undergraduates.* Prepared at the Institute for the Study of Human Problems, Stanford University. Washington, D.C.: U.S. Office of Education, 1967.

KATZ, J., and Associates. *No Time for Youth: Growth and Constraint in College Students.* San Francisco: Jossey-Bass, 1968.

KATZ, M. M., WASKOW, E., and OLSSON, J. "Characterizing the Psychological State Produced by LSD." *Journal of Abnormal Psychology,* 1968, *73* (1), 1–14.

KEELER, M. H. "Adverse Reactions to Marijuana." *American Journal of Psychiatry.* 1967, *124,* 674–677.

KENISTON, K. *The Uncommitted: Alienated Youth in American Society.* New York: Harcourt, 1965.

KENISTON, K. "The Sources of Student Dissent." *Journal of Social Issues,* 1967, *23,* 108–137.

KLEBER, H. H. "Student Use of Hallucinogens." Unpublished manuscript, 1965.

KLECKNER, J. H. "Personality Differences between Psychedelic Drug Users and Non-Users." *Psychology,* 1968, *5* (2), 66–71.

KOGAN, N., and WALLACH, M. A. *Risk Taking: A Study in Cognition and Personality.* New York: Holt, 1964.

KOHN, H. "Youth Movements," in *Encyclopaedia of Social Science.* New York: Macmillan, 1935.

KRUGMAN, H. "The Appeal of Communism to American Middle Class Intellectuals and Trade Unionists," in Smelser, N. J., and Smelser, W. T. (Eds.) *Personality and Social Systems.* New York: Wiley, 1964.

LANE, R. "Political Personality and Electoral Choice." *American Political Science Review,* 1959, *49,* 173–191.

LANE, R. *Political Ideology: Why the American Common Man Believes What He Does.* New York: Free Press, 1962.

LANE, R., and SEARS, D. *Public Opinion.* Englewood Cliffs, N.J.: Prentice-Hall, 1964.

LEAKE, C. D., and SILVERMAN, M. *Alcoholic Beverages in Clinical Medicine.* Chicago: Year Book Publishers, 1966.

LETTVIN, J. "You Can't Even Step in the Same River Once." *Natural History,* 1967, *76* (8), 6–19.

LEVINSON, D. "An Approach to the Theory and Measurement of Ethnocentric Ideology." *Journal of Psychology,* 1949, *28,* 19–39.

LEWIN, L. *Phantastica: Narcotic and Stimulating Drugs.* Berlin: George Stilke, 1924. Reissued, New York: Dutton, 1964.

LIPINSKI, E., and LIPINSKI, B. G. "Motivational Factors in Psychedelic Drug Use by Male College Students." *Journal of the American College of Health Association,* 1967, *16* (2), 145–149.

LIPSET, S. M. "University Students and Politics in Underdeveloped Countries," *Comparative Education Review,* 1966, *10,* 132–162.

LIPSET, S. M., and WOLIN, S. (Eds.) *The Berkeley Student Revolt: Facts and Interpretations.* New York: Anchor Books, 1965.

MACCOBY, E., MATTHEWS, R. E., and MORTON, A. S. "Youth and Political Change." *Public Opinion Quarterly,* 1954, *18,* 23–29.

MALLERY, D. *Ferment on the Campus: An Encounter with the New College Generation.* New York: Harper, 1966.

MANDEL, J. "Myths and Realities of Marihuana Pushing," in Simmons, J. L. (Ed.) *Marihuana, Myths and Realities.* North Hollywood: Brandon House, 1967.

MASTERS, R. E. L., and HOUSTON, J. *The Varieties of Psychedelic Experience.* New York: Holt, 1966.

MCCLOSKEY, H., and SCHAAR, J. "Psychological Dimensions of Anomie." *American Sociological Review,* 1965, *30* (1), 14–40.

MCGLOTHLIN, W. H., and COHEN, S. "The Use of Hallucinogenic Drugs among College Students." *American Journal of Psychiatry,* 1965, *122,* 572–574.

MCGLOTHLIN, W. H., COHEN, S., and MCGLOTHLIN, M. S. "Personality and Attitude Changes in Volunteer Subjects Following Repeated Administration of LSD." Paper presented before the Fifth International Congress, Collegium Neuropsychopharmacologicum, March 1967.

MCNAMARA, N. T., and KELLER, T. "Children of Paradise." Report to the Clinical Society of Commissioned Officers' Association, U.S. Public Health Service, March 29, 1968.

MIDDLETON, R., and PUTNEY, S. "Political Expressions of Adolescent Rebellion." *American Journal of Sociology*, 1963, *68*, 527–535.

MILLER, J. L. United Press report, 1967.

MILLER, M. V., and GILMORE, S. (Eds.) *Revolution at Berkeley.* New York: Dell, 1965.

MORISON, R. S. *The Contemporary University.* Boston: Houghton-Mifflin, 1966.

NEWCOMB, T. M., and FELDMAN, K. A. *The Impact of Colleges on Their Students.* Ann Arbor: Institute of Social Relations, 1968.

NEWFIELD, J. *A Prophetic Minority.* New York: New American Library, 1966.

NOWLIS, H. H. "Responsibility of the Institution for Developing Student Maturity," in *Higher Education Reflects on Itself and the Larger Society.* Washington, D.C.: American Association for Higher Education, 1966.

NOWLIS, H. H. *Drugs on the College Campus.* Detroit: National Association of Student Personnel Administration, 1967.

O'DEA, T. F. *American Catholic Dilemma.* New York: Sheed and Ward, 1958.

O'DONNELL, J. A., and BALL, J. C. (Eds.) *Narcotic Addiction.* New York: Harper, 1966.

PEARLMAN, S. "Drug Experiences and Attitudes Among Seniors in a Liberal Arts College." Report prepared for the Brooklyn College of the City University of New York, 1966. (Mimeograph.)

PEARLMAN, S. "Drug Use and Experience in an Urban-College Population." Paper read at the Annual Meeting of the American Orthopsychiatric Association, Washington, D.C., March 1967.

PERVIN, L. A., REIK, L. E., and DALRYMPLE, W. (Eds.) *The College Drop-Out and the Utilization of Talent.* Princeton: Princeton University Press, 1966.

PETERSON, R. E. "The Scope of Organized Student Protest in 1964–65." Princeton: Princeton Educational Testing Service, 1966.

PRATT, J. B. *The Religious Consciousness.* New York: Macmillan, 1924.

PRICE, C., in "Letter to Parents," Castro Valley, California, Unified School District (M. Smith, Supt.), 1967.

ROBINS, L. N. *Deviant Children Grown Up.* Baltimore: Williams and Wilkins, 1966.

ROKEACH, M. *The Open and Closed Mind.* New York: Basic Books, 1960.

ROKEACH, M. *Beliefs, Attitudes, and Values.* San Francisco: Jossey-Bass, 1968.

RUDOLPH, F. *The American College and University: A History.* New York: Knopf, 1962.

SAMPSON, E. E. "Student Activism and the Decade of Protest." *Journal of Social Issues,* 1967, *23*, 1–33.

SANFORD, N. *The American College.* New York: Wiley, 1962.

SANFORD, N. *Where Colleges Fail.* San Francisco: Jossey-Bass, 1967.

SCHIFF, L. F. "The Obedient Rebels: A Study of College Conversions to Conservatism." *Journal of Social Issues,* 1964, *20*, 74–95.

SEELEY, J. R., SIM, R. A., and LOOSLEY, E. *Crestwood Heights.* New York: Basic Books, 1956.

SHERIF, M. *The Psychology of Social Norms.* New York: Harper, 1936.

SHILS, E. *Torment of Secrecy.* New York: Free Press, 1956.

SIMMON, G., and TROUT, G. "Hippies in College—From Teeny Boppers to Drug Freaks." *Trans-Action,* 1967, *5,* 27–32.

SIMMONS, J. L., and WINOGRAD, B. *It's Happening.* Santa Barbara, Calif.: Marc-Laird, 1966.

SMITH, M. B., BRUNER, J., and WHITE, R. W. *Opinions and Personality.* New York: Wiley, 1956.

SMITH, S. N., and BLACHLY, P. H. "Amphetamine Usage by Medical Students." *Journal of Medical Education,* 1966, *41,* 167–170.

SPENCER, S. M. "The Pill that Helps You Remember." *The Saturday Evening Post,* 1966, *20* (Sept. 24), 64–68.

STARK, R., and LOFLAND, J. "Becoming a World Saver: A Theory of Conversion to a Deviant Perspective." *American Sociological Review,* 1965, *30* (6), 862–875.

State of California, Department of Justice, Bureau of Criminal Statistics. "Drug Arrests in California—1967 Mid-Year Preliminary Survey." Sacramento, 1967. (Mimeograph.)

STEIN, M. R. *The Eclipse of Community.* Princeton: Princeton University Press, 1960.

STEVENSON, G. H. "Drug Addiction in British Columbia." 3 vols. Vancouver: University of British Columbia, 1956. (Mimeograph.)

SUTHERLAND, R. *Personality Factors on the College Campus.* Austin, Tex.: Hogg Foundation, 1962.

TOCH, H. *The Social Psychology of Social Science.* New York: Macmillan, 1935.

TOCH, H. *The Social Psychology of Social Movements.* New York: Bobbs-Merrill, 1965.

TRENT, J. W., and CRAISE, J. "Commitment and Conformity in the American College." *Journal of Social Issues,* 1967, *23,* 34–51.

UNGERLEIDER, J. T., FISHER, D. D., FULLER, M., and CALDWELL, S. "The Bad Trip —the Etiology of the Adverse LSD Reaction." *American Journal of Psychiatry,* 1968, *124,* 11 and 1483–1490.

WAGNER, H. "The Protestant Ethic: A Mid-Twentieth Century View." *Sociological Analysis,* 1954, *25* (1), 38.

WALTERS, P. A. "Therapist Bias and Student Use of Illegal Drugs." *Journal of the American College Health Association,* 1967, *16* (1), 30–34.

WATTS, W. A., and WHITTAKER, D. N. "Some Sociological-Psychological Differences Between Highly Committed Members of the Free Speech Movement and the Student Population at Berkeley." *Applied Behavioral Science,* 1966, *2,* 41–62.

WEAKLAND, J. H. "The Thought of Mao Tse-tung: Communications Analysis of a Propaganda Movement." Technical Report #3. Palo Alto: Mental Research Institute, 1968.

WEBER, M. *Sociology of Religion.* Boston: Beacon Press, 1963.

WESTBY, D., and BRAUNGART, R. "Class and Politics in the Family Backgrounds of Student Political Activists." *American Sociological Review,* 1966, *31,* 690–692.

WILSON, R. R. *Sects and Society.* Berkeley: University of California Press, 1961.

WITKIN, H. A., DYK, R. B., PATERSON, H. F., GOODENOUGH, D. R., and KARP, S. A. *Psychological Differentiation.* New York: Wiley, 1962.

Name Index

Subject Index

395